The Sounds of Commerce

FILM AND CULTURE   *John Belton, General Editor*

The Sounds of Commerce

MARKETING POPULAR FILM MUSIC

JEFF SMITH

COLUMBIA UNIVERSITY PRESS

NEW YORK

COLUMBIA UNIVERSITY PRESS
Publishers Since 1893
New York   Chichester, West Sussex

Library of Congress Cataloging-in-Publication Data
Smith, Jeff (Jeffrey Paul)
    The sounds of commerce : marketing popular film music / Jeff Smith
        p.   cm.— (Film and culture)
    Includes bibliographical references (p.   ) and index.
    ISBN 0–231–10862–1 (cloth : alk. paper). —ISBN 0–231–10863–X
(pbk. : alk. paper)
    1. Motion picture music—Economic aspects. 2. Music trade—United
States. 3. Motion Picture music—History and criticism.   I. Title.
II. Series.
ML2075.S65   1998
781.5'42'0688—dc21   98–17923

Casebound editions of Columbia University Press books are printed
on permanent and durable acid-free paper.
Printed in the United States of America
Designed by Brady McNamara
c 10 9 8 7 6 5 4 3 2 1
p 10 9 8 7 6 5 4 3 2 1

The lyrics for "So Long Trash" (copyright © 1998) in chapter 3 are by Pat
Ballard from the March 2, 1960, issue of *Variety* and are reprinted by
permission of Variety, Inc.

*For Michele and the Green Bay Packers, who have
respectively inspired and distracted me in my efforts to
complete this book*

———

Contents

Acknowledgments

As with any project of this nature, there are many people to whom I owe a considerable debt of gratitude. First, I wish to especially thank David Bordwell for his penetrating commentary throughout the writing of earlier drafts of this work. In addition, thanks go to Tino Balio, Don Crafton, Vance Kepley, Noël Carroll, Lea Jacobs, and Ben Brewster for offering valuable questions and insights regarding various aspects of my argument. Ronald Radano also merits special recognition for encouraging me to rethink certain musicological issues.

I am also grateful to a number of friends and colleagues who have in various ways aided the completion of this monograph. Special acknowledgment goes to Richard Allen, Toby Miller, and Bill Simon; and to the graduate students who have aided my teaching and research efforts, including Stefanie Cohen, Peter Decherney, Yuin Shan-Ding, Matt Fee, Keith Harris, Roger Hallis, Mia Mask, Jason Schlossberg, Shawn Shimpach, and Amy Shore. Greg Taylor, Renae Edge, and Derek Kompare have my heartfelt appreciation both for their friendship and for their recommendations of particularly interesting scores. Bob and Judy Clark deserve mention for hosting me during a research trip and seeing to it I got around in Westwood and Beverly Hills. And very special thanks goes out to Lisa Edmondson, who enabled me to examine the orchestral sketches for *Breakfast at Tiffany's* in Henry Mancini's business office, and especially Mancini himself, who generously consented to an interview.

Special thanks also go to Sidney Herman and Famous Music Corporation for graciously allowing me to reprint the lyrics and a short excerpt of the melody from "Moon River." Lastly, I also wish to recognize the staff at Columbia University Press for their help in preparing the manuscript, especially John Belton, Jennifer Crewe, and Roy Thomas, whose careful reading of my manuscript helped save me from some potentially embarrassing errors. Any mistakes that remain are most assuredly my own.

Most of all, however, I wish to thank my wife, Michele, whose love and support throughout this undertaking have been absolutely unwavering.

The Sounds of Commerce

Did They Mention the Music?

TOWARD A THEORY OF POPULAR FILM MUSIC

Since the 1950s, the production of motion picture soundtrack albums has flourished both as an important tool of film promotion and as an aesthetic and cultural phenomenon in its own right. The remarkable success of the *Wayne's World* soundtrack during the early nineties is a case in point. The album was not only a best-seller on *Billboard*'s charts but also revived interest in the rock group Queen, spurring sales of the group's greatest hits package and bringing the single "Bohemian Rhapsody" heavy radio play more than fifteen years after its initial release. The latter's success came in large measure from the way it was featured in the film. With the art-rock chestnut booming out their car stereo, Wayne, Garth, and friends bopped their way down suburban streets in a comic set piece that is in many ways the equivalent of the song and dance numbers of classical Hollywood musicals.

The *Wayne's World* example is particularly interesting not only because the film itself pokes fun at Hollywood promotional practices like product placement, but also because it offers a view of the mall culture that is so important to the contemporary filmgoer's experience. Whereas a previous generation's exploitation of a film's soundtrack involved setting up special display cases in theater lobbies or making special agreements with local record merchants, modern film patrons, upon leaving the mall multiplex, can simply go to the mall record store and, more than likely, purchase the soundtrack album for the film they have just seen. The spatial contiguity of theaters and record stores suggests the extent to which such reciprocal arrangements between corporate interests have institutionalized what was once an expensive and time-consuming aspect of film marketing. The "one-stop shopping" concept makes the mall a haven for film promoters with soundtrack albums available at record stores, novelizations purchasable at bookstores, posters on display at video stores, T-shirts on sale in department stores, and the film itself playing at the mall multiplex.

Such interlocking business arrangements between film and music interests are, of course, nothing new. Hollywood has long used music to sell films and vice versa.[1] Yet, as Irwin Bazelon notes, what makes these last forty years since the 1950s somewhat different is the development of an "organized machinery behind the manufacture of hit songs in films."[2] The development of this "machinery" came in response to a number of industrial, historical, and sociological factors in the 1950s and early 1960s, including the trend toward diversification and conglomeration in film distribution, the emergence of studio-owned record labels, the establishment of radio and records as important ancillary markets, and changes in popular music tastes and consumption patterns.

Over the years, Hollywood's investment in music subsidiaries has yielded several economic benefits. First of all, film companies earn millions of dollars in ancillary revenues from the outright sale of records and sheet music. Second, through their ownership of publishing and record ventures, film companies also derive additional monies from their control of various copyrighted materials. Generally speaking, these revenues come from two sources—synchronization licenses and master licenses. The *synchronization license* is negotiated with the publishers of a particular song, and this entitles the licensee to use the notes and lyrics to a particular piece of music. The *master use license*, on the other hand, is negotiated with a record company, and it enables licensees to use a particular recording. To use "Bohemian Rhapsody" in *Wayne's World*, filmmakers paid both kinds of licensing fees, one to the song's publisher and one to Queen's record company. To license the song "Mickey" in the same film, however, producers paid only a synchronization fee since they used just the song rather than Toni Basil's recording of it. ("Mickey" is briefly sung by Wayne and Cassandra as they ride in his car.) Finally, with the growth of radio and records as important ancillary markets, theme songs and soundtrack albums became valuable cross-promotional tools. Through its repeated airplay, a title song effectively becomes a kind of free three-minute advertisement for its accompanying film. Similarly, though valued more for their sales than for their promotional value, soundtrack albums serve as an effective means of circulating a film's title and imagery through rack sales and retail displays.

Despite popular music's economic importance for Hollywood, the development of title songs and soundtrack albums as economic and cultural forms has generally been ignored in film music criticism. Although several factors in film music scholarship can account for this, two are especially pertinent to my interests here. The first is the persistence of a "masterpiece" approach to film music history; the second is the critical rejection of popular music as an appropriate style for film scoring. These factors are not only causally interrelated, they also reflect a more general tendency in film music studies to weight aesthetic concerns over technological, economic, or cultural mechanisms.

While recent advances have been made on several fronts of film music theory, film music history remains a problematic area of the discipline.[3] Penned mostly by buffs and musicologists, film music history suffers from a number of methodological problems, not the least of which is a general ignorance of film's critical and theoretical literature. The bulk of historical writing falls into the "masterpiece tradition," which emphasizes "great composers" and significant works.[4] *American Film Music* by William Darby and Jack Du Bois both typifies this tradition and makes its theoretical and historiographical foundations quite explicit.[5] Instead of a history that integrates social, economic, cultural, and technological factors, Darby and Du Bois simply present us with a chronology of artists and their creations.

Of course, there are a number of objections to the "masterpiece" tradition and "Great Man" history, the most serious of which are that such approaches devalue context and overvalue human agency.[6] In countering the "masterpiece" tradition, my research attempts to situate film music's forms, styles, and techniques within their respective historical contexts. One of this project's assumptions is that our understanding of film music is greatly enhanced by an awareness of the various economic, cultural, and technological factors that govern its production. One way of achieving this awareness is by locating film scores in a detailed historical framework, one that is sensitive to film music's commercial functions as well as its more general circulation throughout a culture. The innovation of the soundtrack album is particularly significant in this regard since it remains one of the most common, if least understood, ways in which viewers and listeners come into contact with film music.

This is especially true of the so-called *pop soundtrack*, which emerged as an alternative to the classical Hollywood score during the mid-fifties. Often deemed musically inappropriate and unsophisticated, the pop soundtrack is usually dismissed as a concession to the greed and commercialism of film producers. Describing the reasons for the pop soundtrack's sudden rise, Irwin Bazelon griped:

Through the mass-media loudspeaker system, the pop-music culture has rammed its product down the audience's throat and instilled in people, especially film personnel, a way of associating success and hit songs. By using instantaneously acceptable music, already packaged and presold in the pop culture, the filmmakers display an adroit awareness of their audience's fashionable taste buds, and this audience, in turn, is a sitting duck for the industry's sales psychology.[7]

This view, held by traditional musicologists and film music scholars alike, suggests that popular music has no intrinsic aesthetic value and is only interesting as a sociological phenomenon. Not surprisingly, sixties pop scores were routinely explained away with a simple-minded causal explanation that depicts young filmgoers as mindless consumers and film producers as conniving and manipulative salesmen.[8]

This notion of aesthetic impoverishment has led a number of film music scholars to suggest that pop music's banality makes it singularly unsuited to the expressive and narrative demands of film scoring. Writing on the use of popular songs in *Breakfast at Tiffany's* (1961) and *A Man and a Woman* (*Un homme et une femme*, 1966), Bazelon asserts, "It is a debatable point whether these films and similar types have been 'scored' in the strictest sense of the word. Any one of a thousand songs could serve the identical purpose."[9] Moreover, Mark Evans says of rock and roll, "Harmonically primitive and rhythmically dependent upon a constant throbbing beat, it lacked the capacity to adjust to a variety of moods, so essential to screen scoring."[10] For most critics and historians, pop scores simply do not compare with the dramatically forceful and musically sophisticated offerings of the classical Hollywood composers. Interested in salvaging their object of study from scholarly neglect, academics typically turn to the works of David Raksin, Hugo Friedhofer, Erich Wolfgang Korngold, and others. Few, if any, have given comparable attention to the likes of Henry Mancini, John Barry, Ennio Morricone, and the other pop composers discussed in this study.

Thus, given popular music's low standing in film music studies, it is necessary to do some ground clearing before situating the pop score's development within its historical, economic, and cultural context. One of the first tasks in this regard is to sketch out a provisional definition of the pop score, which I will argue fits two criteria: (1) it must be composed or compiled in one or more popular musical styles, and (2) it must be formally accessible to the average moviegoer. The ensuing discussion of these criteria should not be construed as either an exhaustive or authoritative theory of popular film music, but rather as a useful starting point for a historicized reading of the pop score in terms of its forms, its commercial functions, and its textual operations. The explication of each criterion will not only distinguish the pop score from its classical Hollywood predecessors but will also show how the pop score pertains to some broader issues in film music theory.

The Composer as Tunesmith: The Pop Score as Pop Music

The premise of the first criterion, that a pop score must be predominantly written in a pop style, may seem self-evident or even tautological, but it isn't. Although the pop score shares strong stylistic similarities with pop music, the length and form of a score's cues—and the dramatic functions they serve— often differentiate the pop score from the typical pop song or pop record. Occasionally, to achieve a particular effect, a pop composer will harken back to a more traditional style of orchestral scoring. This kind of eclecticism is nothing new, but rather is common to a great deal of film scoring, where the length, form, and style of music are partly determined by the moment-to-moment requirements of the film's narrative. The effect of this, as Royal S. Brown observes, is that the pop scores of Henry Mancini and John Barry emerge as a kind of stylistic mishmash which frequently moves from pop tunes through jazz to more modern classical styles.[11] Accordingly, a pop score may not be written entirely in a pop style, but it should use pop music as its central set of stylistic components.

Generally speaking, spectators, consumers, and film music scholars all exhibit a commonsensical view of what a popular film music entails. As an umbrella term, popular film music covers a number of commercial genres which have largely been adapted from various strands of African-American and folk music, and includes such styles as funk, blues, rags, reggae, rock, and country and western music as well as certain strains of jazz.[12] During the late fifties and early sixties, pop composers predominantly worked in jazz and Tin Pan Alley traditions, but by the late sixties the form gradually came to encompass such divergent styles as rock, funk, and rhythm and blues. While this tacit conception of popular music is not theoretically rigorous, it is nonetheless serviceable as a means of highlighting the differences between popular and classical film music.

Of course, the pop score's formal organization was also influenced by its narrative functions. As early as 1949, composer Aaron Copland offered a very useful summary of these functions by suggesting five general areas in which film music serves the screen: (1) it conveys a convincing atmosphere of time and place; (2) it underlines the unspoken feelings or psychological states of characters; (3) it serves as a kind of neutral background filler to the action; (4) it gives a sense of continuity to the editing; (5) it accentuates the theatrical buildup of a scene and rounds it off with a feeling of finality.[13]

In serving these functions, the pop score often adapted popular musical forms to the particular needs of the film it accompanied. Traditional devices, such as ostinatos, pedal points, and sustained chords, were written in pop idioms and combined with sixteen- and thirty-two-bar song forms. Through this process of adaptation, pop song forms were sometimes shortened, fragmented, and varied to fit the temporal constraints of the scenes they accompanied. This adaptation enabled the pop score to serve both dramatic functions within the film and commercial functions within the record industry in the somewhat different format of the soundtrack album.[14] The pop score's formal properties will receive more detailed analysis in later chapters, but for now I will give a brief overview of these properties in order to distinguish the sixties pop score from the classical scores that preceded it.

During film music's so-called Golden Age, classical film scores adhered to Western classical traditions of rhythm and orchestration, and adopted many of the stylistic parameters of the late nineteenth-century Romantic idiom. Certainly individual composers offered different talents and skills to producers—Victor Young, for example, was noted for his melodic gifts, Miklós Rózsa for his skill in scoring historical epics—but they operated within a paradigmatic range of classical norms. The combination of these stylistic parameters yielded a remarkably uniform group style among Hollywood composers that emphasized leitmotivs, theme writing, and symphonic orchestrations.[15]

Romanticism's importance to the classical film score can be traced to a number of factors.[16] To begin with, the silent film score's use of nineteenth-century techniques provided an obvious precedent for their later use in the sound era. Second, many Hollywood composers were European émigrés trained in the late Romantic style. Max Steiner, for example, began his career conducting and arranging operettas. Erich Wolfgang Korngold, on the other hand, grew up as the son of a Viennese music critic, and composed two operas by the time he was seventeen.[17] Finally, Romanticism added a High Art sheen to the work of Hollywood film composers. This not only elevated film music in the eyes of film producers, it also enhanced Hollywood composers' own claims of authorship and creativity. As Kathryn Kalinak points out, the composers most thoroughly schooled in nineteenth-century Romantic techniques were usually the ones who received the most prestigious assignments and industry accolades.[18]

The Romantic idiom continued as an option throughout the fifties, but it no longer wielded as strong an influence as Hollywood composers began to broaden the classical score's range of styles. At one end of the spectrum, strong dissonances, polyphonic textures, modal writing, and atonality surfaced more regularly in the works of Bernard Herrmann, Miklós Rózsa, Leonard Rosenman, and Jerry Goldsmith. At the other end, various jazz and pop elements appeared in the scores of David Raksin, Elmer Bernstein, Johnny Mandel, and Henry Mancini. And despite a major revival in the Korngold-styled scores of John Williams, Romanticism's hold on film scoring was further weakened by the incorporation of rock, folk, and soul elements in the 1960s and 1970s, and electronics, minimalism, and even New Age elements in the 1980s. By the 1990s, Romantic-styled film music was still being composed, but it was merely one stylistic option among many.

To some extent, the pop score's differences from the classical Hollywood score can be measured in terms of the more general differences between jazz and pop idioms and their Western classical forbears.[19] To begin with, pop scores relied more heavily on song forms than did their classical Hollywood counterparts. Song forms, of course, have a long history in Western music that encompasses such diverse genres as hymnody, *chansons*, consort songs, art songs, ballads, and *lieder*. Moreover, within the Anglo-American tradition, strophic and modified strophic forms are common to various kinds of folk music which have appeared in the United States since the eighteenth century. In developing the formal organization of the pop score, however, composers largely drew on the repertory of Broadway and Tin Pan Alley music of the thirties, forties, and fifties. Songwriters like Irving Berlin, Cole Porter, and George Gershwin were obvious models for sixties pop composers insofar as the latter aspired to the craft of such songwriting while at the same time fashioning their scores around salable themes and tunes.

In its emphasis on song forms, popular film music maintains a strong connection with functional tonality. Like various kinds of Western folk music, popular music typically utilizes some sort of song structure with a formalized pattern of verse, chorus, and bridge. Moreover, these song structures use traditional Western classical harmonic progressions and they develop repeated symmetrical phrase patterns. Thirty-two-bar song forms, for example, are structured as either AABA or ABAB patterns, which consist of a musical nucleus of two eight-measure cells. Twelve-bar blues forms, on the other hand, are developed from an even simpler AAB structure, with each phrase being a four-bar cell. In addition, popular music also utilizes a basic formal building block that is a kind of counterpart to Romantic music's leitmotiv.

Like the leitmotiv, riffs and hooks are brief snatches of melody or sonorial novelty, usually only a few notes, which provide the starting point for the development of phrase structures.

However, unlike the leitmotiv, riffs and hooks in pop music are not repeated, varied, and developed in any systematic manner. They may be used as the basis for an improvised solo by a jazz or rock musician, but even here the development of musical ideas stays within a stable harmonic and structural framework. Unlike motivic cells, which are used to give a classical piece a sense of organicity and unity, riffs and hooks are designed only to engage a listener's attention, to "sell" the song, as it were, by providing a unique and instantly memorable musical idea within the confines of a standardized song form. In other words, the riff's value as a structural component is that it is perfectly suited to popular music's economy of means. The riff provides moments of melodic interest that are easily exhausted within a pop song's three-minute running time, and do not work against the pop song's standard twelve-, sixteen-, or thirty-two-bar form.

In his landmark work *Introduction to the Sociology of Music*, Theodor Adorno argues that these strophic phrase patterns establish a rigid extrinsic form which defines popular music in terms of a kind of standardization and contrasts it with Western art music's motivic and harmonic complexity.[20] However, such standardization itself depends on a number of extramusical factors regarding pop music's production and reception. Popular songwriters operate within a commercial industry, and thus a complex network of corporate interests establishes the various constraints and limitations on popular music production. As Adorno forcefully points out, popular music forms are inextricably linked to economic and social considerations, factors that for many scholars are seemingly absent in the production of serious music.

Perhaps more importantly, pop scores also opened up new possibilities of rhythmic inflection and coloristic expression. In rhythmic terms, pop scores are generally distinguished from classical scores by their use of a freer rhythmic inflection, a greater emphasis on syncopation, and a less strict sense of vertical harmonic and rhythmic synchronization. In fact, in many pop and rock scores the rhythm section's parts are not notated. Instead, the composer will give the rhythm section a role model or a description of the style and allow the musicians themselves the space to achieve the proper feel and inflection of the idiom.[21] By anticipating or delaying notes within a pattern, these rhythmic inflections give rise to a complex interplay between distinct but concurrently sounding rhythmic figures. As dance music, pop, rock, and soul are especially noted for this interplay, which produces both syncopations and subtle cross-rhythms.[22]

Moreover, like much functional tonal music, pop scores often tend toward pentatonic melodic lines, but frequently these lines are placed in opposition to the diatonicism of functional tonality. Pop scores frequently rely on melodic inflections in which the melody is colored by bending between pitches and a slight flattening of the third and seventh tones of the scale, the so-called *blue notes*. Like rhythmic inflection, this melodic inflection shares certain affinities with the more fluid pitch patterns of everyday human speech and vocalizing.[23]

Finally, pop scores differ strongly from classical scores in terms of their approach to timbre. As with some forms of African-American music more generally, pop scores are noteworthy in their use of highly personal timbres, through which the jazz or pop musician's individual sonorities and inflection constitute a distinctive performance style. Unlike the studied tone of classical vocalists, pop stars often cultivate a guttural, nasal, or falsetto sound as a specific resource of musical expression.

The importance of timbral distinctiveness in popular music cannot be overemphasized. For one thing, distinctive individual timbres are instantly recognizable as a feature of a popular musician's personality, and act as a literal acoustic voiceprint marking the differences between one performer and another. Jazz saxophonists like Lester Young are noted for their silky smooth, almost breathless tone quality, which directly contrasts with the more squawking or honking attack of a John Coltrane or Ornette Coleman. Similarly, the satiny sheen of pop singers like Peggy Lee, Aaron Neville, Julee Cruise, and Mel Torme, the latter known affectionately as the "Velvet Fog," differs markedly from the reediness of a Bob Dylan or Mick Jagger, on the one hand, and the gruff, raspy shouting of an Otis Redding, Bobby "Blue" Bland, or Tom Waits, on the other. When combined with individual approaches to phrasing and attack, these tone colors further indicate more subtle differences in performance style within particular subclasses of popular music like blues or country and western.

Second, the use of personal timbres differs markedly from the comparatively rigorous performance standards of classical music, which adheres to particular conceptions of proper pitch control, attack, dynamics, phrasing, and tone color. Certainly, classical music offers a range of interpretive possibilities, but this range is much narrower than that of popular music. The bending of "blue" notes and the sliding portamento of much pop vocal delivery, for example, is possible in classical music only in very specific and clearly defined contexts, typically instances that are either idiomatic or are specially notated by the composer.

Lastly, because individual sonorities and inflections in popular music are instantly and readily identifiable, they require no special musical training on the part of the listener. While the more narrow range of interpretive possibilities in classical music encourages a kind of connoisseurship to discern the nuances and subtleties of classical performance, the larger "grain" of the voice in popular music is observable even among listeners who lack formal musical training, and thus proves more suited to the mass distribution and consumption of pop music.[24]

In summary, much of what is distinctive about pop music—its greater sense of rhythmic and melodic freedom and its emphasis on unique timbres—are things that cannot be captured in traditional Western notation, but rather are identifiable by a certain "feel" to the music, a feel that is only actualized in the process of performance. Unlike classical music, the individual character of a pop piece is not inherent in its form, but rather in the materiality of its sound.

Because these distinctive characteristics cannot be strictly notated, some film music practitioners have stressed the importance of giving freedom to pop music performers during scoring sessions. In their "how to" manual of contemporary film scoring, *On the Track*, Karlin and Wright note that "in any rhythm-oriented style, if you write everything, the performance may sound stiff and nonidiomatic." As a result, film composers looking for a contemporary sound will usually give the performers a chord sheet, a general description of the style, and, in some cases, a list of artists and even songs that can serve as role models. According to Karlin and Wright, "The goal is to give them all the direction necessary to ensure the proper results, but let them be as free as possible so they can add the style and flavor of the idiom."[25]

Of course, it is for this and other reasons that pop music was long thought to be unsuited to film scoring. Classical Hollywood scores were carefully timed and edited to fit the editing rhythms and movements within the frame. Because the overarching musical form was "generated" by the motivic cell, leitmotivs were extremely adaptable to the various fluctuations and shifts of the visual track. In contrast, popular musical forms were thought to impose an extrinsic and rigid structure onto the visual material of the film, one that, as Mark Evans notes, was "unrelated to the aesthetic and emotional demands of motion pictures."[26] For Evans and others, song forms generally could not accommodate the irregularities and asymmetries of the film's visual action.

This is not to say that popular music was completely or wholly inappropriate. To return to Copland's model of film music functions, popular music was entirely capable of giving a film a convincing sense of an urban contemporary or modern setting, and was often used as such throughout the sixties in such films as *Breakfast at Tiffany's*, *The Graduate* (1967), and *Easy Rider* (1969). Yet despite its ability to signify a kind of contemporaneity, many critics argued that pop music's dramatic function was limited to aspects of settings. Whether a twelve-bar blues, a jazz samba, or a pop ballad, pop music did not appear able to suggest a character's unspoken feelings, provide a sense of mounting dramatic tension, or round off a sequence with any sense of finality.

By structurally equating the pop song with the pop score, however, critics perpetuated a common fallacy. Although the pop score was based on song forms, it was not strictly speaking identical to a collection of songs. As I noted earlier, the pop score commonly combined songs with more conventional devices, such as "stingers" (sudden sforzando chords that are used to emphasize visual actions, underscore characters' reactions, or punctuate moments of suspense) and ostinatos. The one exception to this rule is the compilation score, which sometimes uses prerecorded, preexisting popular music to furnish all of its cues. But as we will see in chapter 6, even the compilation score functions in relation to the film's narrative, albeit according to a quite different logic of association and allusion.

As Kathryn Kalinak notes, the use of jazz and pop idioms challenged the classical Hollywood score, but did not subvert it altogether.[27] Though the idiom was contemporary, the pop score itself served many of the traditional score's functions by establishing setting, by representing characters' points of view, and by expressing a scene's overall mood. Significantly, by combining popular styles and song forms with the developmental forms of the orchestral score, composers like Mancini and Barry deftly juggled the pop score's commercial and narrative functions. This negotiation of filmic and extrafilmic demands would prove to be a crucial feature of the pop score, and I will discuss it in more detail in subsequent chapters.

Putting the Buzz in the Eardrum: The Pop Score as Accessible

The second criterion of the pop score is that it be formally accessible to ordinary listeners. This trait was vital to a score's commercial prospects for obvious reasons. If a score is beyond the ken of most moviegoers, then they are not very likely to seek it out at their local record store. Consequently, it was imperative that pop composers work with devices, forms, and styles that were already familiar to film audiences. Not only did this facilitate proper communication with respect to the film's narrative, it was a necessary precondition for a score to be marketable. During the early sixties, this meant working within styles that had predominated in previous decades, such as Big Band, Tin Pan Alley pop, and rock 'n' roll. As the decade wore on, other styles were added to the pop score palette, including folk-rock, acid-rock, and rhythm and blues. Working within these styles, pop composers used associations between music, culture, and film genre to signify certain aspects of setting and character. This will receive more detailed explication in later chapters in the analyses of *Breakfast at Tiffany's*, *Goldfinger* (1964), *The Good, the Bad, and the Ugly* (1966), and *American Graffiti* (1973). Before considering them, however, I will discuss how the issue of formal accessibility relates to a broader question regarding the musical competencies of ordinary listeners.

While it is difficult to contemplate the issue of listening competencies outside specific historical and cultural contexts, Leonard Meyer's distinction between primary and secondary stylistic parameters proposes one way to generalize this question beyond the realm of particular composers, idioms, genres, or national traditions.[28] The primary parameters of music, such as melody, harmony, and rhythm, are syntactic, and thus establish a set of articulated proportional hierarchical relationships within the temporal unfolding of a piece of music. As a kind of musical grammar, the syntax developed through such hierarchies is rule-governed, learned, and conventional. In contrast, the secondary parameters, which include dynamics, sonority, tempo, and timbre, are not syntactic and cannot be divided into proportional relationships. Instead they tend to be characterized in relative terms of amounts. Tempi may be faster or slower, timbre can be brighter or duller, but in neither case do they offer anything that corresponds with the specifiable proportionality of intervallic or rhythmic relations. As such, secondary parameters establish relative continua that are not hierarchical, but processive and emergent. Perhaps most significantly, secondary parameters do not rely on learned rules and conventions, and thus are more readily apprehended by all listeners.[29]

In applying this distinction to the Romantic idiom, Meyer notes that composers often increased the relative weight of these secondary parameters to accommodate the growing patronage of a larger but less well-educated middle-class audience. With the rise of subscription concerts and public recitals, Romantic ideology evinced a concern with the democratization and egalitarianism of form that had important consequences for musical performance and composition. The need to fill larger auditoriums with sound led both to an increase in the size of orchestras and in increase in the use of instruments to extend the range of orchestral sound (e.g., piccolos, contrabassoons). The increase in magnitude, Meyer argues, served as a sign of the growing social status of the bourgeoisie and thus reaffirmed the social position of its audience.[30]

The growth of social power among this group, however, was inversely proportional to their musical training. According to Meyer, leitmotivic construction was emphasized in Romantic music as a formal structure that was brief and striking enough to facilitate its memorization. In this way, leitmotivs in the Romantic era not only provided a strategy of musical unity through diversity but also made a virtue of necessity by shortening the basic unit of composition to fit the listening constraints of its audience.[31] Additionally, programs and extramusical reference became increasingly important for composers who were fearful that inexperienced audiences might fail to respond to their music's affective components; programs and references provided a conceptual framework that could clarify emotive qualities for listeners. The Romantic emphasis on character pieces, tone poems, and tone paintings belies this tendency toward using extramusical materials to offset an audience's lack of musical expertise.

Because they operated against an ideological background of egalitarian-sim, Meyer argues that Romantic composers emphasized texture, dynamics, and orchestral color in a way that their Baroque and classical predecessors had not. Romantic music's emphasis on leitmotivs and secondary parameters established a system of communication aimed at a vast, heterogeneous audience. At one level, the emphasis on secondary parameters established a plane of comprehension that was shared by all, the musically trained and untrained alike. The use of leitmotivic structures in lengthier and more emergent forms, however, established a second plane of communication aimed at connoisseurs who, it was assumed, could follow the increasingly complex development of musical material.

Meyer's discussion of Romanticism contains a number of observations that are especially relevant for film music theory. Like the Romantic composers of the nineteenth century, the first Hollywood composers were confronted with an audience that was largely made up of musically untrained, middle-class patrons. Faced with such an audience, it made sense that Hollywood composers would seek a direct and straightforward means of musical communication, and during the early sound era the various stylistic parameters of the Romantic idiom fulfilled these criteria. As I noted earlier, Romanticism's early predominance in Hollywood scoring was furthered by the familiarity of its musical conventions and the training and background of the composers.[32] Yet this was not simply a matter of filiation or the continuity of musical conventions, but as Meyer notes, a necessary condition for the audience's understanding of the music. Primary parameters are by their very nature rule-governed, and thus necessitate that their "grammars" be widely circulated and internalized within the culture to enable musical comprehension. Such familiarity suggests one more reason why Romantic works rather than twelve-tone or serial compositions provided a model for Hollywood scores. The "grammars" of the latter simply did not have the widespread cultural circulation of other idioms.

However, it should be noted that this familiarity was a necessary but not a sufficient condition for the Romantic idiom's dominance. Certainly, the "grammars" of the Baroque and classical idioms would have been equally widespread, but they were clearly not as central to the concerns of Hollywood composers. The reason for this, I would argue, was that the stylistic parameters of the Romantic idiom proved to be uniquely suited to the needs of classical Hollywood narrative and classical Hollywood audiences. The Romantic period's emphasis on leitmotivic construction and secondary parameters served the particular needs of Hollywood composing in a way that the parameters of Baroque and classical music could not.

First of all, the relative brevity of the leitmotiv was especially suited to the irregular and shifting demands of the film's narrative. As Graham Bruce notes:

> At the level of the single musical cue, the brief musical cell, because of its flexibility, offers the potential of an active interrelation with dialogue, action, and editing. The importance of the musical modules, however, lies not merely in their flexibility in relation to any single image sequence. The structural potential of these simple, cellular units lies also in their generative qualities, their possibilities for expansion, variation, and development, giving rise to a score of organic unity.[33]

The flexibility of leitmotivs allowed them to function in almost any dramatic context while their repetition, variation, and development allowed composers to create works with both formal unity and musical interest.

The assumption that films required original music further supported the use of leitmotivs as the classical Hollywood score's basic formal unit. Because leitmotivs were inspired by the particular characters, settings, and dramatic situations of a unique and individual film, and because the overall structure of the score was generated by these leitmotivs, classical Hollywood composers were assured of writing works that were unique, unified, and dramatically appropriate. Leitmotivs were also well suited to the limited musical memory capacity of an untrained audience. As Meyer notes, such thematic conservation and repetition serves such constraints in that the varied recurrence of a leitmotiv imprints it upon short-term memory and lessens the number of competing musical ideas in a way that ensures it is efficiently stored.[34] In such a way, Hollywood composers were assured that even for untutored listeners the music could reinforce the impression of the film's structural unity.[35]

Much of Meyer's work is also pertinent to our understanding of popular music in films. For one thing, pop scores, like other film scores, depend quite heavily on those same secondary parameters that Meyer sees as central to Romantic style. Despite the change in idiom, the fast tempi of rock and roll are still used to suggest a character's agitation and excitement, or to accompany action sequences. Sudden changes in a song's dynamics still punctuate moments of suspense, surprise, or reaction. Individual sonorities and timbres still work to underline aspects of setting and character. The formal accessibility of these secondary parameters enhanced their utility to pop composers; changes in tempo, dynamics, texture, and tone color are immediately graspable and thus facilitate clear musical communication to trained and untrained listeners alike.

Moreover, the emphasis on immediacy in popular styles suggests that there are other similarities between popular music and Meyer's description of Romanticism. In terms of ideology, for example, popular music, like Romantic music, evinces a concern for egalitarianism. Indeed, much rock and roll mythology relies rather strongly on the notion that anyone, regardless of education or social status, can play or understand it. Similarly, popular musical forms offer something quite comparable to Romantic music's economy of means. The emphasis on melody, the repetitiveness of harmonic and rhythmic patterns, and the relative brevity of the pieces suggest that pop forms are especially well suited to the memory constraints and cognitive limitations of a musically untrained audience.

This is especially true of the pop hook, which I noted earlier was the pop score's formal counterpart to the leitmotiv. As defined by Monaco and Riordan, the hook is "a musical or lyrical phrase that stands out and is easily remembered."[36] Because of its prominence and memorability, the hook is the chief means by which pop songs attract the attention of their audience. Gary Burns points out that the term itself carries the connotations of being snagged (as when a fish is hooked) or addicted (as when someone is hooked on drugs). Within the context of pop music, both connotations relate to the notion of a song's marketability. Radio listeners are caught, so to speak, by an infectious bit of melody or clever turn of phrase, and are hooked in the addictive sense as a consequence of the hook's memorability and repetition. In Burns's view, repetition is not essential in a hook—some hooks are absolutely unforgettable on a first hearing—but it nonetheless enhances the probability that the hook will remain firmly lodged in the listener's memory.[37] Some well-known examples of hooks include the unusual I-bII harmony in Jefferson Airplane's "White Rabbit" and the five-note fuzz guitar line that begins the Rolling Stones' "Satisfaction."

Virtually any aspect of a song's musical structure, performance, or production may serve as a hook, but most share one integral feature: hooks are generally compact enough to fit the constraints of listener memory.[38] An eight-bar rhythm intro, a skipped beat, a two-bar guitar riff, an unusual chord change, or even a snatch of foreign or nonsense language are all capable of functioning as hooks within the proper context, and none take longer than a few seconds to be stated. In this regard, hooks share strong similarities with leitmotivs, which functioned in a similar way to address the limitations of untutored listeners. As Meyer points out, the length of music's structural units is not solely a matter of convention. Musical phrases tend to range between four and eight measures, since that length roughly coincides with the density of information that can be efficiently stored in short-term memory.[39] Pop hooks typically take this a step further by combining their structural brevity with a syntactic and hierarchical simplicity. In doing so, the pop song reduces the possibility of "interference" from other musical parameters and increases the likelihood that the hook will be gleaned from the musical surface.

The importance of this for the pop score is twofold. First, it suggests that the pop score's adaptation of song forms serves as an efficient means of repeating pop hooks. Whether AABA or ABAB, the song form assures a certain amount of recurrence for its basic structural units. Hooks—be they melodic, harmonic, or rhythmic—thus achieve a high degree of repetition and are more apt to be noticed and remembered by listeners. And since the pop song is largely a commercial form, this repetition of hooks also increases the likelihood that listeners will consume the product in the form of records and sheet music.

More importantly, the link between repetition and listener awareness also helps to explain the pop score's reiteration of themes across the film. By restating the theme in different contexts, the pop score furthered the possibility that a theme would remain lodged in viewers' minds, and that they would then seek out the tune in one of many ancillary markets. To some extent, the commercial impetus for this structural repetition of themes was already present in the monothematic scores of the fifties (and to a lesser degree in earlier decades), which were organized around the pervasive use of a single melody. *Laura* (1944) is perhaps the paradigmatic example of the monotheme score, but its formula was successfully duplicated in *High Noon* (1952), *Love Is a Many-Splendored Thing* (1955) and *Around the World in Eighty Days* (1956).[40] During the fifties, producers demanded these scores in order to capitalize on the promotional value of a marketable tune, and as the examples above demonstrate, they were frequently rewarded with the revenues from both a hit film and a hit song.

In the 1960s, the pop score expanded the number of themes to fit the format of the soundtrack album, but retained the principle of structural repetition to highlight an individual theme that was simultaneously promoted via radio, records, and television performances. Songs like "Goldfinger," "Moon River" from *Breakfast at Tiffany's*, and "Lara's Theme (Somewhere My Love)" from *Doctor Zhivago* (1965) were amply repeated within their respective films in order to strengthen their prospects as commercial singles. In fact, some historians report that *Zhivago*'s director, David Lean, went back after the score was finished and added more cues featuring "Lara's Theme" to boost the score's profit potential. Whether the changes had any effect is open to question, but *Doctor Zhivago* went on to sell over two million soundtrack albums and millions more in various single versions of the theme.

Using Gary Burns's typology of hooks, a brief analysis of the title theme from *Goldfinger* (which is discussed in more detail in chapter 4) reveals both the formal accessibility of its component parts and the various ways in which pop hooks interact to make a film theme memorable. The first hook is one that Burns himself notes—the unusual tonic-flatted submediant chord change that begins the song (figure 1.1).[41]

FIGURE 1.1

After its initial statement, this harmonic hook is then repeated three times in succession to complete the tune's introduction. The novelty of the chord change by itself is almost enough to guarantee its memorability, but composer John Barry repeats it three more times to underline its importance both as a hook and as a foundation for the rest of the song.

Following the initial statement of the harmonic hook, a second hook (figure 1.1) is introduced which uses sonority and tone color to grab the listener's attention: a blaring, cupped trumpet that slides between an E and G# and hovers between the two chords of the introduction. This style of playing is not especially unique within a jazz context, but it sounded fresh in 1964 against a predominantly rock 'n' roll, pop, and rhythm-and-blues background.[42] Like the harmonic hook, the trumpet hook is then repeated three times, the last two an octave lower, to similarly reinforce its memorability.

FIGURE 1.2

The third hook is a melody hook that begins the tune proper (figure 1.2). The first three notes are played over the song's harmonic hook and derive their importance as a melodic unit by establishing the song's title and by using an appoggiatura to underline the distinctiveness of the underlying harmony. Varied recurrences of this melody hook appear later in the song's verse and coda sections.

FIGURE 1.3

The first variation (figure 1.3) expands the opening interval by a semitone and adds a chromatic passing tone between the second and third notes of the hook. The second variation (figure 1.3) inverts the contour of the hook by outlining a G flat triad that then moves up a whole step to resolve on a sustained A flat. Neither of these recurrences is a direct transposition of the hook, but they maintain its overall shape of a leap followed by a whole step. According to Burns, these varied recurrences sometimes result in the variation and modulation of individual hooks. As such, they add formal interest to a tune while simultaneously bolstering the melody hook's memorability.

The fourth type of hook in "Goldfinger" is a subset of the melody hook, one that Burns defines as a form of melodic intertextuality. This hook is the chromatically rising countermelody introduced in the song's bridge section, and it makes direct reference to the film's other main musical theme, the well-known "James Bond Theme" (figure 1.4):

FIGURE 1.4

Later in the coda, this intertextual hook will find a formal counterpart in a second reference to the "James Bond Theme" (figure 1.5):

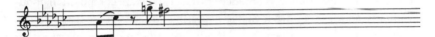

FIGURE 1.5

Of course, both of these intertextual hooks require the listener's familiarity with the original, and they reinforce the quote by referencing other structural elements from their source, namely its rhythm and harmony.[43]

Finally, pitch itself functions as a hook in the song's coda. As Burns notes, many songs have a single highest note, which usually appears near the end of the song to mark its climax. "Goldfinger" uses pitch in a similar fashion by employing its highest note—a long, sustained E flat—as the last note of the song. The late appearance of this hook does not negate its importance, but rather suggests how hooks function in subsequent hearings. The appearance of this high E flat may surprise listeners on a first pass, but on repeated hearings listeners will anticipate it as a satisfying climax to the record.

In "Goldfinger," harmonic, melodic, and instrumental hooks work together both to grab the listener's attention and to lodge the song firmly in his/her consciousness. Moreover, the formal operations of these hooks illustrate the significance of formal accessibility in the creation of hit songs, especially hit film themes. Each of these hooks fits the constraints on short-term memory, and most are repeated a number of times to enhance the probability that they will be retained by the listener. The hook's brevity and simplicity accentuates the song's formal accessibility by enabling both musically trained and untrained listeners to comprehend the basic features of the tune's musical surface. As in other great pop songs, the combination of these factors gives "Goldfinger" an "addictive" appeal. Whether it is played on the radio or in a theater, the song's hooks are designed to snag listeners and to motivate their consumption of the theme in single or album form. *Goldfinger*'s other cues strengthen the theme's appeal by repeating it in other dramatic contexts. These varied recurrences restate the theme's various hooks and assist the score's development of a rich and efficient memory imprint. Both within the tune and within the score, the formal accessibility of "Goldfinger" promised a broad appeal to potential consumers and helped "sell" the film's music in a number of ancillary markets.

Despite contemporary criticism of the pop score, film music composed in popular idioms appeared with increasing frequency from the 1960s to the present. Generally speaking, these scores share two criteria that distinguish them from their classical Hollywood predecessors: (1) they are composed in popular idioms, and (2) they are formally accessible to the average listener. The development of these criteria was largely governed by commercial rather than aesthetic concerns. When jazz scores began to fall out of favor in the mid-sixties, composers began incorporating rock as well as rhythm-and-blues idioms in response to a general change in audience tastes.

Yet while commercial exploitation was preeminent in the pop score's development, it was not the only factor that concerned these pop composers. *Breakfast at Tiffany's*, *Goldfinger*, *The Good, the Bad, and the Ugly*, and other films revealed that pop music might be used in ways that satisfied a film's dramatic requirements. Working with different compositional strategies and untraditional musical forms, composers like Mancini, Barry, Morricone, Francis Lai, Lalo Schifrin, and Quincy Jones were able to do what had appeared to be impossible only ten or twenty years earlier: they created music in popular idioms that enhanced emotions and moods, cued characters and settings, and signified psychological states and points of view. In doing so, they also subtly altered the spectator's experience of film music. By integrating music with plot and action, the pop score moved from a position of subordination within the hierarchy of sound and image to a position of equivalence.

Because of its complex interrelation of convention and invention, innovation and tradition, the pop score is an ideal site for demonstrating the range and diversity of compositional practices that emerged alongside the development of the soundtrack album. To plot this development, I have structured the remainder of this book into roughly equal parts of history and critical analysis. The second chapter supplies a detailed historical framework for the pop score by specifying the economic, social, and historical factors that governed the structural interactions between the film and record industries. Chief among these was the rise of radio and records as the primary ancillary markets for film music. When film companies began either creating or purchasing record subsidiaries in the late fifties, they began to explore a number of different strategies for exploiting these ancillary markets. Chapter 3 examines the market for film music and the variety of techniques used to promote it, including multiple single releases, sales-order screenings, and movie theaters as point-of-purchase retail outlets.

Chapters 4 through 7 offer readings of particular films and film scores. The choice of these films was governed by a couple of criteria. Primary was the fact that each of these scores successfully serve both dramatic and commercial functions. More detailed information about each score's marketing is presented later, but for now suffice it to say that these four soundtracks were among the top-selling albums of their decade. I should note here, however, that for the sake of clarity I have chosen to analyze the scores of comedies and dramas rather than musicals. Although musicals were among the highest-selling soundtrack albums of the period, the genre poses special problems for a discussion of film scoring because of its relative emphasis on spectacle and musical performance. Rather than entangle myself in these issues, I have considered the musical largely outside the scope of this study insofar as my interest lies mainly with the influence of film music's commodity functions on the development of specific styles and scoring practices. My second reason for choosing these films was that each of these particular scores reveals a different facet of the range and diversity of compositional practices during this period. Although the three composers who are the subject of this study—Henry Mancini, John Barry, and Ennio Morricone—share an interest in melodic hooks, unusual tone colors, and song structure, they employed very different strategies for showcasing the tunes that appear on the film's soundtrack albums. Mancini utilized diegetic cues as opportunities to flesh out his scores with light jazz instrumentals. Barry used the popular "girls and guns" credit sequences of the James Bond films as a means of highlighting its series of commercially exploitable songs. Morricone turned the spaghetti western's showdowns and reckonings into highly stylized cinematic set pieces, ones that combined stunning visuals and rapturous music to create memorable marriages of image and sound.

The chapter on Henry Mancini focuses on *Breakfast at Tiffany's*. More specifically, it describes Mancini's development of a multitheme formal organization as a means of adapting the pop score to the format of the typical album. Additionally, it also examines the film's treatment of its central musical theme, "Moon River." Ironically, the theme both supports and undermines the film's treatment of heterosexual romance by signifying the incestuous wish that drives Holly Golightly's narrative goals.

Chapter 5 discusses John Barry's work on the James Bond series, particularly his score for *Goldfinger*. The Bond series is especially notable since its producers innovated the idea of using pop songs as a regularized element of the films' promotion. By adapting film music to this process, Barry developed a potent formula for the typical Bond score. This chapter describes each of the components of this formula and how it interacts with the archetypal Bond narrative. In the case of *Goldfinger*, this interaction creates a striking parallel between the film's villain and its ambiguous hero, and implicitly questions the film's treatment of its female characters.

Chapter 6 examines the work of Italian composer Ennio Morricone on *The Good, the Bad, and the Ugly*. Although Morricone partly operated in the context of Italy's film and record industry, he is central to the development of the pop score for two reasons: his use of tone color, particularly that of the electric guitar, paved the way for many rock composers who followed him; and Morricone's treatment of sound and image relations proved to be an extremely effective means of showcasing particular musical themes to encourage sales of the film's soundtrack album. Working against a background of film jukebox technologies, Morricone epitomizes a more general trend toward highlighting music within cinematic set pieces, and thereby integrating sound and image to create a unified stylistic whole.

Chapter 7 looks at the reemergence of the compilation score. As a form that frequently uses prerecorded songs as dramatic underscore, the compilation score represents the most radical departure from classical Hollywood scoring practices. Despite its formal differences, however, the compilation score nonetheless serves many of the same dramatic functions, particularly in terms of setting and characterization. As the analysis of *American Graffiti* reveals, the compilation score often achieves its dramatic aims through a process of association and allusion. As such, it typically relies on an audience's familiarity with the music to fill in gaps in character motivation or to comment on a character's actions.

The final chapter discusses the continuing cross-promotional value of soundtracks in the age of the Hollywood blockbuster and the compact disk. The ascendance of pop and rock music on soundtrack albums in the 1970s resulted in a number of significant changes for composers, publishers, and record companies. As record companies developed specific soundtrack divisions, rock stars, music supervisors, and MTV all emerged as important players in the industry. Furthermore, film and record producers also began to target their market much more specifically, with many soundtracks serving as a sampler of a particular style or genre. By narrowing their market potential to a particular fan base, producers redefined contemporary notions of cross-promotion. Pop scores became ends in themselves as certain films sometimes became little more than a pretext for record promotion.

By adopting contemporary sounds and musical forms, the pop score established an identity that functioned outside the confines of both the film's textual economy and the theatrical exhibition situation. For most composers, however, the challenge of the pop score resided in its particular negotiation of dramatic and commercial functions. In the title of his autobiography—*Did They Mention the Music?*—Mancini subtly alludes to this concern for self-identity and the commercial struggles that lay behind it. Yet, as we will see in subsequent chapters, Mancini's anxiety about his music being noticed was quite unfounded. To Mancini's query and for many pop and rock film scores, the sound of the radio and the ringing of record store cash registers answered with a resounding "Yes!"

2

Banking on Film Music

STRUCTURAL INTERACTIONS OF THE FILM AND RECORD INDUSTRIES

In November 1960, Cameo Records released a new single entitled "Theme from *The Young Ones*."[1] According to a Cameo spokesperson, the tune was not actually from a film or television series, but the firm nonetheless chose this title in the hope that the words "Theme from . . ." would sell more records.[2] Though this release is unquestionably a very minor footnote in the history of recorded music, it is nonetheless interesting for what it reveals about the record industry's attitudes toward the market for film scores.

Cameo assumed that the people who buy film themes and soundtrack albums are not necessarily going to see the films with which they are connected. After all, since this was a theme from a nonexistent film, the high sales envisioned by the company was predicated on a public interest in movie music as simply music, regardless of any tie it might have to what was playing at the local cinema. This presumption went against the prevailing wisdom in the industry, which generally treated film music as a promotional tool rather than as a self-sufficient musical product. As it turns out, Cameo was probably wrong in this first assumption. Though it is impossible to generalize from a single case, the failure of "Theme from *The Young Ones*" to achieve any meaningful sales suggests that films did indeed play some part in attracting the attention of record buyers.

This is not to say, however, that Cameo's decision was foolish or imprudent. At a time when film music reportedly accounted for 20 percent of all album sales, the company simply took note of the fact that more and more soundtrack albums were being released and record companies were selling more of each individual title. At the start of this cycle, some thirty-eight soundtrack albums were released in the first nine months of 1958.[3] That figure grew incrementally over the next three years until it stabilized at about seventy to eighty releases a year.[4] Whereas an earlier album like *Around the World in Eighty Days* was deemed a success if it sold more than 100,000 copies, albums like *Exodus* (1960), *The Alamo* (1960), *The Apartment* (1960), and *Never on Sunday* (1960) were selling two to five times that number.[5] Recognizing this growth market, Cameo assumed consumer interest in film music would continue and released "Theme from *The Young Ones*" to cash in on the trend. By the time of *The Graduate* (1967) and *Easy Rider* (1969), soundtracks were no longer simply promotional tools but were intrinsically valuable musical commodities.

In this chapter, I will examine the emergence of the soundtrack album as a vehicle for cross-promotion. To do this, however, we must first situate film music more generally within its economic, industrial, and historical context. The reasons for such contextualization are simple; theories of film music can explain certain aspects of film music's form and function, but they cannot account for everything. One must also consider the economic and cultural factors that engendered its development. In this instance, such factors include both the economic structures of the film and music industries, and the emergence of radio and records as the most important means of circulating film music.

Recent work in the fields of musicology and ethnomusicology has been especially sensitive to the ways in which this mix of ideological mechanisms helps to shape specific musical forms, styles, and patterns of consumption.[6] By emphasizing culture and ideology, such work questions the treatment of music as an autonomous art, one that somehow transcends the realms of society and culture. Film music would seem especially fertile ground for exploring these relations since, by its very nature, it is not an autonomous art form. Rather, a film score is always fundamentally a component of a larger signifying system, the motion picture, and as such film music would seem doubly suspect in its contingency. Not only is the music dependent on its filmic context, it is also part of a cultural form that is itself all too entangled in issues of commercialism and social relevance.

Paradoxically, however, in the case of the sixties pop score, film producers and record companies sought a kind of musical autonomy, albeit one that strongly differed from that described by aestheticians and musicologists. Like the aesthetician, film producers hoped to free the score from its immediate filmic context, but unlike the aesthetician, they did so by commodifying it and reinscribing it in alternative marketplaces. Thus, in bringing film music to another audience, producers did not pursue the rarefied airs of concert halls, but ventured instead into the more prosaic, commercialized spaces of radio airwaves and record sales charts. In separating the music from the film it accompanied, the pop score was not made to be raptly appreciated; it was made to be bought and sold.

Many film composers thus responded to an overriding imperative to make their music widely heard. In doing so, they satisfied the film industry's desire for ancillary profits and effective promotion while increasing their own commercial value. To achieve these ends, composers explored a set of formal parameters (unusual orchestrations, the emphasis on melody, the treatment of themes rather than leitmotivs) that adapted film scores to the pop album's emphasis on self-sufficient tunes and melodic/instrumental hooks. Later chapters will take a closer look at how these formal principles structured the pop score and influenced the filmic texts these scores accompanied. For now, however, I will examine the economic and social factors that served as preconditions for the soundtrack album's emergence.

Creating Kingdoms of Song: The Film and Music Industries Unite

The 1950s were a period of moderate upheaval for both the film and music business. After lengthy terms of oligopoly control, the major companies of both industries faced changes in corporate organization and market structure. They also confronted the challenges of new lifestyles and new entertainment technologies. In the case of the film industry, many of these industrial changes were precipitated by the Supreme Court's *Paramount* decision of 1948, which ended unfair distribution practices, such as block booking, and forced the divestiture of the studios' theater holdings. By effectively ending Hollywood's system of vertical integration, the *Paramount* decision helped to weaken the Production Code Administration, renewed an emphasis on foreign markets, and encouraged the rise of independent film production.

Not coincidentally, the strengthening of independent production also became important within the music business. Between 1948 and 1955, the record industry was dominated by four firms: Capitol, Columbia, Decca, and RCA Victor. After 1955, however, this oligopoly was challenged by a major influx of new artists and independent record labels.[7] Much of this new competition was linked to the emergence of rhythm and blues and rock 'n' roll. Atlantic, Chess, Monument, Sun Records, and other labels utilized these new forms to break the majors' stronghold on the record charts. Between 1955 and 1959, aggregate record sales increased by 261 percent, and by the end of the decade retail record sales totaled more than a half billion dollars. These independent labels accounted for approximately 60 percent of the total sales of 45-rpm singles and for about 75 percent of the tunes that made it onto *Billboard*'s most important sales charts.[8]

While several factors contributed to the soundtrack album's emergence in the late fifties and early sixties, the most important was the trend toward diversification and conglomeration that followed the *Paramount* decree. Beginning with the takeover of Universal Pictures by Decca Records in 1952, several motion picture producers and distributors became subsidiaries of huge conglomerates with active and interrelated entertainment divisions.[9] Through such diversification, companies could spread their risks by creating additional "profit centers" to amortize production costs and exploit various kinds of cross-promotional marketing practices.[10]

Historically, music subsidiaries have traditionally served as prime sources of cross-promotion and diversification. A relatively recent instance of this is the idea of *synergy*, which is discussed in more detail in chapter 8. The term, coined by music supervisor Danny Goldberg, became a marketing buzzword during the 1980s. According to R. Serge Denisoff and George Plasketes, the strategy of synergy held that the common cross-promotion of films and records could benefit both industries in almost equal measure. For a film company, sales of soundtrack albums could amortize production costs while radio airplay of film themes served as a cheap and practical form of advertising. For a record company, on the other hand, the link to a film gave a soundtrack album needed name recognition in a highly competitive market. When all cogs of the promotional machine were smoothly functioning, interest in one component "synergistically" fed off interest in the other until both film and soundtrack album reigned supreme over box offices and record charts.[11]

Although the term *synergy* is of more recent vintage, the idea that film music played an important economic function within the industry goes back at least to the early 1910s. For the most part, this economic function operated at the level of live exhibition during this period of silent films. As Chuck Berg points out, one way that exhibitors could differentiate themselves was by promoting the musicians themselves as a kind of special attraction. Musicians typically earned their reputations either through the quality of their performances or through the character of their personality. According to Berg, some accompanists were known as "film funners" for the humor they displayed in their performances:

The film funner would, for example, accompany a dramatic scene where bur-
glars are craftily entering the heroine's home with the strains of the romantic love song, "Meet Me in the Shadows." Such a performer often became a
distinct feature of the house for which he played and was sure of an audience
of his own which came largely "to see what he would do with the pictures."[12]

Other musicians became known for their ability to ply the audience with
familiar melodies. Satisfying a particular audience sometimes meant soliciting
requests, playing currently popular songs, or matching the musical accompaniment to the specific composition of the audience, such as playing Italian
pieces for a predominantly Italian crowd.

Most of these early cross-promotional efforts concerned the sale of sheet
music, which by 1910 had surpassed thirty million in annual aggregate sales.
To capitalize on this emerging new market, several exhibitors included song
slides and singers as special attractions in their programs. The singers were
frequently employed by music publishers for the express purpose of "plugging" a particular tune. In exchange for the plug, the exhibitor typically sold
copies of sheet music in the theater and retained a small percentage of the
monies from such sales. Both publishers and exhibitors benefited from these
kinds of arrangements. Publishers gained increased promotion for their
music while exhibitors enjoyed greater attendance and received the services
of top-notch singers for little or no cost.[13]

The heightened awareness of music in cinema led to several tie-ins between
the film and music industries. In 1914, for example, songwriters created a
minor fad for tunes about serial heroines. One of the earliest was "Kathlyn,"
a hesitation waltz honoring two-reeler star Kathlyn Williams, and it was
swiftly followed by the similarly themed "Zudora," "Runaway June," "Lucille
Love," and "Poor Pauline," a spoof of Pearl White's classic *The Perils of
Pauline*. In fact, the vogue for "serial" music nearly overshadowed two other
cinematically inspired tunes published in 1914: "Those Charlie Chaplin Feet"
and "He's Working in the Movies Now," the latter a comic ditty depicting an
indolent father's transformation into an industrious movie stuntman.[14]

Sales of all sheet music exploded between 1910 and 1918, much of it driven by the opening of music counters in "five and dime" stores like
Woolworth's, Kresge, and McCrory. With more than one thousand stores,
Woolworth's became the largest retailer of sheet music, selling some two
hundred million copies in 1918 alone. With a standard selling price of ten
cents and a wholesale price of six cents, Woolworth's made a tidy 40 percent
profit on every piece of sheet music that it sold.[15]

This same period also witnessed the rise of the "musical illustration" as a specific film genre. According to Berg, these films were a variation of the song slide principle as they were not only created to go with a specific song but also illustrated that song dramatically. Interest in this genre culminated in the late 'teens with two series of song illustrations produced by Harry Cohn and Carl Laemmle, respectively. By featuring song slides and filmed "illustrations" of music, movie theaters joined department stores, music shops, and vaudeville as important venues for song-plugging and as hubs of a multimillion dollar industry.[16]

The practice of using song slides gradually died out in the 1920s when composers began writing specific theme songs for films. Although sheet music sales for film themes were generally modest in the early twenties, the music industry nonetheless took note of the promotional possibilities tendered by a specially composed or compiled film score. In 1920, for example, Columbia Records advised their retailers that "each week the tune studded talking picture leaves customers of yours with impressively presented theme songs echoing in their ears."[17]

According to Russell Sanjek, the first attempt at coordinated cross-promotion occurred in 1918 when Marshall Neilan commissioned a title song for Mabel Normand's *Mickey* that went on to become an unlikely hit. Written and published by Kansas City songwriter Charles N. Daniels, the sales of "Mickey" were undoubtedly boosted by a featured photograph of Normand and ad copy that called attention to her role in the film. Still, the unforeseen fortunes of "Mickey" were clearly the exception rather than the rule. For the most part, the stiff opposition of the American Society of Composers, Authors, and Publishers (ASCAP) served as an unassailable obstacle to the regular use of Tin Pan Alley songs as film promotion.[18]

Late silent and early sound films reversed this trend, however, with the estimable success of "Charmaine" from *What Price Glory?* (1926) and "Diane" from *Seventh Heaven* (1927). The introduction of prerecorded musical soundtracks not only wrested away the last element of film presentation that was under the exhibitor's purview, but it also undermined ASCAP's putative control over silent film music. For years, ASCAP had battled with theater owners over licensing fees for ASCAP-owned music used in silent film accompaniment. Exhibitors countered with lesser-known tunes and original compositions, which were often provided by production companies and studios. However, these efforts were ultimately thwarted by the relative paucity of high-quality, unlicensed music. This became especially evident when ASCAP's reorganization precipitated the sudden withdrawal of huge lists of previously unlicensed music. Much of this music was prepared for the 13,000 members of the Motion Picture Theater Owners Association, but ASCAP's new copyright control made it virtually untouchable. Both factions reached a compromise in 1926 when some 11,000 theater owners became ASCAP licensees and paid over a half million dollars in fees, a figure that comprised more than 50 percent of the association's income that year.[19]

The coming of sound altered this balance of power as Hollywood invested in songwriters, composers, and music publishing houses. Since filmmakers could now be assured that the same music would be played during every showing of an individual film, the new technology had, in effect, standardized the film score. More importantly, by commissioning original songs and scores, producers were able to free themselves from the dependence on ASCAP-owned music. This did not necessarily help exhibitors, who continued to pay a dime-per-seat licensing fee, but it did shift ASCAP's attention away from theater owners and toward the film studios themselves.

Despite Warner Brothers' initial protestation that it was protected under the mechanical licensing provision of copyright law, ASCAP's control over licensed music threatened to halt Warner's production of vaudeville and musical shorts before it even got started. Recognizing its vulnerable position, Warner signed an agreement with ASCAP that obliged the studio to pay a $100,000 minimum annual royalty for recorded or synchronized music rights. RCA Photophone and the East Coast Sonoraphone Company soon followed suit, and in 1928 it was announced that ASCAP and the Music Publishers Protective Association (MPPA) would receive at least a million dollars per year in royalties in exchange for the synchronization rights to their music.[20]

Hollywood soon realized that the film industry had to control a large enough number of music copyrights to make it totally independent of any combine of music publishers and songwriters.[21] Although Paramount and Loew's were the first to buy their own publishing houses, it was Warner Brothers' purchase of the original Tin Pan Alley house, M. Witmark & Sons, in January 1929 that signaled Hollywood's more aggressive stance toward ASCAP. Five months later, Warner added to its newly formed music division when it took control of Max Dreyfus's music publishing holdings, which included the Harms Music Publishing Company, a 50 percent interest in the Remick Music Corporation, a smaller share of DeSylva, Brown, and Henderson, and a host of smaller music houses. By mid-1929, Warner's music division alone commanded a major share of the music publishers' vote in ASCAP policymaking. As studios either bought or formed their own music publishing subsidiaries, Hollywood not only freed itself from the threat of outrageous synchronization fees but was also now in a position to generate added revenues from the songs it featured in original musicals.[22]

It is important to note, however, that these revenues came in two forms. There was the actual monies earned from music publishing royalties and licensing fees. In 1935, for example, Warner estimated that it would earn more than a million dollars a year from its music publishing interests.[23] And from 1937 to 1939, the thirteen music houses affiliated with Hollywood earned about two-thirds of the total monies distributed to publishers by ASCAP. Second, there was the added box office revenues generated by the successful exploitation of a film's theme song or featured music. According to a 1939 estimate, a combination of radio airplay, record sales, and sheet music plugging added as much as a million dollars to an individual film's box office gross.[24]

Between 1930 and 1943, Hollywood's control of the music publishing industry and its employment of the industry's top songwriters prompted the film song's greatest period of success. Although the bulk of these songs were culled from original movie musicals (especially those written by Irving Berlin, Rodgers and Hart, and George and Ira Gershwin), notable film songs also came from westerns, romances, and melodramas. Between 1936 and 1942, film songs were regularly found atop *Variety*'s weekly roster of the twenty-five most-played songs. Additionally, a Peatman survey showed that Hollywood and Broadway together accounted for more than 80 percent of the most-performed songs in 1942.[25]

Although during the Depression radio had gradually replaced sheet music as the film industry's most important ancillary market, World War II brought renewed prosperity to the printed music business. The combination of gas rations and luxury taxes encouraged families to stay home for their entertainment, a factor that greatly boosted sheet music sales during the early part of the war. Annual aggregate sales of sheet music rose to forty million copies in 1943. By the end of the war, the music publishing industry anticipated a $10 million gross from ASCAP distributions and royalties on sheet music and record sales.[26]

The resurgence in sheet music sales was also abetted by the emergence of the music rack business as an important new distribution outlet. After a deal was struck between the MPPA and the Hearst Corporation in 1940, sheet music display racks were installed in some five hundred newsstands across the country. So-called rack jobbers were employed to stock these new display units, which customarily carried two copies each of the twenty best-selling new songs. By 1944 the number of racks had grown to about 13,000, a number that guaranteed each best-seller an initial order of at least 93,000 copies. In addition, because of its portability, music racks made sheet music available in more different kinds of retail outlets than ever before. Places like barbershops, newsstands, and stationery stores, which had never before carried sheet music, were now selling it to their customers.

In the years that immediately followed the war, however, film songs no longer reigned supreme over radio and sheet music markets. According to the Peatman survey, Hollywood's and Broadway's share of the most performed songs declined to a total of about 40 percent between 1944 and 1951. Publishers blamed this downturn on three different factors: (1) the failure of films to adequately highlight new songs; (2) the changing tastes of film producers and directors; and (3) a decline in the overall quality of songwriters' outputs.[27]

Perhaps the most important factor, however, was one that publishers did not wish to acknowledge—the growth of the market for recorded music. With the advent of the LP (long-playing record), the 45-rpm single, and the transistor radio, the downward spiral continued over the next several years. Initial orders for sheet music racks dropped to about 75,000 copies, and most songs were unable to sell out even this amount. The top sheet music tune of 1958, "Volare," sold less than 250,000, a far cry from the 3.5 million copies of "Till We Meet Again" that were sold some forty years earlier. By the end of the 1950s, the number one song on the weekly *Your Hit Parade* averaged only 15,000 copies in print form. As the market for sheet music declined, publishers soon realized that their revenues would come from royalties and licensing fees rather than outright sales. By the late fifties, the music racks that had once stocked thousands of copies of sheet music were selling record albums instead.

Establishing a "Sound Track" Record: The Majors and Their Record Subsidiaries

The weakening of the sheet music market, however, did not mean that Hollywood had given up on the idea of film and music cross-promotion. Rather, the majors simply redirected their efforts toward the burgeoning market of recorded music. According to figures released by the Recording Industry Association of America (RIAA), the total sales of all types of records increased dramatically between 1946, during which eight million disks were sold, and 1951, during which some 180 million disks were sold.[28]

Furthermore, this upward trend continued steadily, if less spectacularly, throughout the 1950s. Between 1951 and 1959 the annual sum of records' retail sales had grown from $191 million to $514 million. Of course, Hollywood's investment in the record industry goes back at least to 1930 when Warner Brothers followed its purchase of several music publishing houses by acquiring Brunswick Records. At the time, Warner had envisioned the possibility of not only owning the music in its films but also releasing it on records. Warner's initial involvement in the record business was short-lived, however, as the studio sold its Brunswick subsidiary to the American Record Company about a year later.[29] After Warner's dalliance, Hollywood had little involvement in the record industry until MGM started up its own subsidiary in the mid-1940s.

After Decca's landmark purchase of Universal, the five other Hollywood majors sought to start up or acquire record subsidiaries between 1957 and 1958. Their activity was prompted by several causal mechanisms, among them the overall climate of diversification and conglomeration, the shrinking sheet music market, and the sudden boom in record sales. Besides the opportunities for cross-promotion, these studios hoped to create subsidiaries that were profitable ventures in themselves. As *Variety* noted in January 1958, "The film companies want in to the record business for more than just pic tie-in reasons. They realize it's a booming business and they want a share."[30]

Paramount was the first to take the plunge in early 1957 with its buyout of Dot Records, one of the most successful of the current crop of indie labels. Paramount paid a fairly high price for the label, some $2 million and a hefty chunk of company stock. By purchasing Dot, the film company not only gained a label with a 12 percent share of the singles market, they also profited from the expertise of Dot's rising young executive, Randy Woods. Under Wood's careful management, the label grossed over $10 million in its first year as a subsidiary, and earned back its parent company's initial investment within five years.[31]

In October 1957, United Artists followed Paramount's lead by launching two new subsidiaries, the UA Records Corporation and the UA Music Corporation. Unlike Paramount, however, United Artists did not purchase existing companies but started their own from the ground up. As Sanjek notes, UA Music began largely as a "desk-drawer operation" that controlled only about fifty copyrights.[32] With virtually no artists or repertoire, UA Records set up distribution agreements similar to that of its parent company. In its first year of operation, UA Records did not produce any of its own music but instead leased masters from outside sources. UA Records offered financing, distribution, and a 50 percent share of a record's net profits on a production-to-production basis. Although these terms brought some proven songwriter-producer teams to UA Records, the label's most important assets were undoubtedly the soundtracks leased from films distributed by its parent corporation. Using these film scores as the centerpiece of its sales and distribution program, UA Records set a rather ambitious goal of grossing $10 million within two years.

By the middle of 1958, Warner Brothers, 20th Century-Fox, and Columbia Pictures had all leapt into the disk business with companies that were, like UA Records, started from scratch. The film companies benefited from the growing stature of the record business as well as the added exploitation angles for studio product and increased exposure for contracted performers. Since none of these companies was able to purchase established labels, the studio's film exchanges provided ready-made promotional outlets for its own record subsidiaries' product.[33] Such arrangements had an obvious disadvantage in that film distributors knew little about record marketing. However, it did allow these newly formed subsidiaries to overcome an enormous barrier to entry and maintain the close coordination of film and soundtrack sales programs.

Ironically, the hopes of these new labels were boosted by the somewhat mixed fortunes of one of their competitors. In February 1958, Loew's Inc. issued its annual financial statement and reported some rather surprising news. Although films were undoubtedly the company's bread and butter, the firm's most profitable enterprises were its music and broadcast subsidiaries. In fact, although the company had lost almost $7.8 million from its motion picture production and distribution operations, its fortunes were salvaged by the $4 million earned by Loew's theaters and the $5.5 million income from MGM Records, its subsidiary the Big Three Music Company, and WMGM Radio in New York City. All told, Loew's realized a net profit of $1.3 million in 1957, which the firm largely attributed to its disk and music publishing ventures.[34] Moreover, in an attempt to maximize its resources, MGM named Arnold Maxin the new president of its disk label and announced in early 1958 that the studio was instituting a stronger program of coordinated disk and film promotion, one that emphasized both musicals and nonmusicals alike.[35]

As *Variety* reported in early 1958, the sudden influx of film companies into the disk market had subtly altered the industry's geographical balance of power. New York City, the site of Columbia, Decca, and RCA Victor's corporate headquarters, had long been the center of the disk business. However, with Capitol Records as the solid nucleus of a flourishing new industrial sector, Hollywood had suddenly emerged as a significant rival to New York's dominance. In the face of Hollywood competition, a number of record companies and music publishers sought to upgrade their West Coast operations and improve their fortunes in the film music market. RCA Victor, for example, revamped its entire West Coast setup in order to compete with the new labels for soundtrack product. Additionally, the Harry Fox office, a music publishing agent and trustee, set up a Los Angeles branch in late 1957 for the specific purpose of collecting mechanical royalties and synchronization fees.[36]

By the end of 1960, *Variety* had proclaimed the sales of soundtrack albums one of the most significant commercial trends of the year:

> Along with comics and percussion, motion picture music had one of its most successful years in 1960. It was a throwback to the time when every film had a title song, even if it came out like "Woman Disputed, I Love You." This year, the titles were no block to the pic songs and scores being cut in bulk and hitting with a remarkably high average.[37]

Billboard added, "The record and motion picture industries are working in closer and more effective harmony today than they have since the golden days of movie musicals."[38]

By the middle of 1961, however, industry analysts also proclaimed an end to the "era of the high flying indie diskers."[39] A number of independent labels had made significant inroads into the pop singles market, but the huge volume of releases, approximately a hundred a week during the late fifties, had oversaturated the market and thinned out the sales potential of all but a few genuine hits. More importantly, small independents were severely hurt by the payola scandal that erupted in the latter part of the decade. With major market stations receiving some five thousand new releases each year, small indies were deprived of an important weapon for influencing disk jockeys and radio airplay, and consequently many of them were unable to get their disks even auditioned. Lacking established artists, durable distribution, and consistent operational patterns, small independent labels scrambled for the scraps of a risky, hit-or-miss business. And with the pop singles trade returning to the control of a dozen major labels, a number of independent record companies simply fell by the wayside.

The film-owned labels were among the independent survivors, but they experienced varying degrees of success. Warner Bros. Records, for example, floundered during its first three years of operations and racked up a $2 million deficit by the middle of 1961. The company considered shutting its doors, but changed its mind when it uncovered a large number of unpaid distributors' accounts. After signing such artists as the Everly Brothers, Bob Newhart, Allan Sherman, and Peter, Paul, and Mary, Warner's fortunes experienced a rapid turnaround and the firm was solidly in the black by May 1963.[40] With the company's prospects more secure, Warner then renewed its efforts at sound-track promotion in late 1963 with André Previn's *Dead Ringer* (1964), Manos Hadjidakis' *America, America* (1963), and Neal Hefti's *Sex and the Single Girl* (1964), which featured performances by Count Basie and his Orchestra.[41]

Columbia's subsidiary, Colpix Records, experienced slow but steady growth in its first five years of operations. Under the management of Paul Wexler and Jonie Taps, Colpix developed a number of teen idols as singles artists, such as James Darren and Shelley Fabares, but generally failed to exploit the potential of the album and film music markets.[42] That changed in the middle of 1962 when Columbia Pictures made a series of moves to consolidate its various music subsidiaries. First of all, Columbia Pictures announced that it was minimizing its ties with ASCAP firm Shapiro-Bernstein in favor of BMI subsidiary Gower Music and its own publishing house, Colpix Music. According to Leo Jaffe, the executive vice president of Columbia Pictures, the parent company also named Marvin Cane as vice president and general manager of both Gower and Colpix in an effort to consolidate and strengthen the firm's music publishing activities.[43]

This announcement was followed some six weeks later by the news that Columbia was also planning a major buildup of its disk subsidiary. According to Colpix head Jerry Raker, the label would now concentrate on the album market with a bevy of LPs that equaled almost 25 percent of the company's output over the previous four years. Among these were a number of film and television soundtrack packages, including *The War Lover*, *The Interns*, *Damn the Defiant*, *Barabbas*, *The Flintstones*, and *Top Cat*.[44] The fruits of this new policy would be realized the next year when the label scored a major hit with its *Lawrence of Arabia* soundtrack. By far the most important move, however, was Columbia's $2.5 million purchase of Al Nevins and Don Kirshner's budding publishing and record empire. In the deal, Kirshner received Colpix's top managerial slot and a $75,000 annual salary while Colpix obtained Kirshner's Dimension record label, all the copyrights of the duo's Aldon Music, and future services of the brilliant group of songwriters known as "Brill Building Pop," which included such notable teams as Carole King and Gerry Goffin, Jeff Barry and Ellie Greenwich, and Neil Sedaka and Howard Greenfield.[45] By late 1963, Colpix was ambitiously broadcasting its intentions of entering the ranks of the major labels.[46]

With new management and talent in place, Screen Gems-Columbia's

Creative Music Group specifically directed its employees to concentrate on the company's television and motion picture products. The idea, according to *Billboard*, was to "get music written which is applicable for commercial recordings."[47] In the months that followed, Columbia put its promotional muscle behind the scores of six upcoming films, including *Ship of Fools*, *Cat Ballou*, *Major Dundee*, and *Lord Jim*, all due for release in 1965. The latter film was especially important to Columbia's plans since it hoped to sell some 500,000 copies of the soundtrack on its Colpix label over the next eighteen months. Unfortunately, neither *Lord Jim* nor any of the other five scores performed up to Columbia's expectations.[48]

Twentieth Century-Fox Records struggled throughout its first five years of operations, and clearly made the poorest showing of the four so-called "movie babies." After a period of shuffling and reorganization, the label reined in its operations in 1962 and announced plans to closely coordinate all music activities with 20th Century-Fox Film Corporation. According to Ted Cain, 20th-Fox's director of musical affairs, virtually all aspects of the label's enterprise, from selecting and building artists to developing a back catalog, would be governed by the parent company's film and television output. This new mandate meant that performers were now chosen not only for their disk appeal but also for their potential as film and television stars. Moreover, greater emphasis in marketing would now be placed on the label's soundtrack packages and on the title tunes culled from 20th-Fox's film productions.[49] Unfortunately, the new policy paid very few dividends and the record company's only sign of encouragement came in 1963 with the release of Alex North's *Cleopatra* score.

In 1965, 20th-Fox's artists and repertoire chief, Bernie Wayne, tried to upgrade the label's moribund soundtrack sales by adopting changes in its album format. The label announced that all film scores would be edited such that no individual track would exceed a maximum length of two and a half minutes. According to Wayne, this would give each band on the album the same running time as a pop song, and would thus encourage airplay for 20th-Fox's film music by pop disk jockeys. A second change involved exploiting both a film's dialogue and its background score. Fox had already successfully experimented with this approach on *Zorba the Greek* (1964), which featured Anthony Quinn's spoken introductions to each musical track, and Fox executives planned on a wider application of this format wherever it was appropriate. According to Wayne, *The Agony and the Ecstasy* (1965) and *Those Magnificent Men in Their Flying Machines* (1965) were among the upcoming Fox releases to get the dialogue-music treatment, and the album for *Flying Machines* even included dialogue in the middle of the album's music tracks in order to "inject the film's comedy flavor into the LP."[50] Wayne added that the label was also considering the release of straight dialogue soundtracks. Interest in this genre, however, proved to be very short-lived and soon the label returned to its concentration on title tunes, dramatic scores, and screen musicals.[51]

UA Records quietly inaugurated its release schedule in 1958 with the soundtrack of the Bob Hope/Anita Ekberg vehicle, *Paris Holiday*.[52] Though the album flopped, it nonetheless signaled UA's staunch commitment to exploiting its library of film music, not only for promotional purposes but also as a means of sustaining the label's own sales and distribution activities. Sales were slack during UA's first two years of operations, but vice president and general manager Art Talmadge remained optimistic at the company's first annual distribution meeting in July 1960. At the assembly, Talmadge unveiled UA's new "selective album" policy, which called for a cutback in the label's general album output to concentrate on established artists and soundtrack packages. The policy was designed to cut down on costs and allow the company's promotional staff to focus their efforts on a smaller number of potential LP hits. Talmadge admitted that UA Records had very little proven talent on its roster, but stressed that the label's film alliances offered more than a million dollars' worth of product to carry them through this rebuilding period. To demonstrate the new "selective album" strategy, Talmadge announced that UA's upcoming releases included soundtrack packages for *Inherit the Wind*, *West Side Story*, *The Misfits*, and *The Alamo*.[53]

Within six months, UA's "selective album" policy began to bear fruit, but it did so, ironically, in the singles market. The themes from *Never on Sunday*, *Exodus*, *The Apartment*, and *The Magnificent Seven* emerged as chart-topping singles, a phenomenon that *Billboard* credited to the careful planning of film and record executives during these films' preproduction stages. According to David Picker, who served as a liaison between parent company and subsidiary, UA Records was working "closer than ever with UA's indie film producers," and was using these consultations to discuss which types of composers and styles offered the best potential in the singles and album markets. As an example, Picker noted his own success in convincing the producers of *Paris Blues* to add three new Duke Ellington songs to the four classics that were already featured in Ellington's film score.[54]

By March 1961, UA's "selective album" program was fully in place and sales of all types of records were booming. Spurred by the million-selling *Exodus* single and the *Great Motion Picture Themes* LP, which went on to rack up over 450,000 in sales, UA's gross billings for January and February were

300 percent higher than that of the previous year.[55] As the year wore on, UA's sales dipped slightly from its early peak, but continued to be very strong. The label's fall sales program spotlighted fifteen new albums and pulled in nearly $1.7 million in billings.[56] UA's gross sales for 1961 topped $5 million, a figure more than double the amount of the previous year. Among the label's big hits were *Great Motion Picture Themes*; the *Never on Sunday* soundtrack, which sold over 350,000 copies; and Ferrante and Teicher's *West Side Story* LP, which attained a more modest 150,000 in sales.[57]

During this time, UA also sought to upgrade its image in foreign markets because, before 1961, the company's disks were released in Europe under a variety of different regional labels. Under a new agreement between UA and its foreign distributors, the firm's records would now be released under the UA stamp. As Talmadge noted, this arrangement offered the record label a number of advantages. The foreign offices of United Artists Pictures offered a ready-made corps of salesmen who could be utilized to market the label's European output. Moreover, UA Records could also better exploit its movie tie-ins. This factor was particularly important in foreign markets since radio exposure for new releases was scarce, and theaters thus became the central outlet for promoting film music abroad. Lastly, UA Records could eliminate administrative problems that arose when UA's foreign distributors also handled competing products. An example of this occurred when British Decca, UA Record's English distributor, not only released UA's smash Ferrante and Teicher recording of the *Exodus* theme, but also its own version performed by Mantovani.[58]

Over the next two years, UA Records expanded into the jazz, country, and children's music markets, but continued to plumb its film resources with great success. In March 1962, UA announced two rather ambitious spring sales programs, one that spotlighted eight new album releases and one highlighting nineteen different movie music LPs. The latter program, dubbed "All Out for Oscar," was timed to coincide with the presentation of the Academy Awards and gave special emphasis to the soundtrack packages of all UA nominees.[59] The effort to expand its stable of artists and repertoire, combined with its film music sales, drove UA Record's gross billings to a $7 million peak in 1962, and as Tino Balio notes, by 1964 the subsidiary could legitimately call itself "the foremost record company in the film music field."[60]

Despite the expansion, however, the fortunes of UA Records remained closely tied to its parent company's films. In 1966, for example, *Variety* reported that the label's immediate future was pegged to a slate of thirteen new soundtrack albums. Among these were the scores for *Hawaii, The*

Russians Are Coming, the Russians Are Coming, Lord Love a Duck, Duel at Diablo, and *After the Fox*.[61] While none of these titles managed to dent *Billboard*'s album charts, UA returned to form a year later with smash soundtracks from *A Man and a Woman, You Only Live Twice*, and *The Good, the Bad, and the Ugly*.

Still, while the new film-owned labels sought to establish themselves, MGM once again demonstrated just how valuable a film company's existing music subsidiaries could be.[62] According to a 1965 financial report, MGM Records and its subsidiary the Big Three Music Company together grossed some $21 million during the previous fiscal year. This figure not only yielded a $2 million profit for the conglomerate, it also accounted for nearly 13 percent of the firm's total income during that period. Moreover, as label executive Robert H. O'Brien noted, MGM's record division, which had enjoyed one of its most profitable years since its inception, would continue to aggressively broaden its scope through "new artists, new lines of production, and new channels of distribution."[63]

Such optimism was undoubtedly buoyed by continuing reports of the music industry's general economic health. A ten-year study by the CBS/Columbia group, for example, showed that total record sales had grown from $250 million to $650 million between 1956 and 1966. Moreover, the annual number of new record releases had also swelled from 6,157 to 10,662. While these releases catered to a variety of tastes, including classical, jazz, country and western, and folk music, consumers clearly indicated a preference for pop and rock music, which accounted for nearly half of all album purchases.[64] In sum, the record industry enjoyed unprecedented prosperity in the mid-sixties, and the film-owned subsidiaries were quite keen on riding the coattails of this success.[65]

The period of growth that dominated the record industry between 1964 and 1969 was, however, gradually replaced by a trend to market concentration and corporate conglomeration.[66] During the latter half of the decade, five major companies—MGM, Columbia, Capitol-EMI (Electrical and Musical Industries), RCA Victor, and Warner/Seven Arts—controlled over half the record market. The film-owned record labels were greatly affected by this development as either they or their parent companies found themselves taken over by larger disk companies or highly diversified conglomerates.[67]

In 1966, Columbia signaled this new drift when it negotiated a distribution deal with RCA Victor for its newly formed Colgems label. According to the agreement, RCA Victor would distribute and promote Colgems' products in hopes of expanding its share in the singles market, but would cede the responsibility for producing records and scouting talent to Don Kirshner, who would function as both the creative director of Colgems Records and head of Columbia-Screen Gems' music division. In creating this new label, Columbia also decided to deactivate its Colpix disk operations, which had limped along in recent years under a series of managerial changes and distribution difficulties.[68]

Shortly after the Colgems move, Hollywood's other foundering record label, 20th Century-Fox, had its distribution and merchandising ventures taken over by ABC Records. Though 20th-Fox's music director, Lionel Newman, insisted that the merger would not affect either label's autonomy, ABC nonetheless made the deal to give itself access to a number of forth-coming film and television soundtracks, an area that it had heretofore not pur-sued. Soon after, ABC proudly announced that its first slate of 1966–67 20th-Fox releases would include the albums for *Batman*, *The Bible*, *Modesty Blaise*, *How to Steal a Million*, and *Doctor Dolittle*.[69]

With fewer worries about distribution, 20th Century-Fox's music opera-tions began a surprisingly ambitious program of expansion some six months after the ABC merger. 20th-Fox severed its longstanding "favored outlet" status with MGM's Big Three and purchased the Bregman, Vocco, & Conn (BVC) music publishing house for some $4.5 million. In addition to gaining control over BVC's catalog, 20th-Fox intended to funnel all of its film scores and soundtracks into its newly acquired publishing interest.[70] With hits from *Doctor Dolittle* (1967) and *The Poseidon Adventure* (1972), 20th-Fox's music operations enjoyed moderate success under this arrangement until it was pur-chased by Warner Communications in 1982 at a cost estimated between $16 million and $18 million.

Like its competitors, Warner Bros. Records also found itself caught up in the fervor of mergers and acquisitions. Unlike its film-owned brethren, how-ever, Warner took a much more aggressive stance toward the issue of corpo-rate expansion. The label asserted itself early on when it merged with Frank Sinatra's Reprise label in 1963. Under the terms of this deal, Warner yielded a one-third share of the company to Sinatra in exchange for Reprise's $3 mil-lion library of master tapes and its stable of recording artists, which included Dean Martin, Trini Lopez, and the Chairman himself.

Both labels experienced short-term gains after the merger, but within three years Warner's music subsidiaries were once again on the brink of financial ruin. The record company experienced a sudden reversal of fortune, however, when Jack Warner negotiated a merger with the Seven Arts Corporation in November 1966. The move immediately placed the revamped Warner-Reprise label among the frontline of disk manufacturers and distributors, a position that was only strengthened by its parent corporation's bold policy of expansion. In 1967, for example, Warner/Seven Arts purchased Atlantic Records for some $17 million and emerged as perhaps the largest combine in the music industry. Under the WB-7 umbrella were several major recording labels, including Reprise, Atlantic, Atco, a host of smaller affiliates, and an impressive assemblage of music publishing interests. The latter included three Atlantic publishing subsidiaries (Cotillion, Pronto, and Walden Music); Seven Arts Music, which published Warner's film and television music; and the Music Publishers Holding Corporation, an ASCAP firm that was then the industry's largest publishing entity.[71]

With each of these components in place, Warner/Seven Arts' disk operations flourished between 1968 and 1975. In the first nine months of 1968, the record division netted approximately $5.3 million on an anticipated $50 million gross, a figure that comprised about 76 percent of WB-7's consolidated corporate profit during that same period.[72] Moreover, even in its subsequent incarnations as part of Kinney National Service and Warner Communications, the Warner-Reprise and Atlantic groups continued to be the most profitable part of their parent corporation's enterprises. In the early seventies, Warner's record division, which now also housed Elektra and Asylum Records, garnered over 25 percent of the slots on *Billboard*'s charts and increased the firm's pretax earnings by almost 50 percent.[73] As the company entered the second half of the decade, Warner's stood well above its Hollywood rivals as the only firm with strong market shares in both the record and sheet music industries.

For Paramount and UA, the reorganization of their disk subsidiaries was directly attributable to the entry of huge outside interests into the film and entertainment industries. Gulf & Western took over Paramount Pictures in October 1966 and attempted to consolidate Paramount's disk and publishing interests under one umbrella. In doing so, Gulf & Western hoped to push Dot more aggressively into the pop singles market. The label had a long string of successes with artists like Billy Vaughan and Lawrence Welk, but it had not been particularly active in acquiring indie-produced masters which could be sold to a thriving market of teenage consumers.

Gulf & Western also wished to renew Dot's efforts in the soundtrack field. The conglomerate's management noted a large number of Paramount releases scheduled for early 1967, but they were disappointed to learn that the scores for these films had already been farmed out to other record labels. Gulf & Western sought closer ties between its film and disk operations, and restructured its music subsidiaries on the model of Metro-Goldwyn-Mayer's

Big Three and MGM Records empire.[74] The Paramount and Dot subsidiaries, however, enjoyed little prosperity over the next several years, and when Gulf & Western retrenched in 1974, the labels were sold off to ABC Records for a $55 million price tag.

Like Gulf & Western, Transamerica hoped to make huge inroads in the entertainment industry when it took over United Artists in 1967. Transamerica added to its empire the following year when it bought the Liberty and Blue Note labels for over $25 million and merged the former with its already existing record subsidiary to create Liberty/United Artists Records. The union produced the sixth largest enterprise in the record industry, but Liberty/UA rapidly became a financial drain only two years after the buyout. After losses of $9 million in 1970 and 1971, Transamerica reorganized its disk subsidiary, renamed it United Artists Records, and gradually began to sell off chunks of its Liberty operation. United Artists Records continued to have occasional successes with its *Rocky* (1976) and James Bond soundtracks, but the revenue from United Artists' music operations remained a steady 25 percent between 1966 and 1976, and as Tino Balio put it, UA "remained primarily a motion picture distribution company throughout its history."[75]

By the end of the sixties, the film-owned labels were firmly ensconced in the record industry either as surviving independents or as subsidiaries of one of the major labels. When Hollywood entered the record industry in the late fifties, film companies shared two general goals for their subsidiaries: (1) to use records and radio as promotional vehicles for their film scores and songs; and (2) to diversify their business interests by creating self-sufficient, ancillary profit centers. The subsidiaries' long term performance, however, suggests that Hollywood ultimately attained only one of these two goals. The efforts of the film companies to sustain a market for film music proved far more successful than their efforts to sustain their own labels.

When the sheet music market collapsed in the late 1950s, Hollywood shrewdly shifted its interests in cross-promotion from music publishing to records and radio. Collections of movie music had long served a small market of connoisseurs, but the albums now became promotional vehicles for a growing audience of record buyers and radio listeners.[76] By buying or creating their own labels, the studios could generate record sales to complement the sizable licensing and performance fees garnered by their longstanding publishing interests. Soundtrack albums were especially apt in this regard in that they were both cheaply produced—their negative costs were already incurred and accounted for by the filmmakers—and offered obvious name recognition for the primary products of their parent companies. When both film and music operations functioned in concert, they not only enhanced a film's box office returns, but they also contributed as much as 25 percent of a film company's total revenues.

Between 1960 and 1969, however, the film companies came to understand that they needed much more than their film scores to survive in an exceedingly costly and competitive record industry. By 1970 the total sales of the record trade surpassed the $1 billion mark, but production expenditures for albums had risen at a comparable rate. As only 40 percent of all albums recovered their initial production costs, labels soon realized that the only way to spread their immense financial risks was by producing enough records to cover the whole spectrum of pop music tastes and thereby increase the likelihood of scoring a gigantic hit.

During their first years of operations, the film-owned independents relied on their financial muscle and cross-promotional resources to subsist in an environment where other indies were rapidly folding. Yet most film subsidiaries never developed enough talent or repertoire to maintain their status as independent labels. When companies like Dot, 20th-Fox, and UA faced financial troubles, they retrenched by containing costs and emphasizing their film-related products. Such strategies fulfilled the promotional interests of the parent companies but hurt the long-term fortunes of the labels themselves. Many labels were swallowed up in the late sixties' trend toward mergers and conglomeration. Warner was the only film-owned label to pursue an aggressive program of expansion. By purchasing talent in its takeovers of Atlantic, Atco, and other companies, Warner was able to survive the industry's reconcentration of resources.

Yet Hollywood's inability to maintain its long-term position in the record market should not be deemed a failure. Although the film-owned labels were the victims of rising costs and huge outside investment, their status as part of larger record groups offered their parent companies the best of both worlds. Film companies could now concentrate their resources on cross-promotion without the worries of record distribution or talent acquisition. Of more importance, film companies were still guaranteed outlets for their film songs and scores, and still could realize the benefits of "synergy," which would shortly thereafter serve as a rallying cry for both industries. The soundtrack album continues to be the most common and vital form of film music exploitation; indeed this may be the most important legacy of Hollywood's entry into the record business.

3

Sharps, Flats, and Dollar Signs

CROSS-PROMOTION AND THE MARKET FOR
FILM MUSIC

The Man with the Golden Arm using a highly jazz-oriented score
for the film, . . . sold 100,000 LPs, which in that day was unheard
of. And once again the response was, "Oh, pop music—
that's wonderful." I began to regret it, because it did open the
door to a particular concept of once again scoring a film in such a
way that it will make records that sell, rather than what it does
for the film. . . .

This trend was, I think, absolutely ruinous for the art of film music.

ELMER BERNSTEIN

Between 1930 and 1950, composers like Max Steiner, Alfred Newman, and
Erich Wolfgang Korngold formulated the symphonic style that defined the
Golden Age of Hollywood film scoring. By the middle of the 1950s, however,
this neo-Romantic model began to break down in a number of ways.
Composers like John Addison began to explore smaller instrumental ensembles and more varied orchestrations. Jazz elements were introduced by
Bernstein, Alex North, and Henry Mancini and gradually became accepted as
a stylistic alternative to the classically oriented, symphonic approach. Dimitri
Tiomkin's *High Noon* (1952) popularized the monothematic or theme score,
which organized its melodic and motivic material around a single popular tune
rather than a group of leitmotivs.

Many of these changes were concurrent with the industrial reorganization
described in the preceding chapter, but Hollywood's sudden arrival in the
record business in 1958 accelerated the development and assimilation of these
stylistic alternatives. The title song mania, for example, which fueled the
development of the monothematic score, became routine once film companies
owned their own record labels. Likewise, jazz musicians like Duke Ellington

and Miles Davis began to score films as a means of exploiting their reputation among record buyers. As records emerged as the primary vehicle for film and music cross-promotion, producers began to pressure composers to create commercially viable scores. Following the lead of show producers, filmmakers began to demand higher price tags for soundtrack rights and more favorable terms from record companies. Otto Preminger, for example, received $250,000 and guarantees of a big promotional push from RCA Victor in exchange for the rights to the *Exodus* track.[1] Similarly, over a dozen labels battled for the soundtrack rights to *The Alamo*, with Columbia Records emerging victorious based on its offer to mount an extensive advertising campaign and its promise to release two singles from the film.[2]

In the late fifties, the asking prices for soundtrack rights were driven up by a number of factors, not the least of which were the rise of independent producers and the use of composers who had founded their own publishing companies. Under the old studio system, music and soundtrack rights would almost invariably pass to the studio's own publishing or recording firms. In the current climate, however, independent producers more commonly retained those rights themselves and sold them off to the highest bidder. In doing so, producers were assured of the best possible music campaigns and the promise of ancillary revenues, some of which might be earned long after a film had completed its run in theaters.[3]

The combination of these factors pressed film composers to write music in various pop idioms. After all, with part of their livelihood staked on music promotions, producers hoped to maximize the performance of their title themes and soundtracks. Elements of jazz, Tin Pan Alley, and later, rock and roll were thought to have greater commercial value in film scores, and the popular image of this era is one in which producers slapped pop songs onto almost every film soundtrack without regard for its effect on the film itself.

Yet the charts themselves tell a rather different story. Jazz scores, like *The Man with the Golden Arm* (1955) and television's *Peter Gunn*, whose title theme was written by Henry Mancini, were joined by more conventional symphonic scores, such as Miklós Rózsa's *Ben-Hur* (1959), Ernest Gold's *Exodus* (1960), and even the reissue of Max Steiner's 1939 *Gone with the Wind*. At first glance, the commercialization of film music that emerged in the 1950s would appear to be a much more complex situation than that depicted by subsequent film composers and music critics.

In this chapter, I will take a closer look at the market for early soundtrack albums and at the promotional strategies used to tap that market. The first part of the chapter examines the ways in which Hollywood's approach to the marketplace changed between 1958 and 1970. Because of various concerns regarding rock and roll's aesthetic worth, producers initially shied away from teenage record buyers. Instead they pursued a more upscale group of adult album buyers, particularly those with tastes for mood music, light classical, and Tin Pan Alley pop. UA's success with the Beatles and *A Hard Day's Night* (1964), however, encouraged both Hollywood and its record subsidiaries to rethink their initial resistance to the use of rock music in major studio releases. By the late sixties, teenagers had replaced adults as the music industry's primary album buyers, and rock 'n' roll had replaced jazz and symphonic music as the film industry's primary focus of music exploitation.

The second half of this chapter examines the promotional strategies that developed around the ancillary markets of records and radio. These included such things as promotional gimmicks, contests, sales-order screenings for disk jockeys, and the use of music racks to sell albums within theaters. The film industry's keen interest in music cross-promotions during this period remains an obscured part of Hollywood's past. By detailing the industrial context for this phenomenon, I hope to articulate both the specific economic pressures faced by film composers during this period and the effects this ultimately had on the film score's formal and stylistic development.

From Mantovani to the Beatles: Changing the Market for Film Music

What segments of the record market were being served by soundtrack albums? What, in a historical sense, is entailed in the notion of "pop"? Joseph Lanza's remarkable *Elevator Music* offers insights into both of these questions as well as some useful observations about film music's relation to "easy listening" services and mood music albums.[4] As Lanza notes, many film scores became staples of "easy listening" formats. In fact, Lanza specifically mentions such mood music favorites as "Theme from *A Summer Place*" (1959), "Moon of Manikoora" from *The Hurricane* (1937), "Fascination" from *Love in the Afternoon* (1957), and "Moon River" from *Breakfast at Tiffany's* (1961). Additionally, a number of composers-arrangers, such as Nelson Riddle, Percy Faith, David Rose, and Henry Mancini, moved back and forth between the worlds of Muzak and film scoring. In fact, Mancini's recordings of "You Don't Know Me" and "Evergreen" were listed in 1983 as two of the top ten "most Beautiful Music instrumentals" ever recorded.[5]

The instrumental and "environmental" qualities of film music made it natural fodder for a number of "easy listening" and mood music auteurs.[6] On albums such as *Film Encores* and *Moon River and Other Great Film Themes*, Mantovani applied his trademark reverberated violin technique to a number of film themes and even scored a major hit with his collection of themes from *Exodus*. The candlelight-and-cocktail piano style of Ferrante and Teicher yielded a number of film-related hits for their UA label, such as the themes from *Exodus*, *The Apartment* (1960), and *Midnight Cowboy* (1969). By 1968 the duo was touted in advertisements as "The Movie Theme Team."[7] Similarly, the Mystic Moods Orchestra mined a motherlode of strings and sound effects on a series of cinematically styled albums in the mid-sixties. *Nighttide* is an exemplar of the Mystic Moods approach as it combines the sounds of ocean waves and horses' hoofbeats with the themes from *Shane* (1953), *The Days of Wine and Roses* (1962), *Doctor Zhivago* (1965), and *Nevada Smith* (1966).

Given the appropriation of film music by "easy listening" performers, it seems reasonable to assume that record labels frequently targeted their soundtracks and film themes at the consumers of mood music albums and services. After all, both forms fit Stravinsky's famous description of film music as aural wallpaper, and both forms would appear to be popular, safe, middlebrow alternatives to classical music, on the one hand, and rock 'n' roll, on the other. As late as 1964, Hollywood record subsidiaries continued to express their interest in tapping this mood music market. After the huge success of *A Hard Day's Night*, UA Records announced that it was grooming Beatles producer George Martin to be a performer in the Mantovani or Percy Faith mold.[8]

This is not to say, however, that film companies or record labels ignored other segments of the music marketplace. On the contrary, it seems equally likely that the neo-Romantic symphonic scores of epic films would hold great appeal for some classical music listeners. In the early fifties, this audience accounted for 20 to 35 percent of the total industry volume, and it remained sizable at the time of the film industry's entry into the recording business.

One indication of the classical audience's importance was the proliferation of classical music record clubs that began in 1955 and continued until the end of the decade. Groups such as the Music Appreciation Record Club, the Concert Hall Society, and the RCA Victor Society of Great Music attracted more than a million members and made up about one third of all classical music purchases during this period. Deluxe packages of Beethoven's complete symphonies and Debussy's "La Mer," the latter featuring a spoken word critique of the piece on the LP's flip side, each sold about 200,000 copies and lured legions of new members into the ranks of their respective clubs.[9]

Despite the apparently lofty aims of these organizations, they maintained a solidly middlebrow appeal. By closely adhering to a roster of classical warhorses, the clubs' offerings from the standard literature were at best unimaginative and at worst a gross misrepresentation of the works. To broaden the appeal of these packages, RCA Victor and Reader's Digest sometimes condensed the works and grouped them in popular twelve-inch "sampler" LPs. As with the "Beautiful Music" campaign, the emphasis on catchy melodies and familiar harmonic language suggests that these classical clubs encouraged facile consumption rather than music appreciation. In sum, though their mandate was ostensibly to foster musical education, the record clubs generally proved far more adept at commercializing classical masterworks by adapting them to pop tastes and formats.

By the late fifties, the clubs began to move away from their exclusive emphasis on classical music and gradually expanded their offerings to include jazz, pop, and original cast albums of Broadway musicals. Soon the same audience that had earlier purchased Beethoven and Debussy selections was eagerly gobbling up albums by Glenn Miller, Bing Crosby, and "mood music meister" Jackie Gleason. According to Sanjek, part of the allure of all club offerings, classical and otherwise, resided in the attractiveness of the packaging itself:

> Adults who had succumbed to the blandishments of advertising that promised high-quality recordings and high-fidelity record players became the prime customers for the boxed sets, multiple-color artwork, and even leather-bound packages that poured from the majors and the most prosperous independents, and often ended as record-club selections.[10]

To be sure, not all classical music buyers were targets of the burgeoning soundtrack industry. Since the craft of film scoring was not universally recognized as an art form, many concert music consumers would undoubtedly disdain film soundtrack albums as unworthy pretenders to the throne of musical masterworks. Alongside this audience of concert music patrons, however, was a substantial bloc of light classical music lovers, who appreciated the film score's emphasis on hummable melodies and tasteful arrangements. With classical music patrons increasingly alienated by the adventurous new works of Milton Babbitt, Pierre Boulez, and John Cage, record executives might well have hoped that scores by Rózsa, Newman, and North would sell alongside the works of Strauss, Wagner, and Tchaikovsky that inspired them. Duplicating the strategy of record clubs, the soundtracks for *Ben-Hur, Mutiny on the Bounty* (1962), and *How the West Was Won* (1962) all featured deluxe packaging, eye-catching cover art, and booklets of full-color movie stills to enhance their appeal to this particular segment of the market.

Producers and composers also looked to pop singers of all types to bolster the appeal of their specially composed title songs. While the emphasis was squarely on Sinatra-style crooners, producers tapped a wide variety of musical stylists that included country stars, teen idols, and even the occasional rock 'n' roller. Dimitri Tiomkin, for example, initially sought Perry Como for the title song of *Friendly Persuasion* (1956), but instead settled for Pat Boone— and a multimillion-selling single—when Como's $50,000 asking price proved to be too high. Other pop singers, such as Frankie Laine, Sammy Davis Jr., and Steve Lawrence and Eydie Gorme, waxed tunes for *Gunfight at the OK Corral* (1957), *The Disorderly Orderly* (1964), and *The Facts of Life* (1960), respectively. Nashville star Conway Twitty recorded two tunes, "Baby" and "Teacher vs. Sexpot," for Albert Zugsmith's *Teacher Was a Sexpot* (aka *Sexpot Goes to College*, 1960).[11] Co-stars Bing Crosby and Fabian both cut tunes from Blake Edwards's *High Time* (1960); and rockers Jerry Lee Lewis and Duane Eddy pounded out the title songs from *High School Confidential* (1958) and *Because They're Young* (1960).[12]

In sum, record release patterns, formats, and stylistic similarities suggest that soundtrack producers sought a number of different segments of the adult music audience, including mood music aficionados, light classical lovers, and more broadly, pop record buyers. Ironically, one area of the market which soundtrack makers initially did not pursue very strongly was teenagers. Although adolescent consumption was a vital economic and cultural force in the 1950s, the major record labels did not view it as commercially significant. Teenagers bought singles rather than albums, and teen tastes for rock 'n' roll and rhythm and blues were widely thought to be passing fads.

Ignored by the majors, teenagers were courted instead by small indie labels, which relied heavily on rock 'n' roll singles, the jukebox trade, and Top 40 radio to fuel their short-term success. Still, according to figures from the Recording Industry Association of America (RIAA), the singles trade represented only 20 to 25 percent of the industry's total dollar volume between 1959 and 1969. The majors had consistently shown interest in signing rock and rhythm-and-blues talent to record singles, but this was done more for strategic economic advantages than for the actual sales. By signing the occasional rock or rhythm-and-blues performer, the majors could spread their risks by maintaining across-the-board music lines and assuring their appeal to various segments of the market. Moreover, by successfully competing with these small labels on their own turf, the majors could mitigate the independents' encroachment on record charts and ultimately eliminate them as serious competitors. With the singularly significant exception of Elvis Presley (who went from Sun Records to his smash career with RCA Victor), the majors realized that their "bread and butter" lay with adult consumers and LPs rather than with teenagers and rock 'n' roll singles.

The singles versus albums debate, however, had special pertinence to soundtrack producers in that it crystallized the sometimes conflicting interests of motion picture companies and record labels. For one thing, theme songs and the singles derived from them had more value to film producers than record companies in that they were an especially effective and cost-efficient means of getting a film's title out to the public. Soundtrack albums, on the other hand, generally had more value for the record company. A hit single provided an attractive album track, but the soundtrack as a whole had to be satisfying to generate the high dollar volume of a hit.[13] Thus, while both theme singles and soundtrack albums were produced to satisfy both sets of interests, the film-owned labels generally hedged their bets by focusing on pop balladeers and instrumentalists as performers. From their perspective, Perry Como or Henry Mancini could sell both singles and albums to adults, but the appeal of Chuck Berry was restricted to a teenage, singles-buying audience.

A second reason why soundtrack producers generally shunned the teen market was that significant portions of the record industry held rock and roll in very low esteem. The clearest indication of these attitudes came in the backlash against rock and roll that developed in the wake of the congressional "payola" hearings of 1959 and 1960. As *Billboard* writer Paul Ackerman noted in testimony, the sheer abundance of products had essentially taken the hit-making process away from Tin Pan Alley song-pluggers and placed it the hands of record manufacturers, radio program directors, and disk jockeys.[14] The last group became the primary target of the congressional probe, but also implicated were the indie labels that supplied the bribes as well as the teenage audience to which these labels catered. According to Herm Schoenfeld:

> While payola existed since time immemorial, the disk jockey phase of this particular institution really came into its own with the advent of rock and roll and the accompanying flood of independent labels. Rock 'n' roll brought with it the amateur singers and combos, the garage made masters, and the smalltime diskers who were ready to cut in anybody who could make their product a hit. The click [*sic*] of indie labels around five years ago stimulated others to enter until the number of releases each week soared to 300 and over. The struggle for air exposure became fierce and the only sure way to get a spin was the payoff route.[15]

Although the various issues involved in the payola hearings were complex, the line of argument espoused both by the Harris Committee and by industry critics was specifically predicated on the low cultural capital of rock 'n' roll and rhythm and blues. According to the committee, teenagers, who were particularly vulnerable to the ploys of unscrupulous merchandisers, were "tricked" by disk jockeys into purchasing music devoid of any aesthetic value. Disk jockeys in turn had been bribed to play this worthless music by crooked A&R (artists and repertory) men whose stock in trade was rock and rhythm-and-blues singles. The bribe itself was taken as evidence of the music's aesthetic vapidness; if a given song was really any good, the argument ran, then disk jockeys would not have to be bribed to program it.[16]

In the wake of the payola hearings, the reaction against rock and roll was swift and strong. Nat "King" Cole complained, "Payola is the reason we were brainwashed and mesmerized by rock and roll."[17] *Variety* added, "While no one expects the 'big beat' to fade for some time, the calibre of the performer and material on upcoming disks will be of pro calibre in contrast to the anything-goes amateurish quality of so many platter hits over the past few years."[18] One writer even blamed corrupt rating services for the longevity of rock and roll. According to *Variety*, New York rating services consistently showed radio rock formats receiving the highest ratings, but informal phone polls revealed that only 14 percent of those questioned gave a "tinker's dam" about rock and roll.[19]

Anti-payola sentiment even found its way into popular songs themselves. A review of Stan Freberg's single, "The Old Payola Blues," notes that the song targets "no talent singers and, by indirection, the jockeys who spin the stuff for a price."[20] Additionally, songwriter Pat Ballard composed the following verse for the March 2, 1960, issue of *Variety*:

> "So Long Trash"
> *(To tune of "Mr. Sandman")*
>
> *Goodbye screamers*
> *So long to trash!*
> *Good songs move slower*
> *But we'll have more cash*
> *No more payolas*
> *Or loud 3-chord blasters—*
> *Just pianissimo from all broadcasters!*
>
> *DJ's clamp down the lids,*
> *Just play mazurkas for all the kids,*
> *No more cut-ins, no more sin—*
> *In the Alley famous for Tin![21]*

Forecasters were soon making dire predictions about the future of rock 'n' roll and the Top 40. In 1959, John Box, the managing director of Balaban stations, boldly predicted that the Top 40 radio format would disappear within five years.[22] Two years later, Roger Coleman, the director of WABC in New York, continued the clarion call by conjecturing that the nation's 1,075 FM stations—which largely programmed classical music, "good pops," and show and film scores—would knock rock and roll "out of the musical box."[23] With broadcasters retreating from Top 40 programs, some observers feared that jukeboxes would become the only public outlet for the music of the "jean set."[24]

As teen tastes came under fire, *Variety* reported a broadcasting trend toward a "better grade of music or to 'adult' songs."[25] The publication correlated this trend with the sharp dip in singles sales and the steady growth of the album market, a scenario that led them to conclude that "there's a 'buying' market for music with a melody."[26] Consequently, more and more broadcasters looked to the LPs themselves as a "treasure trove of programming material."[27] A list of recommendations included in the magazine showed an unusual mix of Brahms, Elvis, Mantovani, Harry Belafonte, and various film scores, more specifically the soundtracks from *Exodus*, *The Alamo*, *The Apartment*, and the UA collection, *Great Motion Picture Themes*.

It is within this larger industrial context that many of the earliest original soundtrack albums were released. The conservatism espoused in these market analyses suggests fairly ideal conditions for the reception of early sixties film music. With radio and the major record labels concentrating on adult audiences, almost any score released on record enjoyed reasonable expectations of wide airplay and solid sales performance. UA's Art Talmadge acknowledged film music's role in this new environment when he claimed that "pic tunes" were "not only sparking the sagging singles market, but also bringing back a better class of music."[28]

Unsurprisingly, in the wake of the payola scandal, film companies' record subsidiaries were reluctant to pursue the teenage record market. This is not to say that Hollywood completely ignored adolescent consumers, but rather that their efforts were directed at film productions instead of recordings. MGM, for example, had been willing to use Bill Haley's "Rock Around the Clock" to create notoriety for *The Blackboard Jungle* (1955), but its only endeavor in the record market was a studio orchestra cover version of the tune released as a single and backed by the film's love theme on the B-side.[29]

When studio record subsidiaries did target the teenage market, their efforts were often wrongheaded or misdirected. A case in point was UA's music campaign for *On the Beach* (1959). About five weeks before the film's release, David Picker announced that UA's *On the Beach* promotion would be the biggest music campaign ever attempted for a straight dramatic picture. Producer/director Stanley Kramer had already sold the soundtrack rights to Roulette Records, but UA would release its own *On the Beach* collection featuring variations on the film's "Waltzing Mathilda" theme on one side and tunes from various other UA productions on the other. Additionally, publisher Phil Kahl and promoter Fred Raphael both touted a wide array of singles from the *Beach* score, including "There's Still Time" on the Roulette, RCA Victor, Hanover-Signature, Columbia, and UA labels, and versions of "Waltzing Mathilda" on the Decca, Mercury, Kapp, Hanover, Roulette, UA, and Dynasty labels, with the latter releasing the tune in eight different languages.[30]

According to UA executives, the teenage market was the primary reason for the scope of this campaign. Citing the social significance of the film's subject matter, UA declared it especially important to reach teenage viewers and they claimed that music and disks were the most direct and effective routes to achieve this.[31] Unfortunately, "Waltzing Mathilda" did not pass muster for teenagers in an era dominated by Elvis, Little Richard, and Buddy Holly. The tune served the film's Australian setting very well, but the huge promotional push for it produced very little in the way of actual sales.

While teen music made very little headway in film scores, Hollywood attempted to reach the market in a number of other ways. As Thomas Doherty notes, independent producers like Sam Katzman made a number of rock and roll musicals specifically aimed at adolescent filmgoers.[32] In addition, studios signed teen idols, such as Frankie Avalon, James Darren, Paul Anka, and Pat Boone, to acting contracts. The industry's perception that rock and roll musicians lacked training and even skill helped to open the door for the studios to exploit film stars, such as Marilyn Monroe, Tab Hunter, Rock Hudson, Robert Conrad, and even Lloyd Bridges, via their record subsidiaries. Hollywood cynics argued that if rock singers without any discernible vocal talent could sell records, then surely Rock Hudson could peddle tunes such as "Pillow Talk" and "Roly Poly."[33]

When the Beatles spearheaded the so-called "British Invasion" in 1964, however, Hollywood's long resistance to rock soundtrack albums began to melt away. UA released the Beatles' *A Hard Day's Night* in the summer of 1964 with modest expectations for the film, but very high hopes for the soundtrack album. In fact, the album was so eagerly anticipated that radio stations around the country threatened to bootleg a WMCA broadcast of it before it was released.[34] UA responded to this pressure by shipping early its initial order of 500,000 copies, but even this was not enough to supply the huge demand. The album sold some 1.5 million copies within its first two weeks, and eventually racked up a $2 million profit for UA Records.[35] Even before its U.S. release, *Variety* reported that *A Hard Day's Night*'s negative costs had already been recouped many times over by advance sales of the soundtrack.[36]

The film itself did almost as well as the album. With equally high demand for previews, UA earned over $500,000 from a series of special screenings and premieres of *A Hard Day's Night* in the weeks before the film's general release.[37] This was followed by a saturation booking plan that sent seven hundred prints to U.S. theaters and brought back some $5.8 million within the film's first six weeks. By the following year, *A Hard Day's Night* had grossed more than $10 million from theaters and an even larger amount in record sales.[38]

After the Beatles' success, a number of filmmakers, both British and American, clamored to get on the rock 'n' roll bandwagon. UA followed up *A Hard Day's Night* with a program of six shorts collectively titled "Swinging U.K." Additionally, UA planned a series of more ambitious projects that featured such artists as Jerry Lee Lewis, the Nashville Teens, Lulu, and the Graham Bond Organization.[39] Likewise, British groups, such as Freddie and the Dreamers, Gerry and the Pacemakers, and the Dave Clark Five, were featured in *Every Day's a Holiday* (1965), *Ferry Across the Mersey* (1965), and *Having a Wild Weekend* (1965), respectively.

In America filmmakers attempted to revive interest in both jukebox musicals and "beach party" movies with *Wild on the Beach*, featuring Frankie Randall, Cindy Nelson, the Astronauts, and Sonny and Cher, and *Gone with the Wave*, featuring Lalo Schifrin's surf–bossa nova score.[40] Independent films like Roger Corman's *The Trip* (1967) also ventured into sixties' drug culture and the music popularly associated with it. Mercury Records released the soundtrack for *The Trip*, which spotlighted blues tunes by Electric Flag and East Indian psychedelia written by Lars Eric and Richard Bond.[41]

By the end of the decade, the huge success of *The Graduate* (1967) and *Easy Rider* (1969) soundtracks had done much to advance the use of rock and pop songs as dramatic underscore. I will discuss this phenomenon in a later chapter, but for now let me simply make a few points regarding the way in which these trends impinged on the notion of a teenage or youth market. First of all, rock-styled film music was no longer solely the domain of low-budget B pictures and exploitation films. Certainly youth-oriented pictures, such as *The Strawberry Statement* (1970) and *Vanishing Point* (1971), continued to use rock music, but the idiom also infiltrated "adult" projects like *Petulia* (1968),

Midnight Cowboy (1969), and *The Owl and the Pussycat* (1970). Ironically, the last starred Barbra Streisand but featured songs by Blood, Sweat, and Tears on the soundtrack.

Second, Hollywood's general acceptance of rock and pop musical forms enabled some filmmakers to use the music itself as the inspiration for their films. Arthur Penn's *Alice's Restaurant* (1969) is a case in point; the film stars singer Arlo Guthrie, and adapts his folk classic to both its narrative and soundtrack needs. The film's box office fortunes were modest, but it did spawn two hit records in United Artists' original soundtrack album and Warner Brothers' reissue of the Guthrie original. Together the two sold more than one million albums and, as composer Garry Sherman noted, turned the cross-promotional process on its head as "a hit record became a film which begat further hit records."[42]

Lastly, rock's presence on soundtracks also reshaped the musical division of labor on a film. Nowadays, films like *Batman* (1989), *Do the Right Thing* (1989), *Dick Tracy* (1990), and *Forrest Gump* (1994) have accustomed us to a soundtrack's separation of functional, dramatic underscore and commercially exploitable tunes. It is worth noting, however, that this collaborative approach to film music was already standard by the late sixties and early seventies. Writing about this process on *Midnight Cowboy*, Garry Sherman notes:

> John Schlesinger . . . used a number of different talents and techniques. John Barry, the musical supervisor, scored the flashback sections. While fulfilling the dramatic-emotional needs of the film, he wove a very successful theme (the hit song "Midnight Cowboy"). A song off a Nilsson album, "Everybody's Talkin," was recreated for the main title sequence, and it also became a hit. To complete the link with popular tastes, I was asked to capture the styles of Aretha Franklin and the Fifth Dimension among a number of other contemporary sounds. Finally, Schlesinger integrated electronic music creating an overall very sophisticated and functional sound track.[43]

By 1970 the machinery for film and recorded music cross-promotion was firmly in place, and rock, funk, soul, and rhythm and blues had all become acceptable stylistic alternatives for film scoring. Composers like David Raksin and Jerry Goldsmith might still voice their distaste for the pop score phenomenon, but after *Easy Rider* and *The Last Picture Show* (1971), even they were willing to sanction pop for certain types of projects. And as rock tunes gradually found their way into more and more soundtracks, the scores themselves began to seem more and more indistinguishable from the pop albums that inspired them.

Music Sells Movies or Movies Sell Music? Early Approaches to Promoting Film Music on Records

With the necessary organizational links in place and a market receptive to film music, the only question that remained for composers and record producers was how to sell this product to its intended audience. In the music industry, sales promotion typically involved such tasks as distributing records to broadcasters, reviewers, and retail outlets; designing advertisements, point-of-purchase displays, and giveaway items; planning a performer's radio and television appearances; coordinating concert tours; and, finally, submitting songs and demo versions to prospective cover artists.[44]

Film music, however, posed certain problems for a conventional record promotion campaign. For one thing, film music had nothing comparable to a performer's concert tours. The film's run served some of the functions of a concert tour in bringing the music to a broad audience of potential record buyers, but a screening was ultimately always a cinematic experience rather than a musical one. Furthermore, many film soundtracks during this period had nothing comparable to a star performer or recording artist. Here again the film itself served as an acceptable form of product differentiation, but the attraction to a record buyer was clearly the score rather than the particular studio orchestra that recorded it.

Most importantly, any promotional campaign for film music had to balance the competing, and sometimes contradictory, interests of record companies, publishers, and film producers. Not only did the music have to be, first and foremost, appropriate to the narrative and continuity requirements of the film, but it also had to generate record sales, radio airplay, and name recognition among potential filmgoers. As Denisoff and Plasketes point out, the participants involved often differed on the best ways to achieve this mutual goal.[45] Record companies, for example, were primarily interested in the sale of soundtrack albums, since the LP format was what bolstered their profit margins and produced the lion's share of their revenues. From the film company's perspective, on the other hand, album sales were vital to sustaining the operations of their music subsidiaries, but they had considerably less promotional value than a successful theme song and the radio airplay that it engendered. Consequently, film producers generally found singles sales far more lucrative than albums in the long run. Publishers, in contrast, were mostly concerned with "working" their catalog, and thus sought the creation of as many different recorded versions of a song as possible.

In the late fifties and early sixties, the resolution of these competing inter-

ests typically meant subordinating the needs of record and publishing subsidiaries to those of the parent company. In other words, the studios exploited
film scores for the added revenues from record sales and mechanical licenses,
but the chief commercial function of film music was still to promote the films
from which they came. Applying the logic of synergy, film promoters reasoned that if exposure to a theme song or soundtrack album were effective in
making the film a hit, a successful film would, in turn, spur further record sales
and mechanical royalties. Film and record promoters debated whether the
music sold the movie or the other way around, but it was clear to all concerned that both benefited from the success of its counterpart.[46]

Some of the earliest promotional efforts used radio as the centerpiece of
their campaigns. During the mid-forties, Ted Wick directed three such campaigns for producer David O. Selznick as his director of radio advertising and
exploitation. For the most part, Wick's job entailed writing and producing
radio spots for Selznick's pictures and hustling free plugs on radio programs.
When Wick heard Max Steiner's score for *Since You Went Away* (1944), however, he suggested creating a promotional record of it that could be used to
drum up some free plugs for the film.

After persuading the film's music editor, Lou Forbes, to both edit the existing score and compose transcription bridges where they were needed, Wick
hired seventy-seven musicians to record a master on a 16-inch transcription
platter. Says Wick, "Since many radio programs were fifteen minutes long, we
limited the length of the recording to fourteen minutes, allowing the stations
a little time to insert a commercial." Over a thousand copies of the record
were pressed and sent to radio stations across the country. Within a month of
the film's premiere, stations were playing either all or part of the record, and
announcers were not only mentioning the film's title but its producer and cast
as well. Wick followed up his initial success with similar campaigns for
Selznick's *Spellbound* (1945) and *Duel in the Sun* (1946).[47]

Generally speaking, however, campaigns such as the one for *Since You
Went Away* were relatively rare prior to Hollywood's large-scale investment in
record subsidiaries. It was only after the gradual breakdown of the studio system that albums of movie music surfaced as attractive promotional tools.
According to Alexander Doty, a number of factors helped to foster this situation, including competition from television, shrinking theater attendance, and
unfavorable film rental terms, all of which forced exhibitors to scale back their
local publicity and advertising campaigns. In order to deal with this new aus-
terity, the film industry developed a plan of cooperative or participatory
advertising in which exhibitors agreed to underwrite the costs of some pro-

motional activities and distributors agreed to supplement limited promotion budgets with additional advertising capital. In most instances, however, promotion and advertising budgets remained low, even with the extra funds furnished by distributors.[48] Within this atmosphere, promoters were very keen on finding inexpensive yet effective alternative sources of publicity. As *Variety* noted, film music was especially useful in this regard since a hit song and album could supply as much as one million dollars' worth of "cuffo promotion."[49]

Initially, disk jockeys and broadcasters had been reluctant to play title songs and soundtrack albums since they feared that the free plug would possibly negate the purchase of spot advertising by local exhibitors. As film music increased in popularity, however, disk jockeys could no longer resist its hit potential, and soon theme songs and albums had gained an important foothold in radio programs across a number of different formats. When this radio time was combined with television performances, sheet music racks, and retail displays, the cumulative promotional value was staggering. As one record executive said in 1961, "A film company *must* have a record arm. It could lose money, and it would still come out way ahead on the promotion of basic product."[50]

Budgetary limitations may have provided some of the impetus for film and record cross-promotion, but the potential success of such campaigns was already demonstrated by the trend toward title songs that emerged in the 1950s. As Michael Fink and other historians note, Dimitri Tiomkin was the "undisputed master of this technique," and his *High Noon* score, in particular, paved the way for the theme scores that followed throughout the decade.[51] Yet as important as *High Noon* was for the techniques of film scoring, it was perhaps more important to the business of film music marketing.[52] UA touted the *High Noon* campaign in internal correspondence as one of the biggest ever, and it featured many of the components that were commonly used in later promotions, such as multiple theme recordings and coordinated radio exploitation.[53]

Even before the film's release, UA publicists were already planting items in the trade and mainstream presses regarding the theme song, "Do Not Forsake Me, Oh My Darlin'," which had been written for the film by Tiomkin and was sung by Tex Ritter. In May 1952, Walter Winchell wrote, "I heard the guitar motif in the Gary Cooper picture, HIGH NOON. It will rival the '3rd Man' theme." *Billboard* favorably compared the song to "Laura" and the "Third Man Theme" and declared UA's promotion one of the heaviest for any song in years. Max Youngstein, UA's vice president in charge of advertising, publicity, and exploitation, reported these efforts to his district and branch managers, and reminded them, "You know how important a selling asset a good song can be."[54] In addition to the publicity for the theme song, a press release prepared by Stanley Kramer's production company described the score as "one of the most unusual musical scores ever composed."[55] To support this claim, the press release not only highlighted the music's monothematic structure but also relayed Tiomkin's own belief that his was the first score ever recorded without the use of a single violin.

Still, while these initial publicity items were crucial to the score's later success, the centerpiece of the campaign was the six single releases of the film's theme song. Frankie Laine and Tex Ritter's versions, for Columbia and Decca respectively, were clearly the most important, but the tune was also recorded by Billy Keith, Lita Rose, Bill Hayes, and Fred Waring.[56] UA had no specific expectations for a particular rendition, but Youngstein was confident that one of them would reach the Hit Parade's Top Ten within two months of the film's release.[57]

In addition to its domestic campaign, UA also exploited records, radio, and sheet music in various foreign markets. For example, during a three-week period immediately preceding the film's release, thirty-two Italian theaters agreed to play *High Noon*'s theme in their lobbies at all intermissions. In Sweden, recordings of the *High Noon* theme were released by four major companies, and Reuter and Reuter Music Publishers agreed to print 50,000 copies of it as sheet music. Additionally, UA's European publicists also arranged live performances and radio plugs of the theme song. On September 14, 1952, for example, Tristen Sjörgsen's popular dance band played the theme as part of a dinner music program, and later that month a well-known Swedish disk jockey recommended the Frankie Laine recording as part of his regular radio broadcast.[58]

In developing *High Noon*'s music promotion, UA approached its campaign much as a publisher or song-plugger would. Whereas a record promoter would seek sales and exposure of a particular version of the theme, UA simply sought as much repetition of the tune as possible. The film itself contributed in some measure with the score's own patterns of structural repetition, but the film text's own "song-plugging" had to be bolstered through the more conventional avenues of broadcasting, radio, and record sales. By releasing multiple versions of the song, Tiomkin and UA not only enhanced the tune's licensing revenues but also its chances for radio airplay and overall record sales. This multiple-release scheme might be considered a kind of shotgun style of promotion; like the spreading pellets of a shotgun blast, the proliferation of single and album versions of a film theme increased the probability that it would hit its target audience.[59]

Not surprisingly, when studios began to exploit their film music more systematically in the late fifties and early sixties, they adopted this shotgun strategy from their earlier approaches to soundtrack promotion. Below is a partial list of sixties' film songs and the number of cover versions they generated. Although not exhaustive, it should give some idea of the range and kind of films that were utilizing this tactic in their promotional campaigns. Numbers in the right-hand column do not encompass all versions of the song that have been produced, but only those recorded within approximately a year of the film's initial release date. Also, all of the following are title songs unless otherwise indicated:

"Midnight Lace"	5 versions
"The Sundowners"	6 versions
"The Dark at the Top of the Stairs"	5 versions
"The Green Leaves of Summer" from *The Alamo*	17 versions
"Tender is the Night"	7 versions
"The Second Time Around" from *High Time*	5 versions
"Moon River" from *Breakfast at Tiffany's*	27 versions
"Love Song" from *Mutiny on the Bounty*	6 versions
"More" from *Mondo Cane*	27 versions
"Lawrence of Arabia"	27 versions
"Hurry Sundown"	11 versions
"The Flight of the Phoenix"	8 versions
"The Shadow of Your Smile" from *The Sandpiper*	100 versions
"A Time for Us" from *Romeo and Juliet*	30 versions

While in some instances the multiple disk coverage served a largely promotional function, most songs benefited from the added exposure afforded by increased broadcast opportunities and larger mechanical license fees. UA's *Never on Sunday* (1960) is a case in point. The initial sales of the song began quite modestly, but grew as more and more versions of the song were cut. Within a year there were some thirty versions of "Never on Sunday" in the United States and more than four hundred worldwide. Together these versions accounted for the sale of between fourteen and sixteen million singles. Don Costa's instrumental and Melina Mercouri's vocal versions, both for UA records, were the top sellers, but they were simply the frosting on a very lucrative cake (see figure 3.1). UA additionally profited from soundtrack album sales of a half-million copies, more than a million dollars in performance royalties and licensing fees, and several hundred thousand dollars' worth of promotion via television.[60]

FIGURE 3.1 With some four hundred versions of it recorded worldwide, the title theme from *Never on Sunday* (1960) sold more than fourteen million copies.

Records, however, comprised only one part of a carefully managed film music campaign. While singles and album receipts were undoubtedly the most significant barometer of a score's overall success, the sales themselves often depended on the close coordination and cooperation of local radio stations, record dealers, and theater owners. In order to merchandise film music more effectively, many record executives began involving themselves in the scoring process at a much earlier stage, often well before the film's production was even under way. UA's David Picker, for example, regularly met with the film company's independent producers before shooting began, and about half of them ultimately proved willing to accept his input regarding the development of the score's overall commercial appeal. According to Picker, this advice policy was formulated when the label first formed, and one of the record company's biggest successes, Johnny Mandel's jazz score for *I Want to Live* (1958), was the first fruit of this kind of collaboration.[61]

Similarly, Jerry Raker, the general manager of the Colpix label, further stressed the executive's involvement in the scoring and recording stages. In supervising the soundtrack for *The Victors* (1963), for example, Raker flew to London to sit in on the screening of rough cuts and the subsequent discussions of the film's score. During these sessions, Raker discussed the overall shape and design of the music with composer Sol Kaplan, producer Carl Foreman, and other Columbia executives. Following these meetings, Raker continued to develop the score with Kaplan and arranger Wally Stott during the actual writing and recording sessions. In Raker's view, the record executive's involvement, both before and during the recording stage, increased the chances of producing a hit. After all, composers may know the craft of scoring, but it is the label executive that must develop and enhance the music's market prospects. In the case of *The Victors*, this collaborative approach, in Raker's view, produced a soundtrack with six different love themes and enormous commercial appeal.[62]

In some instances, however, film and record producers tried to verify their assumptions by using test screenings to, among other things, evaluate the sales potential of a film's score. For *In the Heat of the Night* (1967), producers used an advance screening to ask the audience questions regarding Quincy Jones's underscore and Ray Charles's performance of the title tune. Commentary on Jones's work was quite favorable; though one viewer complained that there was "not enough of Quincy," the audience generally rated the score very good to excellent. Charles's performance, on the other hand, did not receive universal praise from audience members. Approximately thirty-eight of the 240 comments received griped that Charles was too loud, too raucous, or simply "a disgrace to the picture." For the most part, however, the feedback on Charles and the theme song was quite complimentary. Over 75 percent of the comments described the song as "terrific," "fantastic," or just "beautiful baby." One viewer even claimed that he would "definitely buy the record." Though there is no indication that producers used this feedback to gauge actual sales potential, the survey suggests, at the very least, that test screenings were sometimes used to measure the possible promotional value of a soundtrack and theme song.[63]

After a score was finished and recorded, studio and label executives would then coordinate the film's release date with those of the title song or soundtrack album. According to publicists, a music promotion was most effective if the records were distributed to disk jockeys and retailers at least four to six weeks before the film's general release. Ironically, the importance of this window was most clearly felt when record companies failed to meet this deadline. On *Let's Make Love* (1960), for example, conflicts with Marilyn Monroe over the soundtrack's cover art and single selection delayed the album's release until three weeks *after* the film's premiere. The holdup meant that the soundtrack offered very little promotional support in the big money first runs of the major cities. Analysts admitted that the *Love* soundtrack could still conceivably help the film in subsequent runs, but they strongly contended that cross-promotions worked best when the music itself had a few weeks to work its way up the charts and circulate the film's title in radio and retail markets.[64]

In attempting to reach disk jockeys and retailers, promoters developed a number of different schemes for securing radio airplay and record store displays. The most common strategy was to invite dealers and station personnel to special previews of the film as a way of stimulating their interest. Disk jockeys were typically given free promotional copies of the album and singles tied in with the film, and retailers received the opportunity to place advance orders with the records' distributor. In some instances, such as UA's *Jessica* (1962), which starred Maurice Chevalier and Angie Dickinson, label representatives also previewed the soundtrack LP. Then, after dealers had seen the film, heard the album, and perused sample display material, UA took orders on the spot and gave discounts on all sales transacted at the time of the screening.[65]

Because of their broad application, special previews and sales-order screenings were likely the most effective means of reaching dealers and disk jockeys. The strategy could be used for virtually any film, and the screenings themselves could be easily arranged as part of the label's regular contacts with stores and station personnel. Yet special film previews were by no means the only strategy. In fact, promoters explored a number of additional sales tactics, gimmicks, and publicity stunts when they believed they were suited to the particular needs of a film's larger advertising campaign.

MGM Records, for example, attempted to enhance the prestige of its *Ben-Hur* and *Mutiny on the Bounty* soundtracks by arranging special radio programs devoted to the film's music. The *Ben-Hur* soundtrack was featured on a number of radio stations in early 1960, which both played the album and mentioned the film's playdate and local exhibition outlet.[66] Eighteen months later, the *Mutiny on the Bounty* soundtrack was named the "Album of the Month" by the KERR radio service and specially programmed as such on each of the service's 150 stations.[67]

Gimmicks were also commonly used. On *Zorba the Greek*, for example, 20th Century-Fox Records sent disk jockeys free copies of the album and free bottles of Mextaxa, a Greek cognac.[68] For *Lawrence of Arabia*, Colpix hired a "harem girl" to deliver promotional copies of the soundtrack to key disk jockeys around the country. Additionally, the label also shrewdly utilized a certain epithetic coincidence in their correspondence with retailers. Since Colpix's national sales manager, Ray Lawrence, shared his last name with the film's title character, the label printed special sales stationery which said, "Order 'Lawrence of Arabia' through 'Lawrence of Colpix.' "[69]

Not surprisingly, with disk jockeys a major target of film music campaigns, local radio stations frequently participated in the staging of contests and elaborate publicity stunts. In New York, for example, four WINS disk jockeys hyped the premiere of Warner Brothers' new horror film, *The Mask* (1961), by broadcasting thirteen hours of musical programming from the lobby of the Warner Theater. Similarly, rival station WABC promoted Columbia Pictures' *The Devil at 4 O'Clock* (1961), which starred Spencer Tracy and Frank Sinatra, by sponsoring a write-in contest in which people were asked to detail their most "devilish" ideas for the station and its programming. In Hollywood, Paramount sponsored a contest with station KBIG in which listeners were asked to call the station and say, in twenty-five words or less, why they thought they would like the film *Breakfast at Tiffany's*. The winner received an all-expense trip to Las Vegas.[70]

Perhaps the most unusual film and radio promotion, however, was a contest created for UA's *Birdman of Alcatraz* (1962). In cities across the country, UA built special prison cells in the lobbies of local theaters playing the picture and then locked area deejays inside them. While in the cell, these "jailed jocks" both broadcast their regular radio show and continually spun the Highwaymen's "Bird Man" single for patrons waiting inside the lobby. Before the stunt began, however, UA had distributed one thousand keys to people all across the city. If a person opened the cell, then he or she won a batch of prizes that ranged from stereo sets to collections of UA records. The contest had already run in Memphis, Akron, St. Louis, Washington, Cleveland, Los Angeles, and Salt Lake City, and was subsequently scheduled for a dozen other cities within the following week.[71]

The film music boom of 1960 led some record distributors to explore the use of theaters themselves as retail sales outlets. While this type of merchandising was used sporadically before 1960, it was never developed as a regular component of film music promotion. In October 1960, UA became the first to consider the widespread use of this outlet when it installed a new LP rack in Brooklyn's Loew's Metropolitan Theater. *The Apartment* began its neighborhood run there, and UA planned to test its new rack by using it to merchandise the soundtrack album. The rack, which resembled a giant peanut stand, was compact, collapsible, and easily adapted to almost any kind of theater lobby. The LPs were packaged with specially designed polyethylene wrap and were hung by small holes at the top of the album cover. If the initial test was successful, UA intended to offer the rack to theaters across the country and even planned to give exhibitors a small cut of the LP sales.[72]

Though exact sales figures for this merchandising plan are unavailable, *The Apartment* became a huge hit both as a motion picture and a soundtrack album.

Consequently, UA expanded its use of lobby sales outlets and struck gold twice more with *Exodus* and *Never on Sunday*. In order to prevent the perception that UA was encroaching on dealers' markets, Art Talmadge stressed that the company's policy was to feature these soundtracks on a strict individual run basis. This meant that the theaters could only sell the soundtrack from the film being shown and that the album was only available during the film's theatrical run. When the film's run had ended, UA distributors picked up any leftover units and returned them to company warehouses. By January 1961, however, UA's lobby offerings expanded to include other LPs and even singles. To counter these sales, local retailers began setting up their own counter and table displays in theater lobbies. Instead of accommodating local dealers, UA was now forced to compete against them.[73]

Such competition over retail outlets and revenues, however, was relatively unusual. In general, record distributors, theaters, and dealers all benefited from the mutual exploitation of film-related music. Distributors and theaters, for example, profited mightily from retailers' massive window and in-store displays, which not only advertised the soundtrack album itself but also publicized the film's playdates and engagements at local theaters. Twentieth Century-Fox's campaign on *Cleopatra* (1963) revealed some of the promotional advantages of such display material. As the film neared its release date, promoters unveiled window displays in some two thousand record and department stores, including such prominent chains as Sears, Woolworth's, and Gimbel's. In addition, a number of glitzy Manhattan stores installed special window productions. Stern's, for instance, acquired a number of props used in the film and built its entire 42nd Street window around an elaborate display for the film and album.

Arguably, the displays had very little long-term promotional value, but they did create a high early demand for the music. The day after *Cleopatra*'s premiere, 20th-Fox enjoyed the biggest sales day in its history. On that day, the label received orders for over 102,000 soundtrack albums, a figure that placed total sales in excess of 300,000 copies in a little over two weeks' time.[74]

For their part, retailers benefited from soundtrack albums' strong catalog value and the added consumer traffic generated by the film. According to Bernard Braddon, the record department head of New York's Liberty Music Shops, soundtrack albums were among the soundest and most durable items in the recorded music repertoire. Said Braddon, "Movie and show material is absolutely the most lucrative kind of catalog merchandise. These items keep selling year after year. If there is a staple commodity in the record business, this is it."[75]

Because of its catalog value, film music proved an especially valuable asset for small dealers. Rack jobbers and department stores primarily stocked hits and thus did not carry much depth in their film and show music offerings. Since film and show music sold relatively well no matter what the vintage, smaller stores differentiated themselves from their competitors by offering more specialized items not carried by the racks. As Braddon noted, the key to successfully retailing film music was to maintain a well-stocked inventory of soundtrack and show albums. Whether a small or large operation, such inventories effectively brought customers into stores and often interested patrons in the dealer's other products.[76]

The record companies themselves frequently attested to this perpetual sales potential by exploring new ways of repackaging their old film music. In 1960 and 1962 respectively, MGM Records and UA Records took a page from their parent company's merchandising book when they paired previously released soundtracks together as "double feature" packages. UA issued five LPs in its initial program, among them *Exodus* and *The Apartment*; *The Big Country* (1958) and *The Horse Soldiers* (1959); and *I Want to Live* with *Odds Against Tomorrow* (1959), a jazz package that featured the work of Gerry Mulligan and the Modern Jazz Quartet.[77]

When Isaac Hayes received an Oscar nomination in 1972 for his funky soul score for *Shaft*, the accolade served as both a signal of industry change and a harbinger of things to come. Unlike his classical Hollywood predecessors, who were trained in European conservatories, Hayes was an African-American who rose through the ranks of the recording industry. Growing up in Tennessee listening to blues, rhythm and blues, and country music, Hayes began his career in the mid-sixties as a keyboard player and arranger for Stax's legendary session band. Before *Shaft*, Hayes had produced and cowrote a series of smashes for the soul duo Sam and Dave, and had even charted a few minor hits as a recording artist in his own right. This would seem an unlikely background for an Oscar-nominated film composer, but Hayes's emergence clearly suggests the industry's growing acceptance of pop, funk, soul, and rock musicians as legitimate scorers.

Yet Hayes's nomination was in fact the culmination of a number of historical trends that had developed over the previous fifteen years. The entry of film companies into the record industry had created a strong economic base and infrastructure for the exploitation of film music. With little talent and repertoire, these record subsidiaries often organized their limited resources and promotional activities around their parent companies' film products, and in doing so, created a favorable climate for the consumption of motion picture themes and soundtracks. For the first time in history, soundtracks such as *Exodus* and *Doctor Zhivago* sold in quantities that equaled or exceeded the show scores of their Broadway and Hollywood counterparts.

Film and record promoters attempted to capitalize on this market through carefully coordinated sales campaigns, which utilized radio airplay, television performances, and shotgun record-release patterns to achieve as much as one million dollars' worth of inexpensive advertising. In order to stimulate interest in their products, record companies frequently targeted disk jockeys and local retailers through special film screenings and elaborate publicity gimmicks. In some instances, film companies even became record dealers themselves by setting up specially designed sales racks in theater lobbies. Hit films yielded hit albums, which in turn fueled further revenues for both industries.

As Henry Mancini noted in 1979, "The minute you put a song over the titles or in any part of the picture, you're unconsciously trying to play on the viewer's pocketbook—you're trying to get him to listen, to go out and buy."[78] Clearly film music promotions were important in bringing people to the movies, but we should not overlook the contribution that exhibition made to the synergy equation. For record companies, this meant that most film music promotions operated according to a peculiar paradox; while most major labels had from three to eight national sales representatives handling their film music offerings, soundtrack albums and theme songs ultimately had no better salesman than cinema itself.

4

My Huckleberry Friend

MANCINI, "MOON RIVER," AND *BREAKFAST AT TIFFANY'S*

In chapter 1, I argued that the pop score used particular stylistic parameters to make its music both noticeable and memorable to film audiences. In chapters 2 and 3, I examined some reasons why these specific traits were important, namely the increased importance of records as an ancillary market and the use of soundtracks and theme songs as an especially effective form of commercial tie-in. Neither of these discussions, however, had much to say about the pop score's function in particular dramatic contexts. To explore this issue further, one must look more closely at both the films and the scores themselves. In this chapter I will consider how Henry Mancini's music functions within *Breakfast at Tiffany's*. The next two chapters will then consider the work of two other composers—John Barry and Ennio Morricone. Together all three chapters aim to suggest different ways in which the pop score's formal organization adapted to the format of the typical pop album. In Mancini's case, this process of adaptation involved the proliferation of musical themes in order to fit the pop album's multitrack scheme.

In his autobiography, Henry Mancini says of his score for *Breakfast at Tiffany's*:

> It was not the kind of score you'd think would win an Academy Award. Even though it served all of the purposes required of it, it did not seem to be in the dramatic sense parallel to many of the great Alex North and Al Newman scores. In all honesty, without the enormous success of "Moon River," I don't believe the score would have been nominated.[1]

Mancini's sentiment here may well strike one as false modesty. Not only did his music win two Academy Awards and five Grammy awards, it also spawned two hit singles and two hit albums for its showcase song, "Moon River." One of these albums was Mancini's own soundtrack for *Breakfast at Tiffany's*, which remained on *Billboard*'s album charts for more than ninety-six weeks.

Though Mancini had had earlier successes with the television soundtracks for *Peter Gunn* and *Mr. Lucky*, the great accolades for *Breakfast at Tiffany's* firmly ensconced him as one of the top film composers of his generation. With subsequent scores for *Hatari* (1962), *The Days of Wine and Roses* (1962), *Charade* (1963), and *The Pink Panther* (1964), Mancini's soundtrack albums enjoyed an almost unbroken streak on the charts for more than four years. As a leading figure in the shift toward popular music in film scores, Mancini initiated some of the most significant changes in the industry, among them the rerecording of film music specifically for soundtrack albums and the move by film composers to gain copyright control over their music.

Like his classical Hollywood predecessors, Mancini had a considerable amount of formal musical training. After graduating from high school in 1942, Mancini enrolled in the Juilliard School of Music. During World War II, Mancini's education was interrupted by a period of military service, but he later returned to advanced studies in composition and orchestration with Ernst Krenek and Mario Castelnuoveno-Tedesco. Unlike his classical Hollywood predecessors, however, Mancini also had extensive experience as a jazz pianist and Big Band arranger.[2] During Mancini's military stint, he was assigned to the 28th Air Force Band, which was then under the direction of renowned Big Band leader Glenn Miller. After Miller's death, the Glenn Miller Orchestra regrouped with saxophonist-vocalist Tex Beneke at the helm, and Mancini continued to work as a pianist and arranger with the civilian version of the band. As a Miller sideman, Mancini made a number of valuable contacts with other jazz musicians, and later would use members of the Beneke band, such as trumpeter Pete Candoli and drummer Larry Sperling, in his scores for the television series *Peter Gunn*. During this time, Mancini also developed a number of skills that would later serve him well in writing film themes, including a facility with a variety of pop idioms, an ear for catchy melodies, and a familiarity with song forms.

In 1954 Mancini got his big break as an arranger and consultant on Anthony Mann's *The Glenn Miller Story*, a biopic about the late bandleader starring James Stewart. Mancini was a natural choice for the job both because of his experience as a member of Miller's band and his work as a Big Band arranger.

After *The Glenn Miller Story*, Mancini continued to work both on other jazz biographies, such as *The Benny Goodman Story* (1955), and early rock 'n' roll pictures, such as *Rock, Pretty Baby* (1956) and *Summer Love* (1958). At the start of the sixties, Mancini was in the forefront of a group of composers who had come to film scoring with experience chiefly as Big Band arrangers and song-writers. This group initially included such figures as Nelson Riddle, Frank de Vol, and Les Baxter, but would later count Quincy Jones, Neal Hefti, Benny Carter, and Lalo Schifrin among their ranks.

Because of Mancini's jazz background, however, the historical and critical reception of his work has been decidedly mixed. Although Mancini is often praised for his melodic flair and deft arrangements, he earned a reputation as a glib and superficial composer whose work was best suited for light and frothy romantic comedies.[3] Even those who profess admiration for Mancini's work will typically hold him responsible for the pop music muddle they believe followed in his wake. Tony Thomas, for example, notes that while Mancini successfully trod the fine line between pop scoring invention and crass commercialism, his accomplishment was viewed by filmmakers as a commercial formula to be imitated by other, less gifted songwriters and composers.[4] For critics like Thomas, Mancini's reputation is made to suffer as a kind of atonement for the sins committed by his pop music disciples, the latter a group of charlatans and schlockmeisters who lack Mancini's sense of balance and good taste.[5]

Given this mixed critical reception, it is hardly surprising that the most incisive appraisal of Mancini's film work comes from an unlikely source: former Steely Dan member Donald Fagen. In an essay that prefigures Mancini's reemergence among the members of the so-called "Cocktail Nation," Fagen focuses less on the composer's formal and stylistic innovations and more on the way his music evokes moods associated with a particular era. Since Fagen's own work with Steely Dan often exhibited a blend of jazzy hipness and cool irony, it should come as no surprise that Fagen identifies these same traits as vital to Mancini's work. More than any of his contemporaries, Fagen perceptively observes the balance between icy humor and romantic languor that colors Mancini's best scores and marks his break with the hyperstylized, melodramatic tone of much of Hollywood's Golden Age.[6]

However, while Fagen's remarks offer an insightful summary of Mancini's style, his discussion is both too brief and too impressionistic to be of much scholarly value. And at present, there still has not been an extended formal analysis of any of Mancini's scores.[7] With this in mind, my purpose in this chapter is twofold. To start, I will address Mancini's influence on the motion picture industry's gradual acceptance of popular music by placing his work within its historical context. To understand Mancini's contribution to film scoring, it is necessary to situate his use of jazz and song forms within the larger histories of these musical forms in cinema. With the rise of studio orchestras at the major labels in the 1950s, Mancini drew heavily on the style of such notable conductors-arrangers as Marty Paich, Billy May, and Don Costa. Mancini was certainly not the first to use elements of jazz style, but he was among the first to develop entire scores as collections of jazz tunes.

Second, and more important, this chapter will also examine how the main musical theme of *Breakfast at Tiffany's* ("Moon River") functions within the film's larger systems of signification, particularly those that bear on the construction of Holly Golightly's character. As a detailed analysis of the film and its music reveals, Mancini's score establishes an underlying critical voice in the narrative by speaking to larger cultural issues of gender and ethnicity. While "Moon River" often serves as an expressive voice in the film's construction of romantic fantasy and the formation of the classical Hollywood couple, it also cooly undermines that fantasy by hinting at a perverse subtext buried in the film's different levels of meaning.

It is perhaps the larger goal of this chapter to demonstrate that Mancini achieves this not by wholly subordinating his music to Blake Edwards' narrative and visuals, but rather by frequently integrating these elements. In doing so, Mancini proves to be less an innovator than a synthesizer of earlier traditions. A product of larger historical trajectories, Mancini's work is situated at the intersection of two separate trends in fifties film music—the monothematic score and the incorporation of jazz into cinema. As we will see, Mancini's chief contribution to film music came not by inventing a new style, but rather by merging two previous ones.

Mancini's "Le Jazz Hot": Putting Some Swing in Cinema

As Charles Merrell Berg notes, there are several parallels between the historical developments of both jazz and cinema. Both art forms were developed and nurtured on the periphery of official culture around the turn of the century. Both faced and surmounted major challenges from increasingly advanced forms of electronic technology—synchronized sound and television in the case of film, radio and various recorded music formats in the case of jazz. Finally, both jazz and cinema ultimately overcame perceptions of cultural illegitimacy and by the forties and fifties were elevated to the status of quintessential American arts.[8]

However, as Berg also notes, while there are a number of historical commonalities between the two art forms, they have largely moved along separate historical paths. Jazz has been a part of the film music repertoire since the silent era, but has largely remained on the margins of film music practice.[9] Lacking the "high art" patina of classical music, Big Band and Swing were typically used only in musical performances and in settings where it could be motivated as source music. The emphasis on the Romantic idiom and full symphonic orchestration rendered jazz both too tonal and too thinly textured to fit the overall shape and design of the classical Hollywood score.

By the 1950s, however, jazz began to be assimilated into mainstream narrative filmmaking. As bop and progressive jazz made the form more respectable, Hollywood began to make biopics, such as *The Fabulous Dorseys* (1947) and *The Gene Krupa Story* (1959), which took their place in a long tradition of film biographies of musical personalities. Moreover, in films like *A Streetcar Named Desire* (1951), *The Wild One* (1953), *The Big Combo* (1955), *The Man with the Golden Arm* (1955), and *I Want to Live* (1958), jazz elements were also integrated with various forms of dramatic underscore.

While jazz enjoyed unprecedented "audibility" in scores of the fifties, the tacit principles governing its use in cinema remained largely the same. In all the examples mentioned, the integration of jazz elements into dramatic underscore was carefully motivated by aspects of setting and character. In *A Streetcar Named Desire*, for example, Alex North's use of jazz was motivated by the film's New Orleans setting, a city with a great tradition of jazz music and performers. In fact, Christopher Palmer argues that North's use of blues and baleful brass glissandi are a perfect sonic equivalent of Tennessee Williams' stage directions, which call for the constant playing of a tinny "blue" piano in the background of the theatrical production.[10] In *The Wild One*, on the other hand, Leith Stevens' use of jazz is motivated by the musical tastes of the film's youthful and rebellious biker gang.

Otto Preminger's *The Man with the Golden Arm*, however, is particularly notable in that it combines all these strategies and even adds a wrinkle of its own. In Preminger's film, Frank Sinatra plays an ex-junkie pursuing a career as a jazz drummer. By using the protagonist's profession and the film's various nightclub and bar settings, Elmer Bernstein's score became a prototype of how jazz might be dramatically motivated as diegetic music. In addition, the film's linkage of jazz and criminal deviance also proved to be extremely influential. By the late 1950s, jazz in European and American films, such as

Breathless (*A bout de souffle*, 1959), *Rebel Without a Cause* (1955), and *Hot Rod Girl* (1956), was quite consistently associated with crime and juvenile delinquency.[11]

Interestingly, Mancini's music for *Peter Gunn* played an important part in forging a cultural link between jazz and criminality. Many film music critics have remarked on how appropriate Mancini's jazz was to the sleazy waterfront juke joints and nightclubs that Gunn frequented. However, Mancini himself became the target of some of his colleagues' claims that television and film soundtracks were harming jazz's image. In a *Down Beat* profile of Mancini, Fred Binkley quotes an unnamed Chicago pianist as saying, "I think it may kill jazz. All these crime programs with jazz in the background are setting up in people's minds an association between jazz and crime and slick, cheap women."[12] For a number of musicians, jazz's association with sleaze threatened to demean an art form that they had worked hard to make respectable.

In answering these charges, however, Mancini and other film composers distinguished their work, which they described as "dramatic jazz," from more authentic examples of the idiom.[13] As Mancini was quick to point out, this dramatic jazz differed from so-called "real jazz" in a number of respects. It appropriated the blue notes, muted trumpets, bleating saxophones, and swinging rhythms of jazz, but it combined them with the more conventional resources of the symphony orchestra and it subordinated them to the demands of the film's narrative. More importantly, this dramatic jazz of the fifties lacked a fundamental aspect of jazz performance—musical improvisation. This was due not only to the score's somewhat classical conception and orchestration but also to the necessity of fitting music to drama. Since the music itself was as carefully scripted and directed as any of the film's dialogue or camera movements, this dramatic jazz borrowed only the external character of the idiom, and often lacked the spontaneity and improvisatory virtuosity that are hallmarks of jazz artistry.

Yet even as Mancini placed his work under the rubric of dramatic jazz, he nevertheless pushed jazz in cinema in directions heretofore unknown. Unlike the so-called "Leonard Bernstein school" of the fifties, Mancini's music for *Peter Gunn* was not integrated with the conventional orchestra but rather was composed for small ensembles of eleven or twelve instruments. In part this was done owing to the economic constraints of television production, but it also encouraged Mancini to work in a manner more appropriate to the idiom. Working outside the context of a large orchestra, the classic configuration of the jazz rhythm section—piano, guitar, bass, and drums—occupied a more central role in the score's colorations. Devices like the walking bass and Caribbean dance rhythms, which were appropriated from Bebop and Big Band, were more prominent against this thinner instrumental texture. Similarly, Mancini borrowed the device of the obligato, and often used solo instruments, such as trumpets, flutes, or saxes, to decorate and ornament the basic melody of a cue.

While the instrumental resources were comparatively small, Mancini was often able to achieve remarkable dramatic effects from them. In an episode of *Peter Gunn* entitled "Death House Tenement," Mancini's almost aleatoric use of vibes, flute, clarinet, and percussion create a musical equivalent of Gunn's drug-induced nightmare. These instrumental sounds are filtered through an echo chamber to give them an eerie, disorienting ambiance. In addition, sudden blaring brass crescendos and sforzandos punctuate Gunn's sense of the psychic horror embodied in this dreamlike narcotic haze. These musical elements enhance and vivify the show's striking visuals during this sequence, which include a sudden zoom in on a light bulb, a series of "queasy" moving point-of-view shots, and a process shot in which Gunn, seen from overhead lying on a bed, seems to suddenly shrink and disappear in an enveloping darkness.

Another innovation in Mancini's work on *Peter Gunn* was his use of musical improvisation for dramatic underscore. This device does not appear frequently in *Gunn* but nevertheless was used in a way that was a significant departure from classical Hollywood musical practice. Some of these improvisatory moments were extremely conventional, as in the episode, "Keep Smiling," which features a brief diegetic instrumental performance and solo by jazz drummer Shelly Manne and his band. In moments such as this, the band's performance is not unlike a number in a classical Hollywood musical. There is a brief cessation of the narrative flow as the text displays the musical prowess of the performer, in this case Shelly Manne.

At other times, however, these moments of musical improvisation displayed an entirely different character, one that was codified in *Gunn* by its consistent use in the prologue of each episode. Each episode began with a variation of the cue, "Fallout," with a different instrument each week taking a brief, improvised solo. During these solos, a crime would be set up which would then initiate the action of that week's episode. These prologues featured little dialogue and instead relied on iconography, generic expectations, camera work, and mise-en-scène to narrate this initiating event. As each prologue created elements of expectation and suspense, instruments would gradually be added until the music grew to a fever pitch. The music would then suddenly stop, only to be followed by a gunshot or a scream, thus serving to mark the prologue's end.

Though the music in these openings operated according to a certain formula, its improvisatory character is particularly notable. In each, Mancini began with a rough timing of the sequence and a consistent musical framework, not so much a theme as a particular tempo, rhythm, and walking bass pattern. Against that background, Mancini would then allow space for a brief improvised solo lasting a certain number of measures. As the sequence moved inexorably toward its dramatic climax, the solo would suddenly end and be replaced by the entire ensemble and a swift crescendo to a somewhat unexpected musical climax. Though governed by an overarching dramatic shape and a rough timing, the feel of the jazz cues in these prologues is much looser and freer than their classical Hollywood counterparts.

The other notable element about these prologues is the prominence of the music in them. According to Mancini, this was largely because Edwards conceived of these segments as audiovisual wholes. Years after the series, Mancini noted that:

> Especially in *Peter Gunn*, and we did that for three years, Blake Edwards used to delight in shooting sequences without sound and without effects—they'd put them in later—but long things that just went. They had a point, of course, but he would take out all the dialogue and try to make it visual, almost pantomime, like a ballet or something. I used to look forward to seeing what the hell he wanted me to do next because he always used to shoot with the music in mind.[14]

Mancini's reference here to ballet is particularly telling in that it invokes a model of audiovisual relations quite different from that of classical Hollywood scoring, one in which music plays a privileged rather than subordinate role in constructing the text.

Mancini's work on *Peter Gunn* culminated a growing relationship between jazz and cinema throughout the fifties. His use of smaller instrumental combinations and limited improvisation anticipated directions jazz in cinema would later take as legitimate jazz stars, such as Stan Getz, Mal Waldron, Miles Davis, Sonny Rollins, and Herbie Hancock, would themselves take up film scoring. In addition, the prominence of Mancini's music in the series established a precedent for the equivalence of sound and image relations, and was the prototype for the sixties pop scores that followed. With the entry of Mancini and other jazz performers into the field of film composing, many aficionados believed that modern jazz finally had a place in cinema.

That Money-Making "Moon River" Sound: Mancini and the Pop Song

Like jazz, popular songs have played a key role in film music promotion throughout its history. During Hollywood's Golden Age, the lion's share of these songs came from motion picture musicals, such as *42nd Street* (1933), the *Gold Digger* series, the Astaire-Rogers series at RKO, and, of course, *The Wizard of Oz* (1939). Since most composers of dramatic underscore believed that popular songs were appropriate only to musical or comic scenes, it was rare indeed that a theme from a dramatic score was fashioned into a successful popular song.

There were, however, some notable exceptions to this throughout the forties, which showed that successful film songs were not the exclusive province of musicals. Examples include the "Tara" theme from *Gone with the Wind* (1939), "Stella by Starlight" from *The Uninvited* (1944), and the title songs from *Laura* (1944) and *The Third Man* (1949). By demonstrating the way in which a theme might be adapted as a successful tune, these exceptions astutely anticipated the direction film music would take in the following decade.

With the development of the monothematic score in the fifties, the commercial exploitation of thematic material began in earnest. The monothematic score largely adhered to the classical Hollywood model of using thematic material to unify a series of discontinuous cues, but also subtly deviated from that model in terms of the number and variety of musical motifs. By consistently using a single theme for every dramatic situation, it was assumed that audiences would more readily notice the theme and thus would be more likely to purchase it as a record or as sheet music. The success of musical tie-ins for films like *Laura*, *The Third Man*, and *High Noon* (1952) led to a rash of imitators, and soon producers were commissioning pop songs to serve as the basis of monothematic scores.

Like Dimitri Tiomkin, Mancini proved extremely adept at organizing his scores around salable melodies, and his *Breakfast at Tiffany's* score is no exception. As with other film songs, however, the tune's commercial clout was achieved as a result of an aggressive marketing campaign. An article in *Variety* about four months before the film's New York premiere indicates that Famous Music Corp., Paramount's music publishing subsidiary, had already licensed twelve different recordings of "Moon River" and had assigned eight men from its plugging department to a national promotion plan. Mancini himself even participated in this campaign in an April 21, 1962, *Billboard* article written after the song's Oscar win. In this piece, Mancini and the song's lyricist, Johnny Mercer, offer a number of marketing suggestions to record dealers and radio programmers. For example, Mancini and Mercer suggest that an ideal record store window display might be made from the fifteen different albums carrying the song and a single unifying banner with the song's title. In addition, they also suggest that radio programmers might insert different versions of the tune into various program segments during the day.[15] This song-plugging bonanza inspired an even greater proliferation of the song, and by 1966 Famous Music had licensed over 240 recordings of "Moon River."[16]

The accomplishment of the *Breakfast at Tiffany's* score made it a blueprint for Mancini's subsequent work. The scores for *Hatari*, *Charade*, *The Pink Panther*, *A Shot in the Dark* (1964), *The Great Race* (1965), *Arabesque* (1966), *The Party* (1968), and *Gaily, Gaily* (1969) were all designed in some measure to cash in on Mancini's reputation as a commercial tunesmith, and all featured one or more exploitable tunes. Interestingly, with *Darling Lili* (1970) and *Victor/Victoria* (1982), Mancini became one of a handful of film composers to write both dramatic scores and original musical scores.[17]

Yet Mancini's successful entry into the musical genre should come as no surprise insofar as all of his dramatic scores seem to aspire to the condition of the musical. Unlike a monothematic score, a typical Mancini score is not organized around a single prominent, exploitable theme. Instead Mancini's scores emerge as collections of themes with one or two being more prominent than the rest. More importantly, although the films scored by Mancini usually lack the dramatic mechanisms that foreground musical performance, his themes nevertheless retain the shape and formal character of individual musical numbers, and they typically function with a comparable measure of musical autonomy. Like the songs of a musical, Mancini's themes display a mastery of song structures, a plethora of musical hooks, and a surfeit of memorable melodies.

In their orientation toward tunes, Mancini's multitheme scores proved eminently suited to the format of pop albums, and as contemporaneous interviews in *Variety* and *Billboard* show, this added benefit did not escape Mancini's notice.[18] In stressing the commercial nature of his own work, Mancini was openly critical of existing industry practices of soundtrack packaging. Mancini argued that the majority of "background music" soundtracks, many of which were derived from monothematic scores, were successful only in establishing a main theme, usually on the first track of the album. The rest of the album emerged as an assortment of fragments, a collection of bits and pieces that were valueless both musically and commercially. The reason for this, according to Mancini, was that the albums were typically prepared from the actual soundtrack of the film, which was not only inherently fragmented but also generally of poor recording quality.

For this reason, Mancini usually rerecorded his film music for separate distribution on albums. In doing so, Mancini believed his soundtracks gained a number of advantages in the marketplace. For one thing, the rerecording of his scores gave them a better fit within the strictures of radio formats. According to Mancini, "I had an ear and I had an eye on what the record business was. And so what I did with *Peter Gunn*, I made each one of those numbers something that a disk jockey could lay the needle down anyplace and get a tune!"[19]

Moreover, as Mancini noted, he was also able to "impose a real form on the music and thus give the album buyer a sound value."[20] Freed from the confines of the film, Mancini could shape each cue into a separate tune with its own distinct identity. Moreover, during Mancini's album sessions, he would also typically give his performers more freedom in terms of timing and improvisation. The looseness of these album sessions was thought to allow more room for purely musical expression, and thus produce an album that was satisfying even for listeners who had no interest in the film it accompanied.

Mancini's desire to give record buyers a good value had important consequences for his general approach to scoring. Usually only two or three of the themes function nondiegetically as dramatic underscore, and thus a comparatively small number of them are repeated and instrumentally varied throughout the film to perform the score's various narrational functions.[21] The remainder of the themes, which are included in the film largely to give the soundtrack album a sense of variety, typically only appear once and are of relatively limited function in terms of the narrative. These latter are usually light swing or Latin jazz numbers and are commonly motivated within the diegesis either by showing them emanating from an onscreen source or using them as the basis of spontaneous performances.

In fact, Mancini's soundtrack for *The Party* is perhaps the purest distillation of this multitheme approach in that it is almost entirely constructed from this latter type of scoring. There is a lot of music in the film, but virtually all of it is diegetically motivated with very little thematic repetition among the film's various cues. The only underscoring occurs briefly during the credits and in two brief repetitions of the love theme, "Nothing to Lose," to suggest the budding romance of the narrative's two outsiders, Hrundi (Peter Sellers) and Michele (Claudine Longet). By giving almost equal weight to each of *The Party*'s musical cues—"Nothing to Lose" and the title tune are given slightly more weight in terms of their narrative importance—Mancini strips this score of most of its conventional functions. Since it does not signify character, emotion, or point of view, the music provides only a vague sense of setting and a neutral sonic background to set off the film's sight gags and the comic business of performer Peter Sellers. By offering so little in the way of dramatic function, the music is the perfect aural complement of the film's lack of narrative drive.

Mancini's *Breakfast at Tiffany's* score, on the other hand, is both more typical of his other scores and a prototype of the sixties pop score. The film's soundtrack album features some eleven distinct tunes, each of which runs approximately three minutes. Two of these, however, do not even appear in the film and seven are themes that only appear once. Of these seven, six are given diegetic motivation: "Sally's Tomato" and "The Big Blow Out" are played on Holly's phonograph early in the film; "Hub Caps and Tail Lights" accompanies a stripper's performance; and "Latin Golightly," "Something for Cat," and "Loose Caboose" appear during the film's famous party sequence. The two remaining cues, "Breakfast at Tiffany's" and "Moon River," which make up only three tracks on the album (the third being the "Moon River Cha Cha" variation), actually serve as the basis for most of the nondiegetic underscore and thus are the most important cues in terms of the music's narrational functions.

It is in these differences between the film's actual soundtrack and the album prepared from the score that Mancini's contribution to film music history becomes most evident. Like the monothematic score, the narrational music of *Breakfast at Tiffany's* is derived from a relatively small number of musical materials. As such, "Moon River" and the title tune enjoyed a prominence within the film not shared by the other themes, and gave the score a sense of formal unity through their repetition. These same themes, however, were not given the same emphasis on the soundtrack album. Where the prominence of "Moon River" provided unity in the film, its lack of emphasis on the album renders it only a part of a satisfying and heterogeneous variety of musical materials. More than any of his contemporaries, Mancini was able to shape his music to serve different needs in different media, and proved that by balancing the artistic and commercial functions of the music, the film composer could have his cake and eat it too.

Perhaps more importantly, Mancini's multitheme scores altered the conventions of "spotting" (the process by which the composer, director, producer, and music editor determine the placement of music in the film) as well. By conforming to recording industry standards of album packaging, Mancini consistently utiliized the occasion of diegetic music as an opportunity to introduce new melodies and tunes. Through a canny use of "realistic" music, Mancini could thus broaden the score's thematic palette and increase the soundtrack album's musical variety and commercial viability. Mancini's strategy was effective insofar as diegetic music typically served fewer dramatic functions than nondiegetic music. This is not to say that these diegetic cues played no dramatic function, but rather that conventions of realism allowed the music to be more independent in terms of its form and function. Music issuing from a radio, stereo, or dance band could reasonably be expected to adhere to more conventional musical forms, and thus could develop its own formal patterns without regard to the rhythms and shifts of the narrative and visual track. Indeed it would seriously strain the viewer's credibility were the film's characters to listen or dance to music as harmonically open, rhythmically diffuse, and strucurally fragmented as typical dramatic underscore. In this respect, diegetic cues offer the composer the opportunity for comparatively more direct musical expression and the viewer the opportunity for a more fulfilling experience of the score in purely musical terms.

The catch, however, is that this direct expression and apprehension of musical form is not as evident in the film as it is on the accompanying soundtrack album. Within the context of the film, the mediation of the narrative, visuals, and sound mixing complicates our reception of the music. In most cases, diegetic music functions as background to a dialogue scene, and is mixed in a manner that subordinates it to narrative concerns. In other cases, a diegetic cue may be presented as only a relatively brief snatch of a larger musical work, a melodic bit that is motivated only to the extent that it adds variety and commercial value to the soundtrack album.[22] In these latter instances, the form is not so much fragmented as truncated; the tune still has structure, but that structure has not been allowed to develop.

Within the context of the album, on the other hand, our audition of these cues allows for an apprehension of both primary and secondary musical parameters. No longer buried in the mix or cut off mid-phrase, the cue now has greater presence and can develop its formal patterns in the same way that other musical pieces do. In *Breakfast at Tiffany's*, these diegetic cues are shaped according to the conventions of Big Band or jazz combo performances. An initial riff or melodic hook is developed as a sixteen- or twelve-bar theme, which is then followed by a series of improvised instrumental solos. After the solos, the "head" returns, is repeated, and then extended to accommodate a cadence that rounds off and closes the music's melodic and harmonic structures. In this way, Mancini takes cues that were only bits and pieces in the film and develops them into full-fledged tunes.

By shaping his multitheme scores into autonomous soundtrack albums, Mancini anticipated both the commercial explosion of soundtrack sales and the development of scores as collections of popular songs. Moreover, by giving a sound value to soundtrack album consumers, Mancini also greatly expanded the potential market for such products. Whereas a classic Bernard Herrmann score, such as *Citizen Kane* (1941) or *Vertigo* (1958), might appeal to cultists and fans of the film, the pop stylings and intrinsic musicality of a Mancini score made it salable to a more general record-buying public. With *Breakfast at Tiffany's* and other Mancini soundtracks, the multitheme score accommodated the format and conventions of the typical pop album, and in doing so, helped revive consumer interest in film music.

Chasing the Same Rainbow's End: The Meaning and Narrative Function of "Moon River"

As Karlin and Wright note in their typology of film songs, tunes such as "Moon River" bear no direct connection to the events and characters of the narrative, but are oblique statements of their films' overarching themes.[23] In *Breakfast at Tiffany's*, the repetition of "Moon River" in different dramatic contexts and the theme's oblique lyrical content enable it to accrue a number of divergent and even contradictory meanings. On the one hand, "Moon River" functions throughout the film to connote both a nostalgic rural past and a utopian future for the film's heroine, Holly Golightly (Audrey Hepburn). On the other hand, however, the song is simultaneously a cynical reminder of the ways in which Holly's goals are directed, and a signifier of the repressed sexual wish that motivates her actions. By operating at these two different levels, *Breakfast at Tiffany's* is that rare score which simultaneously affirms the narrative's meaning and affective features at one level while ironically undermining those values at another.

Of course, the linkage between music and female sexuality is nothing new to classical Hollywood scoring. Applying this cultural link to Hollywood films like *The Informer* (1935), Kathryn Kalinak argues that composers developed a nucleus of musical practices to construct certain feminine archetypes, such as the vamp. According to Kalinak, the use of woodwind and brass instruments, dotted rhythms, blue notes, and portamento were musical codes that often connoted promiscuity or indecency.[24] Unsurprisingly, some cues in *Breakfast* do adhere to these cultural musical codes. The use of saxophones and bumptious triplet figures in "Hub Caps and Tail Lights," for example, undoubtedly supplies a feeling of bawdiness and vulgarity to the strip show Paul (George Peppard) and Holly are watching.

In this analysis, however, I want to avoid positing an inherent cultural link between music and femininity. While I have no doubt that specific musical codes are employed in this manner, positing such a pervasive cultural link would reduce its complexity to a repository of musical clichés, and would ignore the more subtle and elusive ways music helps to construct femininity as an aspect of characterization.

For this reason, I will examine how *Breakfast* establishes a contextual link between music and femininity by fusing together the two contradictory sides of Holly's personality, her romanticism and sexual predation. Through this fusion, the music becomes a critical voice in *Breakfast*, one that is carefully integrated with the film's other systems of signification and one that speaks to the film's treatment of gender and culture. By this I do not mean to suggest that Mancini actively strives to subvert or undermine the film's narrative meanings. Rather I am contending that the confluence of certain factors—namely, the score's commercial impetus, the structural repetition of the "Moon River" theme, and the multivalence of the song's lyrics—allow the music to underline certain ironies that are at the heart of the film's thematic nexus.

The various cues in the *Breakfast* score range from rather conventional, atmospheric "movie" music to fully developed pop and jazz tunes. In fact, if one saw only certain sequences of *Breakfast*, one might well conclude that Mancini is in reality a composer of a very conventional stripe. Much of Mancini's underscore in *Breakfast* contains a number of well-known musical dramatic devices. As Paul introduces himself to Holly, for example, in the film's second scene, a sudden harp and vibe glissando functions as a stinger to accompany her cat's unexpected leap onto Paul's shoulder. Later in the film, Mancini employs an equally conventional technique as Paul, who has been searching for Holly in her apartment after their night together, suddenly spies his patron-lover, Mrs. Valenson (Patricia Neal), going to his apartment. The cue begins as a repeated four-bar vamp with tinkling piano, but abruptly shifts gears when Paul sees Mrs. Valenson. A furious string arpeggio, played at an agitato tempo, then takes over the scene and accompanies Paul's frenzied run through Holly's apartment and up the fire escape. The diatonic modulation of the string line slyly enhances Paul's sense of panic but does not undermine the overall comic tone of the scene. The cue even further reinforces the action by ending on a sudden cadence just as Paul and Mrs. Valenson simultaneously meet at his doorway.

By far the most important atmospheric cues, however, involve a dramatic rising string line, which is frequently played over an ostinato bass pattern. This rising string line usually circulates around the first four notes of the C-minor scale, and often incorporates motives from the score's other themes.[25] It is first introduced as suspense music during the montage in which the mysterious Doc Golightly (Buddy Ebsen), whose identity the narration has thus far concealed, tries to surreptitiously follow Paul on a walk around the city. Using the low C as a pedal point, Mancini then builds harmonic tension by layering the second, third, and fourth scale tones in clusters in the low strings. This basic pattern is repeated over the series of shots, but is varied by an independently moving upper string line, which decorates the pattern with its own line organized around the sixth and seventh scale tones. The thickening of the music's texture and a slow crescendo further suggest the mounting pressure of the scene. Just as the crescendo reaches its peak, however, the cue abruptly ends on an unresolved note. The brusque ending signals both a change in tone—Doc will be revealed as a harmless country gentleman who needs Paul's help—and the sudden shift of the scene's power relations as Paul turns the tables on his pursuer and asks, "All right, what do you want?" After its initial appearance, the cue will be repeated with slight variations in scenes involving conflict between Paul and Holly, such as their argument in the library or their argument following Holly's drunken declaration that she intends to marry Rusty Trawler.

Perhaps the clearest indication of the functional nature of these cues is the fact that they do not appear on the soundtrack album for *Breakfast*. Written primarily for a dramatic rather than a commercial context, either Mancini or RCA Victor felt that these cues were, like most classical film music, too fragmented and tuneless to fulfill the musical expectations of most album buyers. This is not to suggest, however, that what does appear on the album is entirely extraneous to the film's narrative. On the contrary, all of the cues in *Breakfast* are narratively motivated, and even those that are included largely to add variety to the soundtrack serve very specific dramatic functions.

"The Big Blow Out," for example, a brassy Big Band blues, appears only briefly in the film but is spotted and orchestrated in a way that gives it maximal dramatic impact. The tune appears early on in a scene which opens with Holly's upstairs neighbor, Mr. Yunioshi (Mickey Rooney, in a blatant and embarrassing caricature that mars the film), asleep in bed. After a few seconds of quiet, the music unexpectedly begins from downstairs and awakens Yunioshi. After Yunioshi threatens to call the police, the music just as abruptly ends with the sound of a phonograph needle roughly scratching the surface of the record. Though a rather simple device, the music here functions concisely to make a couple of narrative points. First, it continues a pattern of disruption involving the various ways Holly's parties and dates constantly impinge on Yunioshi's privacy. The blaring, brassy orchestration of the tune functions musically as an objective correlative of the rudeness and impertinence of these interruptions. At the same time, however, the brassiness also suggests the loudness and boorishness of most of Holly's male companions. As we watch Holly fending off a drunken suitor, the music reminds us that her companions are often loutish, rude, and obnoxious slobs.

"Sally's Tomato," on the other hand, is a languid, Latin-tinged jazz ballad, and highlights a somewhat different feature of Holly's dates. Although somewhat speciously motivated—Holly puts the song on her phonograph as she prepares food for Cat—the tune accompanies Holly's description of her arrangement with the Italian mobster Sally Tomato, and initiates a pattern by which Latin jazz is consistently associated with rich, urbane ethnic males. The cultural associations here between Latin jazz and ethnicity remind us that Holly's sexual desires are frequently focalized around men such as Sally, Jake Berman (Martin Balsam), Mr. Yunioshi, and José da Silva Perriera, all of whom embody the wealth and social status Holly craves.

The association between ethnicity, sexuality, and music is something that Mancini exploited throughout his career. In *Touch of Evil* (1958), for example, the use of Latin jazz in association with the film's Mexican characters takes on a certain thematic resonance in that film's treatment of miscegenation, sexual violation, and petty criminality. In *The Pink Panther*, however, the association between music and ethnicity takes on Orientalist hues. The title song, for example, features such Orientalist touches as the use of parallel fifths in the song's introduction and a sinuous, serpentine saxophone melody. Moreover, as William Luhr and Peter Lehman note, the gem itself is consistently linked to Princess Dala (Claudia Cardinale), whose father once owned the gem. The various attempts to steal the Pink Panther parallel the various attempts to steal Dala's virginity, and thus the tune takes on added thematic weight as a signifier of both the diamond and the princess's sexuality.[26]

Perhaps the most telling linkage of ethnicity, sexuality, and music, however, occurs in *Breakfast* itself during the film's most famous sequence, the twenty-minute party scene. According to Mancini, the sequence was one of his biggest challenges since it only involved a half page of description in the script, but ended up being a full-blown comic set piece involving the kind of visual gags and slapstick for which Blake Edwards would become famous. For this sequence, Mancini composed four different pieces of music, each of which reflects the growing raucousness of the party.

The first of these, "Moon River Cha Cha," is a jazzy reworking of the film's signature tune as a light Latin dance number. The second, "Latin Golightly," is a sprightly four beat in the key of F major. The melody, which is played on trumpet, essentially outlines a pentatonic scale but features some chromatic alteration of the third and sixth scale tones. This, along with the supple Latin rhythms and the frequent use of major and minor seventh chords in the harmonization, give the song its idiomatic flavor. The third number, "Something for Cat," is a two-chord riff tune in D major. After a brief vamp on a Latin beat, Mancini introduces the song's driving, syncopated riff in the saxophones. Using this as the song's structural basis, Mancini then adds a simple muted trumpet melody, which, like the sax riff, circles around the fifth, flatted seventh, and ninth of the tonic chord. Though relatively simple, the riff and chord patterns offer a loose harmonic framework for the improvised solos that follow. The last song in the sequence, "Loose Caboose," is used to accompany the most raucous moments of the party and is an appropriately brassy, energetic Big Band tune.

Though they clearly differ from atmospheric movie music, these Latin jazz cues nevertheless perform a couple of important functions within the narrative. First of all, jazz is used in scenes like the famous party sequence to connote both the contemporary urban setting and the casual, cosmopolitan decadence of its characters. Though neither drug use nor sexual deviance is explicitly shown in *Breakfast*, the music nevertheless summons up such themes through jazz's previous filmic association with sensationalist subject matter. Second, the music here also effectively sets off the comic business that makes up a large measure of the sequence. In fact, the autonomy of the music's form during this sequence, its relative separation from the image track, is an important factor in the music's light touch. Rather than highlight the gags through mickey-mousing or broad musical comments, the Latin jazz acts as a neutral background for the comic material and subtly underplays such moments as Holly accidentally setting a woman's hat on fire.[27] Lastly, the music also reinforces Holly's attraction to exotic ethnic types, and foreshadows José's later emergence as her primary romantic interest.

Mancini's use of the provocatively titled "Something for Cat" to accompany the entrance of the film's two biggest "super rats," José and Rusty Trawler, further denotes the specifically predatory nature of Holly's relationship with men. Both musically and narratively, Holly is often linked to sexual predation through a none-too-subtle association between Holly and Cat. Not only is Holly metonymically linked to her nameless feline friend, she is often characterized as catlike in her relationship with Paul, who we learn early on has written a collection of short stories entitled *Nine Lives*, and who steals dog and cat Halloween masks with Holly from a department store. In addition, Holly often describes her male companions as "rats" and "super rats," who give her money for the powder room in exchange for sex. In a drunken speech to Paul midway through the film, Holly says that the typical "rat" expects women to "curl up like a kitten into a little furry ball and feed him." These "rats" apparently forget that when a "kitten" like Holly feeds them, she is only fattening them up for the kill.

This theme is ultimately brought to fruition in the film's final sequence when Holly sets her beloved Cat free in a garbage-filled alley. Saying that they never belonged to each other, Holly seems eager to demonstrate her independence, her separation from any form of emotional entanglement or familial responsibility. However, a second thematic parallel is also evident here; just as Cat will feed off the rats and garbage of the alley, Holly will feed off the rich male "rats" and "super rats" of Brazil.

In all of these ways, *Breakfast* depicts marriage as a form of animal entrapment through its consistent association of sexuality with animality. In fact, the specific association between the feline and the feminine was so significant that it was played up in *Variety*'s ads for the film. In an August 16 ad for the film's engagement at Radio City Music Hall, a bejeweled Audrey Hepburn is shown smoking from an absurdly long cigarette holder, a cat suggestively perched on her shoulder (figure 4.1). Both textually and extratextually the message is clear: Holly's "pussy," to use a vulgar metaphor, is a "rat" trap.

Yet by the end of the film, Holly herself is ensnared by her own sexual and social desires. By casting her relationships as points on a food chain, Holly becomes enmeshed in a cycle that subordinates everything to her search for a proper place in the ecosphere of New York society. Though she strives to be a "wild thing," Holly's deterministic view of social relations paradoxically allows her no freedom and itself becomes a kind of cage in which she is trapped. By submitting to the laws of the social jungle, Holly has unwittingly accomplished what she most feared—she has placed herself in a cage, which, Paul notes, is of her own creation.

The notion that Holly herself is ensnared in predatory sexual relationships is also presented in the film's visual schemes. As Luhr and Lehman note, *Breakfast*'s mise-en-scène often presents Holly in images of entrapment. The use of prison settings, the framing of Holly through banisters and on fire escapes, and the compositional emphasis on a caged and stuffed bird in Holly's apartment all metaphorically depict her as a caged animal yearning to be free of her dependency on rich, older men.[28]

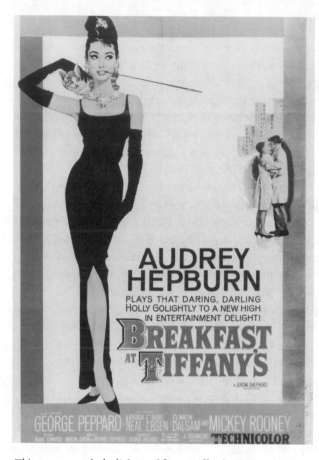

FIGURE 4.1 This poster reveals the link *Breakfast at Tiffany's* (1961) makes between the feline and the feminine.

Significantly, this pattern of dependency is established quite early in Holly's life in her relationship with her former husband, Doc Golightly. Midway through the film, the mysterious Doc, who describes himself as a horse doctor and animal man, tells Paul how he first found Holly, then called Lulamae Barnes, a fourteen-year-old girl stealing milk and turkey eggs with her brother Fred. Holly marries Doc, not out of love, but rather out of a desire to provide a home for herself and her brother. Though Doc has no reason to believe that Holly is unhappy, she nonetheless leaves him and has the marriage annulled.

We later learn in her farewell to Doc at the bus depot that Holly's departure was not because she did not love Doc, but rather simply because of his weakness for "wild things" which he nurses back to health but ultimately leave him when they have the strength and desire to do so. Equating herself with these wild things, Holly urges Doc to understand that her new identity and new environment are part of a natural maturation process, that in leaving him she was merely a bird who was finally old enough to leave the nest. In Holly's eyes, the unfortunate Doc, who is poor, rural, and plainspoken, represents everything from which she has tried to escape. What Holly either ignores or fails to realize, however, is that Doc truly loves her in a way that her rich, urbane, ethnic male companions will not. Doc's kindness, his willingness to nurture Holly and then set her free, is ironically both the mark of his devotion and the character trait that will prevent him from ever possessing Holly again.

Thus, by linking Holly and Cat, sexuality and animality, marriage and entrapment, ethnicity and urban exoticism, Mancini's use of Latin jazz is part of a complex of signifiers which depict Holly as a cynical sexual predator. Yet this bundle of traits represents only one part of Holly's character. Holly's cynicism is usually concealed under an exterior charm, and frequently her frustration and heartache yield a passionate, soulful romantic yearning. Just as Holly's cynicism is suggested in the cool, sophisticated decadence of Latin jazz, Holly's wistful longing is expressed through the film's most important theme, "Moon River."

Throughout the film, "Moon River" is consistently associated with Holly's romanticism and her desire to escape her rural past. With its first appearance under the film's credits, the image and music tracks combine to form a complex signifier of each of these two linked character traits. As befits a song with multiple levels of meaning, however, the first images and sounds of the film provide a kind of incongruity. Under an opening shot of a New York City street and a yellow cab coming toward the camera, we hear the plaintive melody of "Moon River" stated on a harmonica and accompanied by a strummed guitar, instrumental sounds that are more commonly associated with rural America and the western plains. As the song's structure develops, it takes on a more modern hue and quickly establishes a set of thematic oppositions between city/country and present/past. The simple diatonic melody is harmonized with thickly textured jazz substitution chords, which loosen the song's tonality by moving through a series of secondary dominants toward a half cadence at the end of the first verse:

FIGURE 4.2

As the second verse begins and the melody is taken over by the strings, the contemporary urban setting becomes firmly established. We see Holly standing before a Tiffany's store window, casually munching on a croissant and drinking coffee, an image that literalizes the film's title emblazoned on the right half of the frame. Holly, who is elegantly coiffed and exquisitely dressed in a Givenchy gown, appears to be the picture of wealth and sophistication. As we later learn, however, this first impression is false, for Holly only feigns this social position in order to meet wealthy, single men. Viewed in retrospect, Holly's pilgrimage to Tiffany's is a gesture that represents her desire for real wealth and social position, her need to acquire the luxury epitomized by Tiffany jewelry.

Thus, the images and sounds of this rather simple credit sequence economically establish three important facets of Holly's character, traits that will be elaborated and specified through subsequent appearances of the "Moon River" theme. To begin with, the orchestration for guitar and harmonica connotatively suggests Holly's rural roots. Then, the central image of Holly standing before Tiffany's shop windows encapsulates her drive for affluence and status. Third, the jazzy harmonies and subsequent orchestration of "Moon River" for full orchestra and chorus affectively connote the mood of dolorous longing that is the emotional keystone for both Holly and the film.

All of these elements are further embellished by the second appearance of "Moon River" during a later scene in Paul's bedroom. Holly, who is trying to ditch a particularly obnoxious date, climbs through Paul's bedroom window and asks if she might stay there. Holly also remarks that Paul looks a great deal like her brother Fred, and asks if she can call Paul by her brother's name. As Holly reminisces about Fred and his childhood passion for peanut butter, "Moon River" is reprised, once again played on harmonica. Holly says that though she has not seen Fred since she was fourteen, she is saving money so that the two of them can buy a ranch and raise horses in Mexico. Unable to return to her apartment, Holly asks if she might platonically share Paul's bed. As Holly calls out to Fred during a nightmare, "Moon River" briefly returns, but this time is given an eerie shading. Over the ringing vibrato of the vibes, the ghostly sound of the flutes render the melody with a slow, funereal air, one that affectively evokes the wintry cold of Holly's nightmare vision.

While implicitly reinforcing Holly's rural past, "Moon River" also establishes a crucial parallel between Fred and Paul. In addition to their physical resemblance, Paul—in Holly's eyes—also shares Fred's sweetness and guileless good nature. Holly's unspoken trust in Paul is signified when she climbs into his bed, not as a sexual partner, but as a confidante and friend. Holly even dreams of Fred while cradled in Paul's arms, as though her unconscious were stirred by a familiar touch. As before, Mancini's use of harmonica association-ally signifies the wide open landscapes of the West, but here these associations are given clear narrative motivation. Like a character in a classical Hollywood western, Holly speaks of her dreams of operating a ranch in Mexico.

In its next appearance in the film, "Moon River" not only summarizes and reinforces these themes but also more clearly delineates them by adding a tex-tual element which has been absent to this point: the song's lyrics. As sung by Holly in the film (figure 4.3), the lyrics function as a kind of personal and poetic expression of her point of view:

Moon River

Moon River,
wider than a mile;
I'm crossin' you in style
someday.

Old dreammaker,
you heartbreaker,
wherever you're goin',
I'm goin' your way.

Two drifters,
off to see the world,
There's such a lot of world
to see.

We're after the same
rainbow's end,
waitin' 'round the bend,
My Huckleberry friend,
Moon River and me.

—Music by Henry Mancini, lyrics by Johnny Mercer*

The obliqueness of the lyrics leaves the song open to a number of possible readings. At one level, the lyrics draw an analogy between Holly and the

*Copyright © 1961 by Famous Music Corporation. Copyright renewed 1989 by Famous Music Corporation. Used by permission.

FIGURE 4.3 Holly Golightly (Audrey Hepburn) sings "Moon River." Although it was never released on record, it was composer Henry Mancini's favorite version of the song.

moon. Like the moon, Holly holds a certain romantic allure for potential lovers, but remains emotionally distant, cold, and unattainable. In this respect, the analogy metaphorically approximates the poetics of a certain eroticism in that Holly's emotional distance becomes a central feature of her desirability. For most lovers, Holly represents sexual opportunity with no emotional strings attached. Holly does not ask for commitment, fidelity, or romantic devotion; instead she simply asks for Tiffany's jewelry or a fifty dollar tip for the powder room.

For Paul, however, the analogy between Holly and the moon suggests a different link between eroticism and emotional distance. As far as Holly knows, Paul is a man of modest means; she thus has great affection for him but refuses him any kind of long-term commitment. The analogy thus emphasizes Paul's situation as the classic unrequited lover (albeit seemingly caught in a moral quandary of his own making with Mrs. Valenson). At the same time, the analogy suggests that Holly's desirability for Paul is somewhat founded on her unattainability. Like many other romantic figures, Paul wants Holly partly because he cannot have her, and by desiring Holly, Paul is, in a sense, "asking for the moon."

At another level, the lyrics establish an analogy between Holly and the river. As the song's "two drifters," both Holly and the river seem to share a certain path through life, one that is strewn with broken dreams and heartache. Despite the painful past, however, the river continually holds out the promise of a better future "waitin' 'round the bend." Here the imagery of yearning and chasing rainbows stresses Holly's oft-concealed dreaminess, the romantic undercurrent she tries to hide even from herself.

On still another level, the image of "two drifters" is both an apt summary of the film's fantasy of normative heterosexual union and a portent of Holly's plans to marry José and live like royalty in Brazil. This latter aspect is also epitomized in the notion of crossing the river "in style," a phrase that hints at Holly's desire for glamour and social status. The lyrics remind us that these hopes remain unfulfilled and that Holly has not yet found a man to replace the river as that other "drifter."

At the same time, however, an interesting cultural reference reinforces the film's theme of ethnicity as wealthy exoticism, and helps to clarify the paths along which Holly's desire is directed. Mancini himself actually calls attention to it in describing his initial reaction to Johnny Mercer's lyrics. He says:

> Every once in a while you hear something so right that it gives you the chills, and when he sang that "huckleberry friend" line, I got them. I don't know whether he knew what effect those words had or if it was just something that came to him, but it was thrilling. It made you think of Mark Twain and Huckleberry Finn's trip down the Mississippi. It had such echoes of America.[29]

On the one hand, the evocation of Huck Finn extends and refines the sense of opportunity and hope so often associated with Holly. By alluding to Huck's journey down the mighty Mississippi, the song alludes more generally to the sense of freedom, open possibilities, and Manifest Destiny so often signified by the American West, and summarized by Huck's desire to light out for the territories. As such, the lyric's implied reference to Twain and the theme's frequent orchestration for harmonica and guitar mutually reinforce the connotations of rural Americana that accrue throughout the film.

It is wise to recall, however, that the song's "two drifters, off to see the world," are in Twain's novel both Huck and the runaway slave, Jim. The invocation of this famous literary pair reminds us that Holly's sexual drives are often quite cynically directed toward ethnic males like Jim, and that beneath the candy-coated sheen of Holly's romantic fantasy lies a calculated means of achieving it. Within the context of the score as a whole, Mancini's use of Latin jazz to connote ethnicity partly recasts the "Huckleberry friend" of "Moon River" as "Huckleberry's friend." Through this juxtaposition, Mancini's music constructs Holly's feminine desire as a complex and contradictory mix of romantic fantasy and sexual predation.

With the appearance of Doc, "Moon River" returns to the themes of nostalgia and Americana established earlier, but now specifies those themes by fleshing out Holly's background in much greater detail. Through Doc's discussion of his early marriage to Holly, the audience gains a better understanding of her need to escape her past, forge a new identity, and build a life for herself and her simpleton brother. In one sense, Holly's efforts to snare a husband are a continual replaying of her earlier marriage, which she undertook mostly to provide security for herself and Fred. Instead of filching turkey eggs, Holly now filches jewelry and fifty dollar tips for the powder room, and stalks much bigger game than the humble country vet from Tulip, Texas. In harkening back to the earlier image of Holly standing before Tiffany's, "Moon River" underscores the connections between past and present, and clarifies the notion that Holly's present drive for wealth is merely an extension of an earlier struggle for survival.

Yet in underlining the emotions of the various scenes with Doc, the lonesome sound of the harmonica also suggests that Holly's decisions have brought more than their share of regrets. Doc, who does not comprehend either Holly's decision to marry him or her decision to leave him, expresses both his sense of loss and his frustration in failing to understand Holly's needs. In losing his heart to a "wild thing," Doc remorsefully acknowledges that he understands Holly's reasons for action no better than he understands those of the sick animals to which he tends. Holly's chief regret, on the other hand, is that she still loves Doc, but realizes that she is no longer the person that he married.

At the bus station, Holly tearfully says goodbye to Doc in a scene reminiscent of classical Hollywood melodrama. Accompanying this moment of public separation and yielding a feeling of nostalgic sorrow, the music swells to a tremulous, passionate peak, and sentimentally expresses the tender feelings Holly and Doc share even as they part, presumably for the last time. As Holly bids farewell to her past, the film temporarily bids farewell to the musical theme associated with it, albeit with a somewhat flamboyant, romantic flourish. "Moon River" will be reprised only once more in the film, but this final time will be its most important and meaningful.

In its last appearance during the film's closing sequence, "Moon River" supremely epitomizes what Mancini's strategy has been throughout. Combining the functions of both atmospheric scoring and "tune-plugging," the cue also summarizes the polysemic nature of the score as a whole. On one hand, the theme serves as both a musical summary of the various thematic threads of the film and as an affirmation of the classical Hollywood formation of the couple—a climactic plot development not present in Truman Capote's source novel, incidentally.[30] On the other hand, however, the music also acts as an underlying critical voice, one that subtly elevates a theme which has been largely repressed throughout the film: Holly's incestuous desire for her unseen brother Fred. By hinting at this perverse subtext, the music sets many of the film's earlier events in a new light and undermines the climax's consecration of normative, heterosexual romance.

At the start of the sequence, Holly has just been released from jail and plans to leave the country and pursue either José or some other rich single man in Brazil. On a cab ride to the airport, Paul tries to convince Holly to stay by declaring his love for her. Holly, who is eager to show her resolve, sets Cat free in an alley, but then reconsiders and begins to search for him in the rain. As Holly undertakes the search, a motive adapted from the first three notes of "Moon River" is repeated and varied over a shifting ostinato bass pattern. Played in minor mode, the throbbing repetition of this motive underlines the sudden urgency and hysteria of Holly's search, and her sudden realization that Paul deeply loves her. At the same time, however, the cue also represents Holly's inner turmoil at her complicity in the domestication of her sexuality, a thematic element signified by her attempt to recover the cat she had earlier set free. Just before Holly gives up hope, Cat meows from an empty cardboard box, an event signaled by the music in a modulation to D major and a full restatement of "Moon River" by the entire orchestra and chorus. Paul, Holly, and Cat are then reunited on the rain-swept streets of New York City in a moment of classically fervent passion (figure 4.4). Mancini's reorchestration of the theme for full orchestra serves as a sweeping, lyrical, romantic gesture to underscore Holly and Paul's union and to exalt the triumph of Hollywood narrative conventions.

FIGURE 4.4 *Breakfast at Tiffany's* concludes with Paul (George Peppard) and Holly's romantic embrace after finding Cat. The final scene is accompanied by a lush restatement of "Moon River" scored for full orchestra and chorus.

The song's allusion to Holly's rural past, however, also hints at a perverse subtext involving Holly's equation of Paul with her brother Fred. Holly has earlier told Paul that he physically resembles Fred, and indeed calls him by that name for the rest of the film. The coupling of Paul and Holly in this context suggests that their union is the satisfaction of an unexpressed incestuous wish, one that perhaps has served as the unconscious motivation for Holly's actions throughout the film.

In doing so, "Moon River" also retrospectively reveals a consistent narrative pattern in which Fred has been implicitly associated with Holly's sexual activities. Holly marries Doc in order to provide food and shelter for her brother; she trades companionship for money with men like Sally Tomato in order to save for Fred's eventual release from the Army; and she plans on marrying José to provide financial security for Fred in the future (although this future is somewhat thrown into doubt upon the news of Fred's death late in the film). In fact, earlier, when Paul reintroduces Doc to Holly, she momentarily mistakes him for Fred just before Doc carries her off to the bedroom for a night of connubial bliss. When Paul and Holly embrace at film's end, the narrative simply completes the pattern by offering Paul as Fred's substitute. With Fred safely dead, Paul is now free to take his position in Holly's heart as the other "drifter" in her romantic fantasy. In return, Holly can indulge her repressed wish in a socially sanctioned manner by taking Paul as her sexual partner and settling down with him as she would have with Fred.

In addition to undermining the meanings and emotions of the film's resolution, the implied reference to incest also subtly reinscribes the song's lyrical imagery in a number of ways. First of all, by signifying Holly's rural past, the incestuous subtext created through Mancini's patterned use of "Moon River" slyly alters the connotations of the song's "two drifters." Where earlier the phrase had suggested Holly and a future romantic partner (perhaps José), the phrase now suggests Holly and Fred. Viewed from this perspective, the notion of "two drifters" suddenly seems closer to the image of Holly and Fred presented by Doc—vagrants wandering the countryside, stealing and scrounging for meals in order to survive. This additional meaning of "drifter" is in fact further emphasized by a similar inversion of the song's pursuit of "the same rainbow's end." Whereas earlier this might have suggested a fairy tale happy ending shared by Holly and her lover, the hint of incest recasts it to suggest a proverbial pot of gold divided between Holly and Fred. In this respect, the song reminds us that Holly is as much a "grifter" as a "drifter," and that her dreamy eccentricity is driven by a crass materialism. Likewise, the notion of a "Huckleberry friend" undergoes some transformation as well. No longer simply an evocation of Americana or a reference to exotic ethnicity, the phrase coincidentally serves as an oblique description of Fred himself, whose sweet, simple provincialism mirrors that of his literary forebear.

Much of the song's multivalence then inheres in its oblique poetry, its ability to function within a variety of dramatic contexts to achieve a connotative richness. Phrases like "My Huckleberry friend" derive their power from the fact that so many different meanings may be attached to them. Throughout the film, these meanings shift as the song itself shifts in relation to its dramatic context. At one moment, the song evokes the timeless imagery of moonbeams and rivers in its celebration of romantic fantasy. At the next moment, the song hints of Americana and the wide open spaces of the West. At yet another moment, it evokes the popular stereotype of inbred backwoods hill-billies. The climactic use of "Moon River" in the film's conclusion is an emblematic and powerful example of this. While the sweeping, almost monumental arrangement of "Moon River" bestows a sense of romantic grandeur upon Paul and Holly's relationship, it simultaneously reminds us of the dirty little hillbilly secret that drives it.

In the wake of *Breakfast*'s success, Mancini achieved a distinction that few other film composers could claim; he became a household name. Along with his enormous popularity, moreover, came increased industry stature and power for the composer. After receiving a $12,500 fee for *Breakfast*, Mancini now commanded salaries two to three times that figure. In addition, Mancini was also in such high demand that he accepted only one of every ten film offers.[31] Throughout the 1960s, Mancini's celebrity also enabled him to negotiate very favorable terms for publishing royalties. As a 1963 United Artists memo indicates, Mancini's contracts on Blake Edwards' films allowed the composer to designate a company other than United Artists Music Company to hold the copyright. In such an arrangement, UA Music retained a 50 percent interest in monies derived from Mancini's company, with the composer getting the remainder.[32] In early 1965, Mancini even publicly announced that he would no longer score a film if he did not receive the music publishing copyrights.[33] With the continuing success of Mancini's soundtrack albums and the enduring popularity of his most famous themes, his film work remained sweet music to the ears of film promoters. As late as 1975, Mancini was glowingly described in studio promotional circulars as "showmanship plus."[34]

More recently, interest in Mancini's film music has been boosted by the nineties' vogue for "cocktail music."[35] Over the past few years, cuts from *Breakfast at Tiffany's* and other Mancini scores have been turning up in anthologies like Rhino's *Cocktail Mix*, vol. 3, *Swingin' Singles*, and Capitol's *Ultra-Lounge* series. Along with Esquivel, Mantovani, and other composers of "easy listening," Mancini has been tapped as a musical symbol of Kennedy-era optimism and leisure. In his liner notes to *Shots in the Dark*, a collection of Mancini themes covered by various alternative rock bands, Joseph Lanza writes, "Henry Mancini, like Walt Disney, helped to usher in the Cold War escapism that satisfied an over-worked and over-anxious middle class sold on suburbia, satellites, stereophonic sound, super-sonic travel, and arm-chair screen adventures involving espionage and transnational romance."[36] Lanza's assessment of Mancini's cultural import nicely summarizes the reasons for his

appropriation by the "Cocktail Nation." His music's "environmental" qualities—its exoticism, its moodiness, its avoidance of any rough edges or social
relevance—fit squarely within the trend's aesthetic, which not only rejects
rock 'n' roll's codes of authenticity and emotional expression but also celebrates easy listening's evocation of middle-class retro cool.

Yet while Generation X-ers slurp cosmopolitans to his music, historians
would be wise to reconsider Mancini's place in film music history. For one
thing, Mancini's approach to scoring not only helped bring a greater variety
of themes and idioms to film music, but it also established a pattern for soundtrack promotion which would predominate throughout the sixties, seventies,
and eighties. For another, Mancini's work on *Breakfast* brought together the
two most important trends in fifties film music—jazz and popular song. By
shrewdly integrating these two elements, Mancini created a prototype of the
sixties pop score, one that accorded prominence to the film's music in order to
stimulate sales in various ancillary markets. This prominence was achieved
both through the convention of scoring credit sequences with popular songs
and through the careful motivation of diegetic music as spontaneous performance or sourced background music.

As is evident in *Breakfast at Tiffany's*, Mancini's music is never merely an
extraneous promotional tool, but is always an extremely important voice of
the film, adding layers of meaning to the narrative and commenting on the
film's various subtexts. In fact, I would argue that few Hollywood scores can
match the complexity of its dramatic functions or the intricacy of its relations
to the narrative. So closely is the music tied to Holly's character that Jake
Berman's description of her in the film is equally applicable to the film's score.
In its connotations of both romanticism and cynicism, the score is a phony,
but it's a real phony.

5

The Midas Touch

JOHN BARRY AND *GOLDFINGER*

Like Henry Mancini, John Barry has shown himself to be one of the preeminent melodists in the history of film music. As I earlier noted in my brief analysis of "Goldfinger," Barry is especially adept at combining jazz sonorities and short motivic tunes to create forceful and engaging pop hooks. In his James Bond scores, however, Barry modified Mancini's multitheme approach to devise a distinctive musical formula for the series, one that has been utilized in several films and even by different composers. In doing so, Barry proved once again that the structured repetition of themes was a useful technique for reinforcing title songs within the minds of spectators.

In *On Her Majesty's Secret Service* (1969), the sixth of Eon Productions' Bonds, there is an early scene which typifies the textual and extratextual functions of Barry's memorable scores. After an obsessive two-year pursuit of SPECTRE mastermind Blofeld, Bond is abruptly taken off the case by M. In response to this order, Bond dictates a curt letter of resignation to Miss Moneypenny (Lois Maxwell) and storms to his office. At his desk Bond sentimentally rummages through some mementos of his past adventures— Honey Rider's belt and knife from *Dr. No* (1962), Red Grant's lethal wristwatch from *From Russia with Love* (1963), and the tankless, underwater breathing apparatus from *Thunderball* (1965). As Bond picks up each of these objects, Barry plays the musical theme associated with its respective film in brief succession. The cue begins with "Under the Mango Tree" from *Dr. No* and is followed by short snatches of the other two films' title themes.

Although the cue lasts only thirty-four seconds, it is interesting and rather unusual in terms of its form and function. As a series of three discrete themes, the cue clearly diverges from classical Hollywood strategies of leitmotivic and atmospheric composition. It may serve the leitmotiv's function of referring to characters, settings, and situations, but it refers to persons and events that are outside the film's immediate narrative context. For similar reasons, the intertextual nature of the scene poses an interesting problem of interpretation for those unfamilar with the series. Viewers new to Bond would undoubtedly understand the narrative thrust of the scene—Bond is reminiscing about past exploits—but would likely fail to appreciate the specific affective resonance of these objects. Instead of clarifying this resonance, Barry's music only enhances the objects' remoteness. Without an awareness of previous Bond themes, the cue would seem to be so much melodious effluvia, a curious mélange of calypso, gypsy folk music, and Wagnerian "Sturm und Drang."

Still, the intertextual function of the music is only a part of its effectiveness in the scene. One reason why the music also works for nonfans is that each of these themes has an extratextual identity separate from its function in its respective film. Each of these themes was packaged as part of a moderately successful soundtrack album, and each was published and sold as sheet music. Additionally, the latter themes in the cue, "From Russia with Love" and "Thunderball," were released as singles in vocal versions performed by Matt Monro and Tom Jones, respectively. Given the exposure of these tunes on radio and as recordings, the themes in this brief cue address the audience not only as spectators but as consumers as well.

Producers Harry Saltzman and Albert "Cubby" Broccoli have frequently acknowledged the importance of a consistent formula to the durability of the series. This formula contains, among other things, exotic locations, beautiful women, larger-than-life villains, hulking henchmen, elaborate stuntwork, clever gadgetry, Maurice Binder's iconic gun-barrel opening, a spectacular precredit sequence, and an erotic main title featuring a memorable theme. Music has also been a significant, if less noted, ingredient in Bond's recipe for success. Though composers as dissimilar as Marvin Hamlisch, Bill Conti, and Michael Kamen have taken on the scoring duties for individual Bond films, the series as a whole has maintained a remarkable degree of musical consistency. This is largely due to the efforts of John Barry, who developed a musical formula for the series as durable as its narrative formula.

As developed in *From Russia with Love*, this formula consists of four com-

ponents: (1) the "James Bond Theme," used as a signature for the protagonist; (2) "007," a driving, syncopated march; (3) a title song, to serve either
as an action or a love theme; and (4) a leitmotiv for the villain. These basic
components are then incorporated with briefer atmospheric cues and fused
into an integrated whole. The overarching musical unity is further enhanced
by Barry's distinctive style, a brassy, percussive jazz rock that combines menacing low brass with lush, lyrical string passages.

Though the first three of these components are usually employed as recognizable tunes, Barry treats each as a set of discrete motives which can be
repeated and varied to create the score's various atmospheric cues. Over the
years, Barry has typically used one or more motives from the signature
"James Bond Theme" as a starting point for the films' love themes and title
songs. Says Barry, "The [title] song has been a complete part of the theme,
countermelody, and harmonies of an integrated score, and I think that
works."[1] Used in film after film, Barry's compositional strategy not only
assured that the individual Bond score was an integral whole but also that
stylistic and thematic unity was maintained across the entire series.

In the remainder of this chapter, I will look more closely at the economic
and narrative functions of Barry's music for Bond. To begin with, I will chart
Saltzman and Broccoli's efforts to build a market for both the Bond films and
the Bond music. As might be expected, the Bond scores played a significant
role in Saltzman and Broccoli's scheme by amortizing production costs and
by establishing a ready audience for subsequent films in the series. In this
regard, the Bond films are important precursors to the sequels prevalent in
Hollywood throughout the seventies and eighties. Series as diverse as the *Star
Wars* trilogy, the Indiana Jones films, the *Lethal Weapon* films, and the *Batman*
films show time and again that a signature sound is vital to the overall fortunes
of a film series.

Second, I will use the most commercially successful score in the series,
Goldfinger (1964), as a case study demonstrating the specific dramatic functions of Barry's music. Not only is *Goldfinger* an impressive application of the
basic components of the Bond score, its integration of various musical motifs
draws parallels between Bond and the antagonist in a manner which suggests
that one is the inverted mirror image of the other. Through such parallels, the
music offers an inadvertent critique of the ideology embodied in the series'
sexually rapacious hero. Like *Breakfast at Tiffany's*, *Goldfinger*'s score both
popularized a particular image of sixties' cool and dramatized its underlying
ideological tensions.

Creating a Bond Market: Selling John Barry's Soundtracks and Theme Songs

The commercial importance of Barry's music for the series should not be understated. Of the eleven Bond soundtrack albums featuring Barry's work, only two, *The Man with the Golden Gun* (1974) and *The Living Daylights* (1987), failed to have any action on U.S. trade charts. Their lackluster showing, however, perhaps only further points up the importance that a string of more successful title songs from other Bond films have played in the series. Over the years the Bond series has attracted such songwriters as Lionel Bart, Anthony Newley, Leslie Bricusse, Paul McCartney, and Narada Michael Walden, while songs were performed by such stars as Louis Armstrong, Carly Simon, Sheena Easton, Duran Duran, and the Pretenders. With these diverse talents at their disposal, Saltzman and Broccoli reaped the financial benefits of nine charting singles, five of which were Top Ten hits.

While many producers from the fifties onward attempted to exploit title songs as promotional tools, Saltzman and Broccoli innovated the notion of using pop songs as a regularized aspect of production. Earlier efforts at such cross-promotion had been piecemeal and erratic, with each film developing its own textual and extratextual strategies of merchandising music. While these early efforts did have their share of successes, they were somewhat risky from both a commercial and aesthetic standpoint. If the producer and composer greatly misjudged audience tastes, as Stanley Kramer and Ernest Gold did with "Waltzing Mathilda" in 1959's *On the Beach*, the result was often a score that could be dramatically effective in the film itself but of very little promotional value.

To resolve the issue of audience taste, producers frequently commissioned or selected a song to be used for the credits, but which was not integrated with the film's other cues. Commissioned songwriters often understood the need for melodic hooks and clever lyrics better than film composers and thus were frequently more capable of servicing the ancillary markets that helped ameliorate a producer's risks. Since such a tune was often used only during the credit sequence, however, it had a limited chance of ingratiating itself within the collective consciousness of the audience. If a tune failed to make an impression on viewers during this small window of opportunity, then it functioned as little more than a musical announcement of the film's title.

In developing their own approach to marketing film music, Saltzman and Broccoli combined both of these strategies in a way that maximized their benefits. The frequent repetition of the "James Bond Theme" in film after film made this signature tune synonymous with the central character. The almost Pavlovian association of music and character has been a key to the series' success in both domestic and international markets. The twangy, reverbed electric guitar and forceful brass melody transcend language barriers and serve as a simple, economical, and immediately recognizable means of promoting the character. *Variety* estimates that over half the world's population has seen a Bond film, and it is likely that virtually all of them can identify the "James Bond Theme."[2]

Yet by introducing new exploitable tunes with each film, Saltzman and Broccoli were able to hedge their bets by continually offering new product to radio programmers and music vendors. With the films conceived as a series from the outset, each song became an anticipated element in a reliable promotional formula. Just as fans eagerly anticipated the display of the new Bond girl in *Playboy* pictorials, they also awaited the promotional drama concerning who will write and sing a new Bond theme.[3] By pairing the familiar "James Bond Theme" with a new title song, each film conformed to an implicit set of musical norms for the series in a formula that balanced conventionality and novelty, homogeneity and variety.

The groundwork for this formula was laid in June 1961 when Saltzman and Broccoli met with United Artists' Arthur Krim to discuss a distribution deal for their nascent James Bond series. Saltzman had already secured the exclusive film rights to all but one of Ian Fleming's Bond books, but the two producers had not yet received any financial backing for their project. After a fruitless discussion with Columbia Pictures, Saltzman and Broccoli sought out UA, which subsequently agreed in principle to a regular development deal with the pair's Swiss production company, Danjaq. On April 2, 1962, the details of the agreement were finalized in a formal document that gave Saltzman and Broccoli financing for the first film in the series, *Dr. No*, in exchange for UA's standard distribution fees and rights of approval over the main artistic elements of each film.[4]

Also stipulated in this basic agreement was UA's broad control over the various music rights for the Bond series. UA was granted both copyright privileges and the licensing rights for any original songs, instrumental, or background music contained in the films, and was further given the right to manufacture and sell said soundtrack in the form of records, tapes, and written transcriptions. Not only did UA receive authorization to assign these rights to its own publishing and recording subsidiaries, but the parent company also collected two cents on every piece of sheet music sold in the United States, 20 percent of the aggregate net receipts of foreign sheet music sales, and 20 percent of the net receipts from the sale of mechanical and synchronization rights. Additionally, the contract provided that UA and the films' composers would share an aggregate 5 percent royalty on records sold in the United States. The remaining profits were mostly divided among UA's publishing and recording subsidiaries after each had deducted its production and distribution expenses.

For its part, Danjaq got only a small share of these music earnings but retained the power to hire composers and musicians for the films. This privilege was granted to Danjaq with the understanding that it would exercise certain powers over its music personnel. First, Danjaq was to contract composers for no more than customary royalties and provide assurance that music writers would enter into direct agreements with UA assignees. Second, Danjaq was also asked to use its rights as producer to entitle UA to the likeness, name, and biographical data of any Bond composer, performer, or cast member in the promotions of UA's music subsidiaries.[5]

At the same time that Broccoli and Saltzman's deal with UA was formalized, the pair was also finalizing a licensing agreement with author Ian Fleming that would allow them to use the character's name and likeness in promoting various Bond merchandise. Fleming granted Danjaq these rights, but under a number of rather stringent conditions. For one thing, Broccoli and Saltzman were free to make licensing arrangements, but they were not to receive any payment in such deals. Fleming also stipulated that Bond's name would be used with no more than five products, and further that these products would be used only with *Dr. No* and only within one year of that film's release date. Finally, concerned over the proper image of his literary creation, Fleming also specified that Bond would not be used in the promotion of toiletries such as soaps, deodorants, or laxatives.[6]

With limited opportunities for merchandise tie-ins, Saltzman and Broccoli planned to feature only the most obvious angles of the character. Given Bond's well-documented tastes in spirits and cigarettes, Saltzman and Broccoli sought tie-ins with liquor and tobacco companies, including Old Granddad, Smirnoff, Pall Mall, Players, DuMaurier, and Bond Street Tobacco. UA's publicity staff explored additional tie-ins with Gossard for bikinis, Hathaway for men's shirts, and Triumph for automobiles. Since Sean Connery was an unknown actor at the time, UA felt it was particularly important to use these tie-ins as a means of building up the actor's Bondian persona.[7]

It was soon clear, however, that these merchandising angles would play only a minor role in launching the series. Given Fleming's licensing restrictions, UA initially hoped to promote *Dr. No* through publicity photos, television featurettes, and casting gimmicks. Many of UA's early suggestions were centered around Fleming himself, who was at the time the most salable element of their commodity. Perhaps the most interesting of these ideas was the suggestion to cast Fleming in the role of M, a part that UA believed was especially suited to Fleming's authorial persona. Another idea involved arranging a visit by Fleming to Cape Canaveral and having him introduce Connery to President Kennedy and his family.[8]

After an initial flurry of promotional activity in late 1961 and early 1962, UA decided to bide its time until after *Dr. No*'s London premiere. After impressive showings in Europe and the British Isles, UA once again cranked up its publicity machine for the film's U.S. run. In March 1963, UA scheduled a national publicity tour that featured Connery and director Terence Young. As Charles Juroe, then UA's head of European production and publicity distribution, noted years later, it was decided that Bond would always be accompanied by a matched set of ladies—blonde, brunette, and redhead—who would travel with Connery throughout the tour.[9] This tour was followed by a highly publicized Western Hemisphere premiere in Kingston, Jamaica, an area that provided a number of locations for the *Dr. No* shoot.

Yet such campaigns, which constitute the customary prerelease hype, are typically quite ephemeral in nature. Personal appearances and premiere parties bring newspaper notices, magazine coverage, and trade reports for a day or two, but aside from establishing name recognition, they generally do not have any lasting value as publicity measures. Merchandising can often serve as a long-term means of publicity and exploitation, but such angles were relatively limited by Danjaq's agreement with Fleming. Thus, as *Dr. No*'s various promotional campaigns were developed, it became increasingly apparent that the project's music angles would play a significant role in making James Bond a household name. As earlier music tie-ins showed, hit songs and soundtrack albums could keep a film in the public eye for months and even years.

To this end, UA and Danjaq trumpeted the hiring of British songwriter Monty Norman during the latter months of 1961. Before *Dr. No*, Norman was known primarily for his work on the "French" musical *Irma La Douce* and his work as cocomposer on the Terence Fisher film, *House of Fright* (1960). Still while Norman was given the task of writing the score, UA continued to have considerable input regarding the music's overall conception. As a 1962 memo indicates, UA's publicity department made very specific suggestions about music angles they wished to play up. In that meeting, UA executives made two particular requests: they recommended that a "calypso song about the exploits of James Bond somehow be worked into the motion picture," and they recommended that a "Scottish theme be written into the score . . . to distinguish James Bond throughout the picture."[10] From this it seems clear that UA intended to use the music to highlight the film's exotic Jamaican setting and to play up Sean Connery's Scottish heritage.[11]

Upon examining the final product, however, UA evidently decided that Norman's score accommodated only part of this plan. According to Steven Jay Rubin, Norman visited the Jamaican location and became enamored with calypso music. He then incorporated several calypso songs into his score, including "Under the Mango Tree," "Jump Up Jamaica," and an island version of "Three Blind Mice" entitled "Kingston Calypso."[12] By March 1962, Charles Juroe was enthusiastically praising Norman's music in internal correspondence. Writing to fellow publicity staffer Fred Goldberg, Juroe exclaimed, "The music for DR. NO is really exciting, particularly the variation of the theme of 'Three Blind Mice.' I think that we have a chance for a really successful sound-track album for this film."[13]

However, while calypso enlivened Dr. No's prospects on the soundtrack market, the producers experienced difficulty in getting their desired signature theme, although the exact nature of that difficulty is currently a matter of some dispute. Much of this dispute devolves on the question of John Barry's involvement in the creation of the "James Bond Theme." According to Norman, who received the songwriting credit and is legally considered its rightful author, the "James Bond Theme" grew out of a tune he had written for a planned musical adaptation of V. S. Naipaul's A House for Mr. Biswas. After completing the theme, Norman then contacted EMI producer John Burgess, who suggested hiring Barry to do the theme's orchestration. Describing the final product, Norman says:

> I worked with Barry on what I wanted: a rhythmic sustained sound for the opening four-bar figure; low octave guitar for my main melodic theme; big band for the hard riding middle section, etc . . . John Barry did a wonderful, definitive orchestration of the Bond theme.[14]

Barry, however, tells a rather different tale.[15] In Barry's version of events, he was called in on Dr. No by London's UA Music head, Noel Rodgers. Barry claims that the producers were dissatisfied with Norman's attempts to compose a signature theme for Bond, and had asked him to write something for the film's credit sequence. At the time, Barry was considered a valid scoring prospect based on his work for pop singer-actor Adam Faith's film Beat Girl (1959, directed by Edmond T. Greville), and for a string of instrumental hits recorded with his group, the John Barry Seven. Working quickly, Barry adapted the twangy guitar hook of his combo tune, "Bees Knees," and combined it with a swinging, Dizzy Gillespie-like break. Barry says he recorded the theme a few days later with five saxes, nine brass, a solo guitar, and a rhythm section. For his efforts, Barry was paid two hundred pounds and was given the right to record the theme as a single under his Columbia Records contract. Because of their contractual obligations to Norman, though, Saltzman and Broccoli persuaded Barry to give up his songwriting credit in exchange for the promise of future employment.[16] Norman continues to receive the songwriting credit for the "James Bond Theme" as evidenced by the two most recent Bond films, *Goldeneye* (1995) and *Tomorrow Never Dies* (1997).

Whether the "James Bond Theme" was written by Norman or Barry, it gave Saltzman and Broccoli the signature tune they were seeking. Although Barry says that they had initially agreed to use it only during the main titles, the producers went back and began inserting it at several points throughout the film. The most memorable of these was the scene which introduced Bond's character. When we first see him, Bond is playing chemin de fer at a casino. Interestingly, director Young initially keeps Bond's face off camera. Bond's presence is signaled only through an over-the-shoulder shot showing him seated at the gaming table and through a close-up of his hands dealing cards to his opponent, an elegantly dressed Sylvia Trench (Eunice Gayson). After losing a couple of rounds to him, Sylvia remarks, "I admire your luck Mr., er . . ." Young then cuts to Bond's face as he lights his cigarette and utters his famous tagline, "Bond. James Bond." At this point, Barry's theme sneaks in on the soundtrack and creates an indelible link between music and character.

Armed with a distinctive commercial tune, UA's publicity department nevertheless committed only a meager $5,000 to its music advertising and exploitation budget.[17] With limited resources, UA's publicity staff chose to target radio and a burgeoning audience of teenage film patrons. Calling the "James Bond Theme" (here identified as the *Dr. No* theme) a "very important promotional tool," UA's exploitation manual recommended targeting disk jockeys through two strategies. First, the manual suggested that a lovely lady posing as "Bond's woman" conduct a wider than usual tour of radio and television jocks in support of the film; second, the manual advised local theater owners to screen *Dr. No* for local disk jockeys and hand out promotional copies of the UA single, which was set for release in April 1962. Additionally, the manual also encouraged theater owners to play the theme in their lobbies, both before and after screenings, and at school recesses.

Based on their subsequent chart and box office performances, both the film and its music tie-ins were judged only modest successes. *Dr. No* would go on to make some $22 million in domestic and foreign rentals, but much of this was made in reissues. During its initial run, the film made a mere $6 million, with only $2 million coming from domestic rentals. The soundtrack, on the other hand, offered some support for the film, but finished nowhere near UA's high expectations. Released by United Artists Records in May 1963, the *Dr. No* soundtrack would only reach number 82 on *Billboard*'s charts. A UA single version of the "James Bond Theme" fared even worse by failing to make *Billboard*'s "Hot 100" singles chart. The only bright spot was the overseas performance of John Barry's "James Bond Theme" as a single for Columbia. The record, which was produced as part of Barry's initial agreement with Danjaq, was released in October 1962 and peaked at number 13 on U.K. record charts. Still, while the music campaign achieved only nominal success, it nonetheless helped Bond achieve some measure of name recognition, and supported Saltzman and Broccoli's belief that they were on the right track.

With the next film, *From Russia with Love*, Saltzman and Broccoli developed the first of many successful singer-songwriter-composer packages for the series. Clearly the most important component of the package was songwriter Lionel Bart, who was coming off his recent success with the stage musical *Oliver!* Publicity for the film called Bart "Britain's leading theater composer," and noted that the producers were "fortunate" to hire him.[18] The eminent songwriter, however, was packaged with relative unknowns in the singer and composer slots. Singer Matt Monro was viewed as a rising star on the Liberty label, but had nothing comparable to Bart's credentials. Perhaps in deference to an earlier agreement, Saltzman and Broccoli also hired Barry to replace Norman as the series' featured composer. Yet even as UA touted Barry's television work for *The Human Jungle*, it was apparent that publicizing him was something of a problem. Known primarily as a rock and roll instrumentalist, Barry had very few "legitimate" songwriting or composing credits.

In March 1964, UA released the soundtrack album for *From Russia with Love* on their subsidiary record label to coincide with the film's April release. Improving on the performance of its predecessor, *Russia* reached number 28 on *Variety*'s album charts and remained there for over four months. More importantly, though, the title tune quickly became Unart Music's most recorded song. Within a month of the film's release, Bart's tune was featured in eighteen different single versions, both vocal and instrumental, and also turned up as a track on numerous albums. The heavy activity on the *Russia* music was driving UA's music publishing operations to a peak level and racking up considerable licensing fees in the process.[19]

None of these singles, however, was able to crack *Billboard*'s "Hot 100." To some extent, the single's poor performance was likely due to the weak placement of Monro's vocal version within the film. It is heard only twice, first as a snatch of radio music during Bond's picnic with Sylvia Trench, and then later in a more complete version over the end credits. Neither of these instances does a particularly good job of selling the song or reinforcing the film's dramatic material. In the former, the excerpt is so short that it can be easily missed; in the latter, it is easily ignored.

All the elements of the Bond musical formula finally came together with *Goldfinger* in 1964. For the first time, Saltzman and Broccoli gave Barry full musical authority over the score and made him the centerpiece of their musical "package." Barry would not only compose and conduct the score, he would also cowrite the theme song with Leslie Bricusse and Anthony Newley. The song was written in the early months of 1964, and Newley had already recorded two versions of it two months before shooting was completed. Newley's recordings were probably considered at some point for inclusion in the film, but as Scott Shea points out, they presumably failed in some measure to capture the proper tone of the series.[20]

With the composer and songwriters in place, Saltzman and Broccoli brought in Shirley Bassey, a songstress from UA Records' stable of performers, to complete the package. Bassey turned out to be perfect "casting" for *Goldfinger*'s title song for a number of reasons, not the least of which was the great conviction she brought to her performance.[21] For one thing, Bassey was already a star in England and was on the verge of stateside stardom as *Goldfinger* was being produced. For Danjaq, Bassey's name recognition would help gain attention for the film during the buildup to its world premiere in London. For UA Records, on the other hand, the film would be just the thing to propel Bassey to stardom in the States. With a star in the making, Saltzman and Broccoli would not make the same mistake they had made with Monro. Bassey's performance was featured prominently during the film's famous credit sequence, which projects images from the film on the golden body of a bikini-clad woman.

Goldfinger became a huge box office smash and generated a number of hits for UA and its subsidiaries. The film set records during its initial Christmas release and went on to earn nearly $50 million in domestic and foreign rentals. The soundtrack album, released by UA Records in October 1964, eventually topped both *Billboard*'s and *Variety*'s album charts. Within five months of its release, the *Goldfinger* soundtrack had sold 400,000 copies and was certified gold for reaching the $1 million mark in total sales.[22] It was also named one of

Variety's Top Fifty albums of 1965. Though its eventual sales were more modest, Bassey's single was issued in December 1964 and climbed to number 8 on the singles charts. Additionally, Unart Music further profited from the success of some copycat albums: Roland Shaw's *Themes from the James Bond Thrillers* on the London label; UA's own *Music to Read James Bond By*; and Epic Records' *Confidential Sounds for a Secret Agent*, which featured four John Barry tunes, eight originals named after Fleming's unfilmed novels, and one tune by a bass player whose real name was James Bond.[23]

Yet the success of the film and its music were only part of the story. The commercial breakthrough of *Goldfinger* created a veritable mini-industry as Bondmania swept through theaters. The total sales of all of Fleming's Bond novels grew throughout 1964 and 1965 with nearly thirteen million books sold during that two-year period. Similarly, with Fleming's death in August 1964, the floodgates opened on dozens of items of Bond merchandise. These included golf jackets, sheets, jigsaw puzzles, shoes, pajamas, dolls, trading cards, board games, toy automobiles, lunch boxes, and alarm clocks that played the "James Bond Theme." By February 1966 the Licensing Corporation of America estimated that the total sales of Bond merchandise amounted to some $50 million.[24]

With the Bond merchandising machinery operating at full tilt, Saltzman and Broccoli quickly followed *Goldfinger* with *Thunderball*, their fourth Bond production in four years. Budgeted at $5.5 million, *Thunderball* was touted in publicity as "the biggest Bond of all." Shooting began around the time of *Goldfinger*'s initial distribution with the expectation of a Christmas 1965 release date.

Early in the production, Saltzman and Broccoli considered changing the title to *Mr. Kiss Kiss Bang Bang*, a nickname by which Bond was known in Japan. Barry and Leslie Bricusse were asked to write a song for this new title, which was subsequently recorded by both Dionne Warwick and Shirley Bassey.[25] When the title reverted to *Thunderball*, however, Barry had to quickly come up with a second song to accommodate the name change. Since Bricusse was tied up with another project, Don Black was hired to draft new lyrics for Barry's melody. With two exploitable tunes in hand, Saltzman and Broccoli initially decided to use them both, Tom Jones's title tune for the opening credits and Bassey's version of "Mr. Kiss Kiss Bang Bang" over the closing credits. As *Thunderball*'s release date neared, Saltzman and Broccoli changed their minds yet again and decided to leave Bassey's number out of the film completely.

In anticipation of a *Thunderball* music bonanza, Saltzman and Broccoli renegotiated their original distribution agreement with respect to the music rights. As an October 1, 1965, contract amendment indicates, the basic structure of their original deal was maintained, but with three very significant changes. First of all, Saltzman and Broccoli were to form their own music publishing subsidiary under the laws of Switzerland. This subsidiary would operate as an "employer for hire" with Danjaq acquiring the various music rights and subsequently assigning them to UA Music. This new arrangement entitled Danjaq to royalties from both music publishing revenues and record sales. Under the new terms, Danjaq would receive a 10 percent aggregate royalty on records sold in the United States and half of the net publishing profits. For its part, UA Music agreed to bear all the direct costs incurred in the exploitation of the music publishing rights in exchange for the reimbursement of these costs and a 10 percent service fee deducted from the gross music publishing revenues.[26] Seven months after these changes, UA sweetened the deal by extending these arrangements to also cover non-Bonds produced by Saltzman and Broccoli.[27]

At about the same time, publicity for Barry attempted to match the composer with the series' central character. In 1966, for example, *Time* magazine described Barry as a "swinger in the Bond mold—clothes with an Edwardian flair, fashionable Chelsea apartment, Pickwick Club, E-Type Jaguar (white, XK), E-Type wife (brunette actress, Jane Birken)."[28] To further reinforce the parallel between Bond and Barry, the latter is photographed sitting in his Jaguar in an obvious attempt to invite comparison with 007's famous Aston Martin.

Basking in *Goldfinger*'s afterglow, *Thunderball* matched its predecessor's success on record charts and surpassed it at the box office. *Thunderball* amassed nearly $55 million in total rentals and spawned both a Top Ten album and a Top 25 single. As *Thunderball* entered its foreign run, *Variety* estimated that the first four Bond films had accumulated over $100 million in total box office receipts, with Saltzman and Broccoli's share of this sum amounting to some $26 million.[29]

Due to the unprecedented international success of Bond, hundreds of imitators attempted to cash in on the spy craze. More than thirty secret agent films were released in 1966 alone, many of them made by European and British production companies. Among these were the first entries in the Matt Helm (Dean Martin) and Derek Flint (James Coburn) film series, and the second in Saltzman's Harry Palmer series for UA. The latter starred Michael Caine as a "thinking man's Bond," and the series featured such Bond stalwarts as John Barry and director Guy Hamilton.[30] Italy contributed some of the oddest films in this espionage cycle, including *Operation Kid Brother* (1967), which starred Sean Connery's brother, Neil, and featured Bond veterans Daniella Bianchi, Adolfo Celi, Lois Maxwell, and Bernard Lee; and a series of Bond-like westerns which de-emphasized gunplay in favor of explosive gimmickry such as gunpowder cigars and dynamite-laden sombreros.[31]

Outside the domain of cinema, the secret agent fad also began to infiltrate the television and music industries. Borrowing the character names Napoleon Solo and April Dancer from Ian Fleming, producer Norman Felton developed the Bond-inspired *The Man from U.N.C.L.E.* for MGM in 1964. The series became a major success and spawned a number of additional projects for MGM, such as the Stephanie Powers spin-off *The Girl from U.N.C.L.E.* and a group of theatrical features compiled from footage used in the series. *U.N.C.L.E.* was followed by a number of other Bond-inspired shows, including *Get Smart, The Wild, Wild West, Honey West, I Spy, The Baron,* and *Amos Burke—Secret Agent.*[32] Perhaps the weirdest Bond spin-off, however, was an album recorded by popular European jazz organist Ingfried Hoffman, who billed himself as "001." The album, *From Twen with Love,* was produced by the Philips label and featured a number of tunes parodying the Bond persona. Beside straight versions of "Goldfinger" and "Thunderball" were goofy musical spoofs such as "Yeah Dr. No" and "Vabanque in Casino Royale."

By November 1966 many European background music companies were churning out music for commercials, industrial films, and television news programs which was explicitly modeled on Barry's well-known Bond scores. In fact, the demand for jazzy, Bond-ish background music was so high that Mort Ascher, the head of a top background music supplier, complained that the old, straight symphony music could not even be given away.[33]

After the commercial peak of *Goldfinger* and *Thunderball,* sales of Bond songs and soundtrack albums steadily declined throughout the 1960s. Nowhere was this decline more apparent than in 1967's "Battle of the Bonds," which pit producer Charles Feldman's *Casino Royale* against Saltzman and Broccoli's *You Only Live Twice.* Though the latter won the battle at the box office, the former won the battle on the record charts. Burt Bacharach's *Casino Royale* soundtrack album, which featured numbers by Herb Alpert and Dusty Springfield, reached number 12 on *Variety*'s album charts and was a radio staple throughout the summer of 1967. On the other hand, the soundtrack for *You Only Live Twice,* featuring Nancy Sinatra's rendition of the title song, never got higher than number 42 and dropped off *Variety*'s charts after only a month. Continuing this downward trend, the two Bonds that followed, *On Her Majesty's Secret Service* and *Diamonds Are Forever* (1971), failed to match even the dubious chart performance of *Twice.*

With Connery's decisive departure from the series in 1972, Saltzman and Broccoli were once again faced with the prospect of launching a new actor as Bond. After considering Burt Reynolds, Robert Redford, and Paul Newman for the role, they settled on Roger Moore, who had previously starred in the television series *The Saint*. Once he was cast, UA began an extensive promotional campaign to sell Moore as the new Bond, and, as with the *Dr. No* campaign, music would prove to play an important part in the process. With yet another unknown as Bond, it was incumbent on Saltzman and Broccoli to find a major star for the next Bond theme. If Moore could not sell the picture, then perhaps a catchy theme recorded by a major pop star could.

As the production for *Live and Let Die* (1973) was planned, Saltzman and Broccoli appeared to suffer yet another setback when Barry's commitment to another project prevented him from working on the new Bond. To make up for Barry's absence, Saltzman and Broccoli approached Paul McCartney about the prospect of working on *Live and Let Die*. In the deal that resulted from these negotiations, McCartney agreed to write the title song, perform it with his group Wings for the credit sequence, and produce a version of it performed by the Fifth Dimension in the "Filet of Soul" scene.[34] In exchange for his services, McCartney received a $15,000 songwriting fee and a lucrative cut of the music royalties. McCartney and UA agreed to share the copyright on the title song and split the renewals and performance fees fifty-fifty. Additionally, McCartney was granted a 5 percent royalty on record sales, a 75 percent royalty on record club and direct mail sales, a 75 percent cut of the mechanical license fees, and a commitment from UA to pay for recording and reuse costs.[35]

Though signing McCartney was undoubtedly a coup for UA and Eon Productions, his salary demands put Saltzman and Broccoli in a somewhat awkward position. With a $25,000 total music budget, McCartney's songwriting fee left only $10,000 to pay for the additonal scoring, arranging, and conducting services. Clearly Saltzman and Broccoli would not be able to get a composer of Barry's stature since the standard scoring fee was somewhere between $20,000 and $25,000. With this in mind, Saltzman and Broccoli sought out former Beatles producer George Martin. Martin had had very little previous film work, but several other factors worked to his advantage. For one thing, Martin's previous work with both McCartney and UA on previous Beatles films such as *A Hard Day's Night* (1964) and *Yellow Submarine* (1968) made him seem a natural fit for *Live and Let Die*. Moreover, Martin's work on the Bondish orchestral intro to "Help" showed that he had a good sense of Barry's style and orchestration. The most important factor, however, was

Martin's lack of film experience, which allowed UA to negotiate a lower scoring fee and stay within its music budget.

McCartney's single for *Live and Let Die* was released by Apple Records the week of June 18, 1973, and became an immediate chart success. The song peaked at number 2 on *Billboard*'s "Hot 100" singles chart and remained there for three weeks. The soundtrack album, released about the same time, did not perform quite as well for UA records, but nevertheless made an admirable showing by cresting at number 15 on *Billboard*'s charts. With solid record and sheet music sales and an Oscar nomination for McCartney, the Bond theme song reestablished its importance both in film promotion and in shaping popular music tastes. Saltzman and Broccoli had taken a calculated risk in using their first rock and roll performer, but McCartney's reputation and enormous popularity overcame any resistance to his style.

In the films after *Live and Let Die*, Bond themes continued to have their share of hits and misses, but on balance no other film series could boast its long-term success. By the time of *The Man with the Golden Gun*, Barry and company had written enough familiar melodies that pressbooks recommended organizing contests around radio programs of James Bond music. Listeners would be invited to listen for Bond themes and asked to match them to film titles or stills. The wide recognition of Bond music not only made it a vital promotional tool, but also allowed it to function as a remarkably adaptable component of the Bond formula. As we will see in the next section, the interaction of narrative and music formulas enabled the *Goldfinger* score to function in a larger system of textual and extratextual addresses and to provide the basis of an internal critique of Bondian ideology.

A Spider's Touch: Music and Characterization in *Goldfinger*

Although soundtrack buffs have developed an almost cultish appreciation of Barry's Bond music, film music scholars have given it relatively scant attention. Darby and Du Bois, for example, denigrate Barry by claiming that his music is "suited to the slick, hard-edged, dehumanized nature of those films."[36] Simon Frith, on the other hand, damns the composer with faint praise by explicitly comparing him with the British pop group, the Pet Shop Boys, and by titling his piece, "Pretty Vacant—John Barry."[37] Unfortunately, Barry himself has sometimes reinforced this impression with the frequent, offhand dismissal of his Bond music as "Mickey Mouse Wagner."[38]

To understand the effect of this critical scorn, one need only look at Darby and Du Bois's brief discussion of Barry's music for *Goldfinger*, which to date remains the most comprehensive analysis of a Bond score. Though the authors clearly admire Barry's gifts for melody and lyricism, they complain that the composer's approach to developing themes has "a certain ad hoc quality."[39] This in turn gives rise to a score that Darby and Du Bois believe has no consistency, no overall conception, and a surprising number of dramatic incongruities. To illustrate Barry's compositional "laziness," Darby and Du Bois point to such anomalies as the use of a very lyrical theme to accompany the mundane loading of golf clubs and the flagrant use of the "Goldfinger" theme to accompany Bond and Pussy Galore's (Honor Blackman) congenial embrace at the end of the film, a juxtaposition that seems to contradictorily proclaim victory for the villain. Barry's failure in *Goldfinger* to provide motivic consistency leads the authors to conclude that his music "betrays every tenet of dramatic fidelity in film scoring."[40]

Darby and Du Bois's critique of *Goldfinger*, however, is marred by a couple of methodological flaws. For one thing, their notion of dramatic fidelity presumes a rather oversimplified notion of image-music relations as one of strict correspondence. By criticizing the incongruent appearance of the "Goldfinger" theme at film's end, Darby and Du Bois prescriptively imply that film music must either enhance the narrative's tone or reinforce its most obvious levels of meaning. While it is true that *Goldfinger*'s narrative resolves through the formation of the couple, it is unwise to assume that the score's function is to unproblematically support or reflect that resolution. In doing so, the authors not only fall into the familiar trap of subsuming music to the primacy of narrative and image, they also unwisely evaluate the *Goldfinger* score in terms of a model that is singularly unsuited to the typical Bond movie.

Given the tongue-in-cheek quality of the Bond films, dramatic fidelity and unity are not concepts that seem applicable to the films. The penchant for self-parody, the emphasis on fantastic gadgetry, and the excessive representation of such themes as heroism, villainy, and sexuality all tend to mediate against classical notions of verisimilitude. Similarly, the structuring of the Bond narrative around "bumps" (i.e., self-contained action set pieces) tends to mediate against classical notions of dramatic unity and linearity. In both these respects, Barry's ad hoc thematic application and dramatic "incongruity" would seem to be critical virtues rather than vices insofar as they are musical analogs of the Bond narrative's tendency toward fragmentation and farce.

The Bond scores themselves offer some excellent examples of this in their own tendency toward intertextual musical parody. In *On Her Majesty's Secret*

Service, for example, a janitor is heard whistling "Goldfinger," and in *Octopussy* (1983) an Indian snake charmer briefly plays the "James Bond Theme" in the midst of a performance. In later Bonds, allusions to the music of *Lawrence of Arabia* and *The Magnificent Seven* are played as jokes in *The Spy Who Loved Me* (1977) and *Moonraker* (1979), respectively. And in the Arctic teaser of *A View to a Kill* (1985), Barry ironically refers to the Beach Boys by using their song "California Girls" to accompany Bond's "boogie boarding" escape from an attack squad across an expanse of snow. In these examples, the ad hoc thematic application is not a detriment but rather the whole point of the joke. Such references have little effect if they are carefully integrated with a score's themes and motifs.

A second methodological problem emerges with Darby and Du Bois's failure to acknowledge *Goldfinger*'s position within a larger intertextual pattern. As I noted earlier, each Bond score adheres fairly closely to a musical formula that often supersedes the specific context of narrative events. Though the development of this formula was mostly due to market pressures governing the sale of film music, it nonetheless constitutes a level of mediation which contributes to the score's overall design. Each Bond score becomes less a unified, original conception and more a hodgepodge of seemingly interchangeable parts. Because this fragmentation is most apparent at the level of the individual text, a number of musical effects appear anomalous simply because they are bereft of their larger intertextual context.

The use of "007," for example, in *On Her Majesty's Secret Service* illustrates this point insofar as it seems to be yet another instance of Barry's ad hoc thematic application. The theme appears late in the film to accompany the raid on Blofeld's mountaintop retreat (Piz Gloria), and is summarily dropped after the military gains control of Blofeld's forces. However, when placed within the broader framework of the series, "007" takes on significance in relation to other Bond scores. Its single appearance during the raid sequence is not anomalous, but rather is quite consistent with Barry's general use of the theme to accompany large-scale combat, such as the gypsy camp battle in *From Russia with Love*, the underwater clash in *Thunderball*, and the ninja attack on Blofeld's volcano fortress in *You Only Live Twice*.

To begin to approach the Bond scores, it is helpful to consider the musical patterns that develop across the series as well as those that develop within individual films. Not only would such an approach account for certain of the scores' incongruities, it would also offer a more multileveled, nuanced understanding of the Bond music's connotative power. This is not, however, the place to deal with the Bond scores in toto. Such a project would undoubtedly illuminate much about film music, but an examination of some eighteen complete scores is well beyond the scope of this chapter.

Instead I will briefly look at *Goldfinger* as a prototypical Bond score. In doing so, I have two broad aims—to highlight the operations of a characteristic Bond musical formula, and to show how these elements sustained the consumption of subsequent Bond films and soundtrack albums. *Goldfinger* is especially fertile ground for such an examination because it is widely regarded as the best of Barry's Bond scores, and as the composer has noted, it was the first time that "the musical style [in a Bond film] really came together. Everything culminated with that film."[41]

Like Bond's narrative formula, the musical formula creates a set of procedural and stylistic expectations which are intrinsic to the Bond films' appeal. As Tony Bennett and Janet Woollacott point out, such formulas are not overlays which certain readers may ignore and others appreciate, but are rather the very form and substance of the Bond text.[42] Taken together, the various elements of the Bond formula serve a couple of distinct functions. To begin with, they create a unique mind-set among Bond spectators, one that de-emphasizes expectations of versimilitude, consistent characterization, and tight narrative logic in favor of the cartoonish ingredients of the prototypical Bond recipe. Second, the formula's elements also function as a kind of product trademark, one that distinguishes the Broccoli-Saltzman Bonds from their many imitators.

A key part of the Bond trademark is the first and most durable element of the Bond musical formula: the "James Bond Theme" (figure 5.1).

FIGURE 5.1

Given its broad, almost immediate recognition, it is unsurprising that it is frequently used in conjunction with other trademark moments, such as Maurice Binder's famous gun-barrel openings. Using a hole made by a pinprick in a piece of cardboard, Binder filmed an actual gun barrel against a white background. The barrel then appears to scan the image until finally coming to rest on Bond. As the Bond theme plays on the soundtrack, he turns and fires toward the camera. In response to this seeming assault on the spectator's vision, an animated red, bloodlike stain appears to ooze over the image.

Though operating outside the diegesis, this iconic Bond shot, which lasts only a few seconds, economically establishes a number of features of the character and film. Besides establishing motifs of violence and espionage, the shot also establishes Bond himself as the most important recurring feature of the series. In film after film, the shot reminds us that despite changes of actors, directors, screenwriters, and composers, the character remains the stable and unchanging attraction of the series, the "site," if you will, of our continuous and various investments in Bond culture.

It is important to note, however, that although the gun-barrel openings serve as a trademark, they are never exactly the same from film to film. The one malleable element is the arrangement of the "James Bond Theme." Often these small variations in orchestration are done to accommodate more global patterns of instrumentation within the individual Bond score. The shrill and brassy sound of *Goldfinger*'s "Bond Is Back," for example, is consistent with the brighter instrumental textures of the score as a whole. In contrast, *A View to a Kill* begins with a darker toned, more somber rendering of the Bond theme, one that conforms to the score's overall emphasis on traditional orchestral forces, particularly the low brass and strings.

On other occasions, changes in orchestration typically reflect larger changes in popular music style. Note, for example, how the tambourine-heavy mix of the *Diamonds Are Forever* opening gives the cue (and the theme itself) a modern, Motown-ish sound. Likewise, the bass glissandos, swinging drums, and electronic harpsichord tones give the opening of *On Her Majesty's Secret Service* a swanky, mod sound that matches the fuzz guitar and rocking drums of the title theme. These constantly updated variations tend to reinforce the impression of modernity which has traditionally been a key feature of the character's enduring popularity.

Along with the gun-barrel openings, one also expects to hear the Bond theme accompanying the character's signature line of introduction. In *Goldfinger*, this moment takes place in Auric Goldfinger's (Gert Frobe) Miami hotel room. While investigating Goldfinger's card-cheating scam, Bond discovers his secretary, Jill Masterson (Shirley Eaton), using binoculars to surreptitiously look into the hand of Goldfinger's opponent and then relay that information through a radio monitor to a small speaker disguised as a hearing aid. Caught in the act, a surprised Jill asks about the identity of this intruder and thereby provides a perfect setup for the character's trademark reply, "Bond. James Bond."

Throughout *Goldfinger*, however, the "James Bond Theme" is more frequently alluded to than explicitly cited. The two trademark moments noted above are the only ones in which we hear full-blown articulations of the Bond theme. More commonly, Barry will fragment the theme into motivic components which can then be integrated with his atmospheric stock in trade: short syncopated figures, pedal points, sudden sforzandos, and ostinato figures which frequently feature the special harmonic color of minor triads with added seconds.[43] The precredit sequence of *Goldfinger* offers a good illustration of how these motivic variants of the Bond theme operate. Besides affording further opportunities for the Bond theme, the precredit action sequences are vital to the Bond formula for other reasons. As Bennett and Woollacott note, these sequences often show a great deal of stylization and play with film conventions. Such visual gags in *Goldfinger* as the fake seagull which sits atop Bond's head and the removal of his diving suit to reveal an immaculate white tuxedo jacket are designed to give a tongue-in-cheek portrayal of the Bond figure's excesses.[44]

At the same time, these precredit sequences also underscore the character's fantastic resourcefulness and prowess as a secret agent. In *Goldfinger*, Bond is stalked by an assailant while in the midst of a romantic tryst with a naked woman. Remarkably, Bond spies the reflection of the advancing villain in the girl's eyes and quickly turns her to accept the blow intended for him. After a brief fistfight between the two men, Bond pushes the assailant into a bathtub filled with water. As the villain reaches for Bond's holstered gun, which hangs near the bathtub, the quick-witted Bond grabs an electric lamp, throws it into the tub, and electrocutes his assailant. The sequence closes with another signature element, the coolly cynical one-liner, as Bond describes the situation as, "Shocking. (*pause*) Positively shocking."

Although they begin in medias res, these openings are often self-contained mininarratives, the first of the many "bumps" which constitute the typical Bond plot. This is not to say, however, that the precredit sequence bears no relation to the rest of the narrative. In *From Russia with Love* and *The Man with the Golden Gun*, the precredit sequences depict villainous "traps"—Red Grant's (Robert Shaw) lethal watch and Scaramanga's (Christopher Lee) deadly funhouse, respectively—which will later be sprung on our unsuspecting hero. In other instances, the link between the precredit sequence and the rest of the film may involve narrative information that later proves important. In *The Spy Who Loved Me*, for example, one of the men Bond kills in the opening ski chase is later revealed to be Anya's former lover. Thus, when Anya vows to kill Bond in revenge, a seemingly incidental death in the opening becomes a crucial source of character motivation. In *Goldfinger*, on the other hand, the link is more motivic than narrative. Though Bond's tactical sabotage of the heroin plant has no bearing on his later investigation of Goldfinger, the opening fight and electrocution of the villain will later be picked up in Bond's climactic Fort Knox fight with Oddjob (Harold Sakata).

Such tenuous links give these precredit sequences an unusual status. They are never entirely separate from the rest of the film's storyline, but neither are they tightly bound into the narrative's causal chain. As such, they retain a certain autonomy as self-contained set pieces, and they initiate the series of remaining set pieces which comprise the Bond films' mix of gadgets, exotic locations, pretty women, and outrageous humor.

Finally, coming as they do before the credits, the Bond teasers effectively set off and showcase the films' title tunes, which comprise the second element in Barry's musical formula. According to Karlin and Wright, one of the main concerns of film songwriters is the question of where their vocalized number will appear within the film. Relatively speaking, if the song is not prominently featured, it has less chance of succeeding in the commercial music marketplace. As lyricist Dean Pitchford notes, "It doesn't flatter an artist to show them some footage and say 'Listen, we need a song to put on the car radio while they're talking and driving down the street.' "[45] Similar problems occur with more conventional opening and closing credit sequences. If a song is played at the very beginning of a film, late patrons will likely be too concerned with finding a seat to care much about the music issuing from the screen. Played over the closing credits, the song is likely to be ignored as people start to make their way into the aisles and out of the theater.

In contrast to this, the Bond films' opening action sequences easily garner the rapt attention of filmgoers and thus provide a valuable framework for the catchy hooks and memorable melodies of the Bond title songs.[46] Moreover, the matching of visual and musical rhythms in the credit sequences enhances the song's memorability by giving prominence to the music's place within the film's hierarchization of image and sound. The nude silhouettes in the Bond credit sequences "decorate" these title songs by highlighting the double entendres that are featured in the songs' lyrics. In the manner of a modern music video, the song itself becomes the most important channel of signification during the credits, and the tongue-in-cheek sexual imagery serves largely to extend and refine the theme song's meanings.

As Bennett and Woollacott further note, the women in these credit sequences are fetishized as erotic spectacle. Following the guidelines set out in Laura Mulvey's seminal "Visual Pleasure and Narrative Cinema" essay, Bennett and Woollacott not only call attention to the sequences' titillating imagery, but they also note how the credits halt the narrative flow and thus offer a moment of erotic contemplation and scopophilic pleasure that exists entirely outside the film's diegesis. As such, the credit sequences obviate the whole structure of visual pleasure and render the woman irrelevant in a most blatant and flagrant way.[47]

Yet the credit sequence of *Goldfinger* also presents a certain troubling of that eroticism. Though the woman in *Goldfinger*'s titles is also fetishized, it is through her image that we view a streamlined version of the film's plot and central characters. In this respect, the woman's body functions as a complex signifier which condenses a number of the film's narrative and visual motifs. Seductive and tempting as gold, the female body serves as the site of Bond's battles with Goldfinger. This leads Bennett and Woollacott to conclude that the narrative conflict, which is ostensibly about the value and safety of the world's gold supply, is in reality a battle for "woman's body, woman's identity and woman's sexuality."[48]

While I believe that this reading is sound in its broad outlines, it nevertheless oversimplifies a much more complex scenario of male desire. By saying, for example, that the woman's image is made totally irrelevant, Bennett and Woollacott ignore the powerful female voice on the film's soundtrack. Far from being irrelevant, this voice actively depicts Goldfinger's treachery. The lyrics describe the villain's coldness, his insidious lies, and his obsessive, avaricious appetite for gold, a harsh portrait that is completed by an overt comparison between Goldfinger and a poisonous spider. Lustily sung by Shirley Bassey, the song appears to address an unidentified female subject, one who we might assume is any or all of the film's major women characters. Prefiguring the demise of the two Mastersons (Jill's sister Tilly is killed later in the film), Bassey warns that entry into Goldfinger's "web of sin" leads only to deception and death.

The song's description of Goldfinger is certainly in keeping with the Bond films' campy and excessive representation of villainy. The opening three notes of the tune serve as a leitmotiv which recurs throughout the score and continually reminds the viewer of that treachery. At the same time, however, Barry's integration of his two major themes in the score, the "James Bond Theme" and "Goldfinger," complicates both easy notions of good and evil as well as simplistic scenarios of male desire. Barry's music suggests that Bond is a slightly less heinous variant of Goldfinger's greed and sexual predation. The film's famous image of a gold-painted woman is particularly crucial in this regard since it fuses the two halves of this male desire—Goldfinger's obsession with gold and Bond's passion for female conquest.

Formally, Barry's "Goldfinger" theme achieves a similar fusion. The melodic hook I described in the first chapter is merely an abbreviated variation and combination of the two motivic patterns plucked by the Bond theme's signature guitar (figure 5.2):

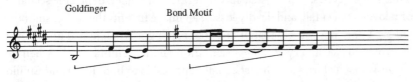

FIGURE 5.2

Simultaneously though, the "Goldfinger" motive also has the basic shape of the Bond theme's other central motive, the famous four-note trumpet blast (figure 5.3):

FIGURE 5.3

Even more telling perhaps is the fact that the opening motive is simply an inversion of the bass line of the alternate Bond theme, "007."

"Goldfinger" is further integrated through the use of the chromatically ascending countermelody which figures throughout the "James Bond Theme" (figure 5.4):

FIGURE 5.4

In "Goldfinger," this countermelody makes a notable appearance in measure 25 at the start of the song's bridge (figure 5.5):

FIGURE 5.5A

FIGURE 5.5B

The bridge's lyrics, which ostensibly describe Goldfinger, depict the scenario of a lover's sweet talk and deadly kisses, an image that fits the suave, smooth-talking Bond more surely than it does the balding, corpulent bad guy. Royal S. Brown makes a very similar observation about "Thunderball" when he suggests that its lyrics are almost equally applicable to both Bond and Emilio Largo (Adolfo Celi), a circumstance that offers "perhaps the ultimate comment on the mythic ambiguity of Fleming's hero."[49]

Brown's reference to Bond's moral ambiguity is particularly revealing in this regard since it hints that the motivic integration of the Bond and Goldfinger themes serves partly to highlight a character trait many see as crucial to Bond's status as an antihero. From the sixties onward, a number of commentators have described this ambiguity in terms of the character's cynicism, brutality, and, to paraphrase Raymond Benson, a less than redeeming attitude toward women.[50] Kingsley Amis, for example, discusses how Bond is portrayed by literary reviewers as "heartless, cruel, even 'sadistic,' a predatory monster."[51] Employing a somewhat skewed notion of transference, Amis attributes this characterization to a tendency among reviewers to displace Bond's violence against his enemies to his treatment of women.

What Amis fails to acknowledge, however, is that this critical impression is as easily imputed to the fact that the novels and films' female characters are frequently endangered or killed because of their romantic involvement with Bond. In fact, the ease with which these women are eliminated serves a couple of purposes in the films. For one thing, the Bond girl's frequent role as "sacrificial lamb" typically provides Bond with a revenge motive that enhances his sense of duty and inspires the violence visited upon his enemies. At the same time, however, the Bond girl's death serves the films' sexual ideology by freeing Bond from the constraints of a hypocritical code of gentlemanly chivalry.

In this context, the notion of moral ambiguity provides a crucial link between Bond's sexual license and his license to kill. Just as Bond's cynicism provides the wellspring for the brutality directed at his foes, it also motivates the hardheartedness and callousness that underlies his free and independent sexuality. By suggesting that Bond and Goldfinger are merely the opposite sides of the same coin, the film will both highlight this ambiguity and spell it out in a series of structural similarities made both in terms of the film's narrative and its music.

The sequence that immediately follows the credits offers a good illustration of how narrative and music work to establish this parallel. After some establishing shots of the new Miami setting, CIA agent Felix Leiter meets with Bond and gives him some background information on Goldfinger. Through this brief dialogue, we learn that Goldfinger is, like Bond, an Englishman who uses his appearance as a businessman to cover his involvement in international espionage. When Bond asks where he can find Goldfinger, Leiter signals the character's entrance by pointing offscreen. The film then cuts to a long shot of Goldfinger walking down a flight of stairs toward the pool deck. At that same moment, a brief snatch of Barry's "Goldfinger" theme sneaks in on the soundtrack and creates a concrete link between music and character. Goldfinger's entrance is paralleled by Bond's introduction to Jill Masterson later in the sequence. Just as Goldfinger's introduction motivates the "Goldfinger" theme, Bond's introduction to Jill motivates the "James Bond Theme."

At one level, the presentation of Goldfinger and Bond closely adheres to the norms of character exposition typically found in classical Hollywood cinema. To this end, Barry's use of the "Goldfinger" and "Bond" themes would seem highly conventional applications of the classical score's association of leitmotivs with characters. Throughout the film, however, Barry broadens and problematizes this association by using the "Goldfinger" theme in a much wider array of dramatic situations. The theme is not only used in sequences which play out the consequences of Goldfinger's murderous plans, but it is also used as a love theme to accompany Bond's scenes with Jill, Tilly, and Pussy Galore.

Two cues are particularly effective at illustrating the marked division between its roles as both action and love theme. The first is "Dawn Raid on Fort Knox," which typifies the ways in which the "Goldfinger" motif connotes either the character's presence or his power. (Other examples of this include Bond's pursuit of Goldfinger through the Alps, Goldfinger's castration threat with the laser beam, and Oddjob's "pressing engagement" with Solo.) Using both the three-note "Goldfinger" motif and the distinctive harmonic shift from tonic to flatted subdominant, Barry constructs "Dawn Raid" as a propulsive march highlighted by strong trumpet lines and urgent snare drum and tympani figures.

Bond's early tryst with Jill Masterson, however, displays Barry's equal emphasis on "Goldfinger" as a love theme. As Jill tells Bond that she likes him more than anyone she has recently met, a light, swinging version of the "Goldfinger" theme sneaks in and covers the ellipsis between their initial flirtation and their postcoital euphoria. The camera tracks past the leftover room service and moves rightward to reveal Bond and Jill lying together on his bed. As the theme reaches the bridge, the phrase "His heart is cold . . ." plays over the image of Bond and Jill kissing. The juxtaposition here explicates what was implicit in Bassey's version of the title song; the "cold heart" alludes not only to Goldfinger's greed but also to the emotional distance that lurks within Bond's cavalier approach to sexuality. The tracking shot further reinforces this reading by creating a metaphorical link between the food displayed on the table and Jill splayed out on Bond's bed. For Bond, Jill is a tempting morsel no different from the food or potables that satisfy his other hungers.[52]

Though the cue fades out at this point, the bridge's lyrics are recalled in subsequent events in this sequence. Oddjob sneaks into the room and knocks out Bond. Goldfinger covers Jill's body with gold paint, thereby causing her skin to suffocate. Through this series of events, Jill becomes the "golden girl" of the song lyrics and credit sequence (figure 5.6). Her lifeless body serves as a warning to Bond, one that is reaffirmed later in the film. As Goldfinger says after the golf match, "Many people have tried to involve themselves in my affairs . . . unsuccessfully." Oddjob then clarifies this veiled threat by using his metal-brimmed hat to cut off the head of a female statue.

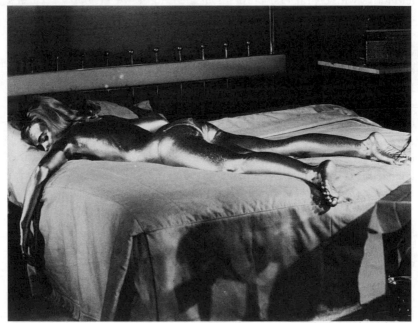

FIGURE 5.6 The famous image of Jill Masterson's body painted gold. She fails to heed the title song's warning not to enter Goldfinger's "web of sin."

Yet here the visual and narrative inscription of the "golden girl" reminds us of the warning issued to her by Shirley Bassey, one that complements the threat issued to Bond. As I noted earlier, the bridge's lyrics, which have already been cued by the music that introduces the sequence, seem much more applicable to Bond than Goldfinger:

> *Golden words he will pour in your ear,*
> *But his lies can't disguise what you fear,*
> *For a golden girl knows when he's kissed her,*
> *It's the kiss of death from Mister*
> *Goldfinger.*

The reference to a lover's golden words and kiss are especially crucial here. Though Goldfinger causes Jill's death, Bond's kiss suggests that he is in some measure equally culpable. In fact, this notion is reinforced by the ellipsis which assures that Jill's death occurs offscreen. Goldfinger never appears in the sequence, and Oddjob appears only as a phantasmic shadow and disembodied hand. By restricting the narration to Bond's point of view, the text ironically implies that Bond's kiss is the "kiss of death," that his cold heart is the real source of Jill's suffocation of the flesh.[53]

Later examples of this thematic application serve to reinforce this structural parallel. For example, a slower, more lyrical rendering of "Goldfinger" underscores Bond's first meeting with Tilly, and once again it is the song's bridge that accompanies this bit of narrative action. As Tilly's Mustang passes Bond's Aston Martin, the sudden welling of Bond's sexual desire is expressed as a revving of his car's engine and an instant gleam in his eye. On the phrase, "It's the kiss of death . . . ," however, Bond ends this pursuit as abruptly as he began it. Remembering his assignment to follow Goldfinger, Bond mutters, "Discipline, 007. Discipline." As with Jill, Bond's involvement with Tilly leads only to her death. Oddjob strikes her down with his lethal bowler in a scene that fuses the two warnings issued earlier. Bond's discovery of Tilly's prone body recalls the scene with Jill while Oddjob's bowler recalls the earlier scene with the statue.

To a great extent, it is this use of "Goldfinger" as a love theme which gives rise to Darby and Du Bois's criticism that the score has an ad hoc quality. According to the norms of classical scoring, it makes more sense to write a new love theme rather than use one that is associated with villainy and greed. I would contend, however, that Barry's thematic application to such scenes is not a "mistake" but rather an adherence to a musical formula which supersedes individual dramatic situations.

Still, it is important to remember that this broad thematic application serves commercial functions as well as textual ones. By utilizing the title theme in a variety of contexts, the sheer number of repetitions helps lodge the melody in the audience's mind. For Barry this was not merely an ancillary benefit but, indeed, one of the primary objectives in scoring. In this respect, the Bond musical formula can be seen as an attempt to provide a scheme in which film music would be serviceable to a multiplicity of listeners in a variety of different reception contexts. And though the "James Bond Theme" and title themes were clearly the most important ingredients, the secondary elements were useful in furnishing the kind of thematic and motivic diversity that contributed to successful soundtrack marketing.

Before concluding this chapter, let me briefly touch on the two remaining elements of Bond's musical formula—the leitmotiv for the villain and the alternate Bond theme, "007." Here again, *Goldfinger* offers a slight wrinkle on the typical Bond formula. Since the "Goldfinger" theme already serves as a leitmotiv for the title baddie, Barry composed a second leitmotiv to be used in conjunction with Oddjob, the villain's henchman (figure 5.7):

FIGURE 5.7

This is somewhat atypical of Barry's usual compositional procedures for the Bond films, but it is not unprecedented. In *Diamonds Are Forever*, for example, Barry composed a solo saxophone line which is consistently used in conjunction with that film's homosexual hit men, Mr. Wint and Mr. Kidd. In *Octopussy*, on the other hand, the evil Gobinda, who wields a lethal razored yo-yo analogous to Oddjob's metal brimmed bowler, is given a fully developed theme that is played in the woodwinds and punctuated by syncopated brass chords. Oddjob's theme actually differs from each of these in that it is composed of two leitmotivs rather than an individual theme. The first is a series of low brass chords and the second is a static, shrill string tremolo. The two are used together when Oddjob bludgeons Bond in his Miami hotel room, but subsequent appearances will typically utilize one motive or the other and will come to connote Oddjob's lethal power. Later appearances of the Oddjob leitmotiv occur during Oddjob's severing of the statue's head, the death of Tilly, and the battle between Bond and Oddjob in Fort Knox.

The last element of the Bond musical formula, "007," does not actually appear in *Goldfinger*. In fact, though it is widely regarded as an alternate theme for Bond, it appears relatively infrequently, and as I noted earlier, it typically underscores scenes of large-scale battle. Interestingly, however, although "007" does not appear, the martial arrangement of "Goldfinger" for the "Dawn Raid" cue very strongly recalls it. The latter's strong trumpet and percussion lines suggest a musical inversion of "007" in much the same way that the "Goldfinger" theme inverts the "James Bond Theme." Through its orchestration and motivic variation, "Dawn Raid" reminds us that Goldfinger's meticulously planned military foray is not unlike those in *From Russia with Love*, *Thunderball*, or *On Her Majesty's Secret Service*. Such set pieces often display the series' emphasis on high production values, spectacular set design, and technologically sophisticated gadgetry.

Taken together, all the elements of the Bond musical formula have created a remarkably stable set of musical expectations for fans of the series. But in *Goldfinger*, more importantly, the formula also functions to highlight Bond's own moral ambiguity and parallels his sexual "greed" with the materialistic greed of the villain. In this respect, *Goldfinger*'s application of the formula could be read as a critique of Bond's embodiment of liberated sexual attitudes. The musical parallel reveals that Bond's charm is founded on a cold, calculated form of sexual predation. Women are lured into Bond's own "web of sin," and they frequently suffer the consequences of his lack of emotional commitment.

Even as it defined its era, the Bond formula has proved remarkably adaptable to a wide range of popular musical styles and idioms. Through the efforts of Barry and the other Bond composers, the scores are a virtual encyclopedia of pop music fads of the past thirty years. At various points, the Bond formula has embraced calypso, jazz, folk, rock, disco, synth-pop, and even funk-tinged ballads. With future Bond films in the offing, one might well see techno or trip-hop incorporated as part of the Bond formula.

The wide circulation of the Bond music did not come about by accident but was of course part of a carefully planned market strategy undertaken by the series' producers and distributors. To assure a market for future entries, the producers demanded a commercially viable signature theme for Bond that would provide broad name recognition for the character both stateside and in the international market. Through this and other measures, the exploitation of music helped defray the risk of the Bond films by contributing ancillary revenues and sustaining a ready market for subsequent films in the series. The Bond music helped to accomplish this through an amazing string of popular title songs and soundtrack albums.

Yet while many people have contributed to the Bond scores, the music remains most closely identified with one person—John Barry. Barry has frequently admitted the obsolescence of his Bond music, but he is also aware of its significance as part of our popular memory of the sixties. As Barry himself noted in a 1981 book on the series, "The Bond music seems to convey the sentiment of the period of the sixties everywhere. The themes actually became nostalgia in their own lifetime."[54] Barry's gift for lyric melody and lush orchestration has brought him a number of gold records and industry accolades. Yet for better or worse, it is his "Mickey Mouse Wagner" which constitutes his most significant contribution to film music history.

6

Every Gun Makes Its Own Tune

ENNIO MORRICONE, *THE GOOD, THE BAD, AND THE UGLY*, AND "L'ESTHÉTIQUE DU SCOPITONE"

In the preceding chapter I described how the James Bond films used teasers to set off and showcase the series' string of successful title songs. While the use of songs during credit sequences was a common practice since the early fifties, the Bond films developed it into a kind of promotional art. Yet, as Fred Karlin points out, filmmakers in the late sixties explored other avenues for showcasing a composer's work within the film. The most significant of these strategies was the interpolated song, which used montages or other devices to halt the film's narrative flow and allow the song an opportunity to sell itself. Karlin names the bicycling sequences of *Butch Cassidy and the Sundance Kid* (1969) as the paradigmatic example of this phenomenon insofar as they mostly served to market Burt Bacharach's theme, "Raindrops Keep Fallin' on My Head."[1]

Ennio Morricone's "spaghetti western" scores constitute an important link in the interpolated song's evolution. Although Morricone did not use songs per se, the formal parameters of his scores bear certain similarities with these interpolated songs, and often his cues similarly invert the normal hierarchy of image and music. Working with director Sergio Leone, Morricone gave prominence to his scores by treating generic elements, such as showdowns and gunfights, as occasions for extended musical exposition. By integrating music and drama, Leone and Morricone made the film's music both noticeable and memorable, and thus enhanced the pop score's two most important characteristics.

Having scored literally hundreds of films, Morricone has become one of the most respected and prolific composers in the industry. Among his most notable works are the scores for *The Battle of Algiers* (1965), *Investigation of a Citizen Above Suspicion* (1970), *Days of Heaven* (1978), *The Mission* (1986), *The Untouchables* (1987), and *Bugsy* (1991). Following the critical and commercial success of his score for *The Mission*, Morricone also experienced a resurgence of popular interest in his career. Virgin Records and RCA have issued three separate collections of Morricone's soundtrack work in the United States; composer John Zorn has recorded a tribute album, *The Big Gundown*; and the Irish rock group, the Pogues, recorded a rollicking version of "The Good, the Bad, and the Ugly" for Alex Cox's 1987 film, *Straight to Hell*.[2] In Switzerland and Holland, critical biographies and musicographies reappraised Morricone's concert and film work.[3] In the United States, Robert Cumbow devoted an entire chapter to Morricone's music in his book-length study of Leone's films.[4]

To a great extent, this critical enterprise attempts to position Morricone's work within a broader set of artistic contexts, including Italian opera, the American western, and postmodernism. What is often overlooked in this discourse, however, is the extent to which Morricone's music is situated within a larger historical context that intersects with the various aesthetic backdrops listed above. Like other sixties composers, Morricone both heralds and reflects a broad historical shift in film-scoring practices. As a composer, Morricone borrowed devices from the classical Hollywood score, but shaped them to the specific design of the commercial soundtrack album. In the process, Morricone created music that startled listeners with its abundance of soaring melodies, its abrupt shifts between lyricism and grotesquerie, and its eccentric but evocative orchestrations.

Although Morricone's style is to some extent merely an amplification of certain classical principles, his work is nonetheless central to our concerns here for two reasons.[5] To begin with, Morricone's melodies and orchestration functioned as pop hooks within the American and European record markets. This is especially true of the electric guitar and vocalized shrieks which flavored Morricone's spaghetti western scores. These sounds not only gave the title themes a certain ear-grabbing appeal, they were also subsumed within a particular rock aesthetic. Moreover, Morricone's work also reflects a broader reconfiguration of sound-image relations in sixties visual media. By developing generic elements into cinematic set pieces, Leone and Morricone elevated sound to a position equivalent to the image and prefigured later uses of songs as underscore in cinema of the 1970s and 1980s. Using *The Good, the Bad, and the Ugly* as an example, I will describe each of these aspects of Morricone's work and place them in their respective contexts within the industry. Although Morricone's style and compositional strategy differ from that of Mancini and Barry, his scores are similar prototypes for supporting and advancing the film's narrative, on the one hand, and for "selling" the film's score, on the other.

A Fistful of Vinyl: Ennio Morricone and the Record Industry

As Morricone's biographers point out, the popularity of Morricone's music is somewhat surprising considering both his classical training and his general disdain for much pop music. Before entering film work, Morricone studied at the Conservatory of Saint Cecilia where he professed great admiration for the work of Palestrina, Monteverdi, Bach, Stravinski, Webern, and Boulez.[6] Morricone has written several chamber pieces and film scores reflective of that background, which reveal a more formally adventurous side of his musical personality, one influenced by atonalism, serialism, minimalism, and the use of electronics. According to Roberto Scollo, this "intellectualist" side of Morricone is the one that best represents the composer's actual musical preferences and interests.[7] Moreover, Morricone's so-called intellectualist preferences are matched by a certain distaste for pop music's ubiquity in contemporary film scoring. According to Anne and Jean Lhassa, Morricone claims that pop has had a disastrous long-term effect on film music by standardizing musical production and limiting the creativity of composers.[8]

Despite these reservations, Morricone's pragmatism and eclecticism allowed him to function within a number of commercial music contexts. After completing his education at Saint Cecilia, Morricone honed his orchestration skills as an arranger for Italian radio and television. In order to support himself, he moved to RCA in the early sixties and entered the front ranks of the Italian recording industry. As a top studio arranger, Morricone provided orchestrations for more than five hundred songs and worked with such recording artists as Mario Lanza, Paul Anka, and Chet Baker. During this period, Morricone developed a facility with a number of pop idioms, including rock, jazz, and Neapolitan love songs. Much of this skill is evident in Morricone's arrangements of American and English songs, such as Hank Williams's "Hey, Good Lookin' " and the Beatles' "I Should Have Known Better." As Gary Radovich notes, these arrangements reveal the instrumental textures that would permeate Morricone's later film work. Says Radovich, "These include the lush and romantic strings, vibrant electric guitars, keyboards, bells, choirs and vocalise, electronics and 'gimmicks.' "[9]

Partly because of his experience in the recording industry, Morricone developed an approach to film scoring which was highly utilitarian. He believed that for film music to communicate with its audience, it was necessary to work in styles, forms, and genres that were already familiar: "The public cannot understand a new musical message in the cinema. Unfortunately it has to find confirmation in what it already knows."[10] This emphasis on accessibility informs many features of Morricone's style, particularly his approach to harmony. When asked why his spaghetti western scores have maintained their popularity over the years, Morricone responds, "When I begin a theme in a certain key, say, D minor, I never depart from this original key. If it begins in D minor, it ends in D minor. This harmonic simplicity is accessible to everyone."[11]

Thus, though Morricone did not initially intend his scores to be popular, the accessibility of their component parts allowed them to function within the context of the Italian and American recording industries. In Italy these traits were especially important, since its disk industry produced soundtrack albums in a quantity that was second only to the United States. Between 1956 and 1962, Italy issued over 250 soundtrack albums, with 111 of these coming in 1962 alone. All of Italy's top film composers took part in this soundtrack boom, including Nino Rota, Mario Nascimbene, and Carlo Rustichelli.[12]

RCA Victor's affiliate, RCA Italiana, led Italy's soundtrack production during the early sixties by releasing albums for over 120 features and fifty documentaries. Although production costs for these records varied between $25,000 and $50,000 per film, depending on a particular project's size and importance, RCA Italiana recorded, packaged, and distributed these albums at its own expense in exchange for a healthy share of the film's various music rights.[13] By 1970, RCA Italiana could boast that the soundtracks of the country's most famous motion pictures were recorded in their Rome studios.[14] And in 1974 one of the country's leading music publishers estimated that film music made up about 30 percent of the entire Italian record industry.[15]

In promoting their film music, however, Italian composers faced certain obstacles not present within the American film and record industries. For one thing, Italian pop singers were hesitant to cover tunes that were already recorded domestically. As a result, before 1964 the title tune as such was something of a rarity. Moreover, Italian composers also complained that record companies frequently rushed out albums which simply reproduced the film's soundtrack, complete with sound effects. As such, these albums often lacked the editing and rearranging necessary to make the music satisfactory to a home listener.[16]

It is within this context that Morricone began scoring films in 1961. His first score was for Luciano Salce's *Il Federale* (aka *The Fascist*), and it was released by RCA Italiana as a seven-track EP ("extended play"). Between 1961 and 1964, Morricone contributed music to some fifteen films, but he did not achieve a commercial breakthrough until the release of *A Fistful of Dollars* in October 1964. The film went on to gross over $4.3 million in its domestic run, its success spurred by Morricone's hit recording of the theme song. The RCA single spent much of 1965 in Italy's top ten where it sold on a par with recordings by the Beatles, Shirley Bassey, and Italian sensation Rita Pavone.

Leone's sequel, *For a Few Dollars More*, surpassed the earnings of its predecessor and in 1967 became the highest-grossing film of any nationality in the history of Italian cinema.[17] RCA tried to capitalize on the success of *For a Few Dollars More* by releasing Morricone's scores for both Leone films on a single LP. Additionally, RCA attempted to expand the market for Morricone's music by issuing the *For a Few Dollars More* soundtrack in Japan, Spain, and Germany. At about the same time, Morricone also gained international exposure through his *Battle of Algiers* soundtrack, which was released in Italy by RCA and in the United States by United Artists Records.

In the latter part of 1966, United Artists announced plans to distribute the first two films of Leone's *Dollars* trilogy in the United States and to finance a third to be budgeted at $1.6 million and tentatively titled *Two Magnificent Rogues*.[18] UA hoped to market the *Dollar* films along the lines of its James Bond series and created a timetable calculated to build interest for its Christmas release of the third film, now titled *The Good, the Bad, and the Ugly*.[19] The film received its domestic release in December and outpaced its predecessors by earning $3.8 million during its first four months.

By the time of *The Good, the Bad, and the Ugly*'s release, American interest in the film was quite high. Amidst rumors that Leone was preparing to remake *Gone with the Wind*, the first two films of the *Dollar* series became box office smashes in the United States, earning $3.5 million and $4 million, respectively.[20] Many theories were propounded to explain the series' stateside appeal, but the most common involved the films' combination of brutal violence and tongue-in-cheek humor. As Robert Landry noted in 1967, "With 'A Fistful of Dollars' the formula has reached a superstereotype, one mouthful of blood short of parody."[21]

An important, if less noted, part of the series' appeal was Morricone's music, which in 1968 enjoyed stateside success nearly equal to that of the films. *The Good, the Bad, and the Ugly*'s title theme and soundtrack album were both Top Ten hits, and the latter went on to earn a gold record for achieving over $1 million in retail sales. Morricone's soundtrack was joined by Hugo Montenegro's *Fistful of Dollars, Etc.*, which compiled themes from all three films in the series and reached the top fifteen on *Variety*'s album charts.

The popular reception of Morricone's score for *The Good, the Bad, and the Ugly* was undoubtedly enhanced by three key components of his authorial signature: his development of long, lyrical melodic lines; his interest in unusual tone colors; and his use of multiple themes as an overarching structural principle. All of these elements were already evident in Morricone's earlier studio and film work, but they strengthened the score's allure to American fans of pop and rock. In fact, as Donald Fagen notes, Morricone's peculiar mix of styles produced a kind of "Dumpster eclecticism" that led fringe rock bands and members of New York's New Music crowd to "adopt Morricone as their spiritual father."[22] Befitting Fagen's description, Morricone's score for *The Good, the Bad, and the Ugly* is a highly evocative postmodernist stew, one that juxtaposes static ostinatos with ear-bending themes; surf guitars with mariachi trumpets; wordless grunts and whistles with mellifluous singing. All in all, these diverse elements added up to a soundtrack that was as tuneful as any late sixties rock album.

Although some of Morricone's predecessors, like Max Steiner and Victor Young, were noted for working with more fully developed themes, Morricone took this principle to an extreme that can only be accounted for by the influence of the song form. This is clear from even a glance at the five major themes of *The Good, the Bad, and the Ugly*, which generally adhere to sixteen-bar song forms as an overarching structural principle. The title theme, for example, is made up of two basic melodies; the first is eight measures and the second sixteen. The melodies for "Marcia," "The Ecstasy of Gold," and "The Trio" are also sixteen measures long while "Story of a Soldier" is eighteen measures (sixteen measures with a two-bar extension).

To some degree, this emphasis on melody is generically and historically motivated. Westerns have traditionally used folk songs and ballads as the melodic materials for their scores. Morricone's interest in melody, however, is also undoubtedly influenced by the tradition of Italian opera writing, a trait shared by fellow Italian composers Nino Rota and Pino Dinaggio.

Yet as I noted earlier, Morricone's approach to melody can also be subsumed within the larger historical shift toward marketable popular tunes. Nowhere is this more evident than in the cases where Morricone composed actual songs for his scores, such as "A Gringo Like Me" in *Gunfight at Red Sands* (1963), "Lonesome Billy" in *Guns Don't Argue* (1964), and "Angel

Face" in *A Gun for Ringo* (1965). The intersection of these three traditions accounts in some measure for the popular appeal of *The Good, the Bad, and the Ugly*'s theme song, the success of which is largely founded on its readily identifiable and eminently hummable melody.

A second aspect of the soundtrack's commercial appeal is Morricone's unusual approach to tone color. While Graham Bruce has argued that Bernard Herrmann's scores of the fifties and sixties extended the possibilities of timbre and musical color in film scoring, Morricone's work in spaghetti westerns extends that principle even further.[23] While Herrmann's use of color is generally motivated by its narrative and representational functions, Morricone often explores timbral possibilities for their intrinsically expressive qualities. To get the precise tone color he desired, Morricone developed a repertory approach to his production of film scores, often using the same musicians over and over again when recording his soundtracks. As such, much of the distinctive tang of Morricone's spaghetti western scores comes from his repeated use of Edda Dell'Orso's soprano, Alessandro Alessandroni's whistling and guitar playing, and the choral stylings of I Cantori Moderni di Alessandroni.[24]

As with his interest in melody, Morricone's use of tone color also exhibits the influence of a popular music aesthetic. Robert Cumbow, for example, identifies the popular guitar instrumentals of the early sixties as an important influence on Morricone's sound. According to Cumbow, the "twangy California sound" of surf-rock was fashionable at the time of Morricone's apprenticeship and was widely copied by a number of European pop groups. Cumbow specifically mentions groups such as the Ventures, the Chantays, and the Tornadoes, which predate or are contemporary with Morricone's western scores and have an instantly recognizable similarity with the composer's distinctive guitar sound.[25]

While absorbing the influences of surf-rock, Morricone's guitar sound would itself inspire several rock musicians who followed him. Reviewing the soundtrack for *The Good, the Bad, and the Ugly*, Dave Marsh writes that "the Italian composer uses electric guitar to create effects more deadly than most rock musicians. Morricone's influence has seeped into several young electric guitarists since this picture appeared in the late sixties." Emblematic of this influence is honky-tonk guitarist Gary Stewart's claim that the *Once Upon a Time in the West* soundtrack is his all-time favorite album.[26]

More broadly, though, Morricone's interest in tone color was mirrored by the mid-sixties' emphasis on studio experimentation. As Morricone was writing his scores for the *Dollars* trilogy, the Beatles and other bands were expanding the tonal palette of basic rock instrumentation. The Beatles' 1964 recording of "I Feel Fine," for example, is allegedly the first recorded instance of electric guitar feedback. It was soon followed by the grungy metallic guitar sounds of the Kinks, the Who, and especially Jimi Hendrix. As rock entered its psychedelic phase, groups began to augment their sounds with odd instrumental touches. Flutes, recorders, harpsichords, and Indian sitars were used with increasing regularity by bands like the Beatles, the Rolling Stones, the Yardbirds, the Animals, and the Doors. While I do not wish to argue that Morricone was influenced by sixties psychedelia or vice versa, I would suggest that his spaghetti western scores may well have been understood within the context of rock's expanding musical horizons. Symptomatic of this is Dave Marsh's description of *The Good, the Bad, and the Ugly* as "a kind of post-Hendrix rock."[27]

Calling Morricone "the line that runs from Puccini to dub," Simon Frith further notes the composer's relation to a rather different tradition of popular music: Jamaican reggae.[28] In Frith's view, this connection is evident in Morricone's rhythmic textures, which often juxtapose pulsing ostinato figures against a random series of other sounds. The sparseness of Morricone's instrumentation and his sense of musical space thus possess certain textural similarities with Jamaican dub production, which itself is noted for playing echoey, reverbed piano and vocal sounds against skanking guitars and plangent bass lines.

Apart from melody and tone color, a third factor influencing Morricone's popular reception was his thematic diversity, a trait that supported the score's profusion of melodic and instrumental hooks but was also entirely adaptable to the specifications and standards of the typical pop album. To illustrate this concept, let me first offer brief descriptions of each of *The Good, the Bad, and the Ugly*'s eight main musical themes.

The title song is easily the most famous and the most complex. It is structured around a motivic cell which is used throughout the rest of the score: a trilled fourth followed by three quarter notes which together outline a D-minor triad (figure 6.1):

FIGURE 6.1

The theme is initially played alone by a flute and a squawk box, but as it is repeated, instruments are added to thicken the musical texture. The entry of the electric guitar in bar seventeen signals the entry of a new theme. This second theme outlines a D-minor and F-major triad using the F on the second beat as a pivot point between them. After this figure is repeated, it is played a third time but is extended upward to outline an A-minor triad and finally comes to rest on a high G and A. A sudden crescendo on this half cadence reintroduces a guitar flourish that harmonically alternates between D-minor and G-major chords before moving melodically and harmonically downward, finally coming to rest on a C that resolves to yet another half cadence. A trumpet bridge leads to the final repetition of the theme. As the piece draws to its conclusion, there is a progressive lessening of the musical texture as it returns to the orchestration of the beginning. Interestingly, the piece does not conclude with a final cadence, but with a single D-minor chord played in the strings.

"The Sundown," the second major theme, consists of a lyrical Spanish guitar line with orchestral accompaniment. Though essentially melodic and in free rhythm, this piece echoes the title theme in some interesting ways. There are, for example, certain structural resemblances to the electric guitar melody of the theme song. In addition, the piece concludes ominously with a repeated motive that is constructed out of perfect fourths and played in the low register of the guitar. The latter appears to be a structural and harmonic anomaly, but it is linked to the opening flute motive, which is itself a repeated perfect fourth.

The third theme, "The Strong," is a mournful trumpet melody in the key of B-flat Major. This theme has a very free rhythm and is largely built out of the following melodic figure (figure 6.2):

FIGURE 6.2

"The Desert," on the other hand, is essentially an orchestral fantasia developed out of a chromatically ascending and descending melodic figure and two repeated motives (figure 6.3):

FIGURE 6.3

Used during the montage of Blondie's (Clint Eastwood) tortuous walk through the desert, the piece is characterized by a high degree of tonal instability and chromaticism and is the most musically ambitious piece in the entire score.

In contrast, a diatonic melody, simple tonic-dominant harmonic alternation, and spare orchestration give "Marcia" an appropriately homespun quality (figure 6.4):

FIGURE 6.4

In its first appearance, the piece is scored quite simply for harmonica and whistle. In later appearances, however, Morricone reorchestrates the piece for full orchestra, slows the tempo, and complicates the harmony to give this theme a more lyrical, melancholy quality.

Much the same can be said of "Story of a Soldier" (figure 6.5), which is harmonically and melodically similar to "Marcia":

FIGURE 6.5

This theme, which is also in D major, has a simple pentatonic melody and is orchestrated for guitar, flute, harmonica, violin, string bass, bells, trombone, and male chorus. "The Ecstasy of Gold" and "The Trio," the seventh and eighth themes, are both more fully developed tunes which alternate free rhythmic and harmonic developments with the piano accompaniment figure from "The Desert." These last two tunes are both scored for full orchestra and feature lyrical, melismatic melodies.

As with other pop scores, the thematic diversity of *The Good, the Bad, and the Ugly* served a commercial function by shaping individual cues into the tracks of a satisfying album. Cues that were either too short or too atmospheric were rejected in favor of those which developed their own thematic identity and structural autonomy. By process of elimination, the score was reduced to eleven cues, which were then molded into eleven discrete album tracks. Most of these tracks display Morricone's melodic flair and most fit within the pop single's typical running time of between two and five minutes.

Morricone's approach to melody, tone color, and thematic structures suggests that the popular success of *The Good, the Bad, and the Ugly* soundtrack was not entirely a fluke. Although all of these elements were extensions of certain classical Hollywood scoring principles, they also accommodated the tastes of a burgeoning youth market and radio audience. Balancing the score's commercial and dramatic functions, Morricone created music that was not only accessible but that also fit into the sixties' growing interest in studio experimentation and pop psychedelia. More than that, through his masterful use of melody and tone color, Morricone redefined the sound of the western and established himself as one of film music's most daring and original composers.

The Ecstasy of Gold (Records): Leone's Image, Morricone's Sound

When discussing Leone's approach to sound-image relations, most critics note that the director's style has certain affinities with operatic form. Robert Cumbow, for example, suggests that the analogy between Leone and opera is almost inevitable and spells out the terms of this comparison in the director's treatment of spectacle, the films' mixing of sentimental kitsch and earthy humor, and the essential musicality of the films' narrative processes. According to Cumbow, "The most important events in Leone's films are always prepared for—and held back—by long, songlike musical passages, calling to mind that operatic cliché, the interminable sung death of the hero."[29]

Laurence Staig and Tony Williams develop the analogy even further by extending it to the entire cycle of spaghetti westerns and by arguing that the film composer's role in this subgenre is unique in the history of film. In Staig and Williams's view, this uniqueness derives from the degree to which music is foregrounded by the Italian western's narrative, which typically contains moments during which the nondiegetic music simply takes over the film. Staig and Williams trace this approach to narrative back to Italian opera, which they believe offers a similar amalgam of music and action.[30]

While I do not doubt that opera is an influence on Leone's work, I question whether operatic form is the only way to conceive of his films' sound and image relations. After all, there are many cultural forms which blend or synthesize music and action, including classical ballet, modern dance, vaudeville, theatrical melodrama, and the Hollywood musical. To single out opera out of all of these forms oversimplifies a very complex scenario of artistic filiation and ignores the influence of more historically pertinent aesthetic forms.

Thus, while I would grant opera's influence, I would also suggest that an important part of the background for Leone's work was the diffusion of various film-jukebox technologies, such as Scopitone and Cinebox, which were designed to showcase the musical talents of actors and recording artists. Scopitone and Cinebox were not the first such technologies, but they did enjoy a significant popularity in Europe and the United States between 1962 and 1967.[31] Although Scopitone's influence on the spaghetti western is difficult to trace, the concurrent development of Scopitone and the pop score nonetheless helped to shape Leone's collaboration with Morricone in two ways. First, as promotional vehicles for records, Scopitone and Cinebox are aligned with a larger trend toward inverting cinema's image-sound hierarchy for the purpose of selling title songs and soundtrack albums. Second, like Leone's films, Scopitone foregrounds music as a primary structural element of cinematic signification, one that sometimes supercedes narrative by reconfiguring the film's visual and editing systems.

Scopitone was a coin-operated, French film-jukebox invented in 1960 by the Compagnie d'Applications Mécaniques et à l'Électroniques au Cinéma et à l'Atomistique (CAMECA). Designed primarily for clubs and restaurants, Scopitone adopted the jukebox format but substituted sound films for records. The machine held a maximum of thirty-six color 16mm films on a revolving drum, which could then be projected onto a twenty-six-inch screen. The Scopitone film's duration was between two and a half and four minutes, and they were played on a continuous running projector with automatic rewinding features. The initial cost of a Scopitone jukebox was $6,500, and by 1961 more than 140 such machines had been licensed by the Société Française Radioélectrique. Early interest in Scopitone was so high that the William Morris Agency purchased its United States sales rights in June 1961.[32]

Cinebox, an Italian film-jukebox, debuted at the San Remo Song Festival shortly after the introduction of Scopitone. The machine differed from Scopitone in that it held a few more films and had separate channels for image and sound. Similar to early Vitaphone technology, Cinebox played 16mm films which were then synchronized with the records they accompanied. Though it followed Scopitone into the marketplace, Cinebox nevertheless generated a great deal of curiosity at the San Remo event. The machines initially cost about one million lira (roughly U.S.$160), and operators hoped to capitalize on their novelty value by installing them in bars, lobbies, and waiting rooms across the country.[33]

By the end of 1961, Scopitone manufacturers had installed more than a thousand machines across the continent, and *Variety* reported that the device was replacing television sets in many cafés and bars. Cinebox sales were a bit sluggish at first, but by 1963 the company operated between 350 and 400 machines in Western Europe and the United Kingdom. Interestingly, advertisers also explored the possibility of interweaving commercials with the Scopitone's filmed performances of orchestras and European pop stars. Marketers believed they could effectively exploit the machine's color and sound for various kinds of "theme" or "mood" advertising, and further believed that the proper placement of commercials could enhance, rather than detract from, the entertainment value of the musical shorts.[34]

Interest in Scopitone continued to grow in Britain and the United States, but operators faced a major obstacle to breaking into those markets; there were few English-language films and fewer still which utilized star performers and chart-topping songs.[35] For example, only six British films were available to U.K. operators in 1962. Since a Cinebox held as many as forty films, the 130 machines operating in Britain were primarily stocked with French and Italian product.[36] To mitigate this problem, Scopitone set up a U.K. unit in 1963 and announced in *Billboard* that it was seeking "ideas, storylines, and scenarists with the talent to compete with the brilliance of French film jukebox products."[37]

As production of English-language Scopitone and Cinebox films increased, both technologies made significant inroads into the British and American markets. Between 1962 and 1965, cinema-jukebox manufacturers placed more than 1,200 of the devices in various locations across the United States. Concentration was particularly heavy on the West Coast where four hundred of the 1,034 Scopitone units sold in the United States were located. To avoid conflict with regular jukebox operators, Scopitone importers targeted hotels, cocktail lounges, and restaurants in large urban areas.[38] The Sparks Pub, on New York's Second Avenue, was a typical Scopitone site. The tavern reported high initial sales from a machine that featured tunes by Françoise Hardy, Johnny Hallyday, Dion, Paul Anka, and Petula Clark.[39]

In 1965, Scopitone launched an ambitious program for the production of films for the American market. In July, Scopitone's U.S. manufacturer, Tel-A-Sign, announced the release of thirteen films featuring such artists as Bobby Vee, Della Reese, Barbara McNair, and Debbie Reynolds.[40] More importantly, Scopitone's U.S. producer, Harman Enterprises, also developed a program for the production of one three-minute film a week. Productions were usually completed with one day of rehearsal and one day of shooting, and using this schedule, Harman set a long-term goal of making forty-eight films a year. Since the artists showcased in these films usually received $1,000 in acting fees and royalties, the typical Scopitone short cost between $6,000 and $11,000 to produce, depending on how many background singers and dancers were employed. Harman handled all the talent acquisition and generally sought out artists who performed material from the standard repertoire and had established track records. Reflecting the conservatism of this policy, future Scopitone productions were to feature James Darren, Frankie Avalon, Leslie Uggams, Vic Damone, and Ella Fitzgerald.[41] Cinebox, in contrast, could not afford any name talent for its films and tried to make do with footage of dancers and go-go girls.[42]

Despite improvements in film quantity and quality, neither Scopitone nor Cinebox achieved the market potential envisioned by their distributors. A. A. Steiger, the chairman of Tel-A-Sign, had estimated the U.S. market for cinema-jukeboxes at about 100,000 locations; the number actually installed in this country, however, never surpassed 10,000.[43] The first sign of trouble came in October 1966 when Tel-A-Sign announced that it was slashing its machine and film prices in order to stay competitive in the coin-machine market.[44] Color-Sonics entered the fray in 1966 with a device that improved on certain aspects of the Scopitone machine, but by 1967 the market for all cinema-jukebox formats had essentially disappeared.[45] Once the novelty wore off, many Scopitone operators simply converted the machines into pornographic peep shows.[46]

Scopitone's failure in the American market can be traced to two persistent problems that plagued the technology throughout its history—a shortage of quality film product and a failure to tap into pop's growing youth market. Despite Harman and Tel-A-Sign's efforts to provide a regular production schedule, they never made enough films to change the industry's view that Scopitone was simply a novelty. Three years after Scopitone's introduction into the United States, Tel-A-Sign's library of shorts comprised only eighty American films and 260 French-made films.[47] With so little product, operators were clearly unable to satisfy the long-term demand for new and better films. Moreover, with few exceptions, Scopitone producers heavily slanted their film content toward adults. Initially, producers reasoned that the machines were located in venues that were off-limits to underage juveniles, but even when they shifted their focus to youth music in 1965, their selection of artists and material was extremely conservative. A sample Scopitone program circulated by the Long Beach Museum of Art featured songs by Nancy Sinatra, Joi Lansing, the Exciters, and jazz trumpeter Clark Terry. The only exception to this adult-music orientation was Procol Harum, but even here their selection, "A Whiter Shade of Pale," was recuperable as a classically orchestrated rock ballad.

For the most part, Scopitone producers, especially those in Europe, traded on their lack of youth appeal by displaying scantily clad women and a *Mondo Cane*-like grotesquerie.[48] In fact, *Billboard* noted the former as a particular selling point within the American market. According to the trade paper, "The color pictures are almost clear and sharp. As a result, the lovely ladies (dressed in high fashion and low bikinis) who prance about in just about every sequence are that much easier to appreciate."[49] Although there are relatively few Scopitone films in circulation today, a sampling of those available generally bears out *Billboard*'s description. Joi Lansing's "The Silencer," for example, depicts the singer as a pseudo-James Bond figure, who appears in various stages of undress amid a group of bikini-clad women. Back Porch Majority's "Mighty Mississippi" contains a silhouetted striptease and close-ups of various female bottoms.

In other Scopitone shorts, however, there is a strong tendency toward the bizarre and the exotic. Princess Leilani, for example, earned a somewhat dubious reputation within the industry for performing an "anatomically astounding fire dance" in one Scopitone short.[50] Similarly, *Time* magazine described the French-made "El Gato Montes" as capturing "the jollity of the annual Pamplona fiesta with trumpet playing, flamenco dancing, and the shrieks of small boys being gored by rampaging bulls in the street."[51]

Scopitone's influence on cinema is hard to pinpoint, but it is nevertheless manifest in certain aspects of late sixties' film and soundtrack production. Perhaps the most obvious influence is found in the work of Claude Lelouch, who directed four hundred Scopitone shorts while breaking into the world of feature production.[52] Lelouch's most famous film, *A Man and a Woman* (*Un homme et une femme*, 1966), became an international hit and spawned a million-dollar soundtrack album for the film's foreign distributor, United Artists Records. Critics have frequently described the film as a feature-length commercial, and indeed this characterization is quite consistent with Scopitone's function as a vehicle to promote music and other products.[53]

A Man and a Woman's stylistic similarity to advertisements is most evident in the film's structure. It proceeds as a series of extended montages depicting Anne's (Anouk Aimee) relationship with her late husband; Jean-Louis's (Jean-Louis Trintignant) preparation of his race car; Anne and Jean-Louis's romantic boat trip; and Jean-Louis's drive to Paris toward the end of the film. Like the production numbers of a musical, these montages essentially "freeze" the narrative flow in order to give composer Francis Lai the opportunity for more sustained musical expression. Music and image are fused in such a way that each of these sequences seem as though it could be excerpted and exhibited as an individual Scopitone short.[54]

In this regard, Lelouch's work prefigures the innovation of the interpolated song, which became increasingly common after 1967. In addition to the *Butch Cassidy* example cited earlier, interpolated songs were also present in *The Thomas Crown Affair* (1968), which uses "The Windmills of Your Mind" to accompany a montage of Steve McQueen gliding; *On Her Majesty's Secret Service* (1969), in which "We Have All the Time in the World" underscores a montage of James Bond's blossoming romance with Tracy; and *Midnight Cowboy* (1969), which uses "Everybody's Talkin' " to accompany Joe Buck's (Jon Voight) efforts to pick up various women in front of New York's Tiffany's store.

All these examples share certain traits which helped to define the interpolated song. First, all of them are nondiegetic. This is particularly significant in that it distinguishes this type of scoring from more conventional numbers, such as those that are performed in musicals or are heard as source music on car radios and home stereos. Second, each tune is not simply run under the opening or closing credits, but instead is placed within the body of the film. According to Gary LeMel, the president of Warner Brothers' music division, such placement greatly enhances the song's commercial potential insofar as it combines the music with memorable imagery. Says LeMel, "It's always better if you can marry the music to an emotional piece of film because that's what makes people react. They're not going to react to a song on the end title of a film."[55]

Applying this model to *A Man and a Woman*, the film's extended montages may be thought of less as interpolated songs and more as "interpolated cues." In each, snatches of jazz or European pop are wedded to affective bits of filmed action to form self-contained sequences.[56] The marriage of music and expressive camerawork—handheld shots, filters, the mixing of color and black-and-white stocks—helped to give these sequences their emotional kick and likely played a major part in making the film's soundtrack album a Top Ten hit in the United States.

While *A Man and a Woman* is perhaps the paradigmatic example of Scopitone's influence on sixties' film style, the latter's traces are evident in a broader effort to reconfigure cinema's normal relationship between image and sound. Adapting the playback techniques used in filming classical Hollywood musicals, Scopitone films were typically shot without sound. Much like contemporary music videos, Scopitone singers simply mimed their performances and lip-synched to prerecorded popular songs. As such, the production of these musical shorts gave logical priority to the soundtrack. Reversing the techniques of classical scoring, the action was staged and the footage shot, framed, and edited to accommodate the music rather than the other way around.

Leone and Morricone's work on *Once Upon a Time in the West* (1969) is especially interesting in this regard since the film was shot in a manner that virtually replicated the production techniques of these Scopitone shorts. While the film was being scripted, Leone asked Morricone to write and record the major themes for the film before shooting got under way. Then, during the film's production, Leone brought huge speakers onto the set and played Morricone's music for cast and crew members. The actors were asked to move and gesture according to the rhythms of the score, and individual sequences of the film were shot while the music was being played. Although this technique is extremely unusual for nonmusical films, Leone had already used it in a more piecemeal fashion on *The Good, the Bad, and the Ugly*, and later used it again for *Once Upon a Time in America* (1984).[57]

Meanwhile, in the United States, a handful of composers and producers explored similar production techniques for the specific purpose of promoting soundtrack albums. On *Harlow* (1965), for example, composer Nelson Riddle recorded his score before the picture started filming. Riddle organized his music around two big themes, "I Believed it All" and "With Open Arms," and wrote cues that could be cut as necessary. The film's sound editors would then match bars of the music to specified frames of the film and simply fade the cues in and out at the proper point of an individual scene.[58]

During the 1967–68 season, television music director Alfred Perry adopted an even more ambitious program for scoring series pilots. Under Perry's system, a composer began developing his score as soon as the pilot was sold. After an initial meeting in which the program's format and script were analyzed, the composer would, according to Perry, "sit down and write 12 musical experiences off the characters in their varying moods."[59] Once the pilot was filmed, then the music was simply selected and matched to particular scenes. As Perry notes, the process had already been successfully implemented on *The Rogues*, *The Big Valley*, and *Honey West*, and it was planned for four other Four Star telefilms. Best of all, Perry had assembled an impressive array of scoring talent, including Lalo Schifrin, Riz Ortolani, George Dunning, and Nelson Riddle, and his prescoring process readily lent itself to the development and release of television soundtrack albums.[60]

Even when a film was scored with conventional techniques, directors began to take a more flexible approach to the editing of image and music tracks. During the postproduction phase of *Shaft* (1971), for example,

Gordon Parks received tapes of Isaac Hayes's music as he composed it, and made changes in his editing to accommodate the score. Said Parks, "The more I heard, the more excited I got. I sometimes cut something to fit his music. . . . And there were times when I said, 'Wow, I wish I had something here to fit this in—how can we use this?' "[61] Similarly, Burt Bacharach described working with George Roy Hill on *Butch Cassidy and the Sundance Kid*:

> He almost set up places where he wanted music to be really important—where they would be free of dialogue—when he shot the film. He was great on the scoring stage, too, and I had a wonderful time on the picture. He'd say, "Hey, you need a few more frames, I'll cut it in. Don't worry about it." Or, "I'll stretch that there."[62]

Viewed within this broader historical context, both Scopitone and Morricone's scores were part of a larger trend in late sixties cinema toward inverting the normal hierarchy of image and sound. In the above examples and in certain cues in *The Good, the Bad, and the Ugly*, music is not subordinate to the image but rather is elevated to a position that is functionally equivalent. Certain characteristics of Morricone's style seem to support the music's elevation. These include the music's presence, its often abrupt entry and exit on the soundtrack, its adherence to strophic formal structures, and its peculiar emotional valences. All these features serve to foreground Morricone's music and make it noticeable to late sixties film audiences. Insofar as Leone's style drew attention to Morricone's music, the films themselves functioned as excellent vehicles for promoting the scores and their respective soundtrack albums.

By this I do not mean to discount the traditional features of Morricone's score. *The Good, the Bad, and the Ugly* employs a number of musical devices that largely serve conventional dramatic functions and occupy a more or less subordinate position within the hierarchy of image and sound. Old-fashioned, over-the-top stingers, for example, are used early in the film to underline characters' reactions to Angel Eyes' (Lee Van Cleef) brutality. Similarly, marches and Confederate ballads are used to suggest the settings of the film's Civil War sections.[63] Finally, flamenco-styled guitar music appears in the early sections of the film to represent the Mexican heritage of Tuco (Eli Wallach), Father Ramirez, and the family killed by Angel Eyes.

If these examples reveal a rather traditional side to Morricone's scores, others show him tweaking certain classical conventions. In another instance of musical characterization, Morricone puts an unusual spin on the

Wagnerian notion of the leitmotiv. As each major character is introduced in a prologue segment, a title appears in the frame to identify their particular ethos. Tuco is identified as "the ugly," Angel Eyes as "the bad," and Blondie as "the good." And as each title appears, there is a freeze frame under which the main musical motive plays as a kind of leitmotiv. However, rather than distinguishing each character by a separate theme à la Wagner, Morricone distinguishes Blondie, Angel Eyes, and Tuco through different orchestrations of the *same* leitmotiv. Blondie's instrumentation, for example, uses the lighter timbres of the flute and harmonica to represent his "goodness," while Angel Eyes' orchestration uses the darker colors of the ocarina and electric guitar to represent his "badness."

Of course, the larger irony pointed up by this device is that the characters' moral codes are virtually indistinguishable. Although the title of the film identifies them in terms of stark oppositions, the melodic identity of the leitmotivs suggests a fundamental similarity between them, and thus, a certain blurring of the lines between "the good," "the bad," and "the ugly." Morricone's peculiar treatment of the leitmotiv underscores one of the most commonly noted themes of Leone's narrative. Since all the characters act out of greed and self-interest, moral designations of "good" and "bad" can only function ironically. To put it another way, if Clint Eastwood's Blondie represents "the good," then all our normal ethical standards must simply be chucked out the window.

While many of the aforementioned examples exhibit some play with the traditional narrative functions of film music, certain other cues reverse the norms of film scoring altogether. This is generally true of Morricone's handling of the genre's stock moments—showdowns, gunfights, and other moments of reckoning—and it seems particularly evident in *The Good, the Bad, and the Ugly*'s most famous set pieces: Tuco's discovery of the cemetery and the final gunfight between the three men. During these scenes, it seems that rather than composing music to match the mood of the narrative, the film appears instead to have been photographed and edited to match the mood of the music.[64]

In the former, Morricone underscores the action with the theme, "The Ecstasy of Gold." Unlike most of the other themes, this appears only once in the film, and both Morricone and Leone seem determined to make the most of it. Just as Tuco falls and hits his head on a grave marker, Morricone introduces the theme with the repeated piano accompaniment figure from "The Desert." As the camera pulls back to show the vast Sad Hill Cemetery, an oboe enters and begins playing the theme slowly and hesitantly (figure 6.6):

FIGURE 6.6

The torpid, melismatic quality of the tune here seems to express Tuco's growing awareness of where he is. Tuco signifies this realization by throwing away his map. Once Tuco begins his search for Arch Stanton's grave (the key to where the gold is buried), the oboe plays the theme's second phrase. Now the oboe plays more assuredly, and Tuco's growing excitement is represented by the introduction of a firmer rhythm. Still the same shot, the camera cranes up to show Tuco moving among a sea of graves. The oboe concludes the second phrase, and as Tuco begins to run, a strong crescendo on a half cadence expresses his sudden welling of excitement.

Edda Dell'Orso's wordless soprano takes up the theme where the oboe left off. Leone then cuts to two lateral tracking and panning shots which follow Tuco as he runs through the graves. The rhythm becomes more insistent and the orchestration fuller as the strings take over the melody. Here Leone cuts to a close-up of Tuco and alternates this with panning point-of-view shots of the gravestones. These images are juxtaposed with a soaring string line that expresses the ebb and flow of Tuco's desperate exhilaration.

By this point, Tuco has moved into a large circular space in the middle of the graveyard. As Tuco crosses this space, the strings, voice, and trumpet alternate the theme in a manner not unlike a fugue. A high extreme long shot shows Tuco as he moves along the edge of this central area. Here the melody reaches a peak and suddenly stops. This is followed by a sudden softening of the dynamics and a much less strict rhythmic articulation as the strings play a brief interlude of transitional material. As Tuco begins running through the graveyard again, the theme begins again in earnest. A chorus enters along with the chimes and a brass countermelody, and each time the theme repeats, it continues to increase in intensity (figure 6.7):

FIGURE 6.7

On the visual track, the camera now frames Tuco closer in lateral tracking shots, which intensifies the visual impression of movement and delirium. These shots are alternated with swish pans, which almost give a vertiginous emotional dimension to the scene. As the music reaches its highest level of cacophony, Tuco spies Arch Stanton's name on a headstone and stops. As if to underline Tuco's discovery, Morricone's music also comes to a sudden halt.

The notion that Leone devised this montage to accompany a prerecorded track is supported by the cue's length and formal autonomy. Running some three and a half minutes, "The Ecstasy of Gold" bears none of the traces of music that has been written to accompany visual action, such as ostinato figures, sustained chords, or unusual shifts in tempo. On the contrary, the cue's harmonic progressions and rhythmic drive suggest that it advances according to a musical rather than a narrative logic.

A similar approach to music and film style is apparent in the film's climactic gunfight (figure 6.8). Much like "The Ecstasy of Gold," "The Trio" starts hesitantly with a solo flute. The texture of the piece thickens somewhat as Blondie places the stone containing the location of the gold in the middle of the circle. A sudden close-up and zoom into the stone is underscored by a dramatic crescendo and the entry of the accompaniment figure from "The Desert" and "The Ecstasy of Gold." Although the piece begins in D minor, the accompaniment functions as an ostinato figure, which alternates with the flute melody and modulates through the keys of F major, C major, G major, and B-flat major. This modulation gives the piece a tonal uncertainty that is expressive of the characters' uncertainty as they take up positions at various points on the circle. After a sudden crescendo on an A-major chord, a mariachi trumpet commences the theme, which is accompanied by the orchestra playing a kind of habanera rhythmic figure. Leone then cuts to a high-angle, extreme long shot to show the three characters finally settling into their positions. The trumpet melody appears to end with another wide shot and a cut to a medium shot of Tuco.

A few seconds of silence suggest that the cue has ended, but the music soon returns with the bells repeatedly playing a soft but insistent descending three-note melody. The piano then reenters playing the four-note accompaniment figure that had earlier been played by the guitar. The alternation of these two figures is punctuated by tympani flourishes, rattling castanets, tinkling bells, and the noise of an electric guitar being plucked at the bridge. When the music reenters, Leone begins to cut more quickly and to closer shots of the three men, poised and ready to draw their weapons. The ostinato figure modulates through two more keys, and then a dramatic crescendo once again announces the entry of the theme. As the melody ascends, the bass line chromatically descends with the opposite movement of the two lines creating an enormous amount of harmonic tension. This musical tension underscores the

FIGURE 6.8 Blondie (Clint Eastwood. *right*), Angel Eyes (Lee Van Cleef, *left*), and Tuco (Eli Wallach, *center*) in Sad Hill Cemetery. Ennio Morricone's "The Trio" provides the accompaniment for the film's final set piece, a showdown between "the Good, the Bad, and the Ugly."

characters' tremendous intensity as each man carefully sizes up his opponents. The full orchestra then takes over the theme as the rhythmic accompaniment shifts to an alternating triplet figure. Leone heightens this shift with even faster cutting and even closer views of the men's eyes and hands. The tension is finally broken as the music stops and a gunshot rings out.

In both sequences, Leone and Morricone combined cutting, framing, and camera movement with the expressive character of the music to create moments of remarkable emotional power. Unlike the musical forms of classical Hollywood scores, which according to Claudia Gorbman are determined or subordinated to narrative, the music of "The Ecstasy of Gold" and "The Trio" is foregrounded as a kind of functional equivalent of the visually represented narrative action. The length of the cues, their melodic songlike character, and their clear formal demarcations suggest that Leone has used cutting and camera movement to develop set pieces attuned to the specific mood and expressive character of the music. Instead of using Morricone's music to score the film, it seems rather that Leone has "imaged" the music.

Like other pop scores, *The Good, the Bad, and the Ugly* shows a number of ways in which Morricone both exemplifies and diverges from the classical

Hollywood film-scoring tradition. Like his predecessors, Morricone organized his score around certain keys, harmonic patterns, rhythmic figures, and motives to give it thematic and formal unity. Also like his predecessors, Morricone utilized the secondary parameters of tempo, dynamics, texture, and tone color to emphasize certain expressive effects in his music. Though both lyrical and expressive, Morricone's music also proved malleable enough to underline character states and emotions, suggest setting, and even comment on similarities of character and narrative actions.

Yet, as Morricone was writing his legendary western scores, traditional film-scoring practices were being modified to fit the economic demands of a growing radio and record industry. Bearing the traces of these pressures, Morricone explored melody and tone color in a way that was consistent with a predominant popular aesthetic. Morricone's approach to orchestration, particularly the electric guitar, proved to be enormously influential on later pop and rock musicians, and the apparent weirdness of the composer's style fit neatly within the context of sixties pop psychedelia.

In addition, Morricone and Leone participated in a broader reconfiguration of image and sound in late sixties visual media, one that reversed their normal hierarchy. Film-jukeboxes, such as Scopitone and Cinebox, were the paradigmatic examples of this trend, but it was also evident in other prerecorded film scores and in a greater flexibility in film editing. In *Once Upon a Time in the West*, Leone took this Scopitone aesthetic to its logical limit by prerecording Morricone's score and then playing it on the set during the film's production. More generally, though, Leone and Morricone showed their affinity with Scopitone by developing stock genre moments into cinematic set pieces. By giving the music a logical priority, they not only elevated Morricone's music from a subordinate position to one that was equivalent to the film's image track, but it also served as a perfect vehicle for selling the score in soundtrack album form.

That the theme for *The Good, the Bad, and the Ugly* was a massive radio hit only proves Morricone's efficacy in negotiating the boundaries between classical scoring practices and popular musical demands. As Morricone's popularity continues, his place in film music history looms larger than ever. As Blondie puts it in *The Good, the Bad, and the Ugly*, "Each gun has its own tune." In understanding the nature of that tune, we make an important contribution toward understanding both the ethos of the spaghetti western and the place of film music within our culture.

7

The Sounds of Commerce

SIXTIES POP SONGS AND THE COMPILATION SCORE

After 1965 composers continued to refine the trend toward thematic expansion and diversification in film music. Since soundtrack albums remained the dominant strategy for film music exploitation, the adaptation of scores to pop album formats prevailed throughout the sixties and has continued to be an important practice up to the present. Each of the composers discussed in the previous chapters offered a slight variation on how this musical transformation from film to album was achieved. Mancini increased the score's thematic palette by using diegetic or sourced cues as opportunities to introduce new musical ideas. Barry adapted the pop score's commercial impetus to the various needs and demands of a serial narrative and a distinctive musical formula. Morricone played up the "operatic" side of the horse opera by treating gunfights and showdowns as though they were production numbers from a musical. Working with prerecorded cues, Morricone and Leone developed cinematic set pieces that fused music and image into a powerful stylistic whole.

For each of these composers, the score was not an afterthought grafted onto the film in postproduction, but rather a calculated element in the film's larger schemes of production and marketing. By the end of the sixties, the trend toward thematic variety culminated with the development of the compilation score. This approach was both the logical extension of the multi-theme pop scores which preceded it and a challenge to the forms and functions of the classical Hollywood score.

Reworking the theme scores of the fifties, the compilation score presented a series of self-contained musical numbers, usually prerecorded songs, which were substituted for the repeated and varied occurrences of a score's theme.[1] These musical numbers would either be grouped together to create a self-sufficient score or combined with more conventional forms of atmospheric underscore. The scores for *The Graduate* (1967) and *Easy Rider* (1969) were among the compilation score's earliest commercial triumphs and were soon followed by somewhat less successful song collections for *Zabriskie Point* (1970), *The Last Picture Show* (1971), *Vanishing Point* (1971), *Superfly* (1972), *O Lucky Man!* (1973), *Mean Streets* (1973), *The Harder They Come* (1973) and *American Graffiti* (1973).[2] Derived from a complex mix of music, marketing, and cinema, the compilation score attained its importance as a commercially self-aware alternative to the neo-Romantic orchestral scores of Hollywood's "Golden Age."

The compilation score emerges as a curious hybrid of the musical and the traditional classical Hollywood score. Like the musical, each song of the compilation score retains a certain measure of structural unity and integrity. The twelve-, sixteen-, and thirty-two-bar phrase patterns of these songs generally resist the fragmentation and variation that are the hallmarks of the classical score's leitmotivic or thematic structure. At the same time, however, the individual songs of the compilation score are typically utilized in ways that are not unlike the cues of the conventional orchestral score. Songs are spotted such that they may perform any or all of the classical score's traditional functions, including establishing mood and supporting the film's construction of formal unity.

What ultimately separates the compilation score from the classical Hollywood score is not the paradigmatic range of narrational functions each performs, but rather the compilation score's tendency to emphasize certain functions over others. Because of its formal autonomy, the compilation score is much less likely to be used as an element of structural and rhythmic continuity. Instead, filmmakers frequently use songs as a way of establishing mood and setting, and as a commentary on the film's characters and action. Moreover, much of the compilation score's expressiveness derives less from its purely musical qualities than from the system of extramusical allusions and associations activated by the score's referentiality. In other words, because of the compilation score's heavy reliance on pop and rock tunes, its meaning within a film is often dependent upon the meaning of pop music in the larger spheres of society and culture.

In the remainder of this chapter, I will explore this dichotomy between musicality and narrativity by looking more closely at the compilation score's history and formal operations. After first briefly tracing the development of the compilation score from a number of diverse historical sources (including such traditions as the "jukebox musical" and the American avant-garde cinema), I will then examine the ways in which the compilation score's self-contained numbers adapt to the demands of scoring by looking at its operations across a number of different films. Finally, I will discuss the film *American Graffiti* as a paradigmatic example of the compilation score, one that illustrates its reliance on both setting and pop music's cultural functions to serve as atmospheric underscore.

The Historical Sources and Reception of the Compilation Score

From a marketing perspective, the logic behind the compilation score's development was plain. Rather than adapt the score to the format of the pop album, why not adapt the album to the forms and functions of the film score? By scoring a film with a series of songs, the compilation score offered a couple of commercial advantages over its predecessors. For example, the larger number of songs within the film—anywhere between four and twenty—gave the record label more potential hits to which the film could hitch its wagon. Furthermore, by 1968 a soundtrack album, unlike a title theme, was more likely to be released on the film company's own record label.[3]

While each of these marketing advantages encouraged the compilation score's emergence during the late sixties, the use of rock songs as underscore was not entirely a move into uncharted territory. As a number of critics and historians point out, rock and cinema have been linked since the inception of that musical idiom.[4] One of rock's earliest hits, "Rock Around the Clock," benefited immeasurably from its exposure under the opening credits of *The Blackboard Jungle*. Before being featured in the Richard Brooks film, the song was a moderate hit for an obscure western swing band called Bill Haley and the Comets. After *Blackboard Jungle*, however, the song acquired new strength on the pop charts, made major stars of its performers, and sold roughly two million copies by the end of 1955.[5]

With the exception of *Blackboard Jungle*, however, filmmakers have generally managed to stay at least one step behind the prevailing trends in rock music.[6] Because of the faddishness of the teenage marketplace, early rock films are especially prone to a kind of bandwagon mentality in which the film attempts to capitalize on a current music or dance craze. The legendary exploitation producer, "Jungle Sam" Katzman, was an exemplar of this approach, and his work illustrates the ways in which rock filmmakers have generally tried to cash in on a flourishing youth market.

Katzman, who earlier had specialized in producing matinee serials and low-budget science fiction, adapted his makeshift "quickie" strategy to rock 'n' roll with the 1956 film *Rock Around the Clock*. According to Thomas Doherty, the timely and controversial nature of fifties rock made it grist for Katzman's production mill.[7] Using the music as a selling point, *Rock Around the Clock* became the first major hit aimed solely at teenagers and was soon followed by other Katzman titles such as *Don't Knock the Rock* (1957), *Calypso Heat Wave* (1957), and *Twist Around the Clock* (1961). As late as 1964, Katzman was still plumbing the teenpic genre with MGM's *Get Yourself a College Girl*, but his once keen sense of musical fashion now failed him. Though *College Girl* featured such rising stars as the Animals and the Dave Clark Five, it also featured more middlebrow jazz talents like Stan Getz and Jimmy Smith and such nontalents as Mary Ann Mobley, Freddie Bell, and Roberta Linn.

Other rock 'n' roll teenpics followed Katzman's, including *Rock, Pretty Baby* (1956), *Shake, Rattle, and Rock!* (1956), and *The Girl Can't Help It* (1956). As other musical fads came and went, other producers proved Katzman's equal in linking a film with a particular movement within youth culture. James Nicholson's "Beach Party" series for American International Pictures, for example, capitalized on the interest in surf-rock with bands like the Kingsmen and Dick Dale and the Del-Tones. In the seventies, producers Robert Stigwood and Allan Carr would cash in on the disco craze with *Saturday Night Fever* (1977) and *Can't Stop the Music* (1980), respectively.

While Katzman and his early imitators are sometimes credited with validating both rock 'n' roll and teenage culture, their contribution to the development of the compilation score is both more particularized and more directly related to the narrative structures of Katzman's so-called jukebox musicals. Working a variation of the backstage musical, the "jukebox" narrative is typically concerned with the problems of putting on a rock 'n' roll show in the face of adult opposition to both the new music and the teenage lifestyle. As such, the narrative is to some extent a pretext for a series of musical numbers performed by a variety of singers and musicians.[8] Rock and rollers played alongside crooners and chanteuses in a manner that not only gave the films a broader appeal but also elevated the tastes of teens to that of adults.[9] At the same time, however, this emphasis on variety is in some measure a clear concession to teenage patterns of consumption. Singles sales and jukebox revenues were markedly dominated by the teen dollar, and in conforming the series of performances to the ebb and flow of the jukebox, the rock 'n' roll teenpics emphasized the collection of singles format that accorded with adolescent subcultural experience.

Thomas Wiener points out that the variety of performers served a second role in the promotion of the film:

> Producers of these films believed in being hip only to the extent that they didn't get caught showcasing a singer or group that would be out of style by the time the film was released. Selecting which acts to employ was risky; thus a wide variety of acts in nearly all the rock movies of this era. If one group's star had fallen by the time of the film's release, then the next might still be on every jukebox in America.[10]

This stress on spreading risk helps to explain the specific form of the compilation score. By using a number of songs and recording artists, film producers and record executives hedged their bets in a couple of ways. For one thing, the careers of lesser-known artists might be boosted by grouping them together with established stars. In addition, the miscellany of recording artists would give the score and soundtrack album broader appeal by reaching a number of different segments of the music marketplace.

Such diversity was especially important in the late sixties when the audience was increasingly fragmented into discrete demographic groups and the charts were splintered by rock's growth into a number of distinct styles. Rock was no longer one entity but encompassed such varied forms as British pop, folk-rock, psychedelia, blues-rock, heavy metal, and even country-rock. Both of these considerations may help explain such odd assemblages as Tony Bennett, Frankie Laine, and Hank Williams in *The Last Picture Show*, and Patti Page, the Grateful Dead, and Pink Floyd in *Zabriskie Point*. Instead of using many performers to market the same song on different labels as was done in the early sixties, the compilation score assembled many performers and many recordings to market a single product—the soundtrack album.

While variety is one distinguishing feature of the compilation score, another is the use of discrete tunes as underscore. In many ways, this is the more significant of the two features in that it clearly differentiates the compilation score from the adapted score of the film musical. Each is structured as a series of numbers, but the compilation score does not feature its songs as part of a narratively integrated, diegetically motivated performance. In contrast, the typical pop song in dramatic films is, according to Claudia Gorbman, "set within the context of naturalistic acting, [and] is most often performed on the soundtrack by musicians with no pretense of a relation to the diegesis."[11] Though Gorbman here is characterizing film music in the age of MTV, her description applies as well to late sixties scores like *Easy Rider*, *Zabriskie Point*, and *The Graduate*.

The latter films were groundbreaking in their use of rock music as underscore, but their approach to the narrative relations of image and sound was not entirely unprecedented. While critics point to films as diverse as *Baby Doll* (1956), *Viridiana* (1961), and *What's New, Pussycat?* (1965) as sources of this scoring practice, two films are particularly pertinent for my purposes: *A Hard Day's Night* (1964) and the underground classic *Scorpio Rising* (1963). The former presaged the development of the aural-visual set piece that later became a staple of rock scoring while the latter used rock as a kind of referential intertext capable of commenting on or satirizing the image track.

At first glance, *A Hard Day's Night* would seem to be precisely the type of backstage musical I earlier argued was distinct from the compilation score. A fictional depiction of a typical day in the life of the Beatles, the Fab Four are featured rehearsing, playing, and dancing to a collection of songs recorded especially for the film. During the occasional moments that use nondiegetic underscore, musical director George Martin displays an array of different approaches to the relation between music and image. The police chases at the end of the film, for example, show Martin adhering to the conventions of theme scoring. Like Mancini, Martin uses a Big Band swing arrangement of the title tune as a neutral background which plays against the knockabout farce of the chase. For other moments, such as Ringo's escapades while parading, Martin uses an instrumental version of the Beatles' song "This Boy" to bring out the character's sudden sense of isolation and awkwardness.

While both of these instances seem conventional in their use of songs as themes, the famous "Can't Buy Me Love" sequence was altogether different. When the boys decide to play hooky from answering their fan mail, they run outside to a nearby field. To the strains of their song, John, Paul, George, and Ringo joyfully jump, hop, and romp in a series of quickly cut shots. Mixing fast and slow motion with a series of unusual camera angles, director Richard Lester created a rapid montage sequence that was a unified aural and visual whole. As Ehrenstein and Reed note, because the Beatles were not trained dancers, Lester used the rhythm of the music and elements of film style to give the impression of dynamic dancelike movement.[12]

In *Help!* (1965), Lester pushed this style even further by intercutting knockabout scenes of the boys skiing and carousing on a beach with footage of the band performing "Ticket to Ride" and "Another Girl," respectively. As Stephen Holden observes, Lester's work "presaged the music-video era with its jump-cut editing and very loose organization of action around the songs."[13] The importance of Lester's influence was tangibly demonstrated when the "Can't Buy Me Love" sequence from *A Hard Day's Night* was simply excerpted and shown on MTV as a music video.

Yet while the Beatles' films are notable precursors of music video, these sequences had more immediate consequences for film scoring. More than anything else, they proved that rock music could be used as underscore for filmed action; a director simply had to use the music in a proper context or treat it as an element equal to the image. The lyrics of the songs were largely immaterial to the narrative, but the feel of each captured the emotional colors of individual scenes and collectively they reflected the mocking visual and verbal wit often described in commentaries on the film.

Still, the music of *A Hard Day's Night* and *Help!* promised more than it delivered in terms of scoring innovations. Though the music accompanies visual action in each, it remains tied to a loose notion of performance. Sequences of the Beatles rehearsing or performing predominate the films in a manner not unlike the jukebox musical. The "Can't Buy Me Love" sequence would seem an exception, but even here the performance element creeps into the sequence in the notion of the Beatles as either dancers or slapstick comedians.

To find a more thorough application of rock music as underscore, we must look to two other sources: Michael Roemer's *Nothing But a Man* (1964) and Kenneth Anger's *Scorpio Rising*. Roemer's film may well be the first feature-length narrative to avail itself of a pop compilation score. Through an arrangement with Berry Gordy and Motown Records, the film's producers were able to feature songs by such acclaimed rhythm-and-blues artists as Stevie Wonder, Martha and the Vandellas, and Smokey Robinson and the Miracles in this tale of a black man's struggle to overcome the small indignities and humiliations of living in a white-dominated society.

Nothing But a Man uses its slate of rhythm-and-blues songs, however, in a manner not unlike early appearances of jazz in cinema. In keeping with the film's emphasis on realism, Roemer uses very little nondiegetic music and instead motivates these popular Motown hits as part of the film's social milieu. The songs are heard coming out of churches, ghetto radios, and bar jukeboxes, and the music functions largely as a handy signifier of the film's black urban setting. Reinforcing this impression is the relatively modest treatment the music receives in the film. The songs are typically used to underscore dialogue and thus are mixed at relatively low volume on the soundtrack. Because Roemer rarely gives the film's music any prominence—the performance of a gospel choir is a notable exception—these songs are used less for their expressive features than for their textual qualities. In other words, the songs in *Nothing But a Man* serve no dramatic functions other than as ambient background noise and cultural touchstones of the film's contemporary Southern locales.

A more significant precursor of the compilation score can be found in Kenneth Anger's avant-garde classic *Scorpio Rising*. The film is structured around thirteen pop songs which, aside from a few sound effects, make up its entire soundtrack. For Ed Lowry, the songs not only demarcate individual segments, but they also serve as a set of pop culture fragments which the film appropriates and invests with its own meanings.[14]

The most famous example of this is undoubtedly the film's "Blue Velvet" sequence, during which a primping Scorpio dresses to the strains of the Bobby Vinton ballad. As Lowry notes, the juxtaposition of music and image here brings out a disturbing, fetishistic element concealed in the song's apparently innocuous lyrics. At the same time, however, the melodramatic romanticism of Vinton's singing provides a homoerotic slant to the cyclist's adornment of denim and leather. The mutually implicative structure of music and image in this example would prove to be a key feature of the compilation score. As with *Scorpio Rising*, much of the compilation score's power would derive from the manipulation of preexisting associations attached to a particular song or musical style.

Interestingly, the two filmic traditions I have discussed so far, the teenpic and the avant-garde, came together in *Easy Rider*. According to Doherty, "The film is an amalgam of virtually every teenpic type that thrived in the 1950s: vice, motorcycles, rock 'n' roll, delinquency, and even weirdies."[15] By updating the teenpic formula in the late sixties, *Easy Rider* capitalized on youth culture in a manner that promised tremendous profit for very little risk. In cannily adapting the strategies of the fifties exploitation filmmaker, producer Peter Fonda and Raybert Productions turned a $375,000 investment into an estimated worldwide gross of $50 million.[16] Rock and roll was not only a crucial part of that strategy, but it earned its makers additional revenues in the form of a Top Ten soundtrack album.

Besides rummaging through the tropes of the teenpic, *Easy Rider* also appropriates several underground film conventions. David James not only cites *Scorpio Rising* as the model for *Easy Rider*'s rock music but also calls attention to the film's borrowing of avant-garde visual and narrative motifs, such as the use of flash cutting between shots, the subjective camerawork of the psychedelic interlude, and the loose journey structure, which he sees derived from the work of Bruce Baillie and Stan Brakhage. Moreover, the film's depiction of drug use, sex, and "free love" broke representational taboos in a manner not unlike Andy Warhol, Jack Smith, or the Kuchar brothers. According to this line of argument, *Easy Rider* may have borrowed certain aspects of motorcycle and rock teenpics, but such borrowing was itself made possible through *Scorpio Rising*'s refashioning of the genre, and nowhere was this more apparent than in *Easy Rider*'s use of rock music as structural and ironic counterpoint.[17] *Easy Rider*'s nondiegetic rock score not only underlined the film's setting and highlighted traits of the two main characters but also served as ironic counterpoint in a way that decisively showed that the multi-artist pop compilation could be employed to pointed dramatic effect.

By the mid-sixties, the general emphasis on prerecorded songs not only altered scoring practices but had a number of consequences for the film music industry itself. For one thing, the compilation score's album orientation encouraged producers to shun Tin Pan Alley and look instead toward contemporary rock and pop artists as the source of film songs. Where producers had earlier hired specialized songwriters like Sammy Fain, Johnny Mercer, and Jimmy van Heusen, they now sought out pop and rock performers like Steppenwolf, Harry Nilsson, and the Association. For another, the compilation score diminished the importance of film composers and increased the value of music supervisors and engineers. If a film were entirely scored with prerecorded music, then the special skills of a craftsman like Elmer Bernstein, Alex North, or Dimitri Tiomkin were simply not needed.

Partly because it threatened to reduce their employment opportunities, established film composers strongly resisted the advent of the compilation score. After working for years refining the tradition of classical Hollywood film music, composers were not about to cede their position to a group of unwashed ruffians whom they believed could neither write, arrange, nor even read music.[18] Complaining of rock's ubiquity in the sixties, David Raksin declared: "It is one thing to appreciate the freshness and naïveté of pop music and quite another to accept it as inevitable no matter what the subject is at hand—and still another to realize that the choice is often made for reasons that have little to do with the film itself."[19]

Yet though composers sneered at the influx of rock music into films, it became increasingly obvious that the idiom was here to stay. While formally limited, the familiarity of pop and rock made them ideal for establishing contemporary settings and characters. The strongly referential element of rock and pop music, frequently provided by such nonmusical signifiers as lyrics and song titles, enhanced that familiarity by forcefully linking tunes to their specific cultural and historical context. It was this latter element that gave popular music its associational potency, a power that more than compensated for its formal limitations.

The Forms and Functions of the Compilation Score

In the liner notes for the *Zabriskie Point* soundtrack album, Mike Curb, the president of MGM Records, wrote, "Contemporary music doesn't merely tell a story or set a mood; it *is* the story and it *is* the mood."[20] Coming from Curb and other record executives, such self-aggrandizing claims for the value of popular music in films are unsurprising. Rock and roll helped to sell motion pictures to a burgeoning and highly desirable youth market while at the same time swelling the coffers of the parent company's subsidiaries. Though *Zabriskie Point* largely failed to reach this audience, its use of rock music as a marketing tool typified the industry's approach to youth culture during this time period. Even if kids were turned off by Michelangelo Antonioni's rather thin plotting, they could still groove to *Zabriskie Point*'s evocative imagery and music, which consisted of tunes by the Rolling Stones, the Grateful Dead, and Pink Floyd.

Still, despite its commercial impetus, *Zabriskie Point* does not represent the compilation score in its purest form. With original music specially composed for the film by Pink Floyd and Jerry Garcia, *Zabriskie Point* is one among a group of films, including *The Graduate*, *Superfly*, *Midnight Cowboy* (1969), and *Shaft* (1971), which combine a collection of songs with more traditional kinds of functional music. Though none of these films adheres to the neo-Romantic, symphonic principles of the classical Hollywood score, their composers and music supervisors nonetheless used their respective idioms—jazz, folk, and funk—to create music that was written directly to accommodate the moods, actions, and editing patterns of the film's image tracks.

In contrast to these hybrid compilation scores were films that relied exclusively on pop and rock tunes as their *only* form of music. These include not only the aforementioned *Easy Rider* but also such films as *The Harder They Come*, *The Last Picture Show*, *Mean Streets*, and *American Graffiti*. In such instances, the element of original musical composition was eliminated entirely, and the whole scoring process became simply a matter of spotting and song selection.

As Kathryn Kalinak points out, however, the chief problem with all of these compilation scores resided less in their commercialism than in the formal difficulties posed by the song's structural unity and integrity. Using Bernard Herrmann's music for *Citizen Kane* (1941) as a prototypical example, Alan Williams neatly summarizes these formal differences between the motivic cells of the classical score and the pop songs of the compilation score:

> The Kane motif (or any other of comparable length) may be heard in its entirety in a few seconds. It can slip in and out of the musical background serving as a punctuation device as well as musical characterization. It is not long enough to interrupt (unless desired) a chain of actions visually or linguistically depicted. Motifs that seem to "rise up" briefly to fill a gap in dialogue or action are frequent in the symphonic scoring of the fiction film. The popular song, on the other hand, is not nearly so malleable. Although it can be and often is thematized . . . its length renders it both more obvious—its smallest complete version would last over a minute—and more recognizable as musical entity, since it is more structured both through tonality and repetition.[21]

Because they cannot be segmented in the manner of themes or leitmotivs, the songs that comprised these rock scores seemed to ignore certain fundamental principles at the heart of the classical score. According to Kalinak, these include the use of music to illustrate narrative content, particularly the direct synchronization of music and image; the use of music to provide structural unity; and the use of music as an inaudible component of narrative signification.[22] Echoing Curb's claims, she believes that rock music committed the cardinal sin of film scoring; it failed to support the story and mood because it *was* the story and mood.

Though a number of reasons may be given for this autonomy, there are a few that are particularly pertinent to the present discussion in that they were crucial in determining the kinds of dramatic functions which compilation scores would largely serve. First of all, as I noted earlier, the pop songs of compilation scores were typically selected for a film rather than specifically composed for it. As such, these scores broke with a long-standing taboo in Hollywood scoring against using well-known music. Though this prohibition was initially directed toward classical warhorses, its underlying principles were equally applicable to preexisting popular music. Well-known music of any kind was thought to carry associational baggage for the spectator, and not only was this potentially distracting but these associations might also clash with those established by the narrative.

In the case of popular music, this associational element is exacerbated by the music's close connections with its historical and social context. Unlike classical music, which is often regarded as having a kind of universality, the perpetually changing fads and fashions of popular music furnish a kind of built-in obsolescence to the idiom, which in turn imparts a certain historical specificity to individual styles, performers, and songs. Because of this specificity, popular music is an especially effective means of denoting particular time periods. One requires very little musical acumen, for example, to recognize ragtime as a signifier of the early 1900s, Benny Goodman and "swing" as a marker of the 1930s, Elvis and rockabilly as a touchstone of the fifties, and the Eagles and disco as emblems of the seventies.

Many young filmmakers of the so-called "New Hollywood"—like Peter Bogdanovich, Martin Scorsese, and George Lucas—grew up listening to early rock and roll, and they were quick to make use of pop music's power to denote time and place. In *The Last Picture Show*, for example, the use of Hank Williams and Tony Bennett is used to evoke the atmosphere of a dying Texas town in the mid-fifties. Similarly, the mixture of opera and contemporary pop in *Mean Streets* gives viewers a strong flavor of the film's Little Italy locales.[23]

In some films, the close connection between music and setting was expressed through the comprehensive motivation of the music within the diegesis. In *American Graffiti*, for example, the radio is virtually a character in the film, one whose constant chatter and music work to provide background filler and embellish the mood of individual scenes. In *The Harder They Come*, the radio's importance is matched by that of the dance hall and recording studio. Together these spaces—and the music in them—serve as crucial reminders of the protagonist's central goal of achieving success as a reggae singer. In *Mean Streets*, on the other hand, the jukebox in Tony's bar serves as the privileged purveyor of the film's songs. Like the car radio in *American Graffiti*, the jukebox in *Mean Streets* functions at the center of the characters' cultural rituals and provides an aural backdrop for their dancing, drinking, debauching, and fighting.

In a manner not unlike Mancini's work, such motivation typically serves a couple of important functions. On the one hand, it creates convenient opportunities to include new tunes that will flesh out the score into a satisfying album. On the other, it allows the filmmaker to locate the music in a particular sociocultural milieu by subtly reminding viewers that the film's characters are also consumers of this music.

As Simon Frith and others point out, the consumption of particular styles of pop music and clothing often work together to create a sense of subcultural identity.[24] When these subcultural markers are widely circulated, they can serve as a quick-and-dirty means of establishing or reinforcing the traits of a character. Currently, this is illustrated by the frequent use of rap music and sports apparel to denote urban "blackness," but it is also evident in character-izations of forties hep cats (bop and zoot suits), fifties rockers (rockabilly and leather jackets), and sixties hippies (psychedelia and long hair).

But while the notion of social and historical context is vital to our compre-hension of the compilation score, the element that most commonly confers ref-erential meaning on music is undoubtedly language. As Peter Kivy, Leonard Meyer, and other music scholars point out, the meanings of a piece are often constrained by the inclusion of a title, lyrics, or program notes. In program-matic classical music, such as Berlioz's *Symphonie fantastique*, this form of rep-resentation is expressed as a relation between the piece's musical parameters and its specified subject matter.[25] According to Meyer, the significance of such works depends on the interactions of "a set of stimuli (the sounding music), a competent listener, and a cultural context (including what we know about a composition)."[26]

With songs in cinema, however, the interaction outlined by Meyer is fur-ther complicated by the presence of two forms of extramusical material: words (song titles, lyrics, and dialogue) and images. The titles and lyrics of popular music thus appear to pose many of the same scoring problems as using a well-known piece of music; the words of a song might not only be distracting but they could also create associations different from those intended by the filmmakers.

Yet as many compilation scores show, the lyrics of popular music proffer a kind of double-edged sword. Indeed they carry a certain potential for dis-traction, but their referential dimension can also be exploited to "speak for" characters or comment on a film's action. Later I will describe this aspect of the compilation score in more detail, but for now I will simply offer some clarification of how this phenomenon works. I do not mean to suggest here that audiences actively listen and comprehend song lyrics during the course of a film. Indeed, a spectator's attention is mostly directed toward the film's narrative and not toward the decipherment of often unintelligible rock lyrics. However, if the song is already well-known, then the matter of song lyrics becomes more a question of recognition rather than cognition. Instead of deciphering lyrics, viewers simply apply what they already know—a title or chorus—to the specific dramatic context that is depicted in the film.

In *The Big Chill* (1983), for example, director Lawrence Kasdan uses Marvin Gaye's classic "I Heard It Through the Grapevine" to underscore the credit sequence during which each of the film's eight main characters is shown reacting to the news of their friend's suicide. In this example, viewers familiar with the song are encouraged to use the song's chorus ("I heard it through the grapevine, and I'm just about to lose my mind") to interpret the present dramatic situation. As such, the chorus is removed from its original context, which describes a lover's infidelity, and instead serves to highlight the sudden sense of anguish felt in response to a comrade's death. Here, as with other compilation scores, one need not have a thorough understanding of the song's lyrics but simply the minimal information supplied by the song's title and chorus.

In instances such as this one, the compilation score functions as a two-tiered system of communication not unlike that described by Noël Carroll in "The Future of Allusion." In that essay, Carroll considers how filmmakers of the sixties and seventies used allusion to film history as an expressive device. This allusionism involved not only quotations and homages to classic films but also the reworking of genres and the recreation of famous shots, scenes, plot patterns, and themes of canonical Hollywood films. Filmmakers utilized a number of strategies to achieve this allusionistic play, including outright mimicry; the inclusion of famous clips in new films; the reinscription of outdated film styles; and the arch play of titles on theater marquees, television screens, and posters in the background of shots.

According to Carroll, filmmakers used these allusionistic devices such that their films could address two kinds of audiences simultaneously. On one level, the film was a "genre film pure and simple," and it communicated to the average filmgoers who made up the lion's share of Hollywood's audience;[27] on a second level, however, the film engaged a cine-literate audience in a form of self-conscious, referential gamesmanship. At this higher level, the viewer is asked to both remember past films and to recognize these allusions as a kind of "hermeneutic filter" through which audiences distill the director's attitudes toward the characters, plots, and actions of his films.[28] Perhaps this system's most important feature is the complementarity of these two tiers. The second tier does not negate a general audience's understanding of the film's use of genre conventions, but rather enriches the film's expressive qualities for an informed viewer.

Allusions to pop music function in much the same manner as the system described by Carroll. On one level, an audience of uninformed viewers may interpret the song as background music pure and simple. As such, they may make judgments regarding the overall style and its appropriateness to considerations of setting, character, and mood. However, an audience of informed viewers will recognize the song's title, lyrics, or performer, and will apply this knowledge to the dramatic context depicted onscreen. In such a way, musical allusion also serves as an expressive device to either comment on the action or suggest the director's attitude toward the characters, settings, and themes of the film.

Not coincidentally, many of the filmmakers Carroll identifies as practitioners of this cinematic allusionism were also proponents of the compilation score. These include not only Bogdanovich, Lucas, Scorsese, and Dennis Hopper but also such "New Hollywood" luminaries as Francis Ford Coppola (*You're a Big Boy Now*, 1967), Robert Altman (*McCabe and Mrs. Miller*, 1971; *Nashville*, 1975), Hal Ashby (*Harold and Maude*, 1971; *Coming Home*, 1978), and Lawrence Kasdan (*The Big Chill*). As one reviewer noted in 1974, the use of pop music in films had become "virtually a trademark of young directors."[29] And just as these filmmakers used a variety of strategies in making allusions to films, they also used musical allusionism toward a number of different ends. Space does not allow a complete inventory of these approaches, but I will offer a description of two general areas that seem particularly significant—the use of musical allusionism to "speak" for characters, and the use of music to reinforce narrative or generic themes.

As Karlin and Wright point out, a number of approaches can be taken to the issue of a song's lyrical content, but all of them are concerned in one way or another with the problem of character.[30] This was especially true of New Hollywood films where the use of music became an even more important tool for delineating character goals and exploring psychological states. David Bordwell and Janet Staiger have previously discussed the extent to which New Hollywood directors borrowed various techniques and formal principles from the European art cinema.[31] Among these elements was a concentration on ambivalent or unmotivated protagonists, who sometimes spent the bulk of a film searching for the sources of their own disaffection.

Easy Rider, for example, treats its protagonists, Billy (Dennis Hopper) and Captain America (Peter Fonda), as analogs of the rootless, unmotivated characters commonly found in European art cinema. Though the narrative identifies their ostensible goal as reaching New Orleans in time for Mardi Gras, the film only hinted at the unspoken beliefs and aspirations that drove them to undertake their seemingly questless journey. By thematizing this ambiguity in terms of a picaresque narrative, *Easy Rider* utilized music to tell the "story" not told in the film's visuals and dialogue and to fill the void at the characters' hollow center. The film may equivocate about Billy and Captain America's mores and motivations, but the film's music and lyrics offer important thematic cues regarding their self-image. Steppenwolf's "Born to be Wild," for example, sets the film's tone over the credits by capturing the sense of power that fuels the character's nomadic drive. The images of "smoke and lightning" and "heavy metal thunder" at once link the characters with their natural environs and proffer the search for control that underlies the bikers' pursuit of freedom. The Byrds' "I Wasn't Born to Follow" even more explicitly underscores the characters' sense of rugged individuality. If the Steppenwolf and Byrds music hints at a kind of existential freedom at the heart of the "road" experience, Jimi Hendrix's "If 6 Were 9" overtly politicizes this feeling and places it within a cultural context. Describing a world that is literally turned upside down, Hendrix portrays the hippies' "freak flag" as an antiestablishment, antiauthoritarian gesture against the "white collar conservatives" and "businessmen" who symbolize a "plastic" official culture.

With *Easy Rider*'s music providing a detailed, referential system of communication, Captain America and Billy need do little to express this sense of individuality and this desire for freedom. Whether peddling drugs, smoking pot, skinny-dipping, or simply riding, the music provides a schema with which we may interpret the significance of the characters' actions. In other words, Captain America and Billy need not communicate their goals and desires verbally; they simply must embody them, and the music itself will serve to specify these goals through individual character traits.

In *The Graduate*, songs by Simon and Garfunkel serve to similarly flesh out important traits of its young protagonist, Benjamin Braddock. Certainly both the narrative and Dustin Hoffman's performance suggest the awkwardness and uneasiness felt by Ben upon his return from college, but the film's music specifies this discomfort by rooting it in a deeper sense of generational alienation and ennui. "The Sounds of Silence," for example, dominates the first part of the film and cues us to Ben's profound sense of loneliness. "Mrs. Robinson," on the other hand, clarifies the source of this disaffection by alluding to Ben's increasing estrangement from an older generation he sees as hypocritical and morally bankrupt.

In still other instances, the compilation score highlights the element of authorial expressivity by commenting *on* characters rather than speaking from their point of view. These cases differ from the ones just discussed in that musical allusionism is used to underline traits which a character may not wish to acknowledge. An example of this in *Mean Streets* is discussed by Ehrenstein and Reed, who describe how the Rolling Stones' "Tell Me" is used to underscore the narcissistic swagger of Charlie's (Harvey Keitel) entry into his neighborhood hangout. Similarly, in *The Last Picture Show*, "Cold, Cold Heart" is used during a scene in Jacy's (Cybill Shepherd) bedroom to depict her as manipulative and insensitive.[32] Such examples do not offer a more objective view of character, but instead make manifest the element of authorial commentary inherent in this type of musical narration.

Thus, while it is true that New Hollywood directors often strived for art cinema's emphasis on ambivalent protagonists, it is also true that they used pop songs to clarify particularly murky or uncertain aspects of character. The lyrics of these songs gave voice to feelings and attitudes that were not made explicit by other structures of the text. In making these features of character more legible, these filmmakers subordinated one element of art cinema in order to highlight others, namely authorial expressivity and more self-conscious narration. The effect of this was that New Hollywood directors could have their cake and eat it too; by using music to "speak for" characters, filmmakers could fill in some of the problematic gaps of causality and motivation while at the same time maintaining the veneer of more complex and realistic characterization. Like the New Hollywood's use of style and genre, the operations of the compilation score suggest a more self-conscious use of music, but one firmly ensconced within the boundaries of classical narration.

Besides fleshing out characters, musical allusionism was also used to emphasize particular generic or narrative themes. I have already touched on some of these points in my discussion of *Easy Rider* and *The Graduate*. In both films, the score serves to specifically highlight themes of generational disaffection, independence, and identity. More interesting perhaps are those instances in which allusions to theme are rendered as references to performers rather than songs. Although this strategy is relatively rare, a couple of examples are particularly illustrative of pop's ability to convey thematic subtext.

The first instance comes from *Mean Streets*. In a very brief scene, a local Vietnam vet is shown attacking his girlfriend inside Tony's club. This little scene of domestic brutality is staged directly in front of the club's jukebox, which rather ironically bleats Johnny Ace's classic ballad, "Pledging My Love." On one level, the scene offers an example of musical counterpoint similar to the juxtaposition of music and violence seen in the famous "Singin' in the Rain" sequence of *A Clockwork Orange* (1971). In this instance, we see the vet beat this woman, and the soundtrack offers a direct emotional contrast to the action in Ace's promises of everlasting love and fidelity. For viewers familiar with Ace's career, however, this simple musical counterpoint is given richer and darker thematic implications by our knowledge of the performer's biography. During the 1950s, Ace attained a certain ignominy among popular music fans by accidentally killing himself in a game of Russian roulette. For viewers who recognize the allusion to Ace, the music underlines an element of self-destructive fury that is only hinted at in the brief scenario of domestic violence. Perhaps more importantly, the allusion links this peripheral moment to a larger pattern of violent male machismo depicted within the film. The subtext of Russian roulette hinted at by the music recontextualizes the vet's actions by thematizing it as a sort of masculine rite of passage. Like Charlie, Johnny Boy (Robert De Niro), and the other male characters, the vet can only express himself by externalizing a self-destructive inner rage.

The Last Picture Show refers to Hank Williams's life in much the same manner that *Mean Streets* uses Johnny Ace. To be sure, the film clearly thematizes the decline of this stagnant, dying Texas town at a number of points in the narrative, including the closing of the local movie house and the deaths of Sam the Lion (Ben Johnson) and Billy (Sam Bottoms). Nevertheless, this theme of decay is immeasurably enriched by our awareness of Williams's music and our knowledge of his life. On New Year's Day in 1953, Williams died of heart failure in the back seat of an off-duty cab which was driving him to his next show. Only twenty-nine, Williams's pathetic death was hastened by a combination of alcohol and pills. Even before his demise, however, Williams was frequently jailed for his alcohol binges during his early years of stardom. The combination of substance abuse and deep depression contributed to the collapse of his marriage, and in his last days Williams lived as a lonely man, despondent despite the fame that came from his brilliant career as a country and western singer.

Thus, even though the theme of rural decay is clearly expressed in the film's narrative and visual style, *The Last Picture Show*'s most penetrating symbol of this decadence is undoubtedly Williams himself. By constantly alluding to the late singer on the soundtrack, the film underlines the despair that pervades the characters' environs of run-down poolhalls, dumpy cafes, and seedy hotel rooms. In other words, *The Last Picture Show* not only portrays the passing of a frontier—ironically alluded to in Howard Hawks' *Red River* (1948)—but also uses the music of Hank Williams to suggest that what remains is a life of quiet desperation, desolation, and death.

In summary, the compilation score maintains a rather unusual status in the way it typically serves film music's standard narrative functions. Though the formal autonomy of song structures problematizes certain kinds of audiovisual correspondence, filmmakers could overcome these limitations by using the associational aspects of pop music to cue settings, character traits, and dramatic situations. In the next section of this chapter, I will look at *American Graffiti* as a contemporary prototype of the compilation score. In doing so, I will show that the film's careful integration of music and narrative provides a perfect synthesis of the compilation score's narrational possibilities. As the production and critical reception of *American Graffiti* indicate, the narrative structure, themes, and visual style of the film are inextricably interwoven with the meanings of rock and roll itself.

Rock and Roll Is Here to Stay: The Case of *American Graffiti*

While it is perhaps not as historically significant as *Easy Rider* or *The Graduate*, George Lucas's *American Graffiti* is especially apt terrain for close textual analysis. Perhaps more than any other film, *American Graffiti* makes extensive use of the kind of musical allusionism discussed in the previous section. In scene after scene, musical allusions serve to underline the subtext of a scene, offer critical commentary on a dramatic situation, or even foreshadow later developments in the narrative. Moreover, *American Graffiti* also offers an interesting case study in that none of the forty-one songs played during the film is ever repeated. This not only highlights a crucial difference between the rock score and the classical score, it also raises a significant question regarding the compilation score's textual operations. With no structural repetition, the rock score would appear to have no device comparable to the leitmotivs or themes of the classical score. Does the rock score function only at the localized level of the individual scene? Or can the rock score use a different strategy to underscore character, narrative, and thematic patterns that develop across a film?

When *American Graffiti* was released in August 1973, few of those involved in the project had any inkling of the great critical and commercial success the film would earn. Two years later, however, *Graffiti* had become one of the most profitable films ever made. On an initial investment of $1.3 million dollars, *Graffiti* earned more than $50 million in total rentals during the first two years of its release, an almost fifty-to-one profit ratio that even subsequent Lucas hits, such as *Star Wars* (1977) and Spielberg's *Raiders of the Lost Ark* (1981; Lucas was executive producer and cowrote the story), would prove unable to match.[33] In amassing this sum, *Graffiti* not only made enormous profits for its distributor, Universal Pictures, but it also placed its director at the forefront of a new generation of so-called "movie brats."

Central to the film's appeal, of course, was the nostalgic soundtrack of rock 'n' roll oldies heard throughout it. Surprisingly though, Universal executives initially dragged their feet at the prospect of so much music in the film. Citing large licensing fees, Universal urged Lucas to cut his initial list of some eighty songs down to about five or six. A compromise was reached when

Lucas pruned his original list to forty-five songs and cut out many of the most expensive tunes, such as those by Elvis Presley.[34]

Yet even as Universal gave in to Lucas on the issue of mechanical rights, they nonetheless refused his additional request for money to acquire the album rights. According to Michael Pye and Lynda Myles, Lucas asked for a mere $10,000, but was denied when Universal claimed that *Graffiti*'s box office potential did not warrant the extra expenditure.[35] After a successful test screening, during which audience members reportedly sang along with the soundtrack, Universal began to change their tune.[36] When this was followed by a triumphant premiere at Westwood's Avco Theater, Universal did a complete turnaround. Now, however, with the success of the film becoming more obvious, the asking price for the soundtrack rights had suddenly risen from $10,000 to $50,000 for the very same material.[37] As it turned out, *Graffiti*'s $90,000 music budget, a figure that accounted for over 10 percent of the film's production costs, was well worth its relatively high price tag. The *Graffiti* soundtrack was released as a double album by Universal's parent company, MCA, and within five months it had sold more than 500,000 copies. The album went on to sell over a million copies and spent forty-one weeks on *Billboard*'s album charts.

In retrospect, the popularity of *American Graffiti* should not seem as unexpected as Lucas's biographers would have it. In fact, the film and album rode the crest of a rising tide of nostalgia for fifties rock 'n' roll. As *Variety* reported in January 1974, the whole nostalgia cycle had reached a certain saturation point. Music promoter Richard Nader, for example, produced a series of rock and roll revival shows between 1969 and 1973 which grossed over $5 million dollars, including one fourteen-day stint at Madison Square Garden that alone earned more than $1.2 million. Interest in Nader's shows peaked in 1973 when the promoter staged over fifty of them between January and June. Just a few months earlier, Chuck Berry enjoyed his first hits in more than eight years with "Reelin' and Rockin' " and the chart-topping "My Ding-a-Ling." And throughout 1973, fifties music was also showcased on television in late-night programs like *In Concert* and *The Midnight Special*, in various syndicated formats, and in a popular Dick Clark anniversary special.[38] As all these outlets for fifties music indicate, there was a burgeoning interest in nostalgia at the time of *Graffiti*'s release, which the film simply tapped into and exploited.

As important as these oldies were to the marketplace, however, they were perhaps even more vital to other aspects of *Graffiti*'s production and critical reception. The rock music and rock culture depicted in *American Graffiti* infused the creative process of the film in three ways: by serving the overall narrative structure; by informing the film's visual design; and by offering a convenient interpretive schema for the journalists and magazine critics who reviewed the film.

Unlike many films in which the music is spotted and composed after the visual track is completed, the songs of *American Graffiti* were very carefully integrated into the development of the script. In fact, according to Dale Pollock, when Lucas originally pitched his treatment to various studios, he played up the importance of these songs by explicitly defining the film as a "musical." Wrote Lucas, "It has singing and dancing, but it is not a musical in the traditional sense because the characters of the film neither sing nor dance."[39] In developing this "musical" element, Lucas allegedly wrote the first drafts of his screenplay with an old 1941 Wurlitzer jukebox playing in the background.[40]

When screenwriters Willard Huyck and Gloria Katz were brought in on the project, Lucas explained the film's complicated, interwoven plot structure to them and calculated that each of the film's planned forty-eight scenes would run about two and a half minutes, or the length of a popular song. Huyck and Katz were, according to Pollock, initially baffled by Lucas's plan, but soon realized that the song-per-scene strategy kept the story constantly moving.[41] As the script underwent further revisions, Lucas, Huyck, Katz, and sound designer Walter Murch had lengthy discussions about which song should go with which scene.[42] Since he did not wish the songs to mimic the characters' actions, Lucas tried to fit them to scenes "on the basis of mood and melody, rather than lyrics."[43]

Whether by accident or design, the songs in *American Graffiti* played a significant part during the whole process of developing the screenplay, and one does indeed find numerous parallels between songs and situations throughout the film. In explicating his working methods, however, Lucas's comments recall the two-tiered system of communication described by Carroll. In attempting to match mood and melody, Lucas suggests that the music will on one level serve some of the traditional roles of the classical Hollywood score for a general audience. At a second level, however, the allusive aesthetic of the music encourages viewers to discover parallels between music and action. For a coterie of rock fans familiar with the songs, the music serves as a form of authorial commentary regarding what Lucas called the "classic teenage scenes" depicted onscreen.

Besides informing the script development, rock and roll—particularly in the form of rock culture—also helped to shape the film's overall visual design. Most reviewers discussed this influence in terms of the film's iconography. Michael Dempsey, for example, offers a tidy catalog of this imagery in his claim that "*American Graffiti* is stuffed to its customized tailpipes with little deuce coupés, rollerskating carhops, cherry cokes, copped feels, cooties, Clearasil—plus lots of vintage pop songs."[44]

Elements of rock 'n' roll culture also inspired certain aspects of the film's lighting and camerawork. Working with cameraman Haskell Wexler, Lucas sought a kind of "jukebox lighting," an amber ambience that resembled the light from a "1962 'Hot Rods to Hell' jukebox."[45] This lighting motif was originally to be introduced in the film's opening shot, which would begin on a huge amber light and steadily pull back to reveal the various numbers and markings of a car radio dial. Jukeboxes and radios, however, were not the only sources of the film's golden lighting scheme. In a 1974 interview, Lucas cited early rock and roll movies as well, stating that he wanted "the film to look sort of like a Sam Katzman beach-party movie, all yellow and red and orange."[46]

As a virtual inventory of rock 'n' roll cultural markers, the film encouraged audiences and reviewers alike to see the music as the very essence of the picture. Commonly this was expressed as a kind of nostalgia or emotional memory stimulated by the period songs on the soundtrack. In some instances, however, rock and roll supplied an overarching interpretive schemata for the film, one that could be extended to discuss the film's tone and narrative structure. Stephen Farber, for example, writes, "The film has the spirit of rock music—bold, confident, colloquial, casually lyrical, unpretentious, but evocative; it is a tribute to the beauty of American graffiti."[47] Joseph Kanon, on the other hand, staked even grander claims for the film's music:

> But Lucas does more than use pop music for emotional effects (the matching of the pace of scenes with their musical backgrounds is superb); he has taken over the very forms and rhythms of pop music. *American Graffiti* has no traditional structure—it is weakest, in fact, when it interjects "story" elements into the flow—because it works the way pop music does: it depends on pace, energy, and selection of images that will set up resonance with its audience. Its shots are often like rock lyrics—simple, hard, and filled with implications. It's a new, loose way of working in movies and the success of *American Graffiti* may well encourage others to try it.[48]

Despite the amount of verbiage expended on the music of *American Graffiti*, the analysis of its actual operations in the film has been, at best, piecemeal and fragmentary.[49] Critics often describe certain correspondences of music and action, such as the use of "Why Do Fools Fall in Love?" as Curt

(Richard Dreyfuss) first spies the mysterious blonde, but they typically only mention these moments in passing. Certainly, individual scenes offer this kind of musical commentary, but is it accurate to ascribe it to the film as a whole? And does the musical commentary only function in this moment-to-moment fashion, or do the various songs create identifiable motifs, themes, or patterns that can be traced across the entire film?

To answer these questions, I will examine some of the music's narrational functions in *American Graffiti*. Although the allusiveness of the music opens up a number of interpretive possibilities, I will discuss the music in terms of its relation to setting, character, and authorial commentary. Moreover, although I propose to treat the score as a whole, I do not mean to imply that my reading of the music closes off further interpretive possibilities. Rather my reading is merely one of a number of potential interpretations. In fact, a common theme of the film's initial reviews was the notion that the nostalgic aspect of the music opened up vast associational networks of spectatorial memory and affect. The film's ad copy ("Where were you in '62?") even made this element manifest by appearing to engage its audience in a process of personal reminscence.

A good way to start this analysis is by looking at the music's relation to the film's setting, a feature that might seem transparently obvious, but is actually subtly interwoven with the film's various themes. The plot of *American Graffiti* is structured around the events of a single night in the lives of four California teenagers. Two of them, Curt and Steve (then "Ronny" Howard), are celebrating their last night on the town before going off to an East Coast college; the other two, John (Paul LeMat) and Toad (Charles Martin Smith), are simply out for a night of summer fun. The actions of these (and other) characters are accompanied by an almost unending stream of music, which in its own way subtly underscores the temporality of the plot.

The song over the opening credits, "Rock Around the Clock," comically foreshadows this temporal structure by summarizing a twelve-hour period during which the song's narrator will "rock, rock, rock 'til broad daylight." Similarly, the music during the closing credits, "All Summer Long," serves to highlight the film's story time by ironically commenting on summer's end. In it, the song's narrator wistfully remembers the fun of the passing summer, but also cautions that "[It] Won't be long till summertime is through." The tune is not only a fitting comment on the film's plot, which is set on the last night of the summer of 1962, but it extends a seasonal metaphor in the film which symbolizes the protagonists' growth out of adolescence and into adulthood.

Besides this opening and closing musical gambit, the soundtrack's very design underlines the film's plot time in an even more fundamental way. As I noted earlier, the film's soundtrack is structured as a radio show with a duration roughly equivalent to that of the film's plot. The importance of this device is even more apparent when one compares the film's plot time and running time. Several hours of action are condensed during *Graffiti*'s 110-minute running time, and the almost continuous nature of the music thus serves one of the score's traditional narrational functions: to cover temporal ellipses.

By structuring the soundtrack as a radio show, the film consistently motivates the music as a part of the diegesis, and more specifically as a part of the teenage customs depicted in the film. Lucas has frequently discussed the "sociological" dimension of *Graffiti*, and the music is as much a part of this as the other archetypal teenage activities depicted in the film: cruising, drag racing, sock hops, "mooning," and other adolescent pranks. Along with the clothing, hairstyles, slang, and other minutiae of period detail, Lucas's oldies enhance the impression of the film's authenticity. The radio not only serves as an overarching form of realistic motivation for the music, it also adds a certain connotative richness by marking the film's time and place as a distinctly teenage subculture, one with its own particular rituals, dialect, and consumption patterns.

Yet while it is tempting to indulge Lucas's claim to sociological analysis, it is equally necessary to remember that the film presents us with a frankly idealized past. Though the music might initially appear exempt from this idealization, the particular selection of songs serves to romanticize the late fifties and early sixties as a lost Golden Age. As some observers point out, Wolfman Jack's program is less an accurate representation of early sixties broadcasts than it is a sampler of the different styles that predominated the early rock era.[50]

In fact, the two songs that begin and end the film are particularly important in this regard in that they metaphorically demarcate a historical period of musical "birth" and "growth." "Rock Around the Clock" (1955) and "All Summer Long" (1964) chart this evolution in a way that both underscores the film's theme of lost innocence and parallels the music to adolescent development. The Bill Haley classic, for example, not only refers back to the Sam Katzman musicals that served as Lucas's role model, but is also an almost mythical symbol of rock 'n' roll's birth. The Beach Boys' music, on the other hand, has traditionally been constructed as the capstone of an era, a synthesis and culmination of fifties styles just prior to the "British invasion."[51]

The Beach Boys' centrality to the film's evocation of lost innocence is actually highlighted by Lucas himself, who acknowledges that the band informed his own emotional memories of the period during the making of *American Graffiti*. The reasons for this might seem obvious but are worth noting. In explicitly defining a California lifestyle, the Beach Boys are the only band specifically attuned to the film's sense of time and place. Moreover, in their utopian vision of a world of cars, girls, and waves, the Beach Boys represented a time when teenage life had only one major goal: having fun. In the process of making *Graffiti*, Lucas admits that many of the film's most memorable images may have been unconsciously appropriated from Beach Boys hits:

> We discovered that you could make a whole Beach Boys album out of *American Graffiti* songs. The blonde in the T-bird is from "Fun, Fun, Fun." "I Get Around" is about cruising. You listen to the words of that and think of the movie. It wasn't intentional, but they were chronicling the period so true that when we came back and redid my childhood the way I remembered it, their songs blend right into the movie. "Little Deuce Coupe" could be about John and his deuce coupé. "All Summer Long"—which is sort of the theme song of the film—talks about T-shirts and spilling Coke on your blouse. "409" is about dragging.[52]

In between Bill Haley and the Beach Boys, however, are a number of songs that enlarge the motifs of birth, growth, and death. The Crests' "Sixteen Candles," for example, extends motifs of both birth and growth in a series of images portraying a young girl's sixteenth birthday, an event that not only celebrates birth but traditionally marks the growth into womanhood. This motif is picked up later in Johnny Burnette's "You're Sixteen—You're Beautiful (And You're Mine)." In between, Chuck Berry's "Almost Grown" takes this point even further by comically observing how the narrator's good behavior ("They ain't said I broke no rules") leads him to a job, car, and marriage. Lastly, the motif of death is established in Mark Dinning's "Teen Angel," a camp classic that melodramatically describes a sixteen-year-old girl's death in a brutal car wreck.

This death motif is also reflected in characters' comments on the music. Wolfman Jack howls, "We're gonna rock ourselves to death, baby!" John gripes, "Rock 'n' roll's been going downhill ever since Buddy Holly died." And echoing the aforementioned allusion in *Mean Streets*, Toad brags about owning a copy of "Pledging My Love" by Johnny Ace, a reference that eerily foreshadows Toad's own disappearance in Vietnam described in his end title.

Thus, *Graffiti*'s score not only cues the film's setting by aiding in the text's construction of a very particular period—adolescence in the early sixties—

but it also supports the film's thematization of this era as a bygone golden moment. As a number of critics point out, the theme of lost innocence operates on a number of important levels. At a more universal level, the film's characters are situated at a point just before they lose the innocence of childhood. At a more socially grounded level, however, the film depicts a culture historically situated before a different kind of lost innocence, a culture before the Beatles, the Kennedy assassination, Vietnam, and Watergate. Within the popular imagination, the filmic and musical evocation of setting commemorates both a universal rite of passage and a specific time when America seemed untainted by the scandal, violence, and death that would haunt our nation after the mid-sixties.

Still, while *Graffiti*'s music associationally cues setting and theme in a most generalized fashion, it also supports the text's construction of characters by creating specific patterns that develop across the text. Lucas originally planned to reiterate a certain progression in his interweaving of the four protagonists' storylines: Curt to Toad to John to Steve and then back to Curt.[53] Though the pattern proved too rigid to actually be workable in the film, it does provide us with a kind of heuristic device through which we can match the film's songs to specific characters and storylines. In charting the music across the film in this way, we see that allusions to specific songs and performers accumulate fairly stable patterns of meaning, which are keyed to the construction of the four protagonists as archetypal figures: Curt is the dreamer, Toad is the misfit, John is the rebel, and Steve is the lover.

Of the film's four protagonists, Steve is the one with the most consistent musical pattern in the film. Since his plotline concerns his relationship with Laurie (Cindy Williams), Steve's actions are almost exclusively accompanied by doo-wop styled love songs. Examples of this include the Platters' "Smoke Gets in Your Eyes," the Five Satins' "To the Aisle," The Skyliners' "Since I Don't Have You," and the aforementioned "Teen Angel." Most of these songs depict some form of romantic loss, and consequently they serve as apt thematic accompaniment for the events that follow Steve's declaration of his desire to see other people while away at school.

What is more remarkable still, however, is the extent to which these songs quite regularly anticipate or parallel the developments of this subplot. The most famous example of this is one that Lucas claims was entirely accidental. At the hop, Steve and Laurie momentarily set aside their differences to lead a dance; as they go out to the dance floor, the strains of "Smoke Gets in Your Eyes" ironically underscores the strain of their relationship. In almost perfect counterpoint, the words "My love has flown away" comment on the couple's situation—Steve is planning to fly east to college the next day. Shortly thereafter, Laurie's sudden weeping is further ironized by the singer's plaint of "Tears I cannot hide."[54]

Yet while this juxtaposition may well be accidental, the pattern it initiates is simply too explicit to be anything but design. When Laurie asks Eddie to dance, they do so to Herbie and the Heartbeats' performance of "She's So Fine," a song that narrates a young man's sudden desire for a girl and his ensuing success at stealing her away from her boyfriend. When Steve and Laurie make out in her car, the radio plays "To the Aisle," a tune that paradoxically implies that her rebuff will move the couple progressively closer to marriage. Similarly, "Since I Don't Have You" is heard when Laurie flirts with Falfa (Harrison Ford), a juxtaposition that clearly delineates her desire to make Steve jealous. Finally, when Steve learns that Laurie is riding around with Falfa, "Teen Angel" will cleverly anticipate the crash that serves to bring the couple back together.

Music also plays a vital role in constructing John's character, but in his case the songs themselves will be less important than their performers. One thing that distinguishes John from the others is that his songs generally fit the genre of rockabilly or blues. As such, the personae of the musicians themselves act as a mirror for John's character: greasy-haired, hedonistic, and rebellious. Examples include songs by Buddy Holly, Del Shannon, Chuck Berry, Johnny Burnette, and the Big Bopper.

To be sure, there are exceptions to this pattern, but even these sometimes only prove the rule. For example, when "Surfin' Safari" comes on the radio, John turns it off in a huff. Despite Carol's (Mackenzie Phillips) admiration for the Beach Boys, John complains that he hates that "surfin' shit," and laments rock's decline in the wake of Holly's death. Interestingly, John is both bemoaning Buddy Holly's actual death and the death of the rebellious spirit that Holly and other rockabilly stars embodied. Like the release of "Rock Around the Clock," Holly's demise has been constructed as one of the pivotal moments in rock history. With Holly dead, Elvis in the army, and Jerry Lee Lewis in public disfavor, rock was seemingly beset with a series of crooners and teen idols who only intermittently captured the spontaneity and excitement of the early rock legends. Even the Beach Boys, who are generally lauded by rock critics, were open to charges of blandness. As Jim Miller says of them, "Behind the pursuit of fun, you might hear a hint of tedium, or a realization that each passing day blemished the pristine Youth this culture coveted."[55] Holly's passing seems to invoke this "passing of Youth" in John's own mind. As the target of young punks with hot wheels, he has a keen sense of himself as a relic of a previous era, a time when the strip itself was, in John's words, "really something."

Toad, on the other hand, is the film's archetypal misfit, and this dimension is enhanced by the musical genre which usually accompanies his actions. While Steve is linked to love songs and John to rock performers, Toad's comic function is signified by a series of novelty songs. Buster Brown's "Fannie Mae," which is the first song given solely to the character, establishes this pattern early in the film. In fact, the song's opening line, "Won't somebody tell me what's wrong with me," tells the viewer virtually everything about the character. "Almost Grown" chronicles the travails of a young man trying to conform to societal norms, a scenario attuned to Toad's own efforts to fit in. Lloyd Price's "Ya Ya," which accompanies Toad's efforts to procure liquor, fittingly but nonsensically describes a young man's experience waiting for a date he believes will probably not come. Lastly, when Toad attempts to recover Steve's stolen car from two thugs, "Chantilly Lace"—and the allusion to the Big Bopper—acts as an ironic observation on Toad's pathetic attempts to defend himself.

As with John, there appear to be some clear exceptions to this pattern. However, as was also true of John, these exceptions frequently function as authorial commentary on Toad's situation. "He's the Great Imposter" by the Fleetwoods, for example, is clearly a love song rather than a novelty tune, but the reference to the title is an especially apt reflection of Toad's attempts to ingratiate himself with others by lying about his background or pretending to be something he is not. Similarly, "I Only Have Eyes For You," by the Flamingos, is a straight romantic ballad, but when it is juxtaposed against Toad's fumbling efforts to "make out" with Debbie (Candy Clark), the song's function becomes comic as it plays against the physical farce that appears onscreen.

Like Toad, Curt is also something of a misfit, but in his case this is caused more by his indecision than by his clumsiness or awkwardness. Of the four, Curt is clearly constructed as the intellectual, the doubter, the dreamer. Thus, of all the film's characters, he is also the one who most clearly fits the New Hollywood's appropriation of the unmotivated protagonist. As Curt is explicitly identified as directionless and ambivalent, the music associated with him is something of a mixed bag. Nonetheless, though the music selected for his scenes is more hetergeneous than the others, there is a consistent thematic strand that weaves its way throughout his numbers. This strand enhances the inwardness and sensitivity of the character by playing up the philosophical side of his personality. As such, the aforementioned "Why Do Fools Fall in Love?"

sequence not only highlights Curt's sudden infatuation but also expresses a series of apparently unanswerable questions ("Why do birds sing so gay?"; "Why does rain fall from up above?"; "Why do fools fall in love?").

Later, the Platters' "The Great Pretender" touches on Curt's inwardness by linking him to the song's narrator, a forlorn lover who puts on a public face to hide his pain and loneliness. During his visit to the radio station, Curt's search for self is paralleled by Sonny Till and the Orioles' "Crying in the Chapel." In fact, as Curt gets out of his car, the juxtaposition of the steeple-like radio tower with the following lyrics cleverly comments on his continuing self-doubts:

> *I searched and I searched,*
> *But I couldn't find,*
> *No way on earth,*
> *To find peace of mind.*

The religious nature of the song characterizes Curt's interaction with the Wolfman as a kind of epiphanic moment. Not only does Curt know something none of the other characters do (the identity of the Wolfman), he leaves the station with a much stronger sense of purpose. While underlining Curt's dilemma, the song doubly comments on the Wolfman's situation within the diegesis. Having had his share of travel and experience, the Wolfman (figure 7.1) is content to stay within the confines of his "chapel"—the radio station—where he links other young people together during their own search for identity.

The importance of their conversation is further paralleled by the song that follows, the Heartbeats' "A Thousand Miles Away." The reference here specifically underscores Wolfman's entreaty to explore the "great, big beautiful world out there." The Wolfman, like Curt's teacher Mr. Wolfe (who has advised Curt to go East), is one who has experienced the world outside Modesto, California, but who, like the singer of the song, has ultimately returned home. It seems there is little to distinguish these adult role models from the other characters except their own sad recognition that there is very little in Modesto for anyone with hope or ambition.

So far, I have charted patterns of musical significance that correspond with each of the film's four protagonists. Though the overarching form of this correspondence is somewhat unusual, the function itself is not. Indeed, as I noted in previous chapters, a common function of all film music involves underscoring character traits, signifying points of view, and expressing emotional states. *American Graffiti* merely magnifies that function in its roughly one-song-per-scene format. As we move from one storyline to another, the asso-

FIGURE 7.1 The late Wolfman Jack plays a mysterious disk jockey in George Lucas's *American Graffiti* (1973). The radio booth is the source of much of the film's music.

ciational matching of song to situation clearly signals changes in the film's tone and rhythm, and provides a helpful interpretive schema for understanding the dramatic undercurrents of an individual scene.

How do we motivate this continuous correspondence between music and character, song and situation? Two possible explanations present themselves, each of them corresponding to one level of the compilation score's two-tiered system of communication. On the one hand, the incessant sourcing of the music within the diegesis invites us to postulate a realistic motivation. After all, the songs are characteristic of the film's time period, and the consumption of radio music was and is common among real-life teenagers. At this level, the music serves as conventional background to the events of the narrative and communicates elements of setting and character to an amorphous, general audience. On the other hand, however, the knowledgeable spectator's recognition of text and title allows these musical allusions to function as a kind of ironic reflection on the characters and their situations. At this level, the matching of song and situation is simply too consistent to be explained as either verisimilitude or happenstance. Rather it makes more sense to suggest that this more self-conscious musical narration is an element of authorial commentary, and further that this links this score and other compilation scores to the advent of the "New Hollywood." As with the references to films, the pattern of musical allusions here serves as an expressive device by acting as a vehicle for the director's attitudes toward specific characters and situations.

Nowhere is this more apparent than in those instances that "defamiliarize" the song's original context. Reviewers have often called attention to particularly notable cases, such as "Smoke Gets in Your Eyes" or "Why Do Fools Fall in Love?" but *American Graffiti* abounds with examples that function as a kind of nonspecific reference to a song's title or performer. Indeed, some of the film's humor derives from this witty juxtaposition of music and narrative. Apart from several instances already mentioned, Buddy Holly's "Maybe Baby" underscores Toad's comic attempts to illegally purchase booze and to score with Debbie. Similarly, Fats Domino's "Ain't That a Shame" accompanies one of Curt's visions of the blonde, but in this instance he is ironically trapped in a car with the Pharaohs. The Silhouettes' "Get a Job" is used when the Pharaohs loot an arcade of pinball machines, an apparently apt commentary on society's view of these juvenile delinquents. Bobby Freeman's "Do You Wanna Dance" underscores John's impromptu race with Falfa down a city street, a juxtaposition that humorously equates a driver's dare with a lover's plea. Buddy Knox's "Party Doll" accompanies the Pharaohs' claims that the blonde is really a call girl. "Come Go with Me," by the Del-Vikings, acts as a comic invitation for the police to chase down Curt and the Pharaohs; they try to do so, but have the rear axles of their vehicle ripped off. Finally, "Goodnight, Well It's Time to Go," by the Spaniels, aptly underscores the scene of Curt's departure and serves as a fitting farewell to the film's other characters and as an appropriate close to the evening's activities.

Although they strongly differed from their classical Hollywood predecessors, *American Graffiti*'s soundtrack and other compilation scores opened up new possibilities for using rock and other pop idioms in film scoring. As accompaniments to montages or as atmospheric underscore, compilation scores served all of the classical score's paradigmatic functions, but they tended toward those that maximized rock and roll's special sense of sociocultural specificity. For a new generation of filmmakers who had grown up on early rock music, the idiom served as a handy and evocative signifier of specific times and places. Moreover, by alluding to particular titles, lyrics, or performers, filmmakers created a kind of two-tiered system of musical communication that augmented and enhanced a larger pattern of allusions to literature, art, popular culture, and cinema. Like this larger system, the patterns of musical allusions could be interwoven with the text's larger configurations of character, theme, and authorial expression. *American Graffiti* offers an especially good illustration of this, but one might just as easily highlight patterns apparent in such divergent films as *Easy Rider, Zabriskie Point, Mean Streets,* and *The Last Picture Show.*

Once it was firmly established as an option, the compilation score appeared in an increasingly vast array of different musical combinations. It was combined with straight symphonic scoring (*Batman*, 1989; and *Dick Tracy*, 1990), jazz idioms (*Do the Right Thing*, 1989; *Malcolm X*, 1992), or with electronic synthesizer scores (*American Gigolo*, 1980; *Beverly Hills Cop*, 1984). A number of other films, including *Fast Times at Ridgemont High* (1982), *Stand By Me* (1986), and *GoodFellas* (1990), showed that rock and roll songs by themselves could still serve as a viable approach to film scoring.

Few of these scores, however, matched the wit, charm, and elegance of *American Graffiti*. *American Graffiti* may well have capitalized on the marketability of its oldies, but the film itself used them in a way that went beyond simply selling songs. The film and the music opened vistas of emotional memory that touched the very hearts of its audience, and they responded by silently (or vocally) singing along. Like Mancini, Barry, and Morricone before him, Lucas showed that pop songs and film music need not be antithetical concepts; cinema could indeed serve as a jukebox for its time.

8

Pretty Women and Dead Presidents

THEME SONGS AND SOUNDTRACK ALBUMS
AFTER 1975

"Music," says a character in *Empire Records* (1995), "is the glue of the world. It holds it all together." Although the character is speaking here about the urban record store where he works, the statement might also apply to music's current place in the entertainment industry. While film producers and distributors remain the crown jewels of most entertainment conglomerates, the music industry has emerged as the more lucrative segment of the media marketplace. Within the large, highly diversified corporations that presently make up Hollywood's majors, music divisions consistently outpace their film counterparts in terms of both operating capital and profit potential.

In achieving this status, the music industry went through several major changes after 1975. Among these were the successful innovation and diffusion of the compact disk as the industry's standard software format; the emergence of music video as an important promotional tool; the advent of punk, New Wave, rap, and alternative rock as new styles of popular music; and the development of sampling as a new production technique. Despite these changes, however, the recorded music industry itself looked much as it had during the fifties and sixties. The market continued to be dominated by a mix of media giants and equipment manufacturers, who supplied the lion's share of the industry's hardware and software.

By the early 1980s, *synergy* had become the industry's buzzword to describe the phenomenon of successful film and music cross-promotion. As I noted earlier (see chapter 2), the concept of synergy held that a well-coordinated marketing campaign could use a soundtrack album to generate advance interest in its accompanying film, and vice versa. Yet while the soundtrack album remained the linchpin of the cross-marketing scheme, MTV joined radio as an important site for promoting individual songs from films as well as the films themselves. The emergence of MTV yielded a concise formula for effective cross-promotion, which R. Serge Denisoff and George Plasketes describe as "movie + soundtrack + video = $$$."[1] Films such as *Flashdance* (1983), *Footloose* (1984), *Top Gun* (1986), and *Dangerous Minds* (1995) capitalized on MTV's ability to circulate a film's music and imagery, and target it to a youth audience.

In recent years, the idea of synergy has come under a great deal of scrutiny, with several scholars assessing its relative efficacy as a model of industrial organization. Justin Wyatt, for example, suggests that synergy is a key component of "high concept" filmmaking insofar as it not only describes conglomerate activity but also expresses the extent to which almost every aspect of a film is subsumed within the current emphasis on marketing and merchandising.[2] Susan Ohmer, on the other hand, suggests that the term is more appropriate as a description of cross-marketing strategies than as a rubric for present forms of industrial organization.[3] Finally, writing specifically about film and music cross-promotion, Denisoff and Plasketes contend that synergy was largely industry mythology, a strategy more successful in theory than in actual practice.[4]

Denisoff develops this latter point more fully in *Risky Business*, a comprehensive survey of rock music in film coauthored with William Romanowski. Examining the box office and chart performances of numerous films and soundtrack albums of the 1980s, Denisoff and Romanowski argue that the type of symbiotic relationship described by synergy rarely happened. More often than not, the film succeeded while the album bombed, or vice versa. Even when film and album both became hits, their chart actions could not be correlated in any meaningful way, suggesting that their successes occurred as isolated pheonomena rather than as the result of a carefully coordinated campaign.[5]

Yet while Denisoff and Romanowski's overview of rock in film is impressive in its breadth and detail, their argument is flawed by a somewhat simplistic economic model. In their single-minded focus on box office numbers and chart performance, they overlook several factors which account for synergy's longevity as an industrial model. The most significant oversight is their failure to acknowledge the role of scale economies. One of the most basic of economic imperatives, the law of scale economies involves the efficient management of resources to reduce both overhead and per-unit production costs.

Scale economies were extremely important to the studio era where centralized management structures, standardized product, and a highly specialized division of labor served as ways to efficiently administer a film company's financial and human resources.

In the fifties, however, the breakdown of the studio system and the rise of independent production both gradually modified the role of scale economies. As entertainment corporations became more and more diversified, the law of scale economies increasingly involved the sharing of resources among the different divisions of a conglomerate. As such, synergy between film and music divisions fulfilled the law of scale economies in at least two senses. To begin with, the structural interaction of film and music divisions allowed for more efficient management of various kinds of human resources, such as legal staff, marketing departments, management teams, and in-house music supervisors. Moreover, to the extent that the film's score functioned both within the film and outside of it, synergy created many commodities out of one intellectual property that could then be produced and cross-promoted by the conglomerate's various divisions.

A second economic factor neglected by Denisoff and Romanowski is the extent to which synergy spreads financial risks. By creating multiple profit centers for a single property, synergy spreads risk among several different commodities. A successful soundtrack album can help defray the production costs of an unsuccessful film, and vice versa. Thus, to suggest, as Denisoff and Romanowski do, that synergy fails if it produces only a hit film or a hit record is to somewhat simplistically elevate one economic goal over another. If one views synergy solely as a strategy to engender success in two markets, then it truly is a failure. If, on the other hand, one views synergy as a means of spreading risk, then it has been an enormous success.

Finally, Denisoff and Romanowski also overlook the fact that the so-called "blockbuster" has been the primary source of operating capital for both the film and the recorded music industries. In the film industry, the profits of a gigantic hit like *Jurassic Park* (1993) typically funds the production of several much less costly features which the distributor in turn hopes to sell to the public as "sleepers." Much the same is true of the record industry where the enormous sales of Michael Jackson, Whitney Houston, or Mariah Carey titles finance the development of several new artists, which the record label in turn hopes to sell as the "next big thing." In both instances, companies rely on a few big hits to provide operating capital for their other projects.

One might object that if this were true, then it would make sense to produce only a few sure-fire blockbusters. Such a strategy, however, would not only increase financial risks but would also run counter to the law of scale economies. As I noted earlier, scale economies require a certain volume of production in order to lower overhead and per unit costs. For this reason, film distributors find it more prudent to finance a mix of big-budget and low-budget projects. For similar reasons, record companies must have a large and varied slate of artists and repertoire in order to spread risks and develop new stars. When a recording star or musical fad starts to wane in popularity, the company must have several other artists ready to step into the breach.

Thus, instead of viewing synergy and cross-promotion through a filter of individual successes and failures, one must situate both practices within a larger set of economic motivations. Understood within this broader context, film and music cross-promotion can be seen more precisely as a strategy that not only creates multiple profit centers but also serves to spread risk and maximize resources. In the remainder of this chapter, I wish to show how this multifarious cross-promotional strategy gave rise to several important developments in the fields of film scoring and film marketing after 1975. Many of these developments, like the appearance of music supervisors and the emergence of music video, are relatively recent phenomena. Others, like the creation of record subsidiaries, are simply the continuation of industrial practices found earlier in Hollywood's history. Since almost every new film is released in conjunction with a promotional song, soundtrack album, or music video, a complete overview of film and music cross-promotion is beyond the scope of this project. Rather, my more modest goal is to sketch out some of the more significant trends in order to develop a more well-rounded portrait of contemporary industrial practice.

Structural Interactions of the Record and Film Industries After 1975

As Douglas Gomery points out, the seventies was a period in which the film industry's seven major distributors consolidated their control of the market. Although the industry underwent several changes in motion picture financing and marketing, none of these changes fundamentally altered its underlying oligopoly structure. Between them, the Hollywood majors produced and distributed about a third of the films receiving MPAA ratings, but collected almost 90 percent of the total box office revenue. Such figures are remarkably close to similar measures taken at the height of the studio system.[6]

During the 1980s, however, only three of these companies would enjoy the same market dominance that they had in the seventies: Warner Brothers,

Paramount, and Universal.[7] The biggest winner during this period, however, was Disney. Some fifty years after the company's inception, Disney finally realized its aspirations to major status by broadening beyond its niche market of family-oriented films. As Tino Balio notes, although Disney had shrewdly diversified into television production, theme parks, and character merchandising in the fifties and sixties, it was not until the company formed its Touchstone subsidiary that it emerged as an industry power. Under the Touchstone banner, Disney made a series of successful films aimed at adult audiences, including *Splash* (1984), *Three Men and a Baby* (1987), and *Who Framed Roger Rabbit?* (1988). By 1988, Disney's two-pronged strategy, which involved clamping down on production costs but expanding its film output, placed it in the industry's upper ranks with a 20 percent share of the theatrical market.[8] With the reemergence of the studio's animation unit, Disney also became the entertainment industry's most recognizable name, one that was feared by competitors as much as it was beloved by fans.

Like the film industry, the record industry continued to have an oligopoly structure that divided the lion's share of revenues amongst six major music conglomerates. In 1975 these six—CBS, Warner Communications, ABC, RCA, EMI, and Polygram—accounted for about 80 percent of the industry's $2.4 billion in record sales. The remainder was divided by four mini-majors: A&M, Motown, 20th Century-Fox, and United Artists. The market dominance of the Big Six, however, would ultimately force these smaller companies into distribution agreements with the majors. A&M and 20th Century-Fox, for example, signed deals with RCA in the mid-seventies, and Motown finally succumbed to MCA's advances in 1983.

Changes in conglomerate structure would have a lasting impact on the structural interrelationship of the record and film industries. Many of the film and music ties that developed during the fifties and sixties were severed in a whirl of corporate takeovers. The trend toward conglomeration continued in both industries, and as a result many studio music divisions were gobbled up by larger, more powerful record conglomerates. In the mid-seventies, for example, MGM's and United Artists' record labels were bought by Dutch Polygram as part of a long-term growth strategy that also included the purchase of Chappell Music and the development of a very profitable affiliation with the Robert Stigwood Organization (RSO). The move was due as much to the faltering fortunes of each label's parent companies as it was to Polygram's aggressive strategy, but it helped make the latter the world's first billion dollar entertainment concern, earning more than $1.2 billion in 1978. A large portion of these revenues could be traced to Stigwood's success with such music-driven film projects as *Saturday Night Fever* (1977) and *Grease* (1978).

Takeovers and divestitures had similar effects on the music operations of Columbia and 20th Century-Fox. In 1979 Columbia Pictures sold its Arista Records subsidiary for $50 million after the latter experienced a decline in profits. A few years later, 20th Century-Fox's music operation was bought by Warner Communications for an estimated $16 million as part of an effort to consolidate Warner's publishing interests. At about the same time, Warner also sought to purchase United Artists' music catalog and printing operation, but the deal ultimately stalled when the Justice Department insisted on approving the sale, and Transamerica insisted on retaining the music rights to future MGM/UA productions. UA's catalog was sold subsequently to CBS Records for $68 million in a deal that gave CBS the first rights to all MGM/UA soundtrack recordings and a five-year copublishing arrangement for music written for future film projects.

The only studios that managed to withstand threats to their music divisions were Universal and Warner Brothers. Of course, the stability of their music operations was largely a consequence of their parent companies' conglomerate structure and diversification. At the start of the eighties, MCA and Warner Communications each epitomized the modern entertainment corporation. Although they were less diversified than their counterparts in the sixties, they nonetheless retained interests in a number of ancillary markets, such as tourism, toy manufacturing, book publishing, television production, and music publishing.

The concentration of resources would ultimately give rise to the concept of synergy as a thoroughgoing principle of corporate organization. Where the term had earlier referred to the simple proposition of using music to sell movies and vice versa, it now came to cover a whole system of cross-promotional practices designed to reinforce the conglomerate structure both vertically and horizontally. The increasing emphasis on corporate synergy was especially evident in Sony's purchase of both CBS Records and Columbia Pictures Entertainment in 1989. The takeover not only placed Sony among the top tier of film and recorded music distributors, it also enhanced its portfolio as a leading manufacturer of audio and video hardware. With strong production bases in both entertainment hardware and software, Sony emerged from the deal as both a vertically and horizontally integrated conglomerate.

Sony's 1993 hit, *Sleepless in Seattle*, neatly illustrates both the potential cross-promotional advantages of corporate synergy and the extent to which a single intellectual property can enhance the interaction of a corporation's hardware and software divisions. Recalling the vertical integration of the studio era, *Sleepless in Seattle* was financed by Sony's Tri-Star Pictures, distributed by the Sony Picture Corporation, and, at least in some areas of the country, exhibited in a Sony theater. After completing its theatrical run, the film was subsequently distributed by Tri-Star Home Video where it might be played on a Sony videocassette recorder or television. The film also spawned a successful soundtrack album for Sony's CBS Records subsidiary, Epic Soundtrax, which perchance was played on one of Sony's tape or compact disk players. As this example indicates, the integration of hardware and software not only spreads financial risk, it also creates several profit centers from a single intellectual property.

Film's centrality to the synergy equation, however, has gradually been weakened by the emergence of new media and new cultural forms. With the progressive development of markets for home video, video games, and home computer software, film is now simply one element in a much larger set of intellectual properties. Ideas for films currently originate from any number of sources, such as comic books (*Batman, The Crow, The Phantom*), cartoons (*Casper, Beavis and Butthead, 101 Dalmatians*), old television series (*The Addams Family, The Beverly Hillbillies, The Brady Bunch, McHale's Navy, Sgt. Bilko*), and even video games (*Tron, Mortal Kombat, Super Mario Bros.*). Such properties are significant in that they not only presell the film project and thereby serve to minimize financial risk, they also provide a ready-made set of images and narrative elements that can be regenerated in any number of distribution channels.

By the 1990s, the logic of synergy was so pervasive that it had filtered down into rather fine-grained levels of corporate cross-promotion. Among the current Hollywood majors, Disney is widely acknowledged as the most successful in its implementation of these multifarious "synergies" as they were now known. During the 1980s, the linchpin of Disney's synergistic strategy was its pay-cable venture, the Disney Channel. As a television outlet for past and current filmed entertainment, the Disney Channel served an important promotional function for a number of other Disney enterprises.[9] Cartoons from the studio library marketed toys and other merchandise sold in Disney's retail stores. Episodes of the new *Mickey Mouse Club* served as program-length advertisements for the Disney-MGM Studio Theme Park. The television broadcast of various Disney theatrical features (such as *Who Framed Roger Rabbit?*) further worked as tie-ins for programs on the EPCOT Center and other Disney World attractions. Merchandising for the Disney-owned hockey franchise, the Mighty Ducks, served as free promotion for upcoming sequels to the studio's 1992 hit film, and vice versa.[10]

After its merger with ABC in 1995, Disney began to more fully explore the synergistic potential of television. A number of ABC programs, such as *Roseanne*, began to integrate family trips to Disney World into their plots. ABC ran decades-old episodes of *George of the Jungle* in its Saturday morning lineup in anticipation of Disney's live-action film adaptation. Most recently, ABC's sister network, ESPN, used clips from Disney's *Hercules* (1997) in the lead-in to its popular *Sportscenter* program about five days before the film's premiere.

By 1994 the prerecorded music business had become an $11 billion industry while the film industry's box office receipts totaled only about $7 billion. The ownership of these leisure conglomerates is evenly divided between diversified entertainment conglomerates (Time Warner and Sony) and musical hardware manufacturers (Philips and Matsushita). Both kinds of relationships can be considered synergistic in that they involve either the cross-promotion of intellectual properties across a number of different media or they supply software for the other consumer products manufactured by the conglomerate. Table 8.1 indicates the corporate owners, their 1994 market share, and the major labels of each.[11]

TABLE 8.1
Record Industry Majors, 1994

Company	Corporate Owner	Market Share (%)	Major Labels
WEA	Time Warner	21.1	Warner Brothers, Reprise, Atlantic, Elektra, Rhino
Sony	Sony	15.2	Columbia, Epic
Polygram	Philips	12.9	Motown, Island, A&M, Mercury, Polydor, Deutsche Grammophone
BMG	Bertelsman	12.9	RCA, Zoo, Private Music, Arista, Windham Hill, BMG Classics
CEMA	Thorn EMI	11.2	Capitol, Liberty, Virgin, SBK, IRS, Chrysalis
UNI	Matsushita	10.7	MCA, GRP, Geffen

The remaining 16 percent of the market was divided up by various independent distributors. Like the indie labels of the fifties, their nineties counterparts have successfully weakened the majors' overall grip on the market. In 1990, for example, the majors accounted for 93 percent of all sales; by 1995 that figure was down to 80 percent.[12] It remains to be seen whether these independent distributors can establish a long-term niche in the market or if they will be swallowed up by ever larger conglomerates.

Despite the weakening of their market share, the overall revenue figures and higher profit margins of the companies shown in table 8.1 have led some industry analysts to suggest that music companies have been Hollywood's most important corporate assets. The film majors' music divisions have not only subsidized the financial ups and downs of filmmaking, but they are also more consistently profitable than their cinematic counterparts. Consider the relatively recent fortunes of the industry's two largest music groups, WEA and Sony. Both are part of much larger entertainment conglomerates, and both have served to stabilize the financial operations of their parent corporations. In 1994, Time Warner's film division enjoyed an exceptional year with an operating income of $565 million and $5 billion in revenues. Time Warner's music division, however, had an even better year by earning $720 million in operating income on only $4 billion in revenue. If Time Warner's fortunes illustrate the increased profitability of music divisions, then Sony's fortunes illustrate their ability to spread risk. In 1994 Sony's film ventures through Columbia and Tri-Star lost nearly $2.7 billion and generated an operating loss of about $510 million. This shortfall, however, was more than made up by Sony's music division, which earned $550 million in operating income on $4.5 billion in revenues.[13]

Generally speaking, the greater profitability of music divisions can be traced to two factors. First, the sales base of prerecorded music is typically more predictable than that of films. While both industries have their share of flops and breakthrough successes, the relative star power of musical performers often makes their sales potential easier to calculate. In film, an actor's breakthrough performance might well depend on the role, the script, his or her costar, or a popular genre, factors that ultimately make such initial success difficult to duplicate.[14] Ironically, this factor has sometimes worked against the marketing of soundtrack albums. When Mo Ostin headed Time Warner's music division, the company established a policy by which the label only issued soundtracks for the film division's blockbuster releases. According to Ostin, soundtracks were really one-off projects and Warner was committed to building up artists rather than individual releases. Ostin's policy underscores the value of artists as long-term investments for a record label.

The second factor accounting for music divisions' greater profitability is that the production costs of albums are generally lower than that of films. Metallica's self-titled album (1991), for example, cost about $1 million to produce, a relatively high figure by record industry standards but well short of the $30–40 million price tag of the average studio film. Metallica's album easily returned that investment as it sold approximately thirteen million copies worldwide and earned about $100 million in revenue. Moreover, even albums with far fewer sales can prove extremely profitable owing to the lower costs of most record productions. Veruca Salt's first album, *American Thighs* (1995), cost only $6,000 to produce and earned some $4 million in revenue. Even after one adds in the record label's marketing costs, the album still returned a tidy profit to its distributor, EMI America. While such examples are somewhat exceptional, they nonetheless illustrate the greater degree of profitability that compact disks and tapes have when compared with films.

Such logic has led several smaller film companies, like Miramax and New Line, to start up their own music divisions. Danny DeVito's Jersey Films launched a recorded music venture after it saw several successful soundtracks from its films flock to other record labels. The most notable of these was Quentin Tarantino's *Pulp Fiction* (1994), a collection of oldies and surf-rock classics that spent more than one hundred weeks on *Billboard*'s Top 200 album chart and sold more than three million albums for its distributor, MCA. According to Randy Gerston, head of Rysher Entertainment's music division, smaller companies can realize the fiscal benefits of music subsidiaries, but only if they confine themselves to soundtrack releases. Lacking the necessary capital and management experience to promote new recording artists, smaller music divisions run a great risk of overextending themselves.[15]

Of course, record companies have also shown some interest in entering the film business, albeit for slightly different reasons. The record giant Polygram is a case in point. In 1994, for example, the company put some $500 million into independent film productions at Interscope Communications, Island Pictures, Propaganda Films, and Working Title Films. While Polygram's investment equaled only about one-tenth of a major studio's financial outlay, its film ventures nonetheless served as a means of both hedging risk and of avoiding takeover by other entertainment conglomerates. As Polygram chief executive Alain Levy put it, "If you're complacent, you will die or be gobbled up."[16]

Thus, although the names of the players have changed, Hollywood continues to maintain large holdings in the music industry. The situation has obvious advantages since record sales and music licensing fees help sustain a corporation's film division through lean times, and vice versa. Moreover, as entertainment conglomerates grow more interactive, intellectual properties developed by one division of the corporation can be reproduced and exploited by several other divisions. The irony perhaps is that as capital is

increasingly concentrated in fewer and fewer hands, the companies themselves become more and more diversified. Unlike their counterparts in the
fifties and sixties, most studios today operate specialized soundtrack divisions
within their respective record subsidiaries. The creation of such divisions is
perhaps the biggest indicator of the extent to which soundtrack releases have
become an institutionalized practice. It is also a sign of their continued importance for the future.

Contemporary Trends in Film and Music Cross-Promotion

The mutually beneficial, if sometimes uneasy, alliance between film companies, music publishers, and record labels remains a constant of contemporary
efforts at cross-promotion. While the practice has produced its share of hits
and misses, there is a general recognition that the successful implementation
of cross-promotions depends on each participant's awareness of the other's
economic needs and interests. Even in situations where all participants are
part of a single large conglomerate, one subsidiary's short-term economic
interests may impinge on its cooperation with the other two points of the
cross-promotional triangle.

Much as they did before, film companies see soundtracks primarily as promotional vehicles, a function that is often better suited to title songs and music
video trailers insofar as they more clearly concretize the link between a film
and its ancillary products. Publishers, on the other hand, derive their revenues
from licensing fees and thus are often more interested in pushing their back catalogs than in promoting work by new artists. Finally, since record labels realize most of their profits in album sales, they have comparatively less stake in
film theme songs and often show greater concern for breaking in new recording artists than for promoting the film the soundtrack album accompanied.

Because of shifting alliances and competing interests among the three factions, soundtrack marketing went through a couple of major boom and bust
cycles from 1975 to 1995. During boom cycles, successful soundtrack albums
often drove up the cost of licensing fees as a greater number of filmmakers
competed for top talent in the recording industry. As costs increased, however, so did the financial risks associated with soundtracks. When some of
these investments failed to pay off, record labels became more reluctant to put
up the large advances expected by film producers. This reluctance on the part
of record companies would in turn stabilize licensing fees, causing the cycle
to begin all over again.

The success of *The Sting* and *American Graffiti* (both 1973) notwithstand-ing, soundtrack sales were generally weak during the first half of the seven-ties. That all changed, however, with the enormous success of *Saturday Night Fever* in 1977–78. As many film scholars and industry analysts point out, *Saturday Night Fever* provided the model for modern soundtrack promotion, one that continues to influence cross-marketing strategies to this day.[17] Much of the promotion's success is due to Al Coury, a former Capitol vice presi-dent who had been hired by Robert Stigwood to head up Stigwood's RSO record label.

Borrowing a prerelease strategy already proven successful for Barbra Streisand's *A Star Is Born* (1976), Coury released four singles from the sound-track during a four-month period prior to the album's release. The four singles included three Bee Gees' tunes—"Stayin' Alive," "How Deep Is Your Love," and "Night Fever"—and Yvonne Elliman's "If I Can't Have You." Their releases were staggered to maximize exposure for the album, and as one single reached the top of its chart run, another would be released to replace it. Coury supported these initial releases with a concentrated marketing campaign that sent full-color posters to eight thousand record retailers and radio stations, all of them featuring John Travolta's famous disco pose, which would later be used on both the album cover and in all the film's advertising. Having stirred up interest in the record industry with this unusual release pattern, Coury then turned his attention to potential moviegoers. In September 1977 a thirty-sec-ond trailer featuring "Stayin' Alive" and John Travolta's inimitable strut was shown in 1,500 movie theaters. Two months later, Coury distributed a longer trailer for the film which featured excerpts of all four singles and concluded with a plug for the soundtrack album. Capitalizing on the chart success of "How Deep Is Your Love," the longer trailer functioned simultaneously as an advertisement for the film, an advertisement for the album, and as promotion for the three other hit singles.

Coury's campaign left an impressive legacy of chart and box office suc-cesses. The soundtrack album sold some 850,000 units even before the film's mid-December release and went on to sell over twenty-five million units worldwide. Once *Saturday Night Fever* was released in theaters, the sound-track further capitalized on the immediate interest in the film. Retailers sold more than 750,000 copies of *Fever*'s soundtrack during a four-day period between Christmas and New Year's. More remarkable still was the fact that the album experienced little drop-off during the film's theatrical run, averag-ing sales of about 500,000 copies a week.[18] The performance of the various singles from the soundtrack was no less prodigious. All in all, the album spawned seven singles that appeared on trade charts, four of them reaching number one. The three Bee Gees' singles alone accounted for over 6.6 million units in sales. In an even more impressive feat, *Saturday Night Fever* placed four different singles in the Top Ten during a single week in February 1978. Garnering support from its soundtrack, the film itself experienced strong returns earning $74 million in domestic rentals by the end of the year.

The enormous success of *Saturday Night Fever* brought with it a greater awareness of what ingredients were helpful in marketing a hit soundtrack. According to a 1979 *Billboard* article, these ingredients included "commercially viable music. Timing. Film cooperation on advance planning and tie-ins. Music that's integral to the movie. A hit movie. A hit single. A big-name recording star. A big-name composer."[19] While not all these ingredients were absolutely necessary, the absence of one or two could spell the difference between a soundtrack's overall success or failure. As product manager Nina Franklin pointed out, the 1978 *Superman* soundtrack underperformed for two reasons: the music was not an integral part of the narrative, and the film itself simply did not do as well as expected.[20]

For most soundtrack albums, radio exposure and commercially viable music remained key components. According to Columbia Records' vice president of sales, Joe Mansfield, "If there's nothing Top 40 to play, you are not going to sell any records, so you don't spend any money, except trade announcements to let them know the soundtrack is available on this label."[21] Less commercial soundtracks occasionally utilized cross-merchandising campaigns to spur sales. Consumers who presented movie stubs to retailers sometimes received discounts on the film's accompanying soundtrack, and vice versa. In other instances, soundtracks were promoted with gimmicks similar to those that appeared in the early sixties. In 1979, for example, several Los Angeles area Tower Record stores held meatball-eating contests to promote the eponymous Bill Murray comedy. For the *Fast Break* (1979) soundtrack, Motown developed several tie-ins with the National Basketball Association. Besides getting the soundtrack played during NBA games, Motown sponsored a dribbling contest, several radio contests that gave away free tickets to basketball games, and retail displays that featured "backboards with little baskets and little balls to throw through them."[22]

Many producers also developed music-oriented projects in order to capitalize on the soundtrack's sales potential. A number of these were factual or fictionalized biographies of musical performers, such as *The Buddy Holly Story* (1978), *The Rose* (1979), *One Trick Pony* (1980), *Coal Miner's Daughter* (1980), and *Sweet Dreams* (1985). Other music-oriented projects were developed as cinematic adaptations of popular songs. Typically, these films were based on country and western ballads, like "Middle Age Crazy" or "The Night the Lights Went Out in Georgia," but producers optioned several other tunes by popular rock artists. In the late seventies, scripts were developed based on the Eagles' "Desperado" and Elton John's "Goodbye Yellow Brick Road," but neither of these projects reached the screen.[23]

Despite the resurgent interest in soundtracks after *Saturday Night Fever*, sales often did not tally with expectations. Although some twenty-five soundtrack albums reached *Billboard*'s charts in 1979, only one of them, the Who's *The Kids Are Alright*, cracked the Top Ten.[24] Similarly, record labels released some forty pop-oriented soundtrack albums during 1980, but only a handful of these achieved any notable success.[25] The one clear exception to this trend was the John Travolta vehicle *Urban Cowboy* (1980), which earned some $42 million at the box office and spawned a triple platinum soundtrack. According to producer Irving Azoff, the album aided the film by keeping it in the public eye. Although the film's box office performance was initially sluggish, it gathered momentum as the album placed some seven different singles on trade charts. In order to strengthen the connection between the songs and the film, Azoff spent over $1 million on a marketing campaign that targeted radio station managers and branch managers of Asylum Records, the distribution partner of Azoff's Full Moon Records.[26]

Despite the overall sales slump, however, most record companies welcomed Hollywood's interest in soundtracks for the infusion of promotional dollars it brought with it.[27] Since films generally have much larger promotional budgets than albums, cost-conscious record executives viewed the premiere parties and press junkets associated with big films as prepaid promotional campaigns for the soundtracks they accompanied. As Casablanca Records president Bruce Bird explains, "You're getting the expectation of a film that might have a $4 million budget for advertising alone. A $4 million budget for a record company to spend on an album—you'd be out of business quick. But for a soundtrack they can do it."[28]

The most significant changes in soundtrack promotion occurred in the early eighties and involved the emergence of two new vehicles for circulating film music—the compact disk and the music video. Based on research conducted jointly by Philips and Sony, compact disk systems were first demonstrated to industry representatives in 1981. Unlike the phonograph, which used a stylus to retrace the groove of a record, the compact disk system employs a laser beam to "read" a series of pits and lands digitally encoded in the reflective surface of the disk. With no surface noise, no background hiss, and a signal-to-noise ratio of 96 db, the compact disk produced an unusually clean sound, one that more accurately reproduced the higher and lower frequencies often obscured by the vinyl record's emphasis on the mid-range. More than that, however, the compact disk improved on the conventional hi-fi in several other ways. Unlike records and tapes, compact disks could easily access any track on an album and suffered no degradation from repeated plays. Although some vinyl purists complain about the "chilliness" of digital sound, most consumers opted for the compact disk's more user-friendly technology.[29]

Following its commercial introduction in 1982, the compact disk gradually replaced the microgroove vinyl record as the industry's dominant format. In 1986 compact disks sold only 50 million units, a relatively small number compared to the 350 million cassette tapes and 110 million vinyl LPs sold. However, by 1989 that figure reached some 200 million units in sales, and by 1993 the compact disk easily surpassed all other formats with sales of almost 500 million units.[30]

The innovation of the compact disk had important repercussions for the cross-marketing of soundtracks. As the dominant consumer format, compact disks replaced vinyl records as the most important vehicle by which soundtracks achieved cultural circulation. Moreover, as many consumers replaced their old, scratched, and worn LPs with CDs, the innovation of the compact disk paved the way for the reissue of several older scores and soundtrack albums in the new format. The more general interest in reissues and catalog albums helped sustain the fortunes of several specialty labels that catered to a coterie of film score connoisseurs.

While compact disks offered the music industry a new form of software, the music video gave it a whole new form of promotion. MTV, of course, was the primary exhibition outlet for these music shorts, and film companies were quick to recognize certain promotional advantages afforded by the so-called "music trailer." As several record executives pointed out, MTV's target audience was essentially the same demographic sought by film producers during this period. And since a music video could include either actual or additional footage from a film, it gave potential filmgoers a better idea of the film's stars, narrative, genre, and visual style than an accompanying single or album would. Furthermore, music videos added a dimension of flexibility to most film music tie-ins. By circulating the imagery of a film, music videos established a natural connection between film and music that, for the most part, was previously realized only through a title song.

Flashdance provided the initial model for film and music video cross-promotion. In using music to promote the film, Paramount followed the usual route of releasing the title track as a scout single succeeded by the release of the soundtrack album shortly thereafter. Where Paramount deviated from the usual marketing formula, however, was in its emphasis on MTV as a promotional vehicle for the film. Paramount released the video for Michael Sembello's "Maniac" to MTV some four weeks before the film was released, which enabled it to play a key role in the cross-promotion of the film, album, and single. The video, which had no footage of Sembello, essentially served as a four-minute musical trailer. After its success, MTV became sensitive to charges that it offered free advertising time to Hollywood and thereafter stipulated that future film-inspired videos would have to include the recording artist in at least 50 percent of the video's footage. In the wake of this decision, the "Old Time Rock and Roll" clip from *Risky Business* (1983) had to be recut to feature less of Tom Cruise in his briefs and more of Bob Seger in concert.[31]

Flashdance went on to earn some $185 million at the box office and sold more than seventeen million copies of the soundtrack. Several aspects of the film made it especially suitable for music video promotion, among them the film's slick visual style and loose narrative structure. With its emphasis on dance and sex, *Flashdance* was virtually tailor-made for MTV. Director Adrian Lyne adapted several visual tropes from MTV, especially its sleek, often minimalist mise-en-scène, its rhythmic editing style, and of course its specularization of scantily clad female bodies. Particularly notable in this regard are the gym scenes and the "Imagination" dance sequence which take place against stark white backgrounds. A second factor in *Flashdance*'s success was its modular narrative structure. As Paramount executive Dawn Steel notes, the film's plot was so designed such that sequences could easily be moved around during the editing process. Such modularity is significant in that it lays bare the film's structure as a series of discrete set pieces, any of which might be adapted to a music video format. The "Maniac" sequence, which depicts Alex's training regimen, is exemplary in this regard since it was simply excised whole and lengthened by intercutting other dance sequences from the film.

In tangent with its success with *Flashdance*, Paramount attempted to replicate the formula with promotional clips for *48 Hrs.* (1982) and *Staying Alive* (1983). The latter proved to be the studio's other major cross-promotional success as the film yielded both a hit album and a hit single in Frank Stallone's "Far from Over." The performance of Stallone's single was boosted by an accompanying video featuring the film's star, John Travolta, and a Jellybean Benitez remix that garnered the track increased airplay in dance clubs and

Contemporary Hits formats. To aid sales of the album, Polygram incorporated it into a comprehensive merchandising support program entitled "Take the Movies Home with You." This program, reminiscent of United Artists' sales campaigns of the early sixties, not only included *Staying Alive* but also several other Polygram soundtracks, such as *Flashdance* and *Return of the Jedi* (1983). All this promotional muscle helped *Staying Alive* overcome tepid reviews as it went on to earn more than $58 million at the box office.

Besides Paramount, a number of other studios attempted to cash in on the trend by either wholly or partially financing the production of music trailers. Among these were videos for Universal's *Rumble Fish* (1983), Warner Brothers' *National Lampoon's Vacation* (1983), and 20th Century-Fox's *Two of a Kind* (1983) that featured Stewart Copeland, Lindsay Buckingham, and Olivia Newton-John, respectively. The production costs for these videos depended greatly on the extent to which they used footage already shot for the film. For example, a Kid Creole and the Coconuts video for Columbia Pictures' *Against All Odds* (1984) was assembled entirely from footage that ended up on the cutting room floor. As a result, the production costs for the video were only about $15,000, a figure that was considered about average for music trailers that only required editing. For Phil Collins's title track, however, Columbia had a set specially built to match the film's visual design, an expenditure that raised the overall costs of the video to about $45,000.[32]

Film exhibitors also showed interest in the burgeoning popularity of music video. In November 1983, American Multi-Cinema (AMC) began programming music videos as pre-feature shorts in eleven major metropolitan markets. The AMC program (dubbed "Concert Cinema") was developed through an exclusive arrangement with R&R Entertainment, the Los Angeles communications subsidiary that agreed to serve as AMC's music video supplier. R&R's chief contribution to the deal, however, was a newly developed black box process which not only transferred the videos to 35mm film but also expanded their aspect ratio to widescreen proportions of 1.85:1 and remixed them for Dolby Stereo.

To differentiate its product from other music video programs, R&R sought to specialize in concert footage, a market strategy intended to stress both the unique qualities of theatrical exhibition and to distinguish R&R's clips from the conceptual videos favored by MTV. Among the artists featured in R&R's first set of clips were David Bowie, Olivia Newton-John, and Bob Dylan. Using available demographic information, R&R attempted to match these artists with films aimed at a similar audience. Thus, Dylan's appeal to an over-thirty crowd made him a perfect fit for a baby boomer feature like *The*

Big Chill (1983). Similarly, Newton-John's largely male demographics made her an appropriate match to high-testosterone action films like Clint Eastwood's *Sudden Impact* (1983). Although "Cinema Concert" was first shown on some five hundred of AMC's seven hundred screens, R&R hoped to have arrangements with more than two thousand theaters during the program's first year.[33]

The emergence of music video helped spur several soundtracks onto *Billboard*'s charts. During a single week in June 1984, soundtrack albums accounted for some thirteen spots in the Top 200, a considerable increase over the two on the charts exactly one year earlier.[34] The current boom was led by *Footloose*, which yielded four Top Ten singles and was then enjoying its tenth week atop the album charts. Described by one reviewer as "a hit record with pictures," *Footloose* earned over $80 million at the box office, produced two number one singles, and sold more than nine million copies of the soundtrack.[35]

More than this, however, the success of *Footloose* also provided a window on the increasingly complex economics of soundtrack packaging. Since the film itself updated the narrative formula of Sam Katzman's jukebox musicals of the 1950s, screenwriter Dean Pitchford and music supervisor Becky Shargo recognized early on that the film's success would hinge on its careful integration of music and narrative. For this reason, Pitchford insisted on writing the lyrics to all the tracks that would appear in the film. This stipulation not only gave Pitchford and Shargo greater control over the music selection process, it also assured that they would not receive the B-sides and leftover tracks that record companies often pawned off on other film projects.[36]

Both the insistence on Pitchford's collaboration and the emphasis on new material served to drive up the production costs of the music, however. Since Paramount's music budget did not cover all the costs, the soundtrack's distributor, Columbia Records, was asked to pony up a $250,000 advance in exchange for the soundtrack rights. For its part, Columbia was able to load the soundtrack with performers from its CBS subsidiary, such as Kenny Loggins, Deniece Williams, and Bonnie Tyler. Columbia also demanded that the soundtrack feature two non-CBS artists whose latest album sales were at least 500,000 copies. Through Shargo, Paramount complied with Columbia's request by signing both Shalamar and Sammy Hagar to the project.[37] Satisfying all the parties involved required months of dealmaking as Shargo negotiated some forty-seven different contracts for the nine cuts that appeared on the album.[38]

As more and more film companies poured money into their music budgets, the soundtrack boom continued throughout 1985 and 1986. Several films duplicated *Flashdance*'s winning formula of scout singles, concurrent album releases, and music trailers. Among the more notable hits were *Beverly Hills Cop* (1984), *A View to a Kill* (1985), *Back to the Future* (1985), *White Nights* (1985), *Rocky IV* (1985), *Pretty in Pink* (1986), and *Top Gun*. The soundtrack boom also grew to include television as the *Miami Vice* album logged eleven weeks as the nation's number one album and became the biggest-selling television soundtrack since Henry Mancini's *Peter Gunn*.

The growing interest in soundtracks, however, led to an inevitable increase in production costs. As both publishers and record labels became more aware of the film industry's desire for exploitable music, producers and music supervisors saw a corresponding rise in synchronization and master license fees. By 1986 the costs of obtaining a top musical act for the soundtrack reached upwards of $50,000 per track with even lesser known acts able to command fees in the $5,000 to $35,000 range. Consequently, the average music budget for a Hollywood film rose to $400,000. Producers who used a lot of pop music could expect to pay $700,000 or more in licensing fees. Film companies sometimes raised money for the music budget by selling the soundtrack's rights in exchange for a record label advance, but doing so generally meant ceding some control over the film's music. Moreover, since record labels assumed the financial risk of an album, they, rather than the film's producers, would receive the lion's share of the soundtrack's profits.[39]

Besides rising production costs, the industry also faced several related problems associated with film and music cross-promotions. For one thing, the proliferation of soundtracks resulted in a glutted market, and since timing was the key to any successful cross-promotion, the increased traffic in soundtracks added another layer of complication to the process. As both filmmakers and record labels jockeyed for favorable release dates, the coordination of strong cross-marketing campaigns became that much more difficult.[40] A second problem arose from the escalating demand for top recording talent. With more and more film companies competing for the same stable of artists, several record labels began to write "soundtrack exclusions" into their contracts, which limited artists to one soundtrack a year.[41] Such exclusions not only complicated the negotiations for an artist's services, but effectively thwarted efforts to get talent from another record label. Finally, several film producers acknowledged that a hit single from a film might not necessarily enhance its box office performance. Unless a clear connection is made between the two, a song may sell on the strength of its performer rather than its tie-in to a film. For this reason, producers reiterated their feeling that title songs have greater promotional value than soundtrack albums. By drawing patrons to theaters, title songs can help a flop offset its losses or make a big hit even bigger. Illustrating this principle, Gary LeMel, then Columbia's senior vice president of music, estimated that Phil Collins's hit recording of "Against All Odds (Take a Look at Me Now)" added five to six million dollars to the film's box office take while Ray Parker Jr.'s "Ghostbusters" added some $20 million to its gross.[42]

These and other problems led some trade journals to sound the soundtrack album's death knell. While prominent industry spokespersons dismissed this as media hype, they nonetheless cautioned that better cooperation among all participants was necessary to "avoid killing the goose that lays the platinum eggs."[43] Film music executives identified two major problems with contemporary cross-promotion. First of all, according to Paramount's Steve Bedell, film companies need to be wary of oversaturating the market for soundtracks. Second, as Gary LeMel pointed out, filmmakers need to avoid the temptation to use a pop soundtrack as an easy marketing angle. According to LeMel, such a strategy can backfire if a film is aimed at adult filmgoers. A pop song associated with the film may get airplay, but it also may lead its intended audience to assume the film is a teenpic.[44]

Between 1989 and 1993 the market for soundtracks stabilized. Although the industry saw several demonstrations of synergy at work in films like *Cocktail* (1988) and *Batman* (1989), soundtracks more generally held their niche in the marketplace, neither gaining nor losing much ground. The mid-nineties, however, saw a major upsurge in soundtrack sales that recalled the industry's salad days of the early eighties. During the week of June 10, 1995, soundtracks accounted for sixteen spots on *Billboard*'s Top 200 album chart. That impressive figure was eclipsed just a couple of months later when some twenty soundtrack albums made the chart during the week of August 20th.[45]

While album sales offered one measure of film music's importance to Hollywood, its influence was felt in several other ways. In an ironic reversal of the fifties' vogue for title songs, the late eighties and early nineties saw dozens of films taking their titles from preexisting popular songs. Although this practice goes back many years, the current emphasis on pop song titles began in the mid-eighties with films like *Peggy Sue Got Married* and *Stand By Me* (both 1986). It reached its apex in 1991–92 when scads of movies tried to cash in on the trend, among them *Only the Lonely*, *Rich Girl*, *Love Potion No. 9*, *Back in the U.S.S.R.*, *Delirious*, *My Girl*, *Rambling Rose*, *Frankie and Johnny*, *Poison Ivy*, and *My Own Private Idaho*.[46]

For distributors, a well-known song title has a number of advantages as a built-in marketing hook. To begin with, a popular song title gives any film almost immediate name recognition. In addition, a particular title may have a nostalgic resonance for certain audience members. Paramount president David Kirkpatrick described the practice thusly: "It puts them [audience members] in a place that's comfortable, so there is an immediate sort of interest or draw toward the movie in question."[47] Although some production executives deny that the strategy is employed with that much forethought, they nonetheless acknowledge that their marketing teams will typically come up with a list of fifty possible titles for a film and that one or two of these is usually a song title.

Perhaps the best illustration of a song title's impact is Touchstone's *Pretty Woman* (1990), originally titled *$3,000*, in reference to the transaction which made Julia Roberts's character, Vivian, the live-in paramour of Edward, the sleazy corporate raider played by Richard Gere. By changing the title to *Pretty Woman*, Touchstone downplayed the seamy subtext of the film in favor of its Cinderella-ish romance. Moreover, by highlighting the feminine charms of its star, both the title and the Roy Orbison song that inspired it helped spur *Pretty Woman* to a $178 million box office gross and soundtrack sales of more than three million copies. In an effort to duplicate *Pretty Woman*'s remarkable success, several more recent romantic comedies have employed this cross-marketing strategy with varying results. Representative titles include *It Could Happen to You, Only You, Something to Talk About, Thin Line Between Love and Hate, Fools Rush In, One Fine Day*, and *Addicted to Love*.

Songs have also been popping up in movie trailers in recent years in a manner that mirrors their current usage in films. In certain instances, the song serves to highlight the film's title in some way. For example, ads for the summer action flick *Con Air* (1997) used Phil Collins's "Something in the Air Tonight" as a kind of pun on the film's title. Similarly, the trailer for *Liar, Liar* (1997) used the Eurhythmics' "Would I Lie to You?" to highlight both the title and the film's central premise (i.e., that the film's hero is unable to tell a lie). In other instances, however, the song may function less in relation to the title than to the action depicted in the trailer. In such cases, the music plays the ironic, commentative function identified earlier with *American Graffiti*. The trailer for *My Best Friend's Wedding* (1997) is a case in point. When Dermot Mulroney introduces Cameron Diaz as his fiancée to Julia Roberts, Ray Charles's "What'd I Say" cleverly comments on the moment with the phrase, "See the girl with the diamond ring . . ." Likewise, when Rupert Everett counsels Julia Roberts to reveal her true feelings to Mulroney, the Exciters' "Tell Him" slyly underlines the moment. The combination of music and narrative here not only conveys the entire premise for *My Best Friend's Wedding*, it also gives the audience something of the film's comedic flavor. In still other instances, the trailer may simply use one or two tracks that are prominently featured in the film. As is evident in the trailers for *Trainspotting* (1996), *Grosse Pointe Blank* (1997), and *Romy and Michele's High School Reunion* (1997), these promotional clips serve a double function by advertising both the film and the album that accompanies it.

By the mid-nineties, soundtracks were packaged according to two very different philosophies, depending on the type of film they accompanied. For most "event" films, soundtracks packaged several different kinds of artists together in an effort to reach as many different radio formats as possible.[48] A good example of this approach is *Twister* (1996), which grouped hard rock performers, such as Van Halen and the Red Hot Chili Peppers, with country and western singers, such as Alison Krauss and Shania Twain. If anything, the soundtrack for *Batman and Robin* (1997) offered an even broader mix of recording artists. Tracks by R.E.M., the Goo Goo Dolls, and the Smashing Pumpkins provide ready access to modern rock formats while tunes by Jewel and R Kelly are inserted to break into adult contemporary and urban music formats respectively. In the case of *Batman and Robin*, this strategy was especially effective since the prominence of these performers guaranteed almost automatic airplay. At the same time, the *Batman and Robin* soundtrack also provided exposure to up-and-coming talents like Arkarna and Soul Coughing.

For smaller budgeted, independent productions, on the other hand, the soundtrack album was often organized in a way that emphasized a particular marketing angle. This was especially true of films that attempted to exploit a popular musical fad, such as Cameron Crowe's *Singles*, which tapped into the "grunge" zeitgeist of the early nineties, or *All Over Me* (1997), which tried to capitalize on the burgeoning "Riot Grrrl" phenomenon. Musical fads, however, are not the only angles which might be exploited. For films made by contemporary African-American filmmakers, the soundtrack often highlighted the ethnic background of both the director and the film's main characters. Examples include several films by Spike Lee (*Do the Right Thing*, *Malcolm X*, *Crooklyn*, and *Get on the Bus*), John Singleton (*Boyz N the Hood*), Mario Van Peebles (*New Jack City*, *Panther*), Carl Franklin (*Devil in a Blue Dress*) and the Hughes Brothers (*Menace II Society*, *Dead Presidents*). The same was also true of films that dealt explicitly with issues of gender or sexual orientation. The soundtrack album for *Waiting to Exhale* (1995), for example, exclusively featured female rap and soul artists in order to emphasize the film's appeal to women.

To these we might also add those soundtracks that exploited a particular gimmick, one apparent either in the film or in the album itself. *Honeymoon in Vegas* (1992), for example, featured contemporary covers of songs associated with Elvis Presley. As such, the album not only played up the film's flying Elvises gimmick, it also served as a kind of pseudo-tribute album. In other instances, the soundtrack's packaging emphasized unusual collaborations. The *Judgment Night* soundtrack (1993) paired popular rap and heavy metal groups, such as Public Enemy and Anthrax on the former's classic "Bring Tha Noize." Similarly, Allison Anders's *Grace of My Heart* (1996), a fictionalized account of Carole King's life, put well-known sixties songwriters together with their more contemporary counterparts. Emblematic of this strategy was the album and film's showpiece, a track composed by Elvis Costello and Burt Bacharach entitled "God Give Me Strength."

Finally, although they served a much smaller market than the one for pop soundtracks, a number of labels carved their own niche in the industry by focusing exclusively on the market for orchestral scores. Labels like Intrada, Silva Screen, and Varese Sarabande specialized in new soundtrack recordings as well as reissues of classic scores. Since the rights to high-profile scores were typically sold to one of the major labels, these specialty labels generally gained access to scores that were perceived to have somewhat limited appeal. Lacking a broad-based market for their products, these labels were sustained by a core of some two thousand collectors who would "pretty much buy anything with the word 'soundtrack' on it."[49]

For this and other reasons, reissues proved to be the bread and butter for most of these specialty labels. Since the musicians' fees had already been paid, a reissue of a soundtrack required only a modest charge to license the master. By specializing in reissues, these soundtrack labels were generally able to control their costs to the point where sales of two thousand copies pretty much recouped their investment for an individual title. For new recordings, however, musicians' fees ran as high as $85,000, a figure that drove the total cost of acquiring the rights to a new score to more than $100,000.[50] While this figure represented a quantum leap over the costs associated with a reissue, a new orchestral soundtrack usually sold from 12,000 to 15,000 copies, which once again enabled these specialty labels to recoup their investment on most soundtracks they released. Where these labels made most of their profits, however, was on their more popular titles, which sell anywhere from 50,000 to 500,000 copies. Varese Sarabande, for example, had sales of close to a million each for the soundtracks to *The Man from Snowy River* (1982) and *Witness* (1985). Such hits allow Varese Sarabande to release some forty to fifty orchestral soundtracks each year and maintain a catalog of over five hundred different titles.

Although orchestral scores occupy a small but significant niche in the record industry, the pop compilation remains the linchpin of Hollywood's cross-promotional apparatus. It is likely to continue serving that function for any number of reasons. First, as several industry analysts note, soundtrack albums have essentially usurped the position once held by the K-Tel compilations made popular in the 1970s. Not surprisingly, soundtracks offer some of the same attractions as other kinds of song collections, such as tribute albums or anthologies. For consumers, soundtracks are thus a relatively safe bet since they either bring together several golden oldies in one package, or they provide a convenient sampler of a particular genre or style. For this reason, soundtracks sell especially well during soft sales periods in the record industry since casual consumers are more likely to purchase an album that contains many well-known performers rather than buy an entire album by an individual artist.

Second, music video has become an especially effective and important promotional tool for films. By 1995 the formula of combining film, soundtrack, and music video had become so ritualized that it was not uncommon to find all three ingredients represented in the videocassette releases of popular films. Advertisements for a videocassette's accompanying soundtrack album are now almost as common as the trailers which plug a distributor's upcoming releases. Similarly, the videocasssette versions of films like *Trainspotting*, *Dead Presidents*, and even the reissue of *The Graduate* feature music videos that appear either just before or just after the so-called "feature presentation." This, too, is likely to continue as long as music video channels, like MTV and VH1, remain important outlets for both film and record promotion.

The Music Supervisor

As the back catalogs of publishers and record companies became increasingly valuable financial resources for Hollywood studios, the problem of managing various licensing arrangements created a number of new responsibilities, and thus a new position to fulfill those duties: the music supervisor. Over time, the music supervisor's duties would come to include such things as the creation of a music budget, the supervision of various licensing arrangements, the negotiation of deals with composers and songwriters, and the safeguarding of the production company's publishing interests. Yet while the position is largely an administrative one, music supervisors also participate in a number of decisions which shape the overall concept of a score. The music supervisor's input is typically sought for such things as spotting sessions, the selection of preexisting musical materials, the organization of prerecords, the screening of dailies, and the preparation of "temp tracks."

As David Bell points out, the music supervisor often acts as a sort of musical casting director.[51] Once the score's concept is agreed upon by the filmmaker, distributor, and record company, then the music supervisor will assist in providing suitable composers, songwriters, and recording artists to match that concept. In doing so, the music supervisor operates with an eye toward budget considerations, the promotional value of various musical materials, and the dramatic appropriateness of the score's concept.

During the late seventies, many of the first music supervisors came directly from the record business. David Franco, for example, was previously an A&R (artists and repertoire) director at RCA and WEA before he formed International Music Operations, one of the earliest firms devoted to music coordination and consulting for movies. Since then, however, music supervisors have come from a much more varied set of backgrounds. Some, like Harry Lojewski and Bodie Chandler, have worked as professional musicians. Others, like Harry Heitzer, have a business or legal background. Still others come from the ranks of film producers, composers, music editors, or recording engineers.

As Karlin and Wright point out, the types of duties performed by a music supervisor will vary according to their previous background. Heitzer, for example, serves largely as an operations manager overseeing the business affairs of his record company's soundtrack division. Lojewski and Chandler, on the other hand, attend all scoring sessions and usually act as producers during recording sessions. Because of their presence in the booth, music supervisors like Lojewski and Chandler take a more hands-on approach and will typically offer advice on a wide range of concerns, such as intonation problems, mixing adjustments, or even last-minute changes in orchestration.[52]

By the mid-eighties, many music supervision firms saw the diverse backgrounds of their personnel as a definite asset. Consider, for example, the Organization of Soundtrack Services, which began in 1985 as an offshoot of Miles Copeland's music and film ventures. The firm was headed by Derek Power and Mike Gormley, each of whom brought a different specialization to their joint role as music supervisors. Power's background was in the film industry as a former salesman in Dino De Laurentiis's organization and as a producer on such films as *The Last Wave* (1977), *The Funhouse* (1981), and

Running Scared (1986). Gormley, on the other hand, previously held positions at Mercury, Polygram, and A&M Records. During his tenure at the Organization of Soundtrack Services, Gormley continued to manage a number of popular New Wave acts, including the Bangles, Oingo Boingo, and Wall of Voodoo. Although Gormley claimed that his clients never expected him to place them on soundtracks, his role as music supervisor sometimes enabled him to favor acts from his own stable.[53]

Some of the more prominent music supervisors capitalized on their success by directly moving into film production. Irving Azoff, for example, had been a twenty-year veteran of the music business before he became the executive producer for *FM* in 1978. Although Azoff initially griped that he was brought in solely to access his roster of recording artists, he later went on to supervise other successful tie-in campaigns for *Urban Cowboy*, *Heavy Metal* (1981), and *Fast Times at Ridgemont High* (1982). For all four of these soundtracks, Azoff drew from the talent developed at his Front Line Productions, which managed such artists as Boz Scaggs, Steely Dan, Stevie Nicks, and the Eagles.[54]

More recently, the industry has seen a shift toward hiring top recording artists and producers to put their creative stamp on the music supervision process. Kenneth "Babyface" Edmonds, for example, worked as a music supervisor on such successful soundtracks as *Boomerang* (1992) and *Waiting to Exhale*. Similarly, Trent Reznor of Nine Inch Nails served as a music supervisor for the auteurist visions of Oliver Stone's *Natural Born Killers* (1995) and David Lynch's *Lost Highway* (1997). In each case, the role of supervisor was linked simultaneously to both the performer's specific appeal in the marketplace and the film's probable target audience. Babyface's facility with rhythm-and-blues balladry undoubtedly matched the film's appeal to African-American women while Reznor's violent, Gothic, industrial music neatly corresponded with the popular persona of Lynch as an auteur.

Because soundtrack albums are now such a standardized part of most films' marketing plans, many music supervisors are housed within the music divisions of large entertainment conglomerates. As part of the conglomerate's corporate structure, studio music directors often receive easy access to songs and artists that are part of the conglomerate's publishing and recording arms. Moreover, studio music directors also benefit from their place within the conglomerate's hierarchized infrastructure, which typically includes an in-house music editing unit and the film company's music clearance and legal departments. Finally, because of the larger volume of films produced by the majors, studio music directors also enjoy a stronger negotiating position with respect to outside publishers and record companies.

Other music supervisors, like David Franco, Becky Shargo, and Terri Fricon, operate on a freelance basis. While studios occasionally hire outside supervisors for assistance on in-house projects, they are more commonly contracted by independent producers whose work is financed and distributed by the majors. Lacking the support system of studio supervisors, independents often rely on their network of industry contacts or their previous track records. Shargo, for example, assisted Irving Azoff on the supervision of *FM*'s soundtrack before going on to achieve individual success with her work on *Footloose*.

Because of their outside status, the role of independent supervisors as interface between the film and music industries is often complicated by their need to satisfy so many competing financial interests. According to Art Ford, the vice president of film and television music at BMG publishing, music supervisors have one of the most difficult jobs in the entertainment industry: "They have four or five people surrounding them with completely different agendas and they have to make everybody happy: a director, a studio, a record label, many different artists and managers that they're putting together for the soundtrack."[55] And as Denisoff and Romanowski note, many of the top independent supervisors, such as Shargo, Danny Goldberg, and Gary LeMel, rose to the top of their profession because of their keen sensitivity to each component of the synergy equation.[56]

In some instances, though, the music budget for a film may not cover the services of a music supervisor. This is especially true of low- and medium-budget films that contain a great deal of underscore, but that can scarcely afford to license more than one or two songs. When this occurs, the production company will usually turn to a music clearance company, such as the Harry Fox Agency or the Music Bridge. A recent issue of the *Hollywood Reporter* listed almost thirty different clearance houses, most of them located in the film production hubs of New York and Los Angeles.[57] Clearance houses are also useful for songs or recordings where the ownership of a particular copyright may be in doubt. Such research is sometimes necessary for rock or rhythm-and-blues tunes recorded before 1972, many of which were cut for small independent labels that have long since gone out of business.[58]

While their goal is to satisfy all competing interests, many current music supervisors regard the negotiation of synchronization licenses as the key node of the film, record, and publishing triangle. The relative importance of synchronization rights can be traced to two interrelated factors, starting with the fact that, for many directors, "the song's the thing" rather than the specific performer. This is especially evident in films where songs have been specifically written into the script. In cases where the cost of the original recording is prohibitive, music supervisors may have to negotiate a separate deal to license a new "cover" recording of the desired tune. Second, as I pointed out in the preceding chapter, directors will frequently use our foreknowledge of songs to add ironic commentary or a layer of extratextual associations to a specific scene. Such usage of songs places a premium on well-known rather than new musical material since a song must have fairly wide cultural circulation for the director to exploit the audience's familiarity with it. Placement issues are also a consideration as interpolated songs generally receive more prominent positions on the film's soundtrack album. For all these reasons, synchronization licenses are an extremely lucrative source of income for publishers. As music supervisor Budd Carr points out, "It's found dollars. Big found dollars."[59]

All these factors, however, tend to drive the prices for licensing catalog material higher. Depending on the tune and its placement, synchronization fees for a specific song might run over six figures. On *Mermaids* (1990), for example, the film's production company offered $40,000 for the synchronization rights to the Phil Spector classic "Be My Baby." But when the publisher refused to accept less than $200,000, the producers simply cut the song out of the film.[60] More commonly, synchronization fees for a well-known song can run anywhere from $30,000 to $100,000. If the film company can guarantee a spot on the soundtrack album, however, publishers will often agree to a reduced synchronization fee in the hopes that the royalties on album sales will make up any shortfall.

Given the soundtrack's marketing potential for both filmmakers and publishers, both sides are increasingly pushing for earlier involvement in the production process. For Howard Stern's *Private Parts* (1997), music supervisor Peter Afterman had to secure copyrights from a number of major performers, such as Van Halen, Queen, Jimi Hendrix, and AC/DC. To reduce costs, Afterman approached the publishers first and offered a "low but fair" sum to each that was equal for every copyright holder. Through this early intervention in the process, Afterman was able to license all the tunes desired by the filmmakers.[61] Afterman's efforts were doubtless aided by the film's radio station setting and the prospect of terrific placement opportunities for each song.

On *Forrest Gump* (1994) the producers took a different approach by inviting publishing representatives, record executives, and even some artists to a special preview screening of the film. Because the film was initially temp-tracked with some fifty-nine different songs, producers recognized that the cooperation of the music industry would be vital to the film's overall marketing plan. The preview screening was thus intended to get music executives excited by the film in the hopes that they might reduce their normal licensing fees. According to its supervisor, Joel Sill, Paramount's proactive stance proved to be an enormous success as almost every one of the songs on the temp track ended up in the finished film.

For their part, publishers also seek early involvement with film producers. To get filmmakers interested in their holdings, publishers frequently offer them a catalog sampler, which contains up to twelve CDs' worth of material broken down into various categories.[62] Moreover, as MCA Music's Scott James notes, some publishers will also involve themselves in the preparation of temp tracks. They do so in the hope that once one of their songs is included, the director will ultimately be much more reluctant to cut it from the final release print. Lastly, when new songs or new artists are involved, publishers will sometimes try to seal the deal by offering financing for song demos or even for the recording costs of a master.

Patterns of Thematic Organization in Contemporary Film Music

For the most part, patterns of thematic organization in contemporary scores remained consistent with those developed during the sixties and early seventies. In fact, by the mid-seventies the conventions of the theme score and compilation score had become so familiar, director Robert Altman brilliantly parodied them in films like *The Long Goodbye* (1973) and *Nashville* (1975). In *The Long Goodbye*, John Williams's unorthodox score constantly motivates the title theme as a part of the film's diegesis.[63] It is heard successively as two different radio songs over the credits; as a tune on a grocery store's "Muzak"; as a lounge lizard's piano bar number; as a flamenco guitar melody; as a Mexican funeral march; and as the doorbell of the femme fatale's home. In *Nashville*, on the other hand, Altman allowed many of the cast members to write their own songs rather than use more established composers and songwriters.[64] By avoiding more authentic examples of the genre, the soundtrack album that emerged from this process was, thus, a caricatured collection of faux country and western tunes. In a further irony, the gimmick was turned on its head yet again when Keith Carradine won the Oscar for Best Original Song ("I'm Easy").

As Lukas Kendall points out, however, rock and pop's impact on dramatic underscoring generally waned after the late seventies. For the most part, rock's influence has been limited to an increased use of various kinds of percussion for action films and the integration of electric guitar into the composer's palette of instrumental colors.[65] The latter is especially evident in the scores of Ry Cooder, such as *Paris, Texas* (1984) and *Trespass* (1992), and in Michael Kamen's collaboration with Eric Clapton and David Sanborn for the *Lethal Weapon* series. To these we might also add scores resulting from a rock musician's occasional foray into film composition, such as Paul Westerberg's alternative-rock score for *Singles* (1992) or Dave Pirnier's guitar noodlings for *Chasing Amy* (1997).

What Kendall overlooks in his assessment of recent film music history, however, is pop's ubiquity as source music for films. Moreover, Kendall also gives short shrift to the common practice of slugging in recordings for montages, action sequences, and love scenes. Like it or not, both the music montages and the use of pop as source music make up a large part of our contemporary moviegoing experience. The recent John Travolta hit, *Phenomenon* (1996), is a case in point. To underline the film's romantic subplot, the score features several adult contemporary tunes as source music and no less than four music montages, the last of which serves as a showcase for the Eric Clapton and Babyface smash, "Change the World."

Not surprisingly, the fads of the music marketplace have also placed special weight on particular genres of popular music at certain historical moments. Rap, for instance, became the style du jour of several urban crime dramas and youthpics, such as *Colors* (1988), *Boyz N the Hood* (1991), *Deep Cover* (1992), *Above the Rim* (1994), and *Set It Off* (1996). More recently, interest in British dance music has led some filmmakers to compile scores from the work of techno and trip-hop artists. As representative scenes from *Trainspotting* and *The Saint* (1997) show, the stylistic combination of rhythmic propulsion, harmonic stasis, and electronic coloring makes this new dance music an especially appropriate fit for chases and action scenes. In this respect, the current use of techno is a kind of throwback to Giorgio Moroder's groundbreaking electronic scores for films like *Midnight Express* (1978) and *Cat People* (1982).

The incorporation of these new pop styles, however, did not necessarily lead to new patterns of thematic organization. Rather, contemporary film scores generally fit into one of four basic stylistic models, each of which contains its own appropriate pattern of thematic organization: (1) leitmotiv-laden orchestral scores composed within neo-romantic or modernist styles; (2) orchestral scores that feature one or two popular songs; (3) scores comprised entirely of popular recordings; and (4) scores that mix orchestral underscore with several pop tunes. As the ensuing discussion will show, these stylistic models may predominate within the work of certain filmmakers, but they more generally cut across the boundaries of many different genres, national cinemas, and modes of film practice.

At one end of this spectrum, the orchestral score remains an extremely significant stylistic option. As I noted earlier, several specialty labels market these scores directly to a coterie of film music enthusiasts. Although the orchestral score is found in every genre, it is especially common to the historical epic and science fiction film. Notable examples include *Star Wars* (1977), *The Mission* (1986), *Robocop* (1987), *The Last of the Mohicans* (1992), and *Braveheart* (1995). It also includes scores like Vangelis's *Blade Runner* (1982), which are electronic, but which nonetheless mimic the sound and style of traditional orchestral music.

During the late seventies, the overwhelming success of *Star Wars* would help to revive the commercial fortunes of the classically styled film score. Released by 20th Century-Fox's record subsidiary, the *Star Wars* soundtrack sold over four million copies and made a household name of its composer, John Williams. A telling indicator of *Star Wars'* impact is offered by recording engineer Grover Hensley. While working on the Village People's camp classic, *Can't Stop the Music*, Hensley was visited by an executive music supervisor, who, in a moment of sublime absurdity, requested that the film's disco score be replaced with a *Star Wars*-style orchestral score. The supervisor's suggestion was quickly shot down when Hensley reminded the executive that they could not get *Star Wars'* sound out of a five- or six-man rock band.[66]

Ironically, though, *Star Wars* set the course for the symphonic score's future by self-consciously looking toward its past. While Williams's music drew its inspiration from several classical composers, especially Holst, Stravinsky, and Mahler, it also worked as an affectionate tribute to the swashbuckling film scores of Erich Wolfgang Korngold. As Randall David Larson notes, *Star Wars* is structured around a handful of principal themes and several leitmotivs. These include a martial, heroic fanfare for Luke Skywalker that also doubles as the main theme; a more lyrical but nonetheless noble theme for Obi-Wan Kenobi and the mystical Force that he represents; a fairytale nocturne for Princess Leia; and a dark, menacing theme for Darth Vader that is typically played by the bassoons and low brass.[67] Because the score strongly resembles the classical model described by Gorbman, Kalinak, and others, several critics have quite explicitly linked the score to the classical Hollywood tradition of Max Steiner's *King Kong* (1933) or Korngold's *The Adventures of Robin Hood* (1938).[68]

Williams's scores for the *Star Wars* trilogy have continued to spark consumer interest some twenty years after the soundtracks' initial release. In 1994

Arista issued an elaborately packaged, four-CD box set which has since been certified gold with sales of more than 150,000 units. More recently, RCA Victor has reissued Williams's scores in deluxe double-CD collector's editions, timed to coincide with the twentieth anniversary rerelease of George Lucas's trilogy. Besides repackaging each of the three soundtracks, RCA also planned to issue several limited-edition CD singles shaped like Yoda's head and Darth Vader's helmet. To generate interest in the rereleased soundtracks, RCA mounted a $1 million promotional campaign, which included television spots on several science fiction shows, such as *The X-Files* and *Dark Skies*. Additionally, RCA's marketing director, Joe Mozian, said that the label planned to have its sales force don Darth Vader and Storm Troopers costumes to hand out postcards and discount coupons to fans waiting in line at theaters.[69] With advance orders of more than 100,000 units, it surprised no one when the first of these deluxe collector's editions leapt onto *Billboard*'s Top Twenty.

Although it performed less spectacularly than the *Star Wars* album, Ennio Morricone's music for *The Mission* is an equally compelling example of the contemporary orchestral score. *The Mission*'s soundtrack has sold a respectable half-million copies since its 1986 release, with many of these sales coming after the film's distribution on video. According to Jordan Harris, then Virgin America's comanaging director, video helped to sustain public interest in the soundtrack, which enjoyed sales of 2,000 to 4,000 copies a week some two years after the film's theatrical release.[70] More than that, however, *The Mission* is also a personal favorite of Morricone's, music that the composer says "represents me nearly completely."[71]

Like *Star Wars*, *The Mission* harks back to several aspects of the classical score, especially in its spotting and thematic organization. The score's principal themes include "The Falls," which features a soaring, lyrical four-note melodic figure; "Gabriel's Oboe," a florid, melismatic oboe figure that often serves as a theme for the film's priestly hero; and "On Earth As It Is in Heaven," a theme often scored for chorus and Brazilian percussion that combines polyrhythms with a short, staccato melodic figure.[72] Although this theme is initially linked with the slave trader Rodrigo, it later becomes associated with the Indian rebellion that culminates the film. Moreover, in many of the film's battle sequences, Morricone juxtaposes long pedal tones with a menacing, highly chromatic five-note leitmotiv, a musical figure that comes to stand for the bloody imperialism of the Spanish and Portuguese.

Reflecting the film's setting and themes, Morricone's score quite cleverly borrows from both Brazilian folk music and Baroque sacred music. While doing research for the score, Morricone studied the musical practices of seventeenth-century South American Indians and interwove several musical and syllabic chant patterns common to the Guarani tribe depicted in the film. At the same time, however, Morricone also developed a number of source cues from traditional sacred melodies, like the "Te Deum" and "Ave Maria," to represent the Guarani's religious assimilation. As Derek Elley points out, Morricone often quite brilliantly fuses these diverse elements. When the "On Earth" theme is heard together with that of "Gabriel's Oboe," as they are over the film's closing credits, the musical counterpoint becomes an aural signifier of *The Mission*'s dramatic conflict, a consummate representation of the film's opposition of Europe and South America, capitalism and spirituality, nation and church, colonialists and indigenous peoples.[73]

To some extent, the predominance of the orchestral score in science fiction and historical epics can be traced to problems of musical appropriateness posed by each genre's treatment of setting. After all, as the preceding examples show, it is difficult to motivate popular songs within the film when action is set on another planet or in eighteenth-century Brazil. However, this has not stopped some filmmakers from selecting deliberately anachronistic music for their films. Consider, for example, Mario Van Peebles's use of hip-hop for the black revisionist western *Posse* (1993) or Peter Gabriel's proto-world beat score for Martin Scorsese's *The Last Temptation of Christ* (1988). A more commercially savvy—some might say cynical—use of contemporary pop is evident in the pair of power ballads Bryan Adams recorded for *Robin Hood: Prince of Thieves* (1991) and *The Three Musketeers* (1993), respectively. Both songs, "(Everything I Do) I Do It for You" and "All for Love," reached the top of *Billboard*'s singles charts. The latter is especially notable for Adams's collaboration with Sting and Rod Stewart, a marketing gimmick that matched these contemporary pop stars to their cinematic counterparts: Athos, Porthos, and Aramis.

The inclusion of these Bryan Adams tunes places the latter two scores much closer to the second model of thematic organization, which combines the classical Hollywood orchestral score with a handful of popular tunes. Much as Mancini's scores did, this approach serves both artistic and commercial interests by combining the traditional musical language favored by composers with the more contemporary styles favored by record labels and publishers. Besides *Robin Hood* and *The Three Musketeers*, there are several other films which have utilized this approach, among them *Arthur* (1981), *Mad Max: Beyond Thunderdome* (1985), *Edward Scissorhands* (1990), *Batman Returns* (1992), and *Don Juan DeMarco* (1995). The latter features "Have You Ever Really Loved a Woman?"—yet another number one hit from the ubiquitous Bryan Adams.

More than the other patterns of organization, the commercial success of these scores depends heavily on the filmic placement of its few pop tunes. Tina Turner's "We Don't Need Another Hero," for example, may have helped call attention to her role as Auntie Entity in *Mad Max: Beyond Thunderdome*, but its placement over the end credits did little to enhance the record's chart performance. What success the song did have was largely attributable to Turner's star power. In contrast, David Lynch's cult masterpiece *Blue Velvet* (1986) brilliantly showcases the early sixties pop of Bobby Vinton and Roy Orbison. Vinton's "Blue Velvet," for example, is used to accompany the film's memorable opening sequence, which begins with the camera tilting down from a bright blue sky to show vivid red rose bushes and impossibly white picket fences, and culminates with the sudden collapse of the protagonist's father on his front lawn. For Orbison's "In Dreams," on the other hand, Dean Stockwell, playing a completely weirded-out pimp ("suave" Ben), does a hilarious and chilling impromptu lip-synch performance of the tune as town psycho Frank Booth (Dennis Hopper), innocent hero Jeffrey (Kyle MacLachlan), and some of the film's other characters look on. Reflecting the commercial import of such placement opportunities, the amazing latter sequence almost single-handedly revived Orbison's career in the late-eighties.

Maurice Jarre's *Ghost* (1990), however, is perhaps the best recent example of a score that combines classical-style orchestral music with one or two pop tunes. Although Jarre beautifully incorporates the Righteous Brothers' "Unchained Melody" as a love theme, a handful of other themes actually comprise the bulk of the film's underscore. The most significant of these is the theme first heard during the credits, which features a descending melody reminiscent of Debussy played over a low, ominous pedal tone. The theme is an aural correlative to Sam (Patrick Swayze) and Molly's (Demi Moore) unfinished upstairs loft (which comes to symbolize the thwarted hopes of their future life together) and appears at several key moments in the film, such as Sam and Molly's discussion of marriage just before he is killed, Sam's funeral, and Molly's reaction to Sam's pet word "Ditto," which Oda Mae (Whoopi Goldberg) channels from beyond the grave. The second major theme is a suspense motif that first appears when Sam is murdered, and subsequently reappears whenever Molly or Oda Mae is in danger. This "danger" theme is characterized by bursts of percussion and low brass and is more chromatic than either of the film's love themes. Lastly, Jarre's score also contains a theme for the scenes set in New York's subways that is extremely percussive and is structured around a rising, chromatic four-note motif.

While all these themes beautifully capture the film's elements of romance and suspense, it was the film's use of "Unchained Melody" that helped turn *Ghost* into the sleeper hit and box office champ of 1990. A large measure of this success was attributable to a carefully coordinated marketing campaign that targeted women between the ages of eighteen and thirty-four. After positioning *Ghost* as a female alternative to summer's usual action fare, Paramount then opted to downplay the film's dramatic and comic angles in favor of romance. Although the film's title suggested gothic or horror elements, the marketing of *Ghost* as a romance was especially evident in the advertising tagline, which read: "Before Sam was murdered, he told Molly he would love and protect her forever." To more effectively reach this target market, Paramount also bought advertising time during several female-oriented television programs, such as *Roseanne*, *Designing Women*, and several afternoon soap operas.[74]

Of course, the film's music, particularly its treatment of "Unchained Melody," also served to reinforce the romantic angle of Paramount's marketing campaign. Although "Unchained Melody" appeared in only three scenes, these scenes contained the film's most emotionally involving material. "Unchained Melody" first appears in the film's famous love scene in which Sam caresses Molly while she works at her pottery wheel.[75] It returns much later during the scene where Sam's spirit enters Oda Mae's body in order to touch and kiss Molly. Its third use is in the film's last scene in which Sam finally tells Molly he loves her, and his spirit is absorbed into a heavenly white light. In toto, the soundtrack sold nearly 1.5 million copies for Varese Sarabande to become the label's best-selling album ever. Robert Towson, Varese Sarabande's vice president, attributes that success directly to the inclusion of the Righteous Brothers' recording of "Unchained Melody" alongside the rest of Maurice Jarre's score.

The third basic pattern of organization is a score compiled entirely of popular songs. Although *American Graffiti* remains the exemplar of this approach, it has been successfully employed in several other films. Representative examples include *American Hot Wax* (1978), *Coming Home* (1978), *Rock 'n' Roll High School* (1979), *The Big Chill*, *Choose Me* (1984), *Goodfellas* (1990), and *Empire Records*. To this list we might also add such scores as those for *Saturday Night Fever*, *Fast Times at Ridgemont High*, and *Grosse Pointe Blank*, which are largely made up of compiled songs but also include some brief instances of additional scoring.

As was the case with *Easy Rider* (1969) and *American Graffiti*, the use of pop in these films is partly motivated by considerations of character and setting. In teen comedies like *Rock 'n' Roll High School*, *Fast Times at Ridgemont*

High, and *Empire Records*, music is a very important element of the world the characters inhabit. The music serves not only to mark the films' contemporary settings, it also serves to distinguish characters through their musical tastes. *High School*'s Riff Randell (P. J. Soles), for example, is almost completely defined by her love of the Ramones. Similarly, in *Empire Records*, Mark's (Ethan Randall) easygoing nature is partly equated with his willingness to listen to a wide-ranging musical tape containing songs by the Shaggs, the Residents, Pink Floyd, and Led Zeppelin.

In *Grosse Pointe Blank*, on the other hand, the setting not only motivates the constant presence of music in the film but also provides the overall concept for the score. Minnie Driver plays the film's love interest, a disk jockey who programs an "all-Eighties" weekend to commemorate the Class of '87's ten-year reunion. Like Wolfman Jack in *American Graffiti*, Driver's character serves to naturalize the presence of music at various points in the film, and in doing so, *Grosse Pointe Blank* develops its own version of *American Graffiti*'s "Where were you in '62?" Several New Wave groups were recruited to furnish the film's requisite sense of eighties' nostalgia, among them the Clash, the Specials, the English Beat, the Violent Femmes, and Echo and the Bunnymen.

Yet while pop records are extremely effective in suggesting a film's sense of time or place, they remain somewhat limited in terms of their other dramatic functions. This is especially evident in a film like Lars von Trier's *Breaking the Waves* (1996), which uses several glam-rock tunes of the early seventies. Aside from some brief instances of source music, the use of music is almost exclusively restricted to the eight process shots that introduce each of the film's seven "chapters" and epilogue. Each of these shots is composed as a painterly landscape, and each contains a proleptic title describing the main plot development of the film's next segment. More important for my purposes, each is also accompanied by a rather lengthy excerpt of a period rock tune, such as Mott the Hoople's "All the Way to Memphis," Procol Harum's "Whiter Shade of Pale," or Elton John's "Goodbye Yellow Brick Road."

Although there is relatively little music in *Breaking the Waves*, what is present is extremely important to the film's overarching symbology. In the prologue sequence in which Bess (Emily Watson) is questioned by the elders of her conservative religious sect, she identifies music as the one thing of value brought by "outsiders" to their community. Throughout the rest of the film, the commingling of music and sex will serve to underline Bess's sensual awakening to the world outside. During the couple's wedding celebration, Bess and Jan (Stellan Skargaard) dance and sing, and then make love for the first time in the reception hall's bathroom. In chapter three, "Life Alone," Jan and his fellow oil riggers listen to the radio as they engage in horseplay in the ship's shower. This is juxtaposed with a brief scene in which Bess sneaks a radio under the covers of her bed. The scene not only highlights Bess's drift toward her husband's sensual appreciation of life, but also underlines the severity of her religious order, which presumably prohibits such activities. All these moments serve to stress Bess's opening to the world. As Jan puts it, the early days of their marriage allow Bess to blossom.

Of course, this sensual appreciation of life will become depraved and perverse during the second half of the film. When Jan is disabled and can no longer have sex, he urges Bess to take a lover so that he may continue to vicariously enjoy the world of earthly pleasures through her. In a kind of twisted allusion to the Scherazade myth, Bess agrees to perform sex acts outside her marriage so she can relate these tales of love to Jan to sustain his appetite for life. Interestingly, this scenario actually inverts the Scherazade myth insofar as Bess acts not to save her own life but rather to save the life of her husband.

Here again, music and sex are commingled in a way that highlights their place within a world of physical gratification. In a montage depicting Jan's return from the hospital, his bedridden status is ironically underlined by T Rex's recording of "Hot Love." And in a scene that parallels the wedding reception, Bess dances to Elton John's "Love Lies Bleeding" in the apartment of her husband's doctor before stripping bare and offering herself to him sexually. Even though the young doctor rejects her, Bess lies to her husband and tells him that sex ensued, a moment that marks a kind of "second honeymoon" for Jan and Bess insofar as it establishes a new configuration of sex and love in their relationship. In an odd conflation of the physical and the spiritual, Bess reconciles this ever-burgeoning adulterous behavior by suggesting that it proves her devotion both to Jan and to God. As the film nears its conclusion, Bess will become increasingly unstable. Walking a fine line between schizophrenia and devout faith, Bess creates her own mise-en-scène of martyrdom in order to not only keep him alive but also cure his paralysis.

After an ugly scene in which Bess is beaten (and later dies), the film concludes with two "miracles" that seem to confirm her self-sacrifice and religious faith. Jan, now seen inexplicably up and walking, convinces his oil rigger buddies to steal Bess's body to keep her from being consigned to hell by the church's elders. Aboard ship, Jan tenderly kisses her lifeless body before giving her up to the sea. Later, Jan is awakened by his friend, who takes him above deck to hear the mysterious sound of church bells ringing, a sound Bess had always loved, but which Jan and Bess were denied on the day of their wedding.

Providing a final link between the physical and the musical, the mystical peal-
ing of the bells not only reaffirms the couple's marriage but also substantiates
the miraculous nature of Bess's love. Thus, while von Trier uses his seventies
rock tunes somewhat unconventionally within the film, he thematizes the music
in a manner that links it to the narrative's unusual blending of the sexual and
the spiritual, madness and faith, religious patriarchy and feminist liberation.

Moreover, to add to a score's other dramatic functions, filmmakers have, in
spite of their limitations, occasionally selected or adapted instrumental recordings rather than vocalized tunes. This is exemplified by the aforementioned
films that have cashed in on the current craze for electronica and by Quentin
Tarantino's *Pulp Fiction*, which uses several surf-rock instrumentals as score.
Consider, for example, how Tarantino uses the modal twang of the
Centurions' "Bullwinkle Part II" to underscore the montage sequence which
intercuts Vincent's (John Travolta) heroin injection with his later drive to pick
up Marcellus's girlfriend, Mia (Uma Thurman). Consider also how the repeti-
tive rhythms and harmonic ascension of the riff from the Revels' "Comanche"
provide a requisite sense of dramatic tension and dark humor to the scene
where Butch (Bruce Willis) tries out various weapons in the pawn shop before
settling on a samurai sword. Such examples are not unlike *Zabriskie Point*'s use
of sixties psychedelia insofar as they all depend on the music's instrumental
texture to serve each film's respective dramatic functions.

This split between kinds of music and their appropriate dramatic functions
is most apparent in the last pattern of thematic organization, which combines
orchestral underscoring with a number of pop tunes. If anything, the split
between commercial and narrative functions is even more marked. In fact,
several film music aficionados have decried the practice by arguing that the
pop tunes only provide a marketable gloss on the more substantive and dramatically effective work of a Carter Burwell or Rachel Portman. Moreover,
since these pop tunes often predominate the soundtrack albums that accompany the film, film music fans further grouse about the limited circulation
many Hollywood film scores ultimately receive. On a number of soundtrack
albums, a composer's work is condensed into an orchestral suite, which typically represents only a small portion of the score and often wrenches musical
themes and motifs out of their original context. While film composers are ill-
served by these practices, this pattern of organization remains the most common in contemporary Hollywood. Among its most prominent examples are
the scores for several Hollywood blockbusters, such as *Flashdance*,
Ghostbusters (1984), *Back to the Future*, *Top Gun*, *Batman*, *Pretty Woman*, *The
Bodyguard* (1992), *Forrest Gump*, and *Twister*.

Yet while many of these rock tunes are included primarily for cross-marketing purposes, this does not mean that they serve no dramatic functions. Rather, as films like *Forrest Gump* and *The Long Kiss Goodnight* (1996) illustrate, the split between rock and neoclassical underscoring on the soundtrack sometimes entails a very precise division of corresponding dramatic functions. While Alan Silvestri's score for *Forrest Gump* often acts as a signifier of both emotion and character, especially in the film's tearjerking final sequences, its collection of oldies serves several other narrative functions. The most important of these is the marking of the film's time scheme, a function partly necessitated by the narrative's flashback structure. At almost every point in the film, rock and roll either cues or reinforces the temporal aspect of the narrative. Duane Eddy's fifties classic, "Rebel Rouser," plays under the scene in which Forrest's dash away from some bullies in a pickup truck earns him a spot on the University of Alabama football team. Forrest's Vietnam experiences are accompanied by several tunes from the late sixties, such as Credence Clearwater Revival's "Fortunate Son," Jimi Hendrix's "All Along the Watchtower," and Buffalo Springfield's "For What It's Worth." Likewise, a television broadcast of Nixon's resignation and Forrest's discharge from the army are both covered by Tony Orlando and Dawn's early seventies classic, "Tie a Yellow Ribbon." Here as elsewhere, the chronology of music and narrative does not exactly match up—"Tie a Yellow Ribbon" was released in 1972, Nixon resigned in 1974—but the use of rock and pop nonetheless provides a general sense of temporal progression from one decade to the next. In a couple of other instances, *Gump*'s oldies provide spatial rather than temporal cues. Scott Mackenzie's "San Francisco," for instance, signals Jenny's trek from Hollywood to Haight-Ashbury. Likewise, when Jenny and Forrest return to his home in Greenbow, the event is signaled on the soundtrack by Lynyrd Skynyrd's "Sweet Home Alabama."

There are still other instances, however, where *Gump*'s oldies serve another traditional function of film music by covering temporal ellipses. This is especially true of several montage sequences in which a number of songs are grouped together to unify the representation of several related events over time. Forrest's rise to fame as a Ping-Pong champion, for example, is accompanied by three Doors' songs, namely "Hello I Love You," "People Are Strange," and "Break on Through." Similarly, Forrest's jog across America is accompanied by a number of "running" and "road" songs, such as Jackson Browne's "Running on Empty," the Doobie Brothers' "It Keeps You Running," and Willie Nelson's "On the Road Again."

Besides providing temporal cues and continuity, *Gump*'s collection of oldies also contributes to the film's thematics, especially its development of a bird motif that comes to represent both Forrest's destiny and Jenny's desperate attempts to escape her past. The motif is introduced in the film's famous computer-generated tracking shot depicting a feather's slow, wind-blown descent to earth. This opening shot was seen by many reviewers as both a symbol of the interactions of chance and destiny, and as a more specific signifier of Forrest's capricious success. What these reviewers overlook, however, is the extent to which Jenny is also associated with this bird motif. Early in the film, Jenny hides from her abusive father in a cornfield and prays that God will make her a bird so that she "can fly far, far away from here." Later, Jenny's association with birds takes on darker tones as her thoughts of flight are transformed into thoughts of suicide. After Forrest "rescues" her from a seedy strip club, Jenny climbs onto a bridge railing and asks Forrest whether he thinks she could fly. This action is repeated in a later scene in which Jenny climbs onto the window ledge of her hotel room. Lynyrd Skynyrd's recording of "Free Bird" accompanies this scene and emphasizes the linkage between the film's avian motif and Jenny's thoughts of suicide. The linkage underlines the film's political conservatism by suggesting that Jenny's desire for freedom, her experience of social and sexual liberation, is in fact a kind of oedipally motivated death wish, one she ultimately realizes when she contracts AIDS.

The rock tunes compiled for Renny Harlin's action film, *The Long Kiss Goodnight*, play a similarly important role in the thematics of that film. The film tells the story of Samantha Caine, an unassuming teacher and mother, who discovers that she was previously a government-trained assassin. Here again, Silvestri's specially composed score serves a number of more traditional functions of film music. The title theme, for example, features a highly chromatic string melody over a pulsing bass and chugging synthesizer. This theme operates generally as an all-purpose action theme for several of the film's chases and gunfights. Similarly, Silvestri also includes a very lyrical string melody to represent the relationship between Samantha and her daughter Caitlin. Since the film attempts to reconcile its representation of motherhood with its representation of postfeminist heroics, Silvestri's music here plays an important role in the film's thematics by underscoring the maternal half of Samantha's "split" personality. This split is made explicit in the film's credit sequence by alternating shots of Samantha / Charlene (Geena Davis) each writing her name. This split is further emphasized both photographically and iconographically; positive images alternate with negative images and shots of family and Christmas alternate with shots of knives and weaponry.

FIGURE 8.1 The source music in *The Long Kiss Goodnight* (1996) reinforces the gender role confusion suffered by Sam/Charly (Geena Davis).

Yet while the narrative explicitly divides the character into feminine and masculine halves, the film's treatment of gender boundaries is never reducible to a simple division between masculine and feminine. Consider, for example, how both Samantha and her alter ego Charlene have names which are frequently shortened into the more masculine-sounding "Sam" and "Charly." This further linguistic bifurcation of masculine and feminine signifiers reinforces the notion that Charly's toughness is present within Sam from the beginning of the film. Later, Sam's negotiation of gender roles will be used for humorous effect. To free herself and her daughter from an icy death in a walk-in freezer, Sam fills Caitlin's doll with kerosene and creates a primitive explosive to blow off the door. Just before Sam ignites the kerosene, she maternally instructs Caitlin to cover her ears and even asks if the family should get a puppy for Christmas.

The film's blurring of gender boundaries extends to the film's soundtrack, which periodically comments on the heroine's transformation from *femme* to *femme fatale*. This is most evident during the moment when Sam finally makes herself over as Charly, a change signified by a montage of Sam cutting her hair and dying it blonde. The soundtrack ironically underlines this transformation through the choice of Santana's cover of "She's Not There." Playing on the ambiguity of the pronoun "she," the song's double meaning comments on both the narrative and thematic implications of Sam's metamorphosis. On the one hand, the "she" of the song title refers to Samantha herself and Charly's rejection of her previous incarnation as wife, mother, and PTA member. On the other hand, the "she" of the title refers more broadly to the absence of femininity in Charly and her emergence as a phallic heroine more generally associated with the action film. This is later concretized in the film's climactic chase scene in which Charly tells her pursuers to "Suck my dick!" just before she crashes her runaway truck into a wall.

The film's linkage between music and identity is reinforced by the selection of performers for the soundtrack. Sam's problematic reconciliation of maternal and professional roles is emphasized by the presence of Tracy Bonham and Neneh Cherry on the soundtrack, artists whose work quite explicitly touches on the relationship between mothers and daughters. Cherry's 1992 album *Homebrew*, for example, was recorded after a two-year period of semiretirement during which Cherry married her collaborator, Cameron "Boogie Bear" McVey, and spent time at home with her two children. The album cover reflected this newfound domesticity by showing Cherry pushing a baby carriage.

Similarly, several African-American artists, such as Muddy Waters, Jr. Parker, and Marvin Gaye, serve as surrogates for Mitch (Samuel L. Jackson), the black detective who aids Samantha in her search for her identity. In the scene where Sam pushes him out of a moving car, for example, Mitch's reluctance to give up the case is underscored by Gaye's "Stubborn Kind of Fellow." Likewise, the musical theme assigned to Mitch, Muddy Waters' "Mannish Boy," not only reinforces his African-American identity but also fleshes out the film's treatment of problematic parental roles. By underlining the perceptions held by his ex-wife, the song's paradoxical title signifies Mitch's previous inability to fulfill his adult responsibilities as husband and father, a situation that complicates his present efforts to rebuild his relationship with his son. Thus, just as the soundtrack highlights Samantha's negotiation of femininity, it also underscores Mitch's attempts to realize his paternity. In doing so, the narrative parallels both characters' difficult relationship to parenthood, a trope that both borrows but also deviates from the typical "buddy" pairing in the action film.

The growth of the soundtrack market since 1975 has been nothing short of astonishing, and with the undeniable success of the soundtracks for *Space Jam* and *William Shakespeare's Romeo + Juliet* (both 1996), there is no reason to think this pattern won't continue. While scholars like Denisoff and Romanowski are right to question the overall success rate of film and music cross-promotions, the phenomenon continues to be a dominant industrial practice. The situation is perhaps best summarized by a recent advertisement for Arista Records' soundtrack division in which the company boasts, "You shoot. We score. Everybody wins."[76]

The music industry has particularly benefited from the increased popularity of soundtrack recordings. For one thing, since they sometimes group several popular artists on one disk, soundtracks are often seen as relatively low-risk purchases by consumers. As such, like samplers and tribute albums, they have become an especially effective device for launching the careers of new acts or reviving interest in the work of older recording artists. Similarly, the increasing importance of music-licensing for films has greatly enhanced the value of publishers' and record labels' back catalogs. EMI-Capitol Music, for example, has seen its master licensing business nearly quintuple since 1989.[77] Licensing fees have also risen at a comparable rate. According to one label executive, the costs of using a particular recording over a film's opening credits is now five to ten times higher than what it was ten years ago.[78]

Yet while the demand for licensed music is higher than ever, so is the competition to get songs and recordings into feature films. Publishers and record labels must be increasingly proactive in their efforts to place songs in films. Says Scott James of MCA Publishing, "Our sampler goes to music supervisors, music heads, advertisers, merchandisers—anyone who has a need for music." Catherine Farley, the director of special products and licensing at the All American Group, takes a similarly assertive stance. To promote the licensing of masters from All American's urban music label, Street Life, Farley sends all the label's new releases to African-American filmmakers in the hope that one will ultimately use the music in their film.

Because of their involvement with almost every aspect of a soundtrack's preparation, music supervisors have emerged as some of Hollywood's most important dealmakers. While some music supervisors perform mostly administrative tasks, several others actively participate in creating a soundtrack's overall concept and design by taking part in scoring sessions, negotiating licensing arrangements, and in some cases, even organizing "casting calls" for songwriters and performers. One sign of their burgeoning influence is the fact that many top music supervisors, like Gary LeMel and Kathy Nelson, become the heads of major studios' music divisions.

Popular styles of music may come and go, but pop's place in films will undoubtedly continue well into the future. With so much at stake for both sides of the cross-promotional equation, a commercial soundtrack will remain one of the cheapest and easiest marketing angles that a filmmaker can exploit. In his book *Hollywood in the Sixties*, John Baxter summarized the then-current pop score phenomenon as an effort to supply the film industry with "something the kids can whistle."[79] In the film music of the past half century, moviegoers not only found that something, they have been whistling it ever since.

Epilogue

Since the 1950s, the interrelation of the film and record industries has placed certain constraints on the production of film music. In serving both dramatic and commercial functions, scores negotiated a boundary between commercialism and dramatic necessity, unity and fragmentation, formal prominence and narrative subservience. On the one hand, a score needed to be unified to serve its various narrational roles; on the other hand, individual parts of a score had to be excerptable as structurally coherent and musically satisfying theme songs and album tracks. One especially important constraint in this regard was the need to adapt film scores to the format of pop and rock albums.

While negotiating that boundary, pop composers like Henry Mancini, John Barry, and Ennio Morricone emphasized particular formal parameters in their work—long melodies, song forms, and jazz-rock orchestrations—as a means of assuring structural coherence and giving their music a strong pop appeal. In the late sixties, the development of all these parameters culminated in the compilation score, which simply used preexisting or original songs to furnish a film's musical cues. The compilation score sacrificed a formal elasticity when underscoring individual scenes, but it compensated for this loss through a shrewd use of musical association and allusion to reinforce aspects of setting, characterization, and theme.

Of course, part of pop music's importance for film stems from the very fact that it is popular. As director Allison Anders points out, pop music—and popular culture more generally—has become our culture's common reference point:

> Popular music is the only reference point we hold in common anymore. We are not all the same religion, we don't hold the same views on whether we eat meat or we don't eat meat, whether we are monogamous or we're not. There's no common ground except for popular culture, so in a way it's what's holding it all together.[1]

Because it serves as a common reference point, pop music becomes a very handy marker of time and place, and it carries a certain built-in resonance that can be used by filmmakers as part of cinema's larger patterns of signification and intertextual association.

Pop's music's resonance among film spectators and its broad cultural circulation suggest that film music critics have been far too eager to dismiss it. Indeed, if one can draw any conclusion from this study, it is that pop music's place in film ought to be studied much more thoroughly insofar as it bears on current theorizations of postmodernity, intertextuality, and consumer culture. Though this attention is a long time in coming, the study of pop music in film promises to be an important area of scholarly activity in the near future. In fact, as this volume goes to press, there is already a special issue of the *Journal of Popular Film and Video* devoted to the subject as well as a planned anthology to be published by Duke University Press.

Throughout this study I have sought to describe the historical development of the pop score in terms of its relation to economics, culture, and film form. Yet for the sake of space and cogency, I have left untouched numerous other issues which I believe warrant further investigation. While several of these leap to mind, I will concentrate here on three broad subject areas relating to questions of film form, film reception, and film history.

First of all, one of the unequivocal assumptions of my argument is that song forms have played an important role in the overall shape and design of the pop score. While this is certainly the case of source music in films, I have argued that it is also true of the underscores of the films I examined. Indeed, in films like *Breakfast at Tiffany's* and *Goldfinger*, it is the frequent repetition of themes and the organization of cues in nearly complete phrase patterns that encouraged audiences to both remember and subsequently buy the film's music as either sheet music or recordings. Whether or not one agrees with my assessment, it nonetheless suggests that we might also rethink the role of song forms in classical Hollywood composition.

In film music circles, it is commonly thought that the pop score's emphasis on songs sharply differentiates it from classical scoring. Throughout my argument I have accepted this tenet of film music dogma, but increasingly it seems to me that the lines separating these two styles of composition are blurred. James Buhler and David Neumeyer have cautioned against overemphasizing nineteenth-century Romanticism as *the* influence on the classical score. Instead, they suggest that the classical Hollywood score was inherently heterogeneous, a polyglot of musical styles, forms, and influences. If Buhler and Neumeyer are correct in describing Hollywood film music as a "pragmatically-inspired eclecticism" (and I think they are), then it seems reasonable to believe that classical composers commonly plundered songs of various types in concocting their particular stylistic mélange.[2]

With their heavy use of traditional folk songs, the films of John Ford come to mind as one example of the song form's importance, as do films like *Casablanca* (1942), *Beyond the Forest* (1949), and *There's Always Tomorrow* (1956), whose scores are organized around preexisting pop tunes. To these we might also add examples like *The Hurricane* (1947) and *The Uninvited* (1944), in which themes ("Moon of Manikoora" and "Stella by Starlight," respectively) are extracted and elevated to the status of pop tunes. All these examples support the notion that Romanticism's influence must be weighed against other comparable influences, such as operetta, musical theater, melodrama, and popular songwriting. Clearly, film music critics have used Romanticism as a way of ennobling the works of Steiner, Korngold, and other composers, but it would be inaccurate to discuss their work solely in these terms.

A second area that deserves further exploration involves the relation of film music to consumer culture. While sales figures attest to consumer interest in film music, they say little about the ways in which fans make use of soundtracks. What do fans derive from listening to soundtracks? Is it merely the chance to relive a pleasurable cinematic experience or does a film's music relate to fans on some other extratextual level? Previous studies of fan culture, like Henry Jenkins's *Textual Poachers*, suggest that this would be a promising area of further inquiry.[3] There is a voluminous amount of fan writing accessible on the Internet, in newsletters, and in numerous fanzines. As with other analyses of fan culture, a study of film music buffs might support the notion that elements of consumer taste serve as markers of social distinction, and that these in turn become important factors in fans' sense of their own identity and their position in the larger spheres of culture and society.[4]

The third area for further research pertains to the study of film music history. During the past decade, scholarly inquiry into film music has experienced a period of productivity unparalleled in its long, if mostly undistinguished, history. While this work reflects a diverse range of interests and critical approaches, its common thread is a deep concern with contemporary film theory and the place of music within a broader framework of semiotic and ideological activities. Through the application of new analytical models and theoretical concepts, this research has greatly enriched our understanding of both the forms and functions of music in the classical Hollywood cinema.

The one research area generally untouched by this flurry of interest, however, has been the history of film music, which for the most part remains mired in the "masterpiece" approach associated with a much earlier generation of cinema historians.[5] If my argument in this study has a polemical dimension, it is that film music studies would positively benefit from a greater emphasis on historicity. Instead of simply analyzing the oeuvres of great composers, we must place the work within its larger industrial and cultural context. By considering aesthetic issues alongside economic and social issues, we not only derive a richer knowledge of film music art, we also gain a better understanding of film music within the contexts in which it is commonly consumed.

Film music theory would equally benefit from a larger stress on historicity. Concepts like formal accessibility and inaudibility must be tested against specific historical backgrounds and compositional practices. As I noted in chapter 1, notions of formal accessibility changed quite markedly between the 1930s and the 1960s as the relative predominance of the Romantic idiom gave way to more popular styles of music, such as jazz and rock. Similarly, tunes were made more "audible" in the sixties by the development of new approaches to spotting and scoring. Other basic concepts of film scoring, like appropriateness and unity, might similarly profit from an examination in specific historical circumstances and according to specific compositional practices.

As I have noted elsewhere, the prospects for developing a historical poetics of film music are daunting.[6] Unfortunately, the study of film music has been treated as an unwanted stepchild by both disciplines, and this is not likely to change in the foreseeable future. One reason for this, of course, is the inherent interdisciplinarity of film music study. The need to master two very different sets of nomenclature, theoretical concepts, and analytical traditions often proves a difficult obstacle to overcome. If very few music scholars have the background to perform close textual analyses of films, then still fewer film scholars have the specialized training required to analyze complex musical works.

Yet if the challenges to such scholarly endeavors are many, so are its benefits. By situating aesthetic issues within their economic and cultural contexts, we not only gain a more nuanced understanding of the film score's form and history, but we also nudge our object of study closer to the center of our discipline's concerns. It is discouragingly commonplace to hear film music described as a so-called "neglected art."[7] To reverse this trend, film music scholars must directly engage with the predominant critical and historical models of our discipline. Only then will the art of film music gain the attention and appreciation it so richly deserves.

$\mathcal{N}otes$

1. Did They Mention the Music?

1. See Douglas Gomery, *The Hollywood Studio System*; and Alexander Doty, "Music Sells Movies: (Re) New (ed) Conservatism in Film Marketing," *Wide Angle* 10, no. 2 (1988): 70–79.

2. Irwin Bazelon, *Knowing the Score: Notes on Film Music*, 30.

3. See Claudia Gorbman, *Unheard Melodies: Narrative Film Music*; Caryl Flinn, *Strains of Utopia: Gender, Nostalgia, and Hollywood Film Music*; Noël Carroll, *Mystifying Movies: Fads and Fallacies in Contemporary Film Theory*, 213–25; Kathryn Kalinak, *Settling the Score: Music and the Classical Hollywood Film*; Fred Karlin, *Listening to Movies: The Film Lover's Guide to Film Music*; and Royal S. Brown, *Overtones and Undertones: Reading Film Music*.

4. For a discussion of masterpiece histories, see Robert Allen and Douglas Gomery, *Film History: Theory and Practice*, 67–108.

5. William Darby and Jack Du Bois, *American Film Music: Major Composers, Techniques, Trends, 1915–1990*.

6. See Allen and Gomery, *Film History*, 71–91, for a concise and lucid summary of the critique of the masterpiece tradition.

7. Bazelon, *Knowing the Score*, 30.

8. This criticism owes a great deal to the landmark work of Theodor Adorno and the Frankfurt School, but lacks the latter's rhetorical subtlety and elegance (see Theodor W. Adorno, *Introduction to the Sociology of Music*, trans. E. B. Ashton, 21–38). Interestingly, Adorno's view of film music was almost equally dim. For an overview of Adorno's contribution to film music theory, see Hanns Eisler and Theodor W. Adorno (uncredited), *Composing for the Films*; and Philip Rosen, "Adorno and Film Music: Theoretical Notes on *Composing for the Films*," *Yale French Studies* 60 (1980): 157–83.

9. Bazelon, *Knowing the Score*, 11.

10. Mark Evans, *Soundtrack: The Music of the Movies*, 194.

11. Brown, *Overtones and Undertones*, 344–47.

12. The question of the extent to which this definition applies to various kinds of

world music is one that lies beyond the scope of this presentation. My definition of the pop score, as it has been previously construed by film music historians, refers to a very specific musical and cultural formation that can be located within Hollywood scoring practices since the 1960s. That said, I suspect that there are certain continuities in the musical parameters of the pop score and various kinds of world music (functional tonality, rhythmic emphasis, timbral specificity). Although several factors can be mobilized to account for this, these shared parameters are at least partly due to the economic and cultural hegemony of American popular music in world markets, and the role of the diaspora in circulating African musical forms and styles around the world.

13. Aaron Copland, "Tip to Moviegoers: Take Off Those Earmuffs," *New York Times*, November 6, 1949, sec. 6, 28.

14. A number of recent film scores, such as *Batman* (1989), *Do the Right Thing* (1989), and *Dick Tracy* (1990), are interesting in this regard in that they divide the labor of the film composer into two discrete parts, each with its own style and function. In *Batman*, for example, Prince's collection of funk and pop songs function largely as a commercial tie-in and are only occasionally featured in the film in extended moments of spectacle (the Joker's vandalization of the art museum, the Joker's parade through Gotham City). In contrast, Danny Elfman's symphonic score plays the more traditional roles of narrative film music: enhancing mood, signaling story developments, and representing characters' inner states. The importance of this division of labor, itself governed by the different demands of art and commerce, is made more evident in the release of singles that do not even appear in these films, but rather are "inspired" by them. To most film music historians, Prince's "Batdance" and Madonna's "Vogue," inspired by *Batman* and *Dick Tracy* respectively, can only be viewed as rather transparent attempts to link pop superstars and blockbuster productions in order to strengthen the money-making potential of each.

15. For more on the notion of group style, see David Bordwell, Janet Staiger, and Kristin Thompson, *The Classical Hollywood Cinema: Film Style and Mode of Production to 1960*, 6–11.

16. For more on Romanticism's influence on Hollywood film music, see Flinn, *Strains of Utopia*, esp. 13–50; and Kalinak, *Settling the Score*, 66–110.

17. Christopher Palmer, however, argues that conservatory-trained composers in Hollywood were more the exception than the rule: "Roy Webb, Herbert Stothart, Alfred Newman, and Adolph Deutsch all hailed from Broadway; Victor Young was a popular radio conductor and song and light music composer; Bronislau Kaper and Frederick Hollander were pianist-songwriters, refugees from an increasingly Nazified Europe; Franz Waxman, also a refugee from Nazism, was still comparatively inexperienced as a composer; David Raksin was a jazz instrumentalist and arranger; Dimitri Tiomkin was primarily a concert pianist, originally less of a professional composer even than Steiner; and so the list goes on." See Palmer's *The Composer in Hollywood*, 19–23.

Eddy Lawrence Manson concurs, and adds that while most composers have some measure of formal musical education, most also have some experience playing or writing "people music" for theaters, night clubs, bar mitzvahs, or jazz and rock bands. See Manson's "The Film Composer in Concert and the Concert Composer in Film" in Clifford McCarty, ed., *Film Music 1*.

18. Kalinak, *Settling the Score*, 79.

19. See John Shepherd, *Music as Social Text*, 128–32; Iain Chambers, *Urban Rhythms: Popular Music and Popular Culture*, 8–12; Simon Frith, "Towards an Aesthetic of Popular Music," *Music and Society: The Politics of Composition, Performance, and Reception*, 133–49; Bruce Baugh, "Prolegomena to An Aesthetics of Rock Music," *Journal of Aesthetics and Art Criticism* 51, no. 1 (Winter 1993): 24–29; and Graham Vuillamy and Edward Lee, *Popular Music: A Teacher's Guide*, 50–63.

20. See Adorno, *Introduction to the Sociology of Music*, 21–38. In drawing this distinction, Adorno conveniently overlooks the fact that strophic phrase patterns and verse/chorus forms predate the Tin Pan Alley music and Broadway shows he criticizes. Likewise, Adorno also overlooks the fact that many developmental forms, such as sonata-allegro or theme and variations, are themselves "standardized." In this regard, Adorno might more properly draw his distinction between popular and classical music on the basis of musical process rather than on form per se.

22. Fred Karlin and Rayburn Wright, *On the Track: A Guide to Contemporary Film Scoring*, 423.

23. See Shepherd, *Music as Social Text*, 128–31.

23. Ibid.

24. Pop music theorists have sometimes adopted Roland Barthes' concept of the pheno-text as a way of envisaging the idiom's approach to phonology. Simon Frith and Andrew Goodwin, for example, grant that Barthes applied this concept to the role of the voice in classical music, but nonetheless argue that it lays the groundwork for an entire reformulation of pop musicology. See Roland Barthes, "The Grain of the Voice," in Barthes, *Image-Music-Text*, trans. Stephen Heath (New York: Hill and Wang, 1977), 179–89; and Simon Frith and Andrew Goodwin, eds., *On Record: Rock, Pop, and the Written Word*, 275–76.

25. Karlin and Wright, *On the Track*, 423.

26. Evans, *Soundtrack*, 195.

27. Kalinak, *Settling the Score*, 184–88.

28. Leonard Meyer, *Style and Music: Theory, History, and Ideology*, 13–23.

29. Meyer, *Style and Music*, 14–15.

30. Ibid., 163–217.

31. Ibid., 206–208.

32. See Flinn, *Strains of Utopia*, 13–50; Gorbman, *Unheard Melodies*, 78–79; and Kalinak, *Settling the Score*, 100–103. Flinn offers the most cogent analysis of Romanticism's influence on Hollywood composers. Tracing this influence through the classical Hollywood era, Flinn shows that this influence was both musical and ideological, and was figured in legal, institutional, and critical discourses of the period.

33. Graham Bruce, *Bernard Herrmann: Film Music and Narrative*, 36.

34. Meyer, *Style and Music*, 207.

35. I should caution, however, against overemphasizing the leitmotiv as a formal unit. While the leitmotiv is certainly important to classical Hollywood scoring, film music theorists have often privileged it in a way that diminishes the relative importance of a score's secondary parameters. The latter are perhaps more important than leitmotivs in that they are a more direct means of musical expression. As Meyer notes, the apprehension of secondary parameters does not depend upon knowing a set of

tacit rules and conventions, and thus would seem especially well suited to a musically untrained audience. Because of their directness, the secondary parameters of film scores—their texture, sonority, tempi, and tone color—are in fact composers' primary means of musical expression and signification.

36. Bob Monaco and James Riordan, *The Platinum Rainbow (How to Succeed in the Music Business Without Selling Your Soul)* (Sherman Oaks, Calif.: Swordsman, 1980), 178.

37. Gary Burns, "A Typology of 'Hooks' in Popular Records," *Popular Music 6*, no. 1 (January 1987): 1.

38. Burns argues that any number of textual elements (rhythm, melody, and harmony) and nontextual elements (tempo, instrumentation, dynamics, and even sound effects or mixing) can serve as a hook, and he illustrates each with examples culled from well-known pop records. Some of these hooks are produced through simple repetitions; others derive from a more complex manipulation and modulation of structural and sonorous elements.

39. See Meyer, *Style and Music*, 207.

40. For a detailed analysis of David Raksin's music for *Laura*, see Kalinak, *Settling the Score*, 159–83. As Don Crafton pointed out to me in a conversation, the music for *Laura* was itself modeled on the monothematic scores of the twenties and early thirties.

41. Burns, "A Typology of 'Hooks' in Popular Records," 11.

42. Burns points out that particular styles of instrumentation may lose their freshness when they recur on a number of different records. The fuzz box, for example, was new in 1965, and lent a unique instrumental effect to records by the Beatles and the Yardbirds. Today, however, a fuzz box effect is not particularly surprising and would not be considered a hook in most cases. In contrast, older pop styles that have fallen out of favor may be revived in a way that produces a hook effect. Burns notes Bette Midler's recording of "Boogie Woogie Bugle Boy" as an instance where the revival of the Big Band sound made for an ear-catching novelty. Barry's use of a Louis Armstrong-styled trumpet here is an analogous example in which a Dixieland or Swing effect momentarily captures the listener's attention.

43. Burns, "A Typology of 'Hooks' in Popular Records," 9–10.

2. BANKING ON FILM MUSIC

1. This should not be confused with the Rik Mayall sitcom of the same name that appeared on British television some twenty years later. That show featured a theme performed by former Squeeze keyboardist Jools Holland, but it bears absolutely no relation to the Cameo release.

2. "Theme from Nowhere," *Billboard*, November 28, 1960, 9.

3. Russell Sanjek, *American Popular Music and Its Business: The First Four Hundred Years, Volume 3*, 350. Here and throughout this chapter, I am greatly indebted to Russell Sanjek's monumental work on the history of the American popular music industry. His work was particularly helpful in gaining an overview of the economic structures of this industry as well as providing a great deal of background information on the music business. For representative examples of Sanjek's work, see the three-volume work cited above, as well as *From Print to Plastic: Publishing and*

Promoting America's Popular Music (1900–1980), and *The American Popular Music Business in the 20th Century*, cowritten with his son David.

Besides Sanjek's work, I additionally consulted a number of other surveys of the structure and history of the music industry, including Michael Fink, *Inside the Music Business: Music in Contemporary Life*; Paula Dranov, *Inside the Music Publishing Industry*; Sidney Shemel and M. William Krasilovsky, *This Business of Music*; David T. MacFarland, "Up from Middle America: The Development of the Top 40," in Lawrence Lichty and Malachi C. Topping, eds., *American Broadcasting: A Source Book on the History of Radio and Television*; Robert Burnett's *The Global Jukebox: The International Music Industry*; and R. Serge Denisoff's two works, *Solid Gold: The Popular Record Industry* and *Tarnished Gold: The Record Industry Revisited*.

4. Figures are from "Disk Industry's '61 LP Output Hits 5,927 Pkgs," *Variety*, March 21, 1962, 49.

5. These sales are especially impressive when one considers that today an orchestral soundtrack album is deemed successful if it sells 50,000 units. See Karlin, *Listening to Movies*, 232.

6. I am thinking here of such works as Richard Leppert and Susan McClary's anthology, *Music and Society: The Politics of Composition, Performance, and Reception*; Jacques Attali, *Noise: The Political Economy of Music*, trans. Brian Massumi; Richard Norton, *Tonality in Western Culture*; Joseph Kerman, *Contemplating Music: Challenges to Musicology*; Alan Durant, *Conditions of Music*; Christopher Norris, ed., *Music and the Politics of Culture*; and Rose Rosengard Subotnik, *Deconstructive Variations: Music and Reason in Western Society* (Minneapolis: University of Minnesota Press, 1996).

7. For a concise overview of the record industry's economic structure, see Richard A. Peterson and David G. Berger, "Cycles in Symbol Production: The Case of Popular Music," in Frith and Goodwin, eds., *On Record*, 140–59.

8. See Sanjek, *American Popular Music and Its Business* 3:333–66.

9. Doty, "Music Sells Movies," 72.

10. See Tino Balio, ed., *The American Film Industry*, 139–47.

11. R. Serge Denisoff and George Plasketes, "Synergy in 1980s Film and Music: Formula for Success or Industry Mythology?" *Film History* 4, no. 3 (1990): 257–76.

12. Charles Merrell Berg, *An Investigation of the Motives for and the Realization of Music to Accompany the American Silent Film, 1896–1927*, 244.

13. Berg, *An Investigation of the Motives*, 254.

14. Jim Walsh, "Fads, Foibles, and History Reflected in Pop Songs of 50 Years Ago," *Variety*, March 25, 1964, 54.

15. See Russell Sanjek, *Pennies from Heaven: The American Popular Music Business in the Twentieth Century*, 34–35.

16. Berg, *An Investigation of the Motives*, 255.

17. Quoted in André Millard, *America on Record: A History of Recorded Sound*, 160.

18. See Sanjek, *American Popular Music and Its Business* 3:47; and Sanjek and Sanjek, *The American Popular Music Business*, 35. It should be noted here that although Sanjek identifies Neilan as the person responsible for commissioning the title song for *Mickey*, the author also mistakenly credits Neilan for the film's direction. Most reference works cite Richard Jones as the director of *Mickey*.

19. See Sanjek, *American Popular Music and Its Business* 3:47–50.

20. Sanjek, *American Popular Music and Its Business* 3:52–54.

21. Ibid., 55.

22. See Sanjek, *American Popular Music and Its Business* 3:91–114; and Gomery, *The Hollywood Studio System*, 106–110.

23. Sanjek and Sanjek, *The American Popular Music Business*, 43.

24. See Sanjek, *From Print to Plastic*, 19.

25. As cited in Sanjek, *American Popular Music and Its Business* 3:317–18.

26. See Sanjek, *Pennies From Heaven*, 251–53.

27. Ibid.

28. See Sanjek, *American Popular Music and Its Business* 3:245. As the author notes, this spectacular jump in sales was at least partly due to the development of new record formats and technologies. In 1946 the 78-rpm record offered the only kind of format available. In 1951, however, 78-rpm records were competing with 45-rpm singles and 33 $^{1/3}$-rpm LPs, and all three carved up a market comprised of the owners of some twenty-two million record players of all types.

29. See Millard, *America on Record*, 161–67.

30. Mike Gross, "Indies' Inroads on Major Diskeries' Pop Singles; $400,000,000 Record Mark," *Variety*, January 8, 1958, 215.

31. See Sanjek, *American Popular Music and Its Business* 3:344–47; and Gross, "Indies' Inroads," *Variety*, 215. Paramount's acquisition of Dot should not be confused with the already existing ABC-Paramount label. About two years earlier, United Paramount Theaters had joined with the American Broadcasting Company to form ABC-Paramount Records. This venture was part of a larger merger between UPT and ABC in 1953, and it had nothing to do with Paramount Pictures' production and distribution wings.

32. See Sanjek, *American Popular Music and Its Business* 3:346.

33. "20th Century-Fox in Disk Field; Onorati Quits Dot to Head Subsid," *Variety*, February 12, 1958, 53.

34. "Time to Grow Up," *Variety*, February 12, 1958, 53.

35. "MGM Records and Metro Pix Getting Real Chummy; Maxin's 'All One Family,' " *Variety*, February 5, 1958, 53.

36. Herm Schoenfeld, "New Big Street—B'Way and Vine," *Variety*, February 5, 1958, 53.

37. Herm Schoenfeld, "R'n'R and Payola Still with the Music Biz: ASCAP Hassles; Diskeries' All 33-RPM Move," *Variety*, January 4, 1961, 207.

38. June Bundy, "Film Themes Link Movie, Disk Trades," *Billboard*, December 24, 1960, 8.

39. "End of the Indie Disker Era," *Variety*, June 7, 1961, 51 and 54.

40. See Sanjek, *American Popular Music and Its Business* 3:388–89; and Bob Rolontz, "They Laughed When Film Firms Sat Down . . . ," *Billboard*, May 11, 1963, 1 and 6.

41. "WB Label Gets 'Track LPs to 3 Upcoming Pix," *Variety*, December 18, 1963, 45.

42. Rolontz, "They Laughed When," 6.

43. "Columbia Pix' Buildup of BMI Subsid Strains Ties with Shapiro Bernstein," *Variety*, June 27, 1962, 39.

44. "Raker Cooking Major Buildup of Colpix Label," *Variety*, August 1, 1962, 37; "Colpix Steps Up Soundtrack Ties with Columbia," *Billboard*, September 1, 1962, 6; and "Colpix and Parent Film Co. Hiking Cross-Promo Sked on Track LP's," *Variety*, September 5, 1962, 43.

45. See Sanjek, *American Popular Music and Its Business* 3:387; and Rolontz, "They Laughed When," 6.

46. "SG-Col Music Rolls Big Campaign to Build Colpix into Major Label Status," *Variety*, September 25, 1963, 55.

47. "SG-Col Music's Creative Group Places Songs with Top Artists," *Billboard*, January 23, 1965, 10.

48. See " 'Lord Jim' LP Gets Royal Promotion," *Billboard*, February 20, 1965, 12; and "Col. Films Looks to Disks as Promotion," *Billboard*, March 13, 1965, 3.

49. "20th-Fox Label Blueprints Closer Ties with Parent," *Variety*, February 14, 1962, 45.

50. "20th-Fox Label Tests New Slant on 'Track LPs," *Variety*, April 21, 1965, 49.

51. See "20th-Fox Is Making Giant Track Strides," *Billboard*, December 18, 1965, 1. *Billboard* notes that 20th-Fox's winter sales program was organized around some thirteen scores, including *Our Man Flint*, *The Sand Pebbles*, and *The Blue Max*.

52. For a concise history of UA's various music operations, see Tino Balio, *United Artists: The Company That Changed the Film Industry*, 112–16.

53. "UA Sets First Distrib Meets," *Billboard*, June 20, 1960, 4; and "UA Stresses Pic Ties at Its First Annual Conclave," *Variety*, July 27, 1960, 109.

54. Bundy, "Film Themes Link Movie, Disk Trades," 8 and 10.

55. "UA Label Booming 300 Percent Over Last Year," *Variety*, March 1, 1961, 75.

56. See "UA Fall Sales Program Eyes $1,700,000 Billings," *Variety*, August 30, 1961, 44; and "UA & Its Diskery in Joint Push on 3 Oct. Film Bows," *Variety*, October 4, 1961, 59.

57. "UA's 1961 Gross Hits $5,000,000, a 100 Percent Increase Over Last Year," *Variety*, December 13, 1961, 47.

58. "Talmadge Shapes Strong Global UA Image, Toting Label's Name," *Billboard*, March 13, 1961, 4.

59. "UA Goes All Out for Sales Keyed to Oscar Awards," *Billboard*, March 17, 1962, 14.

60. See "UA Records Preps Film Score Projects; Formats to Include a Jazz Tie," *Variety*, August 15, 1962, 41; "UA Adds 3rd Soundtrack Album," *Billboard*, September 15, 1962, 5; "Report UA Net Off Despite Peak $7-Mil Biz in '62," *Variety*, January 2, 1963, 35; and Balio, *United Artists*, 114.

61. "UA Label Pegs Future to Flock of Film Tracks," *Variety*, April 6, 1966, 51.

62. Like other Hollywood subsidiaries, MGM Records maintained close contact with its parent company and frequently participated in the promotion of its film products between 1958 and 1965. For more on MGM's soundtrack interests, see "MGM Label Promoting Two Metro Pic Scores," *Variety*, July 13, 1960, 46; *Variety*, March 18, 1961, 58; "MGM Bountiful on 'Mutiny' Disks," *Variety*, September 5, 1962, 41; " 'Bounty' Disks Get Big Push," *Billboard*, September 8, 1962, 5; "MGM & Its Pub, Disk Affils Join in Big Push on 'West,' " *Variety*, February 13, 1963, 53; "MGM in Summer Soundtrack Ride," *Variety*, June 10, 1964, 4; "MGM to Bow Six

Soundtracks," *Billboard*, July 18, 1964, 35; and "MGM Records Rolls Big Push on 'Zhivago' Theme," *Variety*, December 22, 1965, 46.

63. O'Brien, quoted in "MGM Records, Big Three Annual Gross Hits $20,900,000; Net Over $2,000,000," *Variety*, December 8, 1965, 53.

64. As cited in *Time*, October 7, 1966, 56.

65. See "1965 a Boom Year in Disk Merchandising," *Billboard*, January 29, 1966, 1 and 8; "Retail Disk Sales Up 14 Percent; All-Time High," *Billboard*, June 4, 1966, 1 and 16; "$1.1 Bil. in Sales Racked Up in '67," *Billboard*, July 20, 1968, 3; "U.S. Record Survey," *Billboard* supplement, August 30, 1969, 9–13; and "Recorded Sales Put at $1.7 Bil. for '70," *Billboard*, November 7, 1970, 3.

66. Peterson and Berger, "Cycles in Symbol Production," 153–55. Some record executives recognized this trend toward market concentration much earlier than 1970. In 1967, Liberty Records' Al Bennett predicted that various mergers and acquisitions would consolidate the industry around a group of eight to ten corporate giants. The end result would be a larger oligopoly than that which had reigned during the fifties, but, according to Bennett, the ten labels dominating the market would constitute an oligopoly as powerful as the one in the film industry. See "Disk Mergers to Create 10 Industry Giants, Predicts Liberty's Al Bennett," *Variety*, December 13, 1967, 49.

67. See "Film Trade Powerplays—Its Effect on Industry," *Billboard*, December 16, 1966, 8.

68. "Victor's Col-SG Deal Accents Anew Indie Producer's Role in Disk Biz," *Variety*, June 22, 1966, 47. See also Herm Schoenfeld, "BMI's Fastest Growing Pub," *Variety*, April 13, 1966, 55; and "Col Pix-SG Disk Division Beefs Up Exec Wing in Broad Expansion Move," *Variety*, December 6, 1967, 43.

69. See "ABC to Distrib 20th-Fox Disks," *Variety*, July 6, 1966, 39; and "ABC in Soundtracks with 20th-Fox Pact," *Billboard*, July 9, 1966, 4.

70. "20th-Fox Buyout of BVC Setting Stage for Big Move in Publishing and Disks," *Variety*, February 1, 1967, 57.

71. Herm Schoenfeld, "WB-7 Arts Music Empire," *Variety*, October 25, 1967, 41.

72. "Third Quarter Snappy for W7 Both in Sales, Profits; Big Eye on Disks," *Variety*, May 22, 1968, 30.

73. Sanjek, *American Popular Music and Its Business* 3:510–11.

74. "Gulf & Western to Shuffle Par's Music, Disk Cos. to Beef Up Their Operations," *Variety*, December 21, 1966, 43.

75. Balio, *United Artists*, 116.

76. See Karlin, *Listening to Movies*, 227. Among the earliest albums of movie music were Miklós Rózsa's *The Jungle Book* (1942), Victor Young's *For Whom the Bell Tolls* (1943), and Alfred Newman's *The Song of Bernadette* (1943).

3. Sharps, Flats, and Dollar Signs

1. Bob Rolontz, "Record Firms Find Movie Sound Track Terms Tougher," *Billboard*, September 5, 1960, 1.

2. "Col. Takes 'The Alamo,' " *Billboard*, September 5, 1960, 1. See also "Open Bidding for Sound Tracks," *Billboard*, October 19, 1963, 3 and 6. This later article indicates that the major labels were often thwarted in their attempts to secure sound-

track rights for high-profile films by the arrangements made between Hollywood studios and their record subsidiaries. Because the studios tended to emphasize the promotional value of soundtrack albums, their major label competitors complained that the film-owned labels did not do enough to maximize sales. Columbia's Irv Townsend, for example, argued that soundtracks "aren't reaching their full sales potential because the companies which could do the most for them [i.e., the majors] aren't on the receiving end" (3).

3. See Rolontz, "Record Firms Find," 1.

4. See Joseph Lanza, *Elevator Music: A Surreal History of Muzak, Easy-Listening, and Other Moodsong.*

5. Lanza, *Elevator Music*, 182.

6. Ibid., 67–127.

7. See, for example, an advertisement for Ferrante and Teicher's 126-city concert tour in *Variety*, April 10, 1968, 61.

8. "Martin Getting United Artists' 4-Star Buildup as Performer," *Billboard*, September 19, 1964, 15.

9. For more on the record club business, see Sanjek, *American Popular Music and Its Business* 3:336–39.

10. Ibid., 338.

11. See June Bundy, "Young Disk Talent in Hot Film Demand," *Billboard*, February 22, 1960, 1.

12. In fact, though it occurred rather rarely, Broadway and legitimate theater producers occasionally tried to cash in on the exploitation value of title theme songs throughout the early to mid-sixties. According to *Variety*, Broadway producers modeled their efforts on the campaigns developed by Hollywood filmmakers and usually used this tactic for straight comedies and dramas rather than musicals. The first cycle of legitimate theatrical theme songs occurred in 1962 in connection with *The Fun Couple*, *The Happiest Man Alive*, and *Come on Strong*, the latter of which even attempted to motivate the song through a turntable that appeared in the play's second act. The cycle returned in 1965 with *Any Wednesday*, *Golden Boy*, and *Minor Miracle*. To better exploit the "Theme from *Golden Boy*," producer Hillard Elkins even arranged to have the track recorded for Percy Faith's *Broadway Bouquet* LP. See "Night of the Iguana Twist," *Variety*, August 22, 1962, 43; and "Legit Gets New Trend as Producers Discover Plug Value of a Title Song," *Variety*, September 29, 1965, 43.

13. For a concise summary of the relative merits of film singles and albums in a contemporary context, see Denisoff and Plasketes, "Synergy in 1980s Film and Music," 258–74.

14. See Sanjek, *American Popular Music and Its Business* 3:448.

15. Herm Schoenfeld, "Payola Keys D.J. Eclipse," *Variety*, January 6, 1960, 6.

16. A couple of anecdotes illustrate the extent to which musical tastes and independent competition lay at the heart of the payola debate. In congressional testimony, one disk jockey admitted that he had received money to favor one label's recording of a Tchaikovsky symphony over another, but the committee was uninterested. According to one of their members, the committee was not concerned with anything but pay-for-play as it pertained to "bad" music. (See Sanjek, *American Popular Music*

and Its Business 3:448, and *From Print to Plastic*, 52.) Similarly, Rep. John Moss of California acknowledged that he had received a number of letters from teens asking what is wrong with payola. To this Moss responded that teens had not only been duped by disk jockeys, but they had also failed to receive proper moral instruction from churches and schools. (See "Payola and Teen Morality," *Variety*, April 20, 1960, 141.)

Moreover, even before the Harris Committee's hearings, a number of disk jockeys had already laid blame for payola at the feet of the independents. According to *Variety*, Dallas disk jockeys "indirectly blamed rock 'n' roll for the payola boom, pointing to the sudden creation of small companies flooding the market with rock 'n' roll records. [Dallas disk jockey Nick] Ramsey pointed out that some of the records have been so bad that disk jockeys had to be paid to play them." See "Dallas Jocks Claim They've Been Bypassed by Payola Disk Firms," *Variety*, December 2, 1955, 55.

17. "Nat King Cole Hits Diskeries' Yen for Rock 'n' Roll, But Sez TV Will Kill It," *Variety*, May 25, 1960, 57.

18. "The No-Payola Sound of Music," *Variety*, December 2, 1959, 1.

19. "R & R Ratings Fool Indie AM Stations," *Variety*, December 30, 1959, 1.

20. *Variety*, January 13, 1960, 44.

21. Pat Ballard, "So Long Trash," *Variety*, March 2, 1960, 55.

22. "Top 40 on the Pan Again," *Variety*, September 30, 1959, 45.

23. "FM Throws Block at Rock," *Variety*, August 16, 1961, 43.

24. "Jukeboxes May Become Last Refuge of Rock 'n' Roll and Indie Diskers," *Variety*, May 4, 1960, 45.

25. "The No-Payola Sound of Music," 1 and 64.

26. See Herm Schoenfeld, "Radio De-Rocks, Sales Roll," *Variety*, February 3, 1960, 55 and 60; and Abel Green, "Music Biz in Squeeze as Disk Jocks Play It Too Honestly in Payola Scare," *Variety*, March 2, 1960, 1 and 58.

27. "Programming the Top LP's," *Billboard*, March 20, 1961, 40–41 and 94.

28. "UA Riding High on Tidal Wave of Film Themes," *Variety*, November 16, 1960, 55.

29. See R. Serge Denisoff and William D. Romanowski, *Risky Business: Rock in Film*, 6–20, for a more complete discussion of the *Blackboard Jungle* campaign.

30. See "UA's Teener Prow with Atomic Bally for 'On the Beach,' " *Variety*, November 9, 1959, 60; "Beach Film Score Due for Plenty Wax," *Billboard*, December 14, 1959; and " 'Matilda' Goes Berlitz Day-Dating 'On the Beach,' " *Variety*, December 16, 1959, 43.

31. "UA's Teener Prow," 60. As late as 1963, film and record companies had still not learned their lesson regarding teenage taste. An item in *Variety* reported, "Composer Dimitri Tiomkin, who has written the musical backgrounds for over 140 pix, came into the studio last week for the first time to wax a single aimed at the teenage market." The single was from Tiomkin's *55 Days at Peking* score and it failed as predictably as the *On the Beach* singles. See "Dimitri Tiomkin, Vet Pic Composer, Cuts 1st Single from His 'Peking' Score," *Variety*, July 10, 1963, 57.

32. Thomas Doherty, *Teenagers and Teenpics: The Juvenilization of American Movies of the 1950s*.

33. See Abel Green, "What Is Payola? Part III," *Variety*, December 2, 1959, 55;

and "Pic Stars Get Itch for Disks," *Billboard*, October 12, 1959, 1. Green's argument mirrors the plot of Frank Tashlin's classic rock musical *The Girl Can't Help It* (1956). In the film, mobster Fats Marty (Edmond O'Brien) sees Eddie Cochran sing "Twenty Flight Rock" on television and decides that his "talentless" girlfriend, Jeri Jewell (Jayne Mansfield), can be made into singing star. The irony, of course, is that Jeri hides her genuine musical talent in order to preserve her chances of becoming a wife and mother.

34. "Beatles' Soundtrack Is Blockbuster Before Their 1st Pic's Release," *Variety*, July 1, 1964, 70.

35. Balio, *United Artists*, 251; Roy Prendergast, *Film Music: A Neglected Art*, 147.

36. "First Cream for Beatles Film May Net UA $500,000," *Variety*, July 15, 1964, 52.

37. Ibid., 1.

38. Balio, *United Artists*, 251.

39. "Rock 'n' Roll Pic Trend Returns," *Variety*, December 16, 1964, 24.

40. See the capsule reviews of the *Gone with the Wave* soundtrack, *Variety*, June 30, 1965, 50, and the *Wild on the Beach* soundtrack, *Variety*, July 14, 1965, 42.

41. See "Merc Puts 'Trip' Film in Groove," *Variety*, May 31, 1967, 41, and the capsule review of *The Trip* soundtrack, *Variety*, October 31, 1967, 42.

42. Garry Sherman, "Pic Scores Follow Pop Trends from 'Jazz Singer' to Beatles," *Variety*, May 15, 1974, 59.

43. Ibid.

44. Fink, *Inside the Music Business*, 77–86; Dranov, *Inside the Music Publishing Industry*; 25–28, 108–110.

45. Denisoff and Plasketes, "Synergy in 1980s Film and Music," 272–74.

46. The question of whether a hit film creates hit songs is one of those "chicken and egg" questions which will probably never have a satisfactory answer. The conventional wisdom on the matter, however, is that until 1970, it was usually films that sold film music rather than the reverse. Yet, as *Variety* pointed out in 1961, "Actual experience of late has only served to confuse the issue once more since, in practice, it's actually working both ways, according to the individual case" (see "Pic Tunes Clicking Big Overseas Before and After Films Get Released," *Variety*, April 5, 1961, 59). I certainly have no definitive answer to this question other than to note its essentially symbiotic relationship.

47. See Ted Wick, "Creating the Movie Music Album," *Hi Fidelity*, April 1976, 68–70.

48. See Doty, "Music Sells Movies," 71.

49. Mike Gross, "Pix Promotion's Cuffo Ride," *Variety*, September 6, 1961, 45–46.

50. Ibid., 46.

51. See, for example, Fink, *Inside the Music Business*, 182; Kalinak, *Settling the Score*, 185–86; Palmer, *The Composer in Hollywood*, 142–43; Prendergast, *Film Music*, 102–104; Evans, *Soundtrack*, 191; and Tony Thomas, *Film Score: The Art and Craft of Movie Music*, 122.

52. Stephen Handzo observes that *High Noon* was considered a "certain flop" until Tiomkin peddled the theme song to record companies. See Handzo, "The Golden Age of Film Music," *Cineaste* 21, nos. 1–2 (1995): 52.

53. United Artists Advertising, Publicity, and Exploitation Bulletin, May 16, 1952 (box 4, *High Noon* file), UA Collection Addition, Wisconsin Center for Film and Theater Research, State Historical Society Library, Madison. All letters and contracts are from this collection unless otherwise noted.

54. United Artists Advertising, Publicity, and Exploitation Bulletin, June 23, 1952 (box 4, *High Noon* file).

55. Undated press release, Stanley Kramer Productions, Inc. (box 4, *High Noon* file).

56. UA press release, October 22, 1952 (box 4, *High Noon* file).

57. United Artists Advertising, Publicity, and Exploitation Bulletin, June 23, 1952 (box 4, *High Noon* file).

58. See Continental Division Publicity Round-Up (box 4, *High Noon* file).

59. This multiple-release idea was entirely consistent with Hollywood's general philosophy of film promotion. Film publicity departments typically discussed hundreds of angles for exploiting an upcoming film, and they ultimately incorporated a large number of these ideas into their final plan for advertising and publicizing their product. The studios, of course, had large investments in the music publishing business, and therefore one of their subsidiary's primary goals would be arranging as many cover versions of any song as was possible. Film theme songs were certainly no exception to this practice, and if a theme, such as "Laura" or "Moon River," became a pop standard, then it generated a continuous flow of performance and mechanical royalties each year whether or not it was promoted by its publisher. As Paula Dranov notes, most pop standards were traditionally derived from Broadway musicals, but over the years have increasingly come from motion picture film themes. See Dranov, *Inside Music Publishing*, 17.

The multiple-release scheme, however, does indeed distinguish film music promotion in the fifties and sixties from that which is common today. Current film music promotions depend less on the songs themselves and more on the styles and personalities of the artists that perform them. According to Dranov, this is because the work of most rock artists is tailored to their individual style, and thus does not lend itself to a large number of cover records. Consequently, in today's business environment, an original film song is likely to be promoted through a single recording by a prominent rock artist. Rap songs in film offer a particularly good illustration of this principle; Public Enemy's "Fight the Power" makes a memorable impression during the credits of Spike Lee's *Do the Right Thing*, but much of the song's appeal inheres in the particular style and attitude of its performers. It is absurd to think that any cover version could successfully duplicate or enhance that appeal, or to think that it would increase the record sales of the original.

60. See Gross, "Pix Promotion's Cuffo Ride," 45; "UA 'Sunday' Tune Owner," *Billboard*, July 11, 1960, 2; "France Follows U.S. in Pic Music Click," *Variety*, October 26, 1960, 55; " 'Never on Sunday' Racks Up 10-Mil Sales Worldwide in Over 30 Disk Versions," *Variety*, August 9, 1961, 1; and " 'Sunday' Disks UA Hypo Plus," *Billboard*, March 24, 1962, 12.

61. See June Bundy, "Film Themes Link Movie, Disk Trades," *Billboard*, December 24, 1960, 8 and 10; and Bundy, "Pic Tune Tie-Ups Spark UA Sales," *Billboard*, May 23, 1960, 4.

62. Don Wedge, "Co-Operation Key to Soundtrack Hit," *Billboard*, June 15, 1963, 37.

63. Summary of Music Comments on *In the Heat of the Night* Preview (box 10, file 8), Norman Jewison Collection, Wisconsin Center for Film and Theater Research, State Historical Society Library, Madison.

64. "This Is 'Love'?" *Variety*, September 14, 1960, 43.

65. See "UA Previews 'Jessica' Film, Disk for Dealers & Deejays," *Billboard*, March 24, 1962, 5.

66. " 'Ben-Hur' in Stereo 2-to-1 Over Monaural," *Variety*, February 10, 1960, 55.

67. " 'Bounty' Disks Get Big Push," *Billboard*, September 8, 1962, 5.

68. " 'Zorba' Gets 20th-Fox's Full Drive," *Billboard*, March 27, 1965, 6.

69. "Colpix Pushes Movie Track," *Billboard*, February 2, 1963, 6.

70. June Bundy, "Movie Theme Wax Adds Spark to Disk-Flick Ties," *Billboard*, November 13, 1961, 2.

71. "Imprison Disk Jocks as 'Bird Man' Stunt," *Variety*, July 25, 1962, 91.

72. "UA to Test New LP Rack for Theaters," *Billboard*, September 19, 1960, 18.

73. See "Sell Pic Packs in Theatre Lobbies," *Variety*, January 18, 1961, 53.

74. See " 'Cleopatra' Fever Spreads to Records," *Billboard*, June 8, 1963, 1 and 8; Jack Maher, "The 'Cleo' Disk Gets Giant Splash, But Everybody's Dipping Toe in Nile," *Billboard*, June 15, 1963, 3; and "20th Records in Biggest Day as 'Cleo' Opens," *Billboard*, June 22, 1963, 1 and 8.

75. Ren Grevatt, "Movie, Show Material Spell Big Dealer Profit," *Billboard*, March 24, 1962, 9.

76. Ibid.

77. "MGM Soundtrack LP's to be 'Double Featured,' " *Variety*, April 13, 1960, 45; and "United Artists Lifts Movie Gambit; Now It's Double Feature Sound Track," *Billboard*, July 21, 1962, 5. I wish to remind readers here that the *I Want to Live* score was composed by Johnny Mandel and the *Odds Against Tomorrow* score was composed by Modern Jazz Quartet pianist John Lewis.

78. Karlin, *Listening to Movies*, 221.

4. MY HUCKLEBERRY FRIEND

1. Henry Mancini with Gene Lees, *Did They Mention the Music?*, 106.

2. One should not overstate the significance of Mancini's popular music background, however. As I noted earlier, many classical Hollywood composers came from various popular music backgrounds. Where Mancini most clearly differs from his predecessors is that he continued to use so-called "people music" in his films while his predecessors sought nineteenth-century European classical musical models instead.

3. William Darby and Jack Du Bois, for example, have reaffirmed Mancini's image as a shallow and frivolous composer by arguing that "apart from his pop-oriented films, Mancini's music emerges, for the most part, as a pale imitation of more potent forerunners." See Darby and Du Bois, *American Film Music*, 483.

4. Thomas, *Film Score*, 250.

5. One exception to this general pattern of reception is Timothy Scheurer's "Henry Mancini: An Appreciation and Appraisal," *Journal of Popular Film and Video*

24, no. 1 (Spring 1996): 34. Interestingly, Scheurer begins his essay by remarking on the paucity of tributes and valedictories following the composer's death in 1994.

6. Donald Fagen, "Movie Music: Mancini's Anomie Deluxe," *Premiere* (October 1987): 97–99.

7. There has, however, been a detailed formal analysis of Mancini's "Pink Panther Theme." See Stephen M. Fry, "The Music for the Pink Panther: A Study in Lyrical Timelessness," *The Cue Sheet* 8, no. 4 (April 1992): 14–23.

8. Charles Merrell Berg, "Cinema Sings the Blues," *Cinema Journal* 17, no. 2 (1978): 1–12.

9. Between 1920 and 1950, jazz cues in feature films typically functioned diegetically either as a showcase for popular swing and Big Band performers, such as Cab Calloway, Duke Ellington, Jimmy Dorsey, Woody Herman, and Artie Shaw, or as source music within nightclub settings. Outside the feature film, however, jazz was quite frequently featured in short films called "soundies," which starred a number of popular jazz performers. See Gregory Lukow, "The Antecedents of MTV: Soundies, Scopitones, and Snaders, and the History of an Ahistorical Form," *The Art of Music Video: Ten Years After*, 6–9; and Michael Shore, *The Rolling Stone Book of Rock Video*.

In addition, jazz was also frequently used as underscore in animated cartoons and avant-garde shorts. In studio cartoons for Warner Brothers and MGM respectively, composers Carl Stalling and Scott Bradley frequently developed these jazz elements into a whole series of musical clichés. Muted trombones represented soused drunks; wailing trumpets indicated sultry, hip-wiggling females; and twenties-style jazz stomps signified swinging nightclub life. These clichés could readily and immediately convey broad elements of character and setting in a manner befitting the breakneck pace of cartoons. In avant-garde films, on the other hand, animators like Oskar Fischinger, Len Lye, and Norman McLaren used preexisting performances by Ralph Rainger, Albert Ammons, and Oscar Peterson as the basis of their soundtracks. For these recordings, these animators created visuals that attempted to match the rhythm, pitch, movement, and color of the music.

10. Palmer, *The Composer in Hollywood*, 295–96.

11. For a discussion of the juvenile delinquent film, see Doherty, *Teenagers and Teenpics*, 105–41. For a more complete discussion of how jazz has been represented by Hollywood, see Krin Gabbard, *Jammin' at the Margins: Jazz and the American Cinema*.

12. Fred Binkley, "Mancini's Movie Manifesto," *Down Beat*, March 5, 1970, 16.

13. In Fred Binkley's interview with Mancini, the composer responded to these charges saying: "It was very strange because at no time during the *Peter Gunn* show was any claim made, on the albums or by me in any interview, that it was jazz. It was jazz-oriented, it was dramatic, and jazz was part of it; in that way it was picked up by various critics. But there was no claim ever made—perhaps because it had such a big influence that some of the jazz critics and writers felt they were losing their audience to this thing that was coming out of nowhere" (Binkley, "Mancini's Movie Manifesto," 16).

In a separate interview in *Down Beat*, both Mancini and fellow composer Patrick Williams suggest that these scores are not really jazz, because they come from the

"Leonard Bernstein school." According to Mancini and Williams, these jazz scores grew out of a classical conception of jazz and thus lack a sufficient feel for the idiom. In fact, at one point, the *Down Beat* interviewer asks, "Well it might have had a classical conception, but it still swung, right?" To which Mancini replied, "Oh well, if you can't swing a 6/8, you'd better quit." See Harvey Siders, "The Jazz Composers in Hollywood," *Down Beat*, March 2, 1972, 14.

14. The American Film Institute, *Dialogue on Film* 3, no. 3 (1974): 16. In another context, Mancini reiterated Edwards' emphasis on music as a part of the textual whole. Mancini says: "When I was involved with Blake Edwards on the *Peter Gunn* series, he challenged me weekly with long scenes without any dialogue, already hearing the musical score in his mind's ear. Blake regarded the music as a vital voice in the whole picture." See Thomas, *Film Score*, 256; also see Siders, "The Jazz Composers in Hollywood," 12.

15. Henry Mancini and Johnny Mercer, "Oscar Winner 'Moon River' Spells Hefty Programming, Sales Bonanza," *Billboard*, April 21, 1962, 19.

16. "Mancini's 'Moon River' Royalties Jus' Keep Rollin' Along to the $230,000 Level," *Variety*, March 30, 1966, 1. Ironically, the film's producer Martin Jurow suggests in studio correspondence that Paramount was initially reluctant to undertake such a massive campaign. According to Jurow, Paramount needed some persuasion to promote Mancini despite the fact that the composer had shown time and again that he "sells big." This is doubly ironic in that Mancini was not originally planned as the song's composer. According to his autobiography, Mancini was initially hired only for the score, with another songwriter set to do the over-the-credits song. See Mancini, *Did They Mention the Music?*, 97–98.

17. There is a fine distinction here between writing a dramatic score and an original musical. As the musical directors at MGM and 20th Century-Fox respectively, Johnny Green and Alfred Newman supervised the adaptations of a number of Broadway and original motion picture musicals, but did not actually compose any of the songs. Composers who showed fluency in both capacities were few, and rarely did any composer of dramatic scores try his hand at writing scores for musicals. Perhaps Mancini's only rival in this regard is Michel Legrand, who also was an extremely successful songwriter throughout the sixties.

18. See, for example, "Soundtracks: Single or LP," *Variety*, November 22, 1961, 41 and 43; "Mancini, H'Wood's Hottest Pic 'Track Artist, Grooving 1-Mil. LP Sales Yearly," *Variety*, March 4, 1964, 55. It should be noted, however, that Mancini's conception of an album as a collection of nine or ten distinct tunes adheres much more closely to the conventions of pop album packaging than it does to any classical notion of musical unity or organicity. What strikes one most about Mancini's soundtrack albums when compared with those of his contemporaries is that there is a remarkable and refreshing lack of repetition from track to track. This is not so novel in the cases of *Peter Gunn* or *Mr. Lucky* where Mancini could select cues from many hours of screen time. But it is very unusual for film soundtracks, which by and large rely on a relatively small number of musical materials. Undoubtedly, this variety was a key to the success of his soundtrack albums, which interestingly do not sound much different from his non-soundtrack albums, such as *Uniquely Mancini* and *The Blues and the Beat*.

19. Henry Mancini, interview by author, Beverly Hills, California, May 24, 1993.

20. "Mancini, H'Wood's Hottest," *Variety*, 55. It should be pointed out, however, that years later Mancini would see a deleterious side effect to his rerecording his scores. Mancini has repeatedly noted that dramatic, functional underscoring is the part of film composing he most enjoys and represents the work of which he is most proud. Unfortunately though, as Mancini relates in his autobiography, this work was not desired by record companies, and his soundtracks thus only present a certain side of Mancini's musical personality. In retrospect, Mancini claims that this was something of a mixed blessing. The soundtracks sold in vast numbers, but they also typecast him as a composer of light comedies and light suspense pictures, and may have hurt his reputation as a composer of serious film music. Mancini's comments in *Variety* should thus be taken in their historical context. Whether they represent the sentiments of his record company, RCA Victor, or Mancini himself, his remarks nevertheless made him an important spokesman for the commercialization and exploitation of film music in album formats, and are symptomatic of the historical context that influenced Mancini's innovation of new compositional practices.

21. It is worth noting that the themes used for nondiegetic dramatic underscore are also typically the songs released as singles to promote the film in the radio and record markets. Some examples are "Moon River" and the title tune of *Breakfast at Tiffany's*; "Baby Elephant Walk" from *Hatari*; the title tunes from *The Days of Wine and Roses*, *Experiment in Terror* (1962), and *Soldier in the Rain* (1963); "It Had Better Be Tonight" and the title tune from *The Pink Panther*; "The Shadows of Paris" and the title tune from *A Shot in the Dark*; "The Sweetheart Tree" from *The Great Race*; "We've Loved Before" and the title tune from *Arabesque*; "Nothing to Lose" and the title tune from *The Party*; "There's Enough to Go Around" and "Tomorrow Is My Friend" from *Gaily, Gaily*.

22. Examples of this spotting phenomenon are too numerous to mention. In *Breakfast at Tiffany's*, for example, "The Big Blow Out" appears very briefly blaring out of Holly's apartment, but is given a full musical treatment on the soundtrack album. Because they issue from a primarily commercial impetus, such cues often lay bare the conventions of such spotting. The presence of music at such moments seems to "naturalize" their presence on the album; the inclusion of brief snatches of tunes in these films seems to authorize their usage on the album and make their function appear less nakedly commercial. After all, this is the music to which the characters of the film listen, and to that end, the music either gives the characters some dramatic nuance or it suggests something about their milieu.

23. Karlin and Wright, *On the Track*, 531–32.

24. Kalinak, *Settling the Score*, 120–21.

25. This rising string line will become an important musical figure throughout Mancini's film work in the sixties, most notably in *The Days of Wine and Roses*, *Experiment in Terror*, and *A Shot in the Dark*. This musical figure will often be reorchestrated, but will essentially maintain the same structure and function. It seems as though whenever Mancini requires music for suspense or heightened conflict, he will return again and again to this device.

26. See William Luhr and Peter Lehman, *Blake Edwards*, vol. 2, *Returning to the Scene*, 69–96.

27. Mancini himself offers a similar assessment of his "cat and mouse" theme from *Victor/Victoria*. Says Mancini: "The music doesn't pay any attention to what's going on on the screen. It does not mimic, it just sits back." See Mathias Budinger, "A Conversation with Henry Mancini," *Soundtrack!* 7, no. 26, (1988): 5–9.

28. Luhr and Lehman, *Blake Edwards* 1:62.

29. Mancini, *Did They Mention the Music?*, 100.

30. It is worth noting here that the musical theme used earlier for Paul and Holly's romance was "Breakfast at Tiffany's," which is used for their trip to Tiffany's and their trip to the library. When considering these earlier scenes, which culminate with Holly and Paul at last sleeping together, the decision to use "Moon River" for their final union is all the more curious.

31. "Mancini, H'Wood's Hottest," *Variety*, 55.

32. Letter from Joe Adelman to Arnold Burk UA Collection Addition (box 5, Blake Edwards file), Wisconsin Center for Film and Theater Research, State Historical Society Library, Madison (all subsequent citations are from this collection unless otherwise noted). It should be noted, however, that such power did not extend over the soundtrack albums. Though Mancini maintained a long-term contract with RCA Victor which gave him some royalties, United Artists nevertheless retained the right to designate the release date of the soundtrack album so as to coordinate it with the release of the film.

33. "Mancini Hints He Won't Score Sans Copyrights," *Variety*, January 27, 1965, 47.

34. Promotional circular for *The Return of The Pink Panther* (box 5, *Pink Panther* sequels file).

35. For more on the history of both cocktail music and cocktail culture, see Joseph Lanza's *Elevator Music* and *The Cocktail: The Influence of Spirits on the American Psyche* (New York: St. Martin's, 1995). For more specific discussions of the so-called "Cocktail Nation," see Karen Schoemer, "Sounds of Schmaltz," *Newsweek*, August 22, 1994, 58–59; J. Glenn, "Cocktail Nation," *Utne Reader* (September-October 1994): 83–89; and Randall Rothenberg, "The Swank Life," *Esquire*, April 1997, 70–79.

36. Various artists, *Shots in the Dark: Dol Fi Does Mancini*, Donna Records, 1996.

5. THE MIDAS TOUCH

1. Barry, quoted in Randall D. Larson, *Musique Fantastique: A Survey of Film Music in the Fantastic Cinema*, 318.

2. Roger Watkins, "007 Sights $2-Bil in Ducats Overall," *Variety*, May 13, 1987, 57.

3. Simon Frith, "Mood Music: An Inquiry into Narrative Film Music," *Screen* 25, no. 3 (May-June 1984): 78.

4. See Balio, *United Artists*, 253–74, for a more complete account of Saltzman and Broccoli's relationship with United Artists.

5. Distribution agreement between Danjaq and United Artists, UA Collection Addition (box 3, file 2), Wisconsin Center for Film and Theater Research, State Historical Society Library, Madison. Subsequent citations are from this collection unless otherwise noted.

6. Letter from Ian Fleming to Danjaq, Inc., April 3, 1962 (box 3, file 4).

7. Memorandum from Sam Kreisler to Mort Nathanson, January 9, 1962 (box 3, file 4).

8. Kennedy was widely reported to be an avid reader of Fleming's novels, and in fact *Life* magazine listed *From Russia with Love* as one of JFK's ten favorite books of all time.

9. Charles Juroe, "Launching Sean Required Blonde, Brunette, Redhead," *Variety*, May 13, 1987, 58.

10. Memorandum from Sam Kreisler to Mort Nathanson, January 9, 1962 (box 3, file 4).

11. The character of Bond was also of Scottish heritage. According to an obituary written by "M" in Ian Fleming's *You Only Live Twice*, Bond was born to a Scottish father, Andrew Bond, and a Swiss mother, Monique Delacroix. Yet it is extremely doubtful that the character's literary heritage had any bearing on UA's request. The character's Scottish background has never been a particularly important trait in either the novels or the films. More importantly, Fleming's "obituary" was not published until 1964, two years after the release of *Dr. No*. In fact, as Raymond Benson notes, it is more likely the case that Fleming invented this bit of Bond's background with Connery's film incarnation in mind. Fleming reportedly believed that Connery was too "uncouth" when he was first cast, but changed his mind upon seeing the actor portray his character on-screen. See Benson, *The James Bond Bedside Companion*, 164; and Lee Pfeiffer and Philip Lisa, *The Incredible World of 007*, 16.

12. Steven Jay Rubin, *The James Bond Films*, 18.

13. Letter from Charles Juroe to Fred Goldberg, March 23, 1962 (box 3, file 4).

14. Norman, quoted in Geoff Leonard and Pete Walker, "John Barry and James Bond: The Making of the Music," *Film Score Monthly* 63 (November 1995): 15. The article provides an excellent summary of the internecine struggles behind the composition of the Bond theme.

15. Over the past ten years, Barry has tried to reclaim authorship of the "James Bond Theme" in published interviews. For accounts of Barry's work on *Dr. No*, see Rubin, *The James Bond Films*, 21; Wolfgang Breyer, "An Interview with John Barry," *Soundtrack!* 7, no. 25 (March 1988): 28; Karlin and Wright, *On the Track*, 6–7; and Royal S. Brown, "My Name Is Barry . . . John Barry," *Fanfare* 16, no. 5 (May-June 1993): 121.

16. Though Barry's account is not corroborated by any documents in the archival resources I consulted, there is some very strong circumstantial evidence to support his claim. For one thing, the theme is stylistically quite different from much of the other music in the score. This does not prove that two different men worked on the score, but Barry's claim does offer some explanation as to why such differences exist. Moreover, as Barry himself points out, Norman was known primarily as a lyricist. Here again this does not disprove Norman's authorship, but it does support the assumption that Norman wrote the calypso songs but did not write the instrumental theme music. Finally, and importantly, Barry, of course, went on to score another eleven or so Bond films while Norman did not score another film, Bond or otherwise. If a deal had not been struck by Barry and Danjaq, we would have to conclude that Saltzman and Broccoli rejected the successful composer of their first film in favor of

an untried newcomer. Such a hypothesis makes little sense from a business perspective (why throw away a proven commodity?), and even less sense from an aesthetic perspective. In light of all of these things, and the stylistic similarities between the "James Bond Theme," Barry's "Bee's Knees," and his work on later Bond films, one might conclude that Barry is indeed the composer of the signature Bond theme.

17. In part this was because the overall production budget for *Dr. No* was itself relatively small, approximately $900,000.

18. Undated production summary of *From Russia with Love* (box 3, file 6).

19. " 'Russia' Booms UA Music Firm," *Variety*, May 6, 1964, 67.

20. Scott Shea, liner notes to *The Best of James Bond: 30th Anniversary Limited Edition*, EMI Records, 1992.

21. According to Barry, this conviction was one of the big reasons for the song's success. See Shea, liner notes to *The Best of James Bond*; and "Tunesmith Barry Keeps in Mind the Kid on the Edge of His Seat," *Variety*, May 13, 1987, 66.

22. "UA Label Mines Big Sales in 'Goldfinger' Track," *Variety*, March 10, 1965, 59.

23. See "Epic Riding '007' into Sales Groove with SESAC Deal," *Variety*, March 31, 1965, 53. The bass player referred to here is actually better known as Jimmy Bond.

24. " 'Batman' Merchandizing Bonanza to Surpass 'James Bond' Record Take," *Variety*, February 23, 1966, 1.

25. Shea, liner notes to *The Best of James Bond*.

26. Letter from United Artists Corporation to Danjaq, S.A., October 1, 1965 (box 3, file 3).

27. UA memorandum, March 30, 1966 (box 3, file 3).

28. "Aboard the Bondwagon," *Time*, January 14, 1966, 65. This linkage between composer and character has continued to the present; a May-June 1993 interview in *Fanfare* was titled "My Name Is Barry . . . John Barry" as a spoof of Bond's familiar greeting.

29. See Mike Gross, "Record Men Roll 007's in 'Thunderball' Game," *Billboard*, December 4, 1965, 1 and 6; "As Fantastic as Its Sexy Sleuth, 007 Pix Rentals Hit $100,000,000," *Variety*, October 12, 1966, 1.

30. "Broccoli Bonds Spawned Imitators," *Variety*, May 13, 1987, 62.

31. "Bond-Type Horse Operas in Spain," *Variety*, June 14, 1966, 25.

32. "Broccoli Bonds Spawned Imitators," *Variety*, 74.

33. " 'James Bond Music' Calling Tune in Today's Background Themes," *Variety*, November 23, 1966, 51.

34. Memorandum from Ronald Kass to Harry Saltzman (box 3, file 10). Note that the Fifth Dimension did not end up recording the song for the film. Instead the number was performed by RCA recording artist BJ Arnau.

35. UA Office Rushgram, March 15, 1973 (box 3, file 10).

36. Darby and Du Bois, *American Film Music*, 390.

37. Simon Frith, *Music for Pleasure*, 146–47.

38. Barry, quoted in Arthur Knight, "A Chat with the Composer," *Saturday Review*, July 8, 1972, 71.

39. Darby and Du Bois, *American Film Music*, 391.

40. Ibid., 392.

41. Shea, liner notes to *The Best of James Bond*.

42. Tony Bennett and Janet Woollacott, *Bond and Beyond: The Political Career of a Popular Hero*, 166.

43. For an excellent summary of Barry's style in the Bond films, see Royal S. Brown, "The Sound of 007," *Fanfare* 5, no. 2 (1981): 306–309.

44. Bennett and Woollacott, *Bond and Beyond*, 150.

45. Pitchford, quoted in Karlin and Wright, *On the Track*, 537.

46. It is worth noting that the emergence of the precredit sequence as a common practice occurred roughly about the time that pop music began to make inroads into film scoring. David Bordwell argues that the precredit sequence developed in the fifties as a borrowing of the "teaser" as a television technique. While this is undoubtedly a factor, it seems to me that the growing emphasis on film songs as commercial tie-ins would also lend gravity to the precredit sequence as a narrational option. Since so little scholarly work has been done on precredit sequences in film, it is difficult to posit any concrete link between the two phenomena, but their historical contiguity does suggest that such a relation would be a fruitful avenue for further research. See Bordwell, Staiger, and Thompson, *Classical Hollywood Cinema*, 27.

47. Bennett and Woollacott, *Bond and Beyond*, 153. See also Laura Mulvey, "Visual Pleasure and Narrative Cinema," *Screen* 16, no. 3 (Autumn 1975): 6–18.

48. Bennett and Woollacott, *Bond and Beyond*, 153.

49. See Brown, "The Sound of 007," 307–308.

50. Benson, *The James Bond Bedside Companion*, 74.

51. Kingsley Amis, *The James Bond Dossier*, 40.

52. Note that Bond even calls attention to this through one of his trademark double entendres. Leaning over to a nearby nightstand, Bond turns off a radio report in mid-sentence. The announcer begins his story saying, "The White House says today that the President is entirely satisfied . . ." to which Bond replies, "That makes two of us." The notion of satisfaction expressed here is particularly insightful about Bond's character. As a sixties swinger, Bond seeks sex not for romance but rather to satisfy a physical craving. This depiction of sexuality is in part a consequence of Bond's embodiment of a modern image of male sexuality. Moreover, as Bennett and Woollacott further note, since Bond represents a free and independent sexuality liberated from the confines of marriage and domesticity, the Bond girl is tailored toward those needs as a similarly liberated feminine counterpart. See Bennett and Woollacott, *Bond and Beyond*, 34–35.

Unlike Bond, however, many of these liberated women serve a "sacrificial lamb" function in the narratives. While I think there is a danger in making broad ideological interpretations based on this function, it does remind us that though each figures as a marker of modern sexuality, Bond girls are never accorded the same narrative prominence as Bond and often suffer a threat of textual containment that is never directed at our hero. This double standard and gendered inequality forms an important part of the score's internal critique of the character. Both Bond and the villain ruthlessly pursue a form of ideological domination, but Bond's is sexual in nature rather than political.

53. Since Goldfinger has no sexual relations with these women, Bond is the only character for whom the "kiss of death" is pertinent. Jill stresses that though Goldfinger

likes for Jill to appear in public with him, their relationship is strictly business. Similarly, Pussy Galore actually resists Bond's advances, an action that (along with other sly allusions in the film) tends to support the reading of the character as a closet lesbian.

54. Barry, quoted in Rubin, *The James Bond Films*, 71.

6. EVERY GUN MAKES ITS OWN TUNE

1. Karlin, *Listening to Movies*, 225. Don Crafton reminds me that *The Naked Gun* (1988) offers a clever parody of the interpolated song in which Herman's Hermits' "I'm into Something Good" accompanies a montage of Jane (Priscilla Presley) and Frank's (Leslie Nielsen) budding romance. The romance itself is undercut by a series of pratfalls and visual gags, including Drebbin creating a mishapen mound of cotton candy and the couple squirting ketchup and mustard on each other at a hotdog stand. The sequence itself has been excerpted as a music video and is a mainstay on VH-1.

2. Ennio Morricone, *Film Music*, volumes 1 and 2 (Virgin Records, 1987–88); Ennio Morricone, *The Legendary Italian Westerns* (RCA, 1990); John Zorn, *The Big Gundown: John Zorn Plays the Music of Ennio Morricone* (Icon Records, 1986); The Pogues, "The Good, the Bad, and the Ugly," in *Straight to Hell* (Virgin Records, 1987).

3. Anne and Jean Lhassa, *Ennio Morricone: biographie*; and H. J. de Boer, ed., *Ennio Morricone: The Complete Musicography*.

4. Robert C. Cumbow, *Once Upon a Time: The Films of Sergio Leone*, 199–211. See also Randall Larson's review of Cumbow's chapter on Morricone in *Soundtrack!* 7, no. 25 (1988): 2.

5. Harlan Kennedy offers a similar observation, but gives it a kind of postmodern spin. Describing Morricone's relation to the "golden oldies" approach to film scoring, Kennedy says: "This, too, is postmodernism. It's film music as a playful invocation of history and bygone culture, streamlined by a modern sensibility. If Morricone has achieved anything single-handedly as a film composer, it's the perfection of a fusion between the classical composing methods of the Steiners or Korngolds and the eclecticism that has informed music culture since the 1960s and that is typified by the pile-on-the-pop-songs brand of movie score." See Kennedy's "The Harmonious Background," *American Film* 16, no. 2 (February 1991): 41

6. Anne and Jean Lhassa, *Ennio Morricone*, 23–33.

7. See Roberto Scollo, "Morricone One and Two," in de Boer, ed., *Ennio Morricone: The Complete Musicography*, xxi–xxx.

8. Anne and Jean Lhassa, *Ennio Morricone*, 31.

9. Gary Radovich, "Some Thoughts About Morricone's Arrangements," in de Boer, ed., *Ennio Morricone: The Complete Musicography*, xxxiii. These "gimmicks" include Morricone's incorporation of nonmusical sounds, such as rattling tin cans, ticking clocks, bubbling water, and duck quacks.

10. Morricone, quoted in Scollo, "Morricone One and Two," xxii.

11. Donald Fagen, "Ennio Morricone? Ah, Bellissimo!" *Premiere* (August 1989): 106.

12. "Italo Film Boom Spurs Grooving of Soundtracks," *Variety*, May 15, 1963, 62.

13. "RCA Italiana's Soundtrack Pitch," *Variety*, January 1, 1964, 19.

14. See print ad for RCA Italiana in *Variety*, April 29, 1970, 56.

15. "Film Music Accounts for 30% of Italo Disk Biz; Overseas Angles," *Variety*, May 15, 1974, 59.

16. "Italo Cleffer Beefs at Uncreative Packaging of Pic Soundtracks on LP," *Variety*, December 16, 1964, 47. The presence of sound effects on many soundtrack albums may help explain this feature of Morricone's style. After all, if the sound effects are present on the album as a matter of routine, then there is a certain logic to incorporating them into the texture of the music. In doing this, Morricone may well have made the sound effects less disruptive to record listeners.

17. Sergio Leone, "Hopalong Veneto," *Variety*, October 11, 1967, 34.

18. Hank Werba, "$1,600,000 for Italo Western," *Variety*, August 31, 1966, 20.

19. "UA Gambles 'Dollars' Good as Bonds; Out of Italian West, Boxoffice Raiders," *Variety*, December 28, 1966, 7.

20. See "Sergio Leone on Fertile U.S. Themes," *Variety*, March 29, 1967, 30; and " 'Few Dollars More' Runs 30% Ahead of First Dubbed Italo-Made Western, So UA 'Bond' Analogy Makes Out," *Variety*, May 31, 1967, 4.

21. Robert J. Landry, "It's Murder, Italian Style," *Variety*, February 8, 1967, 7; see also " 'Cool Humor with Gore': As $ Formula," *Variety*, May 31, 1967, 4.

22. Fagen, "Morricone? Ah, Bellissimo!," 106.

23. See Bruce, *Bernard Herrmann*, 75–116.

24. See Laurence Staig and Tony Williams, *Italian Western: Opera of Violence*, 117–20.

25. Cumbow, *Once Upon a Time*, 204.

26. Dave Marsh, *The Rolling Stone Record Guide*, ed. Dave Marsh with John Swenson (New York: Random House/Rolling Stone Press, 1979), 562.

27. Ibid.

28. Frith, *Music for Pleasure*, 141–45. The reggae film, *The Harder They Come* (1973), pays homage to the influence of spaghetti westerns by showing two of its central characters as they watch *Django* (1965).

29. Cumbow, *Once Upon a Time*, 214.

30. Staig and Williams, *Italian Western*, 117–71.

31. As Gregory Lukow points out, the "soundies" of World War II and the Snader TELEscriptions of the 1950s were important precursors of the Scopitone format. For a discussion of all three technologies, see Lukow, "The Antecedents of MTV: Soundies, Scopitones, and Snaders, and the History of an Ahistorical Form," 6–9.

32. See "New French Jukebox Parlays Pix & Music," *Variety*, June 14, 1961, 47; "French Scope-I-Tone is a la Soundies," *Variety*, June 27, 1961, 21; "Scooby-Ooby Scopitone," *Time*, August 21, 1964, 49.

33. See "Singer-Composers Score in San Remo Competition," *Variety*, February 13, 1961, 18; "Cinebox Invades Britain; Italo-Made Device Plays Disks & Screens Artist," *Variety*, March 23, 1962, 47.

34. "Ad Tests for French Movie Juke," *Billboard*, September 11, 1961, 66.

35. John Thompson, "Worthy Pop Product Lack Irks British Phono Fans," *Billboard*, May 25, 1963, 1 and 58.

36. "Cinebox Invades Britain," *Variety*, 47.

37. "British Journalists Dig French Film Juke Box," *Billboard*, March 14, 1963, 88.

38. Ray Brack, "Cinema Juke Box: Just a Novelty?" *Billboard*, July 10, 1965, 45 and 48.

39. "NYC's Second Ave.: Banjos to Juke Box Flick Bikinis," *Billboard*, May 2, 1964, 10.

40. "Scopitone Puts Out Pics by Disk Artists," *Billboard*, July 10, 1965, 1 and 46.

41. "Jukebox Films Pay Structure," *Variety*, August 11, 1965, 3.

42. Brack, "Cinema Juke Box: Just a Novelty?" 48.

43. The actual number was probably much lower; manufacturers in the film-jukebox industry were notorious for inflating their sales figures.

44. "Scopitone Cutting Machine, Film Prices," *Billboard*, October 8, 1966, 71.

45. The Color-Sonics machine is an extremely interesting format which deserves further research, but such inquiry is beyond the scope of this book. Suffice it to say that the Color-Sonics technology improved on the Scopitone model in three specific areas: (1) Color-Sonics used continuous-loop cartridges, which unlike Scopitone's actual reels of film were both more durable and could be replaced in seconds by another cartridge; (2) the Color-Sonics machine had a simpler optics system, which used a single mirror rather than the six employed in the Scopitone device; (3) Color-Sonics films were shot in 35mm Eastman color, and had improved clarity and color quality in their images. Color-Sonics planned to have 5,000 machines on the market by the end of 1968, but unfortunately the fad for all film-jukeboxes had already passed by the time the machine was introduced. See "Color-Sonics into Music and Films Jukebox Market," *Variety*, January 26, 1966, 49; "Color-Sonic to Roll at Paramount Lot," *Variety*, April 27, 1966, 193; Herb Wood, "Color-Sonics Ships in June," *Billboard*, May 28, 1966, 55 and 61; and "Color-Sonics Bows See-Hear Jukebox at Coast Demo," *Variety*, September 7, 1966, 45.

46. Lukow, "The Antecedents of MTV," 8.

47. "Scopitone Cutting Machine, Film Prices," *Billboard*, 71.

48. As with MTV, feminist film and cultural critics are somewhat interested in Scopitone for its representation of female sexuality. Michael Nash writes: "In their effort to distill purely pop elements of music and film into an integrated format, Scopitones provide a paradigm for pre-hippie sixties kitsch Americana. Using this form to attempt to create a pay-per-view financial empire, Scopitones gravitated towards risqué and downright offensive depictions of women; this selection comments on the sexism that arguably is inherent in adapting music media to the dynamics of capitalism." See Nash, "Program Guide," *The Art of Music Video: Ten Years After*, 23.

49. "NYC's Second Ave.: Banjos to Juke Box Flick Bikinis," *Billboard*, 10.

50. "Scopitone Cutting Machine, Film Prices," *Billboard*, 71.

51. "Scooby-Ooby Scopitone," *Time*, 49.

52. See David Meeker, *Jazz in the Movies: A Guide to Jazz Musicians*, 3.

53. See, for example, Roy Armes, *French Cinema* (London: Secker and Warburg, 1985), 212; David Cook, *A History of Narrative Film* (New York: Norton, 1981), 483; or Pauline Kael, *Kiss Kiss Bang Bang* (Boston: Little, Brown, 1968), 126. Armes calls *Un homme et une femme* the equivalent of a "feature-length television commercial," while Kael suggests that the film is "designed and rhythmed more like a trailer."

54. I have found no evidence that these sequences were actually used in this way,

but Lelouch's attempts to integrate music and image in them strongly suggest the influence of his earlier Scopitone work.

55. LeMel, quoted in Karlin and Wright, *On the Track*, 539.

56. In this respect, Lelouch's Scopitone montages are not unlike the proto-MTV sequences in eighties films like *Flashdance* (1983), *Footloose* (1984), or *Top Gun* (1986). As in the case of Scopitone, the development of these segments was the result of a dynamic and fluid interaction between the film and music industries. Filmmakers saw music videos as an excellent vehicle for promoting both films and film music and created sequences that could be easily excerpted and shown on MTV. In order to fit into this latter market, many of these sequences simply adopted the conventions of the musical short, which typically combined performance elements with simple storylines and stylized visuals.

57. See Cumbow, *Once Upon a Time*, 214; Marco Werba, "Ennio Morricone: Once Upon a Time in America," *CinemaScore* 13–14 (Winter 1984–Summer 1985): 3–4; Didier C. Deutsch, liner notes to *Ennio Morricone: The Legendary Italian Westerns* (RCA Victor, 1990); and John Zorn, liner notes to *Ennio Morricone: Film Music*, vol. 2 (Virgin Records, 1988).

As Roy Prendergast notes, certain sections of Eisenstein's *Alexander Nevsky* (1938) were developed in a similar fashion. Though most of the film was scored in the conventional fashion, Eisenstein would sometimes edit sequences to music that was already written and recorded by Sergei Prokofiev. See Prendergast, *Film Music*, 48–52.

58. "Record Music Track Before 'Harlow' Films," *Variety*, March 31, 1965, 7.

59. "4 Star Devises New 'Track LP Technique," *Variety*, January 5, 1968, 209.

60. At the time of the preceding article, two television soundtrack albums had already been released on the ABC-Paramount label and more albums were planned.

61. Parks, quoted in Karlin and Wright, *On the Track*, 18.

62. Bacharach, quoted in ibid.

63. Robert Cumbow (*Once Upon a Time*, 201) observes that "Story of a Soldier" is derived from the Confederate standard "Lorena," which was also used in Max Steiner's score for *The Searchers* (1956) and David Buttolph's music for *The Horse Soldiers* (1959).

64. While I have no direct evidence that these two cues were actually spotted in this way, Robert Cumbow makes a couple of observations that support my assumption. Cumbow notes, for example, that Leone often "designed montages and even shot scenes to fit Morricone's already composed music" (*Once Upon a Time*, 199). Moreover, while arguing that Leone pointedly counters the notion that film editing must be invisible and film music inaudible, Cumbow singles out the "Ecstasy of Gold" sequence as "one of the most remarkable examples of an eminently visible and audible montage" in the history of cinema (ibid., 201). Given our knowledge of Leone's working methods, it seems reasonable to believe that the "Ecstasy of Gold" and "The Trio" sequences are two such scenes specially designed to accommodate Morricone's music.

7. THE SOUNDS OF COMMERCE

1. Kalinak refers to these scores as pop scores in her book *Settling the Score*. Basing her usage on industry nomenclature, Kalinak defines the pop score as "the

'guitar-washed' youth oriented version based in various kinds of rock and roll" (186). Such a description is consistent with Kalinak's own account of film music history, but I prefer to use the term *compilation score*, which I believe is both more precise and does a better job of capturing its album orientation. In contrast to Kalinak, I have consistently used "pop score" to describe a much more general cocatenation of pop, rock, and jazz styles that emerged in the film music of the 1960s. According to my scheme, the compilation score is a particular species of the pop score rather than the other way around.

2. To this list, one might also add *2001: A Space Odyssey* (1968). Though the film does not use any pop songs, the score certainly fits the definition of self-contained musical numbers, and it frequently treats its collection of Johann Strauss ("The Blue Danube"), Richard Strauss ("Also Sprach Zarathustra"), György Ligeti, and Aram Khachaturian as though it were an album of great classical hits. Moreover, it also frequently weds this music to memorable imagery in a series of beautiful and emotionally powerful set pieces: the discovery of the bone as a tool or weapon, the docking of the spaceship, the rebirth of the Star Child. All these factors undoubtedly contributed to the score's great success as a soundtrack album.

Additionally, the MGM soundtrack was programmed on some rock radio stations around the country. San Francisco's KSAN, for example, included three Ligeti tracks ("Requiem for Soprano, Mezzo Soprano, Two Mixed Choirs and Orchestra," "Lux Aeterna," and "Atmospheres") in its regular rock and roll format. See "MGM's '2001' 'Track in Offbeat Exposure," *Variety*, June 19, 1968, 57.

3. In contrast, singles from a film were typically released on the label of a song's performer. As we saw with many of the Bond films, a company could get around this problem by using performers from its subsidiary's own stable of artists. However, if a company desired a particular star from another label, then it would have to sacrifice some record sales to the firm with which the artist was contracted. UA's *Live and Let Die* (1973) offers a typical instance of this latter scenario. In order to get Paul McCartney, UA and Danjaq had to cede the rights to the title single to Capitol Records.

4. See, for example, Doherty, *Teenagers and Teenpics*, 71–108; David Ehrenstein and Bill Reed, *Rock on Film*, 12–20; Marshall Crenshaw, *Hollywood Rock*, ed. Ted Mico, Greil Marcus, "Rock Films," in Jim Miller, ed., *The Rolling Stone Illustrated History of Rock and Roll*, 390–400; and Thomas Wiener, "The Rise and Fall of the Rock Film," *American Film* 1, no. 2 (November 1975): 25–29.

5. Doherty, *Teenagers and Teenpics*, 76.

6. Wiener, "The Rise and Fall of the Rock Film," 26.

7. Doherty, *Teenagers and Teenpics*, 74.

8. Ehrenstein and Reed are rather acerbic in their characterization of the jukebox musical's slight narrative. According to Ehrenstein and Reed, "The sole purpose of movies like *Rock Around the Clock* and *Go, Johnny, Go* was only to squeeze in as much music as possible into their ninety minutes (or less) of running time—with the "dramatic" filler consisting of such will-o-the-wisp concerns as the havoc wreaked by the teen vamp, a band's struggle for stardom, or being allowed to attend the big dance" (*Rock on Film*, 17) Ironically, the one area of contemporary filmmaking which still bears the influence of the jukebox musical is the "rockumentary." In removing the

pretext of a narrative, the rockumentary fulfills the raison d'être of the jukebox musical without having to clutter the film with seemingly extraneous plot considerations.

9. Doherty, *Teenagers and Teenpics*, 94.

10. Wiener, "The Rise and Fall of the Rock Film," 26.

11. Gorbman, *Unheard Melodies*, 162.

12. Ehrenstein and Reed, *Rock on Film*, 56.

13. Stephen Holden, "How Rock Is Changing Hollywood's Tune," *New York Times*, July 16, 1989, sec. 2, p. 18.

14. Ed Lowry, "The Appropriation of Signs in *Scorpio Rising*," *The Velvet Light Trap* 20 (Summer 1983): 42.

15. Doherty, *Teenagers and Teenpics*, 234.

16. Hank Werba, " 'Rider's' $50,000,000 Gross?" *Variety*, November 5, 1969, 29–30. Studio estimates of *Easy Rider*'s total box office take, however, were somewhat optimistic. Though it likely neared that figure, much of this money came in overseas rentals. By the end of 1969, the total gross for the United States and Canada was a respectable $16 million, a sum far short of Columbia's $50 million estimate.

17. David James, *Allegories of Cinema: American Film in the Sixties*, 12–18, 153–56.

18. Kalinak, *Settling the Score*, 186.

19. Ibid., 201. It should be noted that this resistance to commercial rock and pop soundtracks continues to this day. In an interview for Karlin and Wright's *On the Track*, published in 1990, Elmer Bernstein said, "Today the heads of most music departments are basically record-industry people, and their job is basically to sell as many records as they can. That's a legitimate thing for selling records but it does very little for the art of film music." See Karlin and Wright, *On the Track*, 26.

20. Curb, quoted in Roger Manvell and John Huntley, *The Technique of Film Music*, revised and enlarged by Richard Arnell and Peter Day, 260. Interestingly, Ehrenstein and Reed make a similar argument regarding *Quadrophenia* (1979). According to Ehrenstein and Reed, "The Who's songs aren't simply support, supplement, or illustration of the story. Instead, they are the story" (*Rock on Film*, 73). It is worth noting, however, that Mike Curb's claim directly contradicts a statement made by Michelangelo Antonioni regarding his general approach to film music. According to Antonioni, "The only way to accept music in films is for it to disappear as an autonomous expression in order to assume its role as one element in a general sensorial impression."

21. Alan Williams, "The Musical Film and Recorded Popular Music," in Rick Altman, ed., *Genre: The Musical*, 153.

22. Kalinak, *Settling the Score*, 186–87.

23. Pop music's ability to denote setting is itself premised on the idiom's broad cultural circulation, a pervasiveness that was only made possible through changing technologies and patterns of consumption. As a number of critics point out, the transistor radio, the car radio, the boombox, and even Muzak have all contributed to technologically mediated forms of public music consumption. The effect of this is that music, especially popular music, has infiltrated every corner of American culture. As a result, these changes in technology and consumption have had no small effect on the role of popular music in film. As Stephen Holden puts it, "The more ubiquitous pop

music has become, the more it has served as an instant identifier of time and place in movies" ("How Rock Is Changing Hollywood's Tune," 18).

24. See Simon Frith, *The Sociology of Rock* (London: Methuen, 1979) and *Sound Effects: Youth, Leisure, and the Politics of Rock 'n' Roll*; Dick Hebdige, *Subculture: The Meaning of Style*; David Harker, *One for the Money: Politics and Popular Song*; and Angela McRobbie, ed., *Zoot Suits and Second Hand Dresses: An Anthology of Fashion and Music*.

25. See Meyer, *Style and Music*, 126–34; and Peter Kivy, *Sound and Semblance: Reflections on Musical Representation* (Ithaca: Cornell University Press, 1991), 28–60.

26. Meyer, *Style and Music*, 131.

27. Noël Carroll, "The Future of Allusion," *October* 20 (Spring 1982): 56.

28. Carroll, "The Future of Allusion," 53.

29. Joseph Kanon, "The Neighborhood," *Atlantic Monthly*, December 1973, 132. This is from a review of *Mean Streets*.

30. See Karlin and Wright, *On the Track*, 526–32.

31. Of course, the emphasis on ambiguous or unmotivated characters in New Hollywood films stems partly from an appropriation of certain narrative strategies from art cinema. See Bordwell, Staiger, and Thompson, *The Classical Hollywood Cinema*, 372–77; David Bordwell and Kristin Thompson, *Film History: An Introduction*, 707–710; Robert Self, "The Art Cinema and Robert Altman," *The Velvet Light Trap* 19 (1982): 30–34.

32. The version of the song played here is by Tony Bennett rather than the more familiar version by Hank Williams.

33. According to Dale Pollock, the overall budget for *Graffiti* included $775,000 in direct costs and another $500,000 for prints, advertising, and publicity. For a more detailed account of *Graffiti*'s production history, see Pollock's *Skywalking: The Life and Films of George Lucas*, 99–130.

34. Pollock, *Skywalking*, 108–109.

35. Michael Pye and Lynda Myles, *The Movie Brats*, 125.

36. Here I am referring to the May 15, 1973, screening at the Writers Guild Theater in Beverly Hills, not the semilegendary test screening in San Francisco on January 28, which ended in a violent shouting match between Lucas, producer Francis Ford Coppola, and Universal Pictures president Ned Tanen. See Pollock for accounts of both test screenings.

37. Pye and Myles, *The Movie Brats*, 125.

38. "Nostalgia Cycle Goes Thataway; Nader Fades Out Rock Revivals," *Variety*, January 30, 1974, 47.

39. Lucas, quoted in Pollock, *Skywalking*, 105.

40. See Pye and Myles, *The Movie Brats*, 121; and Judy Klemesnid, " 'Graffiti' Is the Story of His Life," *New York Times*, October 7, 1973, sec. 2, p. 1.

41. Pollock, *Skywalking*, 105.

42. Pye and Myles, *The Movie Brats*, 121.

43. Pollock, *Skywalking*, 127. The irony, however, was that the editing process showed the songs themselves to be virtually interchangeable. As Lucas noted: "Walter Murch did the sound montages, and the amazing thing we found was that we could take almost any song and put it on almost any scene and it would work. You'd

put a song down on one scene, and you'd find all kinds of parallels. And you could take another song and put it down there, and it would still seem as if the song had been written for that scene. All good rock and roll is classic teenage stuff, and all the scenes were such classic teenage scenes that they just sort of meshed, no matter how you threw them together." Quoted in Stephen Farber, "George Lucas: The Stinky Kid Hits the Big Time," *Film Quarterly* 27, no. 3 (Spring 1974): 6.

44. Michael Dempsey, "American Graffiti," *Film Quarterly* 27, no. 1 (Fall 1973): 58.

45. Klemesnid, " 'Graffiti' Is the Story of His Life," 13.

46. Farber, "George Lucas: The Stinky Kid Hits the Big Time," 7.

47. Stephen Farber, " 'Graffiti' Ranks with 'Bonnie and Clyde,' " *New York Times*, August 5, 1973, sec, 2, p. 6.

48. Joseph Kanon, "On the Strip," *Atlantic Monthly* (October 1973), 125.

49. James Curtis, "From *American Graffiti* to *Star Wars*," *Journal of Popular Culture* 13, no. 4 (Spring 1980): 598.

50. As John Morthland notes, Wolfman Jack's own radio programs in the 1950s tended to be heavy on blues with an occasional hillbilly tune mixed in. Though this description is open to some interpretation, it would still seem a far cry from *American Graffiti*'s mixture of doo-wop, pop, rockabilly, and surf music. See Morthland, "The Rise of Top 40 AM," in Miller, ed., *Rolling Stone Illustrated History of Rock and Roll*, 93.

51. To illustrate this point, I would like to cite a couple of examples of this historical construction from one of the standard texts, *The Rolling Stone Illustrated History of Rock and Roll*, edited by Jim Miller. In describing the style of the Beach Boys' music, Miller writes: "The first Beach Boys hits managed to sound raunchy and vital, yet clean, somehow safe—for here was a rock and roll band aspiring to the instrumental sleekness of the Ventures, the lyric sophistication of Chuck Berry, and the vocal expertise of some weird cross between the Lettermen and Frankie Lymon and the Teenagers" ("The Beach Boys," 163). Moreover, Lester Bangs offers some insight into rock critics' construction of this juncture in the music's history. Bangs writes, "Rock and roll itself was present, but shapeless; we did have Phil Spector, and the Beach Boys and the Four Seasons, but it took the influx of the British Beatles and a thousand trashy imitators to truly bring us together" ("The British Invasion," 169).

52. Lucas, quoted in Farber, "George Lucas: The Stinky Kid Hits the Big Time," 7.

53. Pollock, *Skywalking*, 117.

54. See Farber, "George Lucas: The Stinky Kid Hits the Big Time," 7.

55. Miller, "The Beach Boys," 163–64.

8. Pretty Women and Dead Presidents

1. Denisoff and Plasketes, "Synergy in 1980s Film and Music," 257.

2. See Justin Wyatt, *High Concept: Movies and Marketing in Hollywood*.

3. Susan Ohmer, "Behind Corporate Doors: The Organizational Cultures of Multimedia Conglomerates," Paper presented at the Society for Cinema Studies Conference in Ottawa, Canada, May 16, 1997.

4. Denisoff and Plasketes, "Synergy in 1980s Film and Music," 258.

5. See Denisoff and Romanowski, *Risky Business*.

6. See Douglas Gomery, "The American Film Industry of the 1970s: Stasis in the 'New Hollywood,' " *Wide Angle* 5, no. 4 (1982): 52–59.

7. The other four majors were plagued throughout the eighties by a combination of bad management and questionable mergers. United Artists never recovered from the *Heaven's Gate* fiasco of the late seventies and was acquired by MGM in 1981 when the latter sought to revive its distribution arm. Kirk Kerkorian installed several new management teams, but they did little to improve its fortunes. Kerkorian raised money in the mid-eighties by liquidating several of the company's assets, but by 1991 the company was on the verge of bankruptcy and was ultimately sold to Giancarlo Paretti of the Pathé Communications Co.

Under Denver oilman Marvin Davis, 20th Century-Fox also fell on hard times in the early eighties. The company experienced a rapid turnaround, however, when it was purchased by Rupert Murdoch's News Corporation in 1985. With the formation of the Fox television network shortly thereafter, Murdoch further diversified a media empire that included arms in book and magazine publishing, film and television production, video distribution, and satellite television systems. Coca-Cola's purchase of Columbia Pictures in 1982 also signaled a major shift in the company's marketing and managerial policies, but the company never met the high expectations of its new owners. Later that year, Columbia launched Tri-Star Pictures as a joint venture with HBO and CBS that assured access to pay cable and network television as ancillary markets. Tri-Star produced few hits, however, and three years later, Columbia bought back half of HBO's interest and all of CBS's.

For more on the market performance of these companies in the eighties, see Tino Balio, *Hollywood in the Age of Television* (Boston: Unwin Hyman, 1990), 270–77; Janet Wasko, *Hollywood in the Information Age*, 41–69; and Thomas Schatz, "The New Hollywood," in Jim Collins, Hilary Radner, and Ava Preacher Collins, eds., *Film Theory Goes to the Movies* (New York: Routledge, 1993), 25–32.

8. Balio, *Hollywood in the Age of Television*, 272–73.

9. Disney's use of television for promotional purposes is, of course, nothing new. Chris Anderson's *Hollywood TV* (Austin: University of Texas Press, 1994) details the company's efforts in the fifties to develop a series that would promote its new Disneyland theme park. The series, which was developed for ABC, enjoyed a three-year run. It was ultimately retitled the *The Wonderful World of Disney* where it served as an outlet for the studio's library of filmed entertainment (cartoons, nature documentaries, live action films, etc.)

10. See Wasko, *Hollywood in the Information Age*, 52–57.

11. The figures for table 8.1 are from the *New York Times*, April 10, 1995, D1 and D8. It is worth noting that UNI has since changed ownership; it was sold by Matsushita to the Seagram Company, which purchased 80 percent of MCA in 1995. Also, Russell Sanjek's *Pennies from Heaven* includes a similar chart which features the majors' market shares for 1995. During that one-year period, WEA's share increased to about 26 percent of the market while the shares of UNI, CEMA, and Sony all fell slightly.

12. Sanjek, *Pennies from Heaven*, 671.

13. James Sterngold, "Seagram's Deal Buys Glamour and a Cash Cow Called Music," *New York Times*, April 10, 1995, D8.

14. The careers of Julia Roberts and Kevin Costner might be cases in point. After the initial success of *Pretty Woman* (1990), Roberts starred in an amazing string of flops, such as *Dying Young* (1991), *I Love Trouble* (1994), and *Mary Reilly* (1995). Costner's career arc is slightly more complicated but contains the same general trajectory. After an early series of successes in *Bull Durham* (1988), *Field of Dreams* (1989), and *Dances with Wolves* (1990), Costner starred in a succession of financial duds that culminated in the 1995 *Waterworld* debacle.

15. Jeffrey Jolson-Colburn, "Making Tracks," *Hollywood Reporter*, August 27, 1996, S19.

16. Levy, quoted in James Sterngold, "Polygram Has Eyes for Hollywood," *New York Times*, July 10, 1995, D1 and D8.

17. For more detailed accounts of *Saturday Night Fever*'s cross-marketing strategy, see Sanjek, *Pennies from Heaven*, 596–99; Wyatt, *High Concept*, 139–45; and Denisoff and Romanowski, *Risky Business*, 219–34.

18. See Denisoff and Romanowski, *Risky Business*, 277.

19. Susan Peterson, "Selling a Hit Soundtrack," *Billboard*, October 6, 1979, ST-2.

20. Peterson, "Selling a Hit Soundtrack," ST-4.

21. Mansfield, quoted in ibid.

22. Peterson, "Selling a Hit Soundtrack," ST-4.

23. "Scripting the Hits," *Billboard*, August 2, 1980, M-6 and M-12.

24. Susan Peterson, "Rediscovering a Built-in Mutual Benefit," *Billboard*, October 6, 1979, ST-2.

25. Paul Grein, "Large Surge in Record and Film Tie-Ins," *Billboard*, May 31, 1980, 1, 33, 42; and Ed Ochs, "Mining Gold from the Silver Screen," *Billboard*, August 2, 1980, M-1.

26. Jane Maloney, "Azoff Says Soundtrack Pulls in Many to See 'Urban Cowboy,'" *Variety*, September 17, 1980, 73.

27. See Grein, "Large Surge in Record and Film Tie-Ins," 1, 33.

28. Bird, quoted in Ochs, "Mining Gold from the Silver Screen," M-3.

29. See Millard, *America on Record*, 346–55.

30. See ibid., 355; and Sanjek, *Pennies From Heaven*, 670.

31. See Richard Gold, "Hollywood Majors Spinoff Videos from Youth Pix," *Variety*, February 22, 1984, 108.

32. Ibid.

33. See Cynthia Kirk, "Music Videos in 35mm Shown by Theater Circuit," *Variety*, November 23, 1983, 1 and 36.

34. Paul Grein, "Film Tracks a Star on Album Chart," *Billboard*, June 23, 1984, 3.

35. Quoted in Denisoff and Romanowski, *Risky Business*, 403.

36. Paul Grein, "'Footloose' Forges New Movie-Music Tie," *Billboard*, February 11, 1984, 82.

37. Richard Gold, "Studios & Labels Pan Soundtrack Gold," *Variety*, April 18, 1984, 216.

38. Grein, "'Footloose' Forges New Movie-Music Tie," 82.

39. See Ken Terry, "Pics Leery of Pop Soundtracks," *Variety*, April 9, 1986, 122.

40. See Chris McGowan, "Soundtrack Fastlane Already Facing Congestion as Labels Strenghten Crossover Links in Marketing Chain," *Billboard*, June 21, 1986, S-4.

41. Grein, " 'Footloose' Forges New Movie-Music Tie," 82.

42. See Rob Tannenbaum, "Soundtracks Thrived in the Summer of '85," *Rolling Stone*, November 21, 1985, 16.

43. Jeffrey M. Sydney, "Putting Soundtracks on a Sound Basis," *Billboard*, February 14, 1987, 9. See also "Film Studio Executives Refute Soundtrack Burnout," *Billboard*, August 30, 1986, 92, and "Studio Execs Seek Automatic Adds with Title Cuts from Soundtracks," *Variety*, August 20, 1986, 83.

44. "Film Studio Executives Refute Soundtrack Burnout," *Billboard*, 92.

45. See Jim Koch, "Music and Movies: For Better or Worse," *New York Times*, June 11, 1995, sec. 1, p. 49; and Steve Pond, "The Soundtrack Boom Leaves Composers at a Loss," *New York Times*, August 20, 1995, sec. 2, p. 26.

46. See Larry Rohter, "In Movies, a Formula Is Born: Hitching One's Star to a Song," *New York Times*, C11.

47. Ibid.

48. I should note that this is not true of every event film. The *Men in Black* (1997) soundtrack, for example, features several rap and soul artists alongside the two tracks by Will Smith, the film's star. In this instance, the soundtrack's packaging appears to be an effort to capitalize on Smith's star power. For other event films, like *Jurassic Park* or *Independence Day* (1996), the studio simply puts out portions of the film's orchestral score in album form. Here the prevailing wisdom seems to be that the film's popularity will help sell the album rather than the other way around.

49. Karlin, *Listening to Movies*, 230.

50. See Charles Fleming, "Soundtrack Label Varese Changes Its Tune on Hit Pix," *Variety*, July 11, 1990, 21.

51. David Bell, *Getting the Best Score for Your Film*, 54.

52. Karlin and Wright, *On the Track*, 25–26.

53. See "Two Milco Copeland Firms Team for Film, TV Music Supervision," *Variety*, January 9, 1985, 182; and Terry, "Pics Leery of Pop Soundtracks," 122.

54. See Denisoff and Romanowski's *Risky Business*, 319–32, for more detailed descriptions of each of these campaigns. As on *FM*, Azoff served as each film's executive producer, but also supervised the production of the soundtrack for each.

55. Ford, quoted in Jon Burlingame, "Getting Songs in Sync," *Hollywood Reporter*, August 27, 1996, 24.

56. Denisoff and Romanowski, *Risky Business*, 461.

57. *Hollywood Reporter*, January 15, 1997, 79–81.

58. Jean Rosenbluth, "Soundtrack Specialists: Maximizing Cross-Market Connections," *Billboard*, July 16, 1988, S-12.

59. Carr, quoted in Burlingame, "Getting Songs in Sync," 24.

60. Karlin, *Listening to Movies*, 226.

61. Afterman, quoted in Burlingame, "Getting Songs in Sync," 23.

62. This practice is not unlike what early music publishers did in compiling volumes of mood music or in preparing handbooks for silent film musicians. Compilers such as J. S. Zamecnik, Giuseppe Becce, and Erno Rapee typically organized cues into groups based on considerations of setting, action, and mood.

63. I should note that the germ of this idea was already present in Leigh Brackett's script, which specified two different versions of the theme for the credit sequence. As with other elements of the screenplay, however, Altman played with the score concept to an unusual degree. Brackett's early script drafts are included in box 2 of the Robert Altman Collection, Wisconsin Center for Film and Theatre Research, State Historical Society Library, Madison, Wisconsin.

64. The actual genesis of some songs is a bit confusing, however. Recently I saw an old *Dick Van Dyke* episode in which guest star Henry Gibson (*Nashville*'s Haven Hamilton) read aloud one of the verses of "Keep A'Goin' " as a kind of inspirational poem. This would suggest that the song (or this incarnation of it) predates *Nashville* by some ten years and was probably one of the comic poems Gibson wrote for his appearances on nighttime talk shows.

65. Lukas Kendall, "The Fifth Element: The Final Frontier?" *Film Score Monthly* 2, no. 4 (June 1997): 31.

66. Hensley, quoted in Karlin, *Listening to Movies*, 244.

67. Randall D. Larson, *Musique Fantastique*, 295–96.

68. Ibid., 297.

69. Jon Burlingame, "Energizer Jedi," *Hollywood Reporter*, January 15, 1997, 6.

70. Rosenbluth, "Soundtrack Specialists," S-4.

71. Morricone, quoted in Jay Cocks, "The Lyrical Assassin at 5 a.m.," *Time*, March 16, 1987, 83.

72. Upon the advice of the composer, I have resisted the temptation to compare this theme with Carl Orff's *Carmina Burana*. Says Morricone, "There is nothing in *The Mission* that reminds one of *Carmina Burana*. When people hear the choir singing loud and staccato, they believe that is *Carmina Burana*, but they are deaf people who don't understand." Quoted in Cocks, "The Lyrical Assassin," 83.

73. Derek Elley, "New 'Mission' in Life," *Variety*, January 22–28, 1996, 92.

74. Geraldine Fabrikant, "Campaign Helps Sleeper Become a Hit," *New York Times*, September 19, 1990, D8.

75. The Zucker brothers would use the tune again to hilarious effect in trailers for *Naked Gun 2 1/2: The Smell of Fear*. In a bit specifically parodying *Ghost*'s famous love scene, Police Lt. Frank Drebin (Leslie Nielsen) and Jane Spencer (Priscilla Presley) make love at a pottery wheel that spins out of control, covering them and the rest of the room with globs of heavy clay.

76. Advertisement in the *Hollywood Reporter*, August 27, 1996, S31.

77. Alan Waldman, "Going for a Song," *Hollywood Reporter*, August 26, 1997, S12.

78. Waldman, "Going for a Song," S66.

79. John Baxter, *Hollywood in the Sixties*, 43.

EPILOGUE

1. Anders, quoted in Jonathan Romney and Adrian Wootton, eds., *The Celluloid Jukebox: Popular Music and the Movies Since the '50s*, 119.

2. See James Buhler and David Neumeyer, "Film Studies/Film Music," *Journal of the American Musicological Society* 47, no. 2 (Summer 1994): 384.

3. See Henry Jenkins, *Textual Poachers: Television Fans and Participatory Culture* (New York: Routledge, 1992).

4. For more on this subject, see Pierre Bourdieu, *Distinction: Social Critique of the Judgment of Taste*, trans. Richard Nice (Cambridge: Harvard University Press, 1984).

5. The one clear exception to this trend is the work of Martin Marks, whose interests have largely focused on the development of the silent film score. See Marks's "Film Music of the Silent Period, 1895–1924" (Ph.D diss., Harvard, 1989).

6. See my "Film Music Criticism: The Last Refuge for Film Aesthetics?" Paper presented at the Society for Cinema Studies Conference, Dallas, Texas, 1996.

7. I am referring here, of course, to the title of Roy Prendergast's seminal work, *Film Music: A Neglected Art*.

Selected Bibliography

Adorno, Theodor W. *Introduction to the Sociology of Music*. Translated by E. B. Ashton. New York: Continuum, 1976.

Allen, Robert and Douglas Gomery. *Film History: Theory and Practice*. New York: Knopf, 1985.

Amis, Kingsley. *The James Bond Dossier*. New York: New American Library, 1965.

Attali, Jacques. *Noise: The Political Economy of Music*. Translated by Brian Massumi. Minneapolis: University of Minnesota Press, 1985.

Balio, Tino. *United Artists: The Company That Changed the Film Industry*. Madison: University of Wisconsin Press, 1987.

——, ed. *The American Film Industry*. Rev. ed. Madison: University of Wisconsin Press, 1985.

Barthes, Roland. "The Grain of the Voice." In Barthes, *Image-Music-Text*, 179–89. Translated by Stephen Heath. New York: Hill and Wang, 1977.

Baugh, Bruce. "Prolegomena to Any Aesthetics of Rock Music." *Journal of Aesthetics and Art Criticism* 51, no. 1 (Winter 1993): 24–29.

Baxter, John. *Hollywood in the Sixties*. London: Tantivy Press, 1972.

Bazelon, Irwin. *Knowing the Score: Notes on Film Music*. New York: Van Nostrand Reinhold, 1975.

Bennett, Tony and Janet Woollacott. *Bond and Beyond: The Political Career of a Popular Hero*. New York: Methuen, 1987.

Benson, Raymond. *The James Bond Bedside Companion*. New York: Dodd, Mead, 1984.

Bell, David. *Getting the Best Score for Your Film*. Los Angeles: Silman-James Press, 1994.

Berg, Charles Merrell. "Cinema Sings the Blues." *Cinema Journal* 17, no. 2 (1978): 1–12.

——. *An Investigation of the Motives for and the Realization of Music to Accompany the American Silent Film, 1896–1927*. New York: Arno, 1976.

Binkley, Fred. "Mancini's Movie Manifesto." *Down Beat*, March 5, 1970, 16–17.

Bordwell, David, Janet Staiger, and Kristin Thompson. *The Classical Hollywood*

Cinema: Film Style and Mode of Production to 1960. New York: Columbia University Press, 1985.

Bordwell, David and Kristin Thompson. *Film History: An Introduction*. New York: McGraw Hill, 1994.

Breyer, Wolfgang. "An Interview with John Barry." *Soundtrack!* 7, no. 25 (March 1988): 28–31.

Brown, Royal S. "My Name Is Barry . . . John Barry." *Fanfare* 16, no. 5 (May-June 1993): 118–25.

——. *Overtones and Undertones: Reading Film Music*. Berkeley: University of California Press, 1994.

——. "The Sound of 007." *Fanfare* 5, no. 2 (1981): 306–309.

Bruce, Graham. *Bernard Herrmann: Film Music and Narrative*. Ann Arbor: University of Michigan Research Press, 1985.

Buhler, James and David Neumeyer. "Film Studies/Film Music." *Journal of the American Musicological Society* 47, no. 2 (Summer 1994): 364–85.

Burnett, Robert. *The Global Jukebox: The International Music Industry*. New York: Routledge, 1996.

Burns, Gary. "A Typology of 'Hooks' in Popular Records." *Popular Music* 6, no. 1 (January 1987): 1–20.

Burt, George. *The Art of Film Music*. Boston: Northeastern University Press, 1994.

Caps, John. "The Lyricism of Mancini." *Film Music Notebook* 3, no. 2 (1977): 12–17.

——. "The John Barry Tryptych." *Film Music Notebook* 2, no. 4 (1976): 6–8.

Carroll, Noël. "The Future of Allusion." *October* 20 (Spring 1982): 51–81.

——. *Mystifying Movies: Fads and Fallacies in Contemporary Film Theory*. New York: Columbia University Press, 1988.

Chambers, Iain. *Urban Rhythms: Popular Music and Popular Culture*. New York: St. Martin's, 1985.

Chell, Samuel L. "Music and Emotion in the Classical Hollywood Film: The Case of *The Best Years of Our Lives*." *Film Criticism* 8, no. 2 (Winter 1984): 27–38.

Cooper, B. Lee. *Popular Music Perspectives: Ideas, Themes, and Patterns in Contemporary Lyrics*. Bowling Green, Ohio: Bowling Green State University Popular Press, 1991.

Copland, Aaron. "Tip to Moviegoers: Take Off Those Earmuffs," *New York Times*, November 6, 1949, sec. 6, p. 28.

Crenshaw, Marshall. *Hollywood Rock*. Edited by Ted Mico. New York: Agincourt Press, 1994.

Cumbow, Robert C. *Once Upon a Time: The Films of Sergio Leone*. Metuchen, N.J.: Scarecrow Press, 1987.

Curtis, James M. "From *American Graffiti* to *Star Wars*." *Journal of Popular Culture* 13, no. 4 (Spring 1980): 590–601.

Darby, William and Jack Du Bois. *American Film Music: Major Composers, Techniques, Trends, 1915-1990*. Jefferson, N.C.: McFarland, 1991.

de Boer, H. J., ed. *Ennio Morricone: The Complete Musicography*. Amsterdam: Postbus, 1990.

Denisoff, R. Serge. *Solid Gold: The Popular Record Industry*. New Brunswick, N.J.: Transaction Books, 1975.

———. *Tarnished Gold: The Record Industry Revisited*. New Brunswick, N.J.: Transaction Books, 1986.

Denisoff, R. Serge and George Plasketes. "Synergy in 1980s Film and Music: Formula for Success or Industry Mythology?" *Film History* 4, no. 3 (1990): 257–76.

Denisoff, R. Serge and William D. Romanowski. *Risky Business: Rock in Film*. New Brunswick, N.J.: Transaction Books, 1991.

Doherty, Thomas. *Teenagers and Teenpics: The Juvenilization of American Movies of the 1950s*. Boston: Unwin Hyman, 1988.

Doty, Alexander. "Music Sells Movies: (Re) New (ed) Conservatism in Film Marketing," *Wide Angle* 10, no. 2 (1988): 70–79.

Dranov, Paula. *Inside the Music Publishing Industry*. White Plains, N.Y.: Knowledge Industry Publications, 1980.

Durant, Alan. *Conditions of Music*. Albany: State University of New York Press, 1984.

Ehrenstein, David and Bill Reed. *Rock on Film*. New York: Delilah Books, 1982.

Eisler, Hanns (and Theodor W. Adorno, uncredited). *Composing for the Films*. New York: Oxford University Press, 1947.

Evans, Mark. *Soundtrack: The Music of the Movies*. New York: Hopkinson and Blake, 1975.

Fagen, Donald. "Ennio Morricone? Ah, Bellissimo!" *Premiere* (August 1989), 106–107.

———. "Movie Music: Mancini's Anomie Deluxe." *Premiere* (October 1987), 97–99.

Farber, Stephen. "George Lucas: The Stinky Kid Hits the Big Time." *Film Quarterly* 27, no. 3 (Spring 1974): 2–9.

Fink, Michael. *Inside the Music Business: Music in Contemporary Life*. New York: Schirmer Books, 1989.

Flinn, Caryl. *Strains of Utopia: Gender, Nostalgia, and Hollywood Film Music*. Princeton: Princeton University Press, 1992.

Frith, Simon. "Mood Music: An Inquiry into Narrative Film Music." *Screen* 25, no. 3 (May-June 1984): 78–87.

———. *Music for Pleasure*. New York: Routledge, 1988.

———. *Sound Effects: Youth, Leisure, and the Politics of Rock 'n' Roll*. New York: Pantheon, 1981.

———. "Towards an Aesthetic of Popular Music." In Richard Leppert and Susan McClary, eds., *Music and Society: The Politics of Composition, Performance, and Reception*, 133–49. Cambridge: Cambridge University Press, 1987.

Frith, Simon and Andrew Goodwin, eds. *On Record: Rock, Pop, and the Written Word*. New York: Pantheon, 1990.

Gabbard, Krin. *Jammin' at the Margins: Jazz and the American Cinema*. Chicago: University of Chicago Press, 1996.

Geduld, Harry. "Film Music: A Survey," *Quarterly Review of Film Studies* 1, no. 2 (1976): 183–204.

Gorbman, Claudia. "Narrative Film Music." *Yale French Studies* 60 (1980): 183–203.

———. *Unheard Melodies: Narrative Film Music*. Bloomington: Indiana University Press, 1987.

Gomery, Douglas. *The Hollywood Studio System*. New York: St. Martin's, 1986.

Grossberg, Lawrence. "The Media Economy of Rock Culture: Cinema, Postmodernity, and Authenticity." In Simon Frith, Andrew Goodwin, and Lawrence Grossberg, eds., *Sound and Vision: The Music Video Reader*, 185–209. New York: Routledge, 1993.

Handzo, Stephen. "The Golden Age of Film Music." *Cineaste* 21, nos. 1–2 (1995): 46–55.

Harker, David. *One for the Money: Politics and Popular Song*. London: Hutchison, 1980.

Hebdige, Dick. *Subculture: The Meaning of Style*. London: Methuen, 1979.

James, David. *Allegories of Cinema: American Film in the Sixties*. Princeton: Princeton University Press, 1989.

Kalinak, Kathryn. *Settling the Score: Music and the Classical Hollywood Film*. Madison: University of Wisconsin Press, 1992.

Karlin, Fred. *Listening to Movies: The Film Lover's Guide to Film Music*. New York: Schirmer Books, 1994.

Karlin, Fred and Rayburn Wright. *On the Track: A Guide to Contemporary Film Scoring*. New York: Schirmer Books, 1990.

Kerman, Joseph. *Contemplating Music: Challenges to Musicology*. Cambridge: Harvard University Press, 1985.

Lanza, Joseph. *Elevator Music: A Surreal History of Muzak, Easy-Listening, and Other Moodsong*. New York: St. Martin's, 1994.

Larson, Randall D. *Musique Fantastique: A Survey of Film Music in the Fantastic Cinema*. Metuchen, N.J.: Scarecrow Press, 1985.

Lees, Gene. "Mancini at Fifty—Mr. Lucky." *Hi Fidelity* (July 1975): 11–12.

Lerdahl, Fred and Ray Jackendoff. *A Generative Theory of Tonal Music*. Cambridge: MIT Press, 1983.

Leppert, Richard and Susan McClary, eds. *Music and Society: The Politics of Composition, Performance, and Reception*. Cambridge: Cambridge University Press, 1987.

Lhassa, Anne and Jean. *Ennio Morricone: Biographie*. Lausanne, Switzerland: Favre, 1989.

Lowry, Ed. "The Appropriation of Signs in *Scorpio Rising*." *The Velvet Light Trap* 20 (Summer 1983): 41–46.

Luhr, William and Peter Lehman. *Blake Edwards*. Athens: Ohio University Press, 1981.

———. *Returning to the Scene: Blake Edwards*. Athens: Ohio University Press, 1989.

Lukow, Gregory. "The Antecedents of MTV: Soundies, Scopitones, and Snaders, and the History of an Ahistorical Form." In Michael Nash, ed., *The Art of Music Video: Ten Years After*, 6–9. Long Beach, Calif.: Long Beach Museum of Art, 1991.

Mancini, Henry. *Sounds and Scores: A Practical Guide to Professional Orchestration*. Northridge Music, 1973.

Mancini, Henry with Gene Lees. *Did They Mention the Music?* Chicago: Contemporary Books, 1989.

Manson, Eddy Lawrence. "The Film Composer in Concert and the Concert

Composer in Film." In Clifford McCarty, ed., *Film Music 1*, 255–70. New York: Garland, 1989.

Manvell, Roger and John Huntley. *The Technique of Film Music*. Revised and enlarged by Richard Arnell and Peter Day. London: Focal Press, 1975.

Marcus, Greil. *Mystery Train: Images of America in Rock 'n' Roll Music*. New York: Dutton, 1976.

Marks, Martin. "Film Music of the Silent Period, 1895–1924." Ph.D. diss., Harvard, 1989.

McAdams, Stephen. "Music: A Science of the Mind?" *Contemporary Music Review* 2 (1987): 1–61.

MacFarland, David T. "Up from Middle America: The Development of the Top 40." In Lawrence Lichty and Malachi C. Topping, eds., *American Broadcasting: A Source Book on the History of Radio and Television*. New York: Hastings House, 1975.

McRobbie, Angela, ed. *Zoot Suits and Second Hand Dresses: An Anthology of Fashion and Music*. Boston: Unwin Hyman, 1988.

Meeker, David. *Jazz in the Movies: A Guide to Jazz Musicians*. London: Talisman Books, 1977.

Meyer, Leonard. *Emotion and Meaning in Music*. Chicago: University of Chicago Press, 1956.

——. *Style and Music: Theory, History, and Ideology*. Philadelphia: University of Pennsylvania Press, 1989.

Millard, Andre. *America on Record: A History of Recorded Sound*. Cambridge and New York: Cambridge University Press, 1995.

Miller, Jim, ed. *The Rolling Stone Illustrated History of Rock and Roll*, 2d ed. New York: Random House, 1980.

Mitchell, Sammy. "Unbuggable Henry Mancini." *Down Beat*, March 6, 1969, 15 and 36.

Mulvey, Laura. "Visual Pleasure and Narrative Cinema." *Screen* 16, no. 3 (Autumn 1975): 6–18.

Nash, Michael. "Program Guide." In Nash, ed., *The Art of Music Video: Ten Years After*, 17–27. Long Beach, Calif.: Long Beach Museum of Art, 1991.

Niogret, Hubert. "Ennio Morricone sur trois notes." *Positif* 266 (April 1983): 2–11.

Norris, Christopher, ed. *Music and the Politics of Culture*. New York: St. Martin's, 1989.

Norton, Richard. *Tonality in Western Culture*. University Park: Penn State University Press, 1984.

Palmer, Christopher. *The Composer in Hollywood*. New York: Marion Boyars, 1990.

Pfeiffer, Lee and Philip Lisa. *The Incredible World of 007*. New York: Citadel, 1992.

Pollock, Dale. *Skywalking: The Life and Films of George Lucas*. New York: Harmony Books, 1983.

Prendergast, Roy. *Film Music: A Neglected Art*. 2d ed. New York: Norton, 1992.

Pye, Michael and Lynda Myles. *The Movie Brats*. New York: Holt, Rinehart, and Winston, 1979.

Romney, Jonathan, and Adrian Wootton, eds. *The Celluloid Jukebox: Popular Music and the Movies Since the '50s*. London: British Film Institute, 1995.

Rosen, Philip. "Adorno and Film Music: Theoretical Notes on *Composing for the Films*." *Yale French Studies* 60 (1980): 157–83.

Rubin, Steven Jay. *The James Bond Films*. New York: Arlington House, 1981.

Sanjek, Russell. *American Popular Music and Its Business from 1900 to 1984: The First Four Hundred Years*. 3 vols. New York: Oxford University Press, 1988.

——. *From Print to Plastic: Publishing and Promoting America's Popular Music (1900–1980)*. Brooklyn, N.Y.: Institute for Studies in American Music, 1983.

——. *Pennies from Heaven: The American Popular Music Business in the Twentieth Century*. Revised and updated by David Sanjek. New York: Da Capo, 1996.

Sanjek, Russell and David Sanjek. *The American Popular Music Business in the 20th Century*. New York: Oxford University Press, 1991.

Scheurer, Timothy. *Born in the U.S.A.: The Myth of America in Popular Music from Colonial Times to the Present*. Jackson: University of Mississippi Press, 1991.

——. "Henry Mancini: An Appreciation and Appraisal." *Journal of Popular Film and Video* 24, no. 1 (Spring 1996): 34.

Self, Robert. "The Art Cinema and Robert Altman." *The Velvet Light Trap* 19 (1982): 30–34.

Shemel, Sidney and M. William Krasilovsky. *This Business of Music*. 5th ed., rev. and enlarged. New York: Billboard, 1985.

Shepherd, John. *Music as Social Text*. Cambridge, Eng.: Polity Press, 1991.

Shore, Michael. *The Rolling Stone Book of Rock Video*. New York: Rolling Stone Press, 1984.

Siders, Harvey. "The Jazz Composers in Hollywood." *Down Beat*, March 2, 1972, 12–15.

Staig, Laurence and Tony Williams. *Italian Western: Opera of Violence*. London: Lorrimer, 1975.

Thomas, Tony. *Film Score: The Art and Craft of Movie Music*. Burbank, Calif.: Riverwood, 1991.

Vuillamy, Graham and Edward Lee. *Popular Music: A Teacher's Guide*. London: Routledge and Kegan Paul, 1982.

Wasko, Janet. *Hollywood in the Information Age*. Austin: University of Texas Press, 1995.

Wiener, Thomas. "The Rise and Fall of the Rock Film." *American Film* 1, no. 2 (November 1975): 25–29.

Williams, Alan. "The Musical Film and Recorded Popular Music." In Rick Altman, ed., *Genre: The Musical*, 147–58. London: Routledge and Kegan Paul, 1981.

Wyatt, Justin. *High Concept: Movies and Marketing in Hollywood*. Austin: University of Texas Press, 1994.

Index